The Compact Beginner's Guide to
Painting

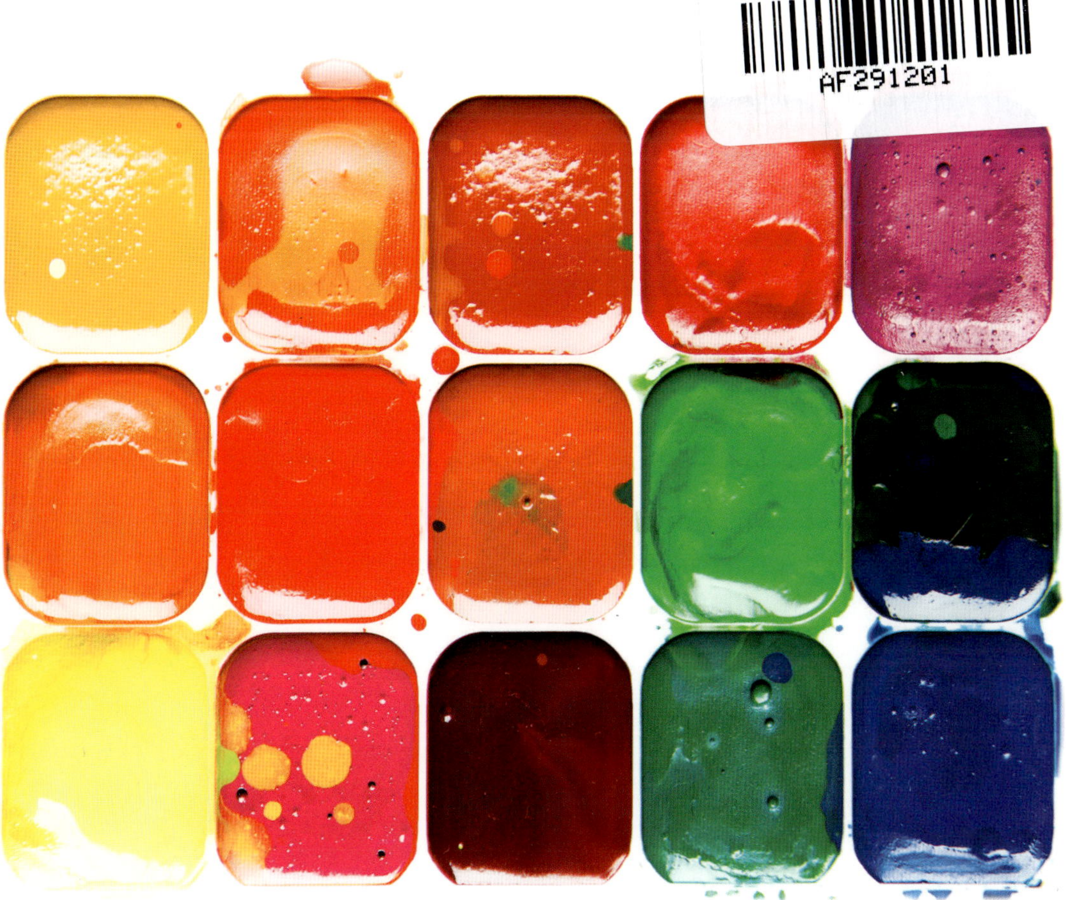

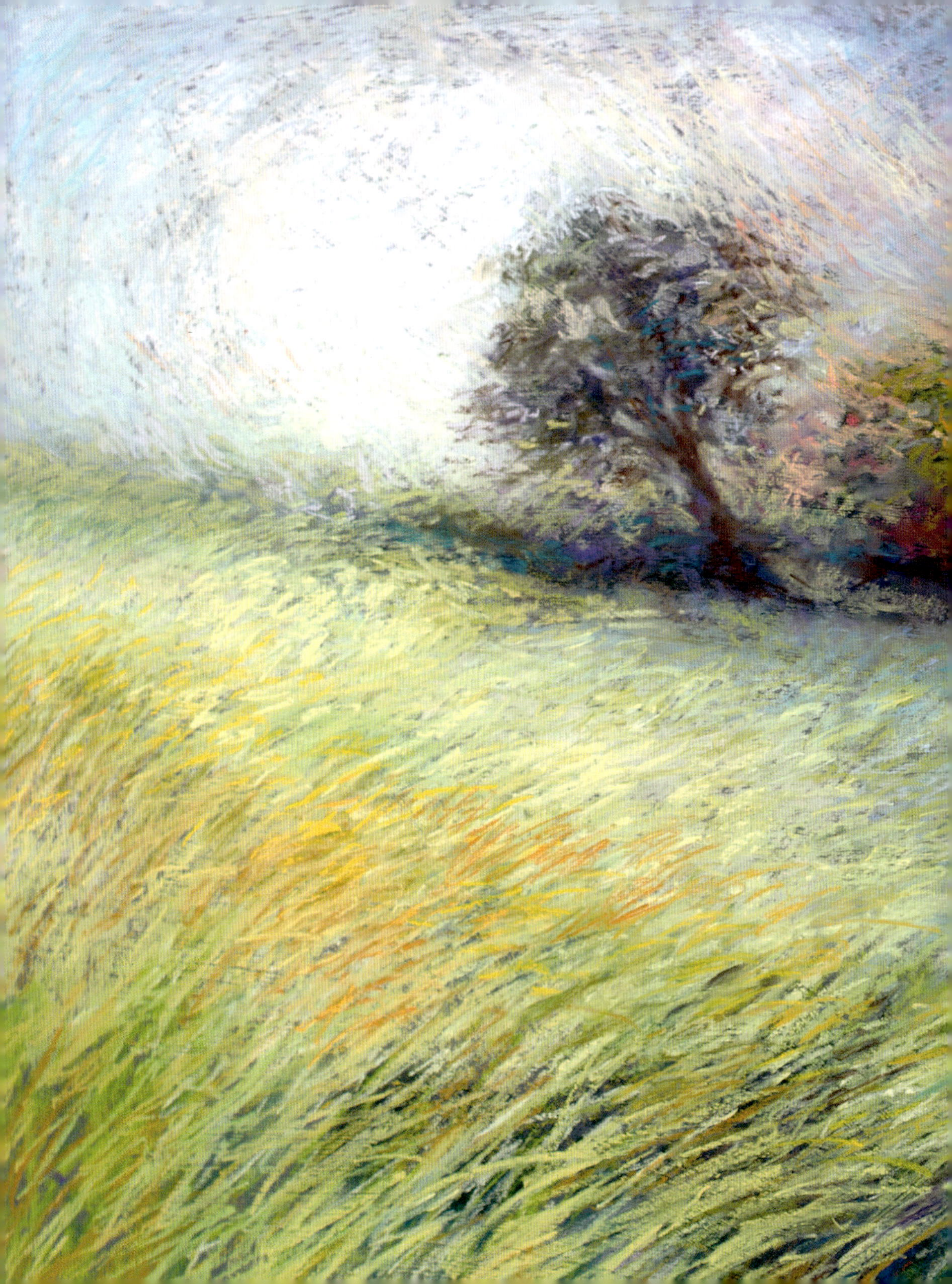

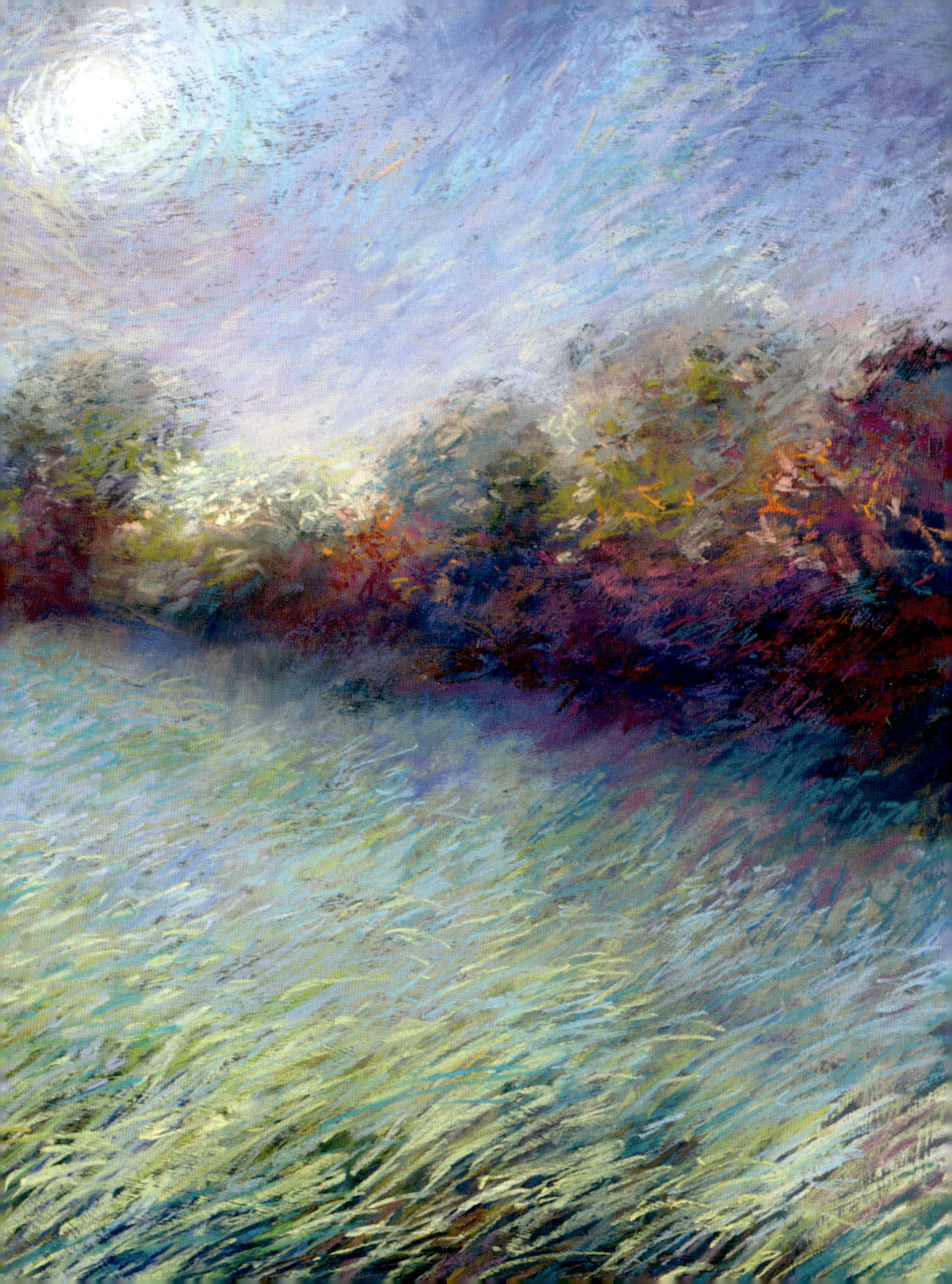

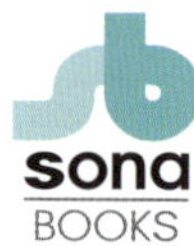

sona
BOOKS

First published in 2022 by Sona Books
an imprint of Danann Media Publishing Ltd.

© 2022 Danann Publishing Limited

Copy Editor Juliette O'Neill

CAT NO: SON0527
ISBN: 978-1-915343-68-0
Made in the UAE.

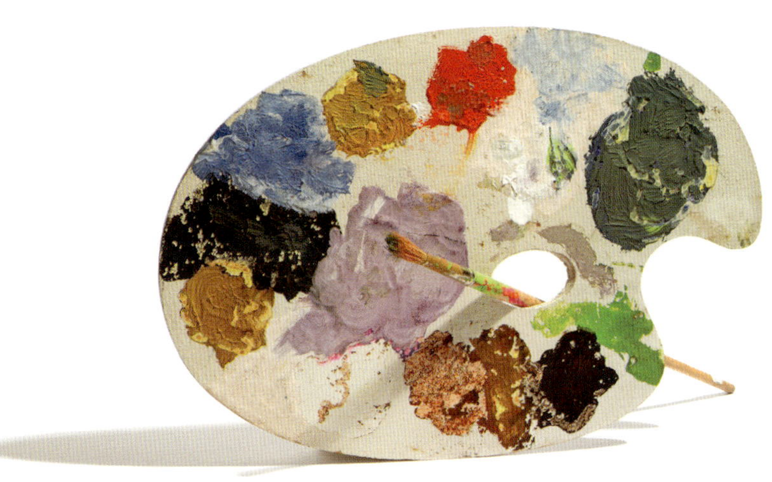

Painting

Contents

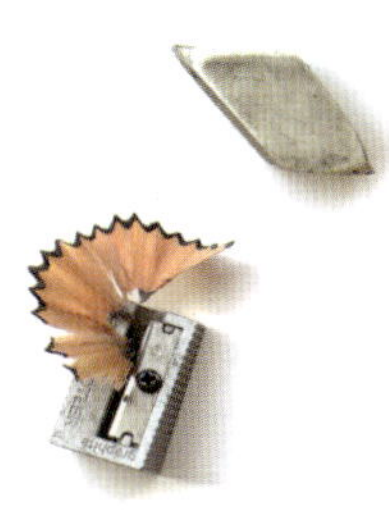

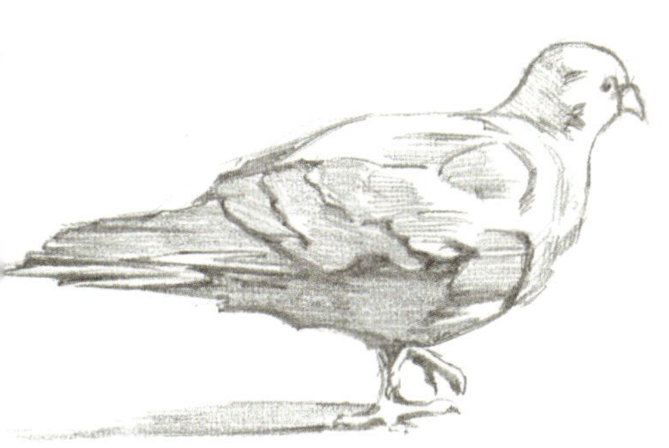

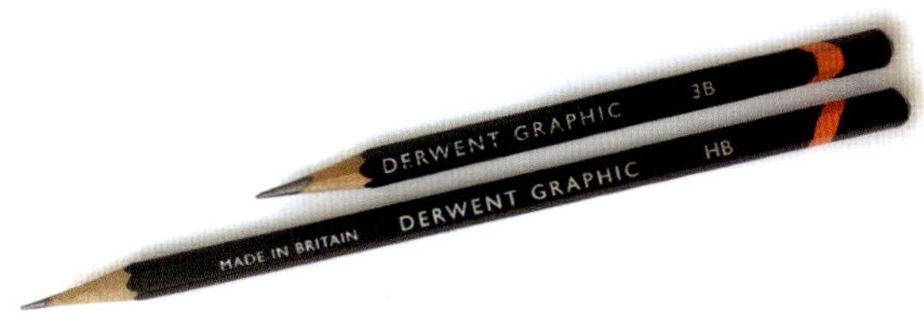

choosing your painting medium

Lancelot Richardson covers the key features of oils, pastels, watercolours and acrylics, and weighs their strengths and weaknesses

There are lots of different options for choosing the right medium for your work. Each has its own qualities that offer different benefits and challenges, so there is no best medium, only the one that is the most suitable for you.

Ask yourself, what does your work require? Is it big or small, tight or expressive? The positives of some materials might be a downside for your approach to painting; for instance, the light, translucency of watercolours wouldn't suit someone looking to get into thick, impasto painting.

The slow drying times of oils might suit a process that requires lots of manipulation of the paint, but would be hard to deal with if you prefer to work in layers.

Practical needs are also important, such as available workspace, climate, or toxicity. While any materials can be used even in fairly compact settings, good ventilation is still essential for oils and should also be considered for pastels. Materials may also work differently in varying climates, with watercolours and acrylics drying rapidly in hot weather. If there are pets or small children around, toxicity is also important.

Using quality materials and maintaining good studio practise is crucial across all mediums. High-quality paint will be more vibrant and stand the test of time. Good studio habits, such as maintaining a clean workspace and equipment, or storing paint properly, will reduce costs and keep materials pleasant to use.

Oils

Pro

Being oil-based, they dry slowly and require solvent to clean and thin the paint. This makes them quite forgiving, as they are reworkable for a while, and can be repainted and removed easily.

Con

Oils have a high starting cost and require lots of equipment, but because they are easy to mix, starting with several tubes of paint is fine. A tube goes a long way, and solvent can be recycled, so in the long term they are affordable. Good quality paints last for decades if sealed properly, too. Student-quality oils are noticeably less vibrant than artist-quality paints, but are usually fine to start out with.

Pro

Oils are reliable and versatile, with an excellent depth of colour that allows for a range of approaches. Paintings are hard-wearing and easy to store.

Con

The initial learning curve is a little tricky with solvents and mediums, picking suitable surfaces and equipment maintenance. Solvents require good ventilation, as nearly all options are toxic. While a set-up can be small, space for a free-standing easel is a significant plus.

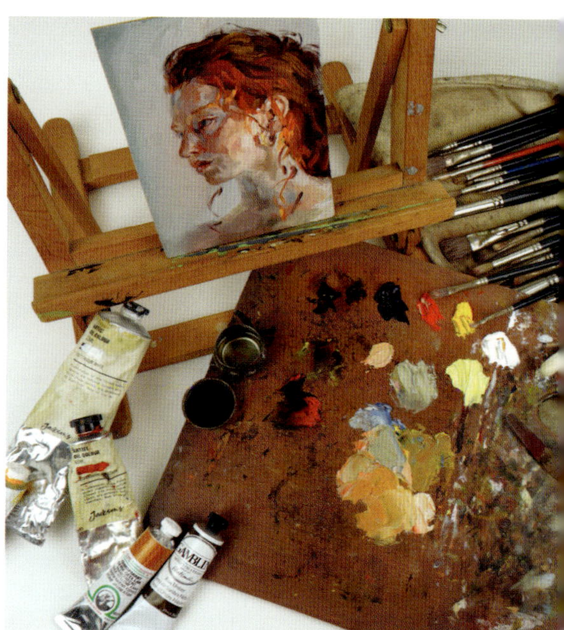

Pastels

Pro

While it is possible to start out with a few core colours, adding more to your selection helps significantly. Cheap sets are affordable, but while they're acceptable to use, they won't hold up to quality materials as they wear down quickly. Pastel paper is also expensive, though some toned papers are fine in a pinch. While pastels are affordable to get started in, they can get expensive when expanding your selection.

Pro

The biggest strength of pastels is the vibrant colour from their high pigment content. They are easy to get started with and require minimal extra space and equipment.

Con

Pastels typically suit medium-sized work; their softness makes detailed work challenging, and they can become difficult to take care of and frame on larger scales.

Con

Unfortunately, soft pastels produce quite a bit of dust, which is messy and makes ventilation advisable. Pastel artworks are vulnerable to smearing, and must be stored carefully. While fixatives such as acrylic or casein help, some artists avoid them as they may alter colours. Despite this fragility, the longevity of the work mainly depends on the support it is made on. The pastels themselves are dry and stable, so work done on high-quality paper or board should last well, and retain its colour if taken care of.

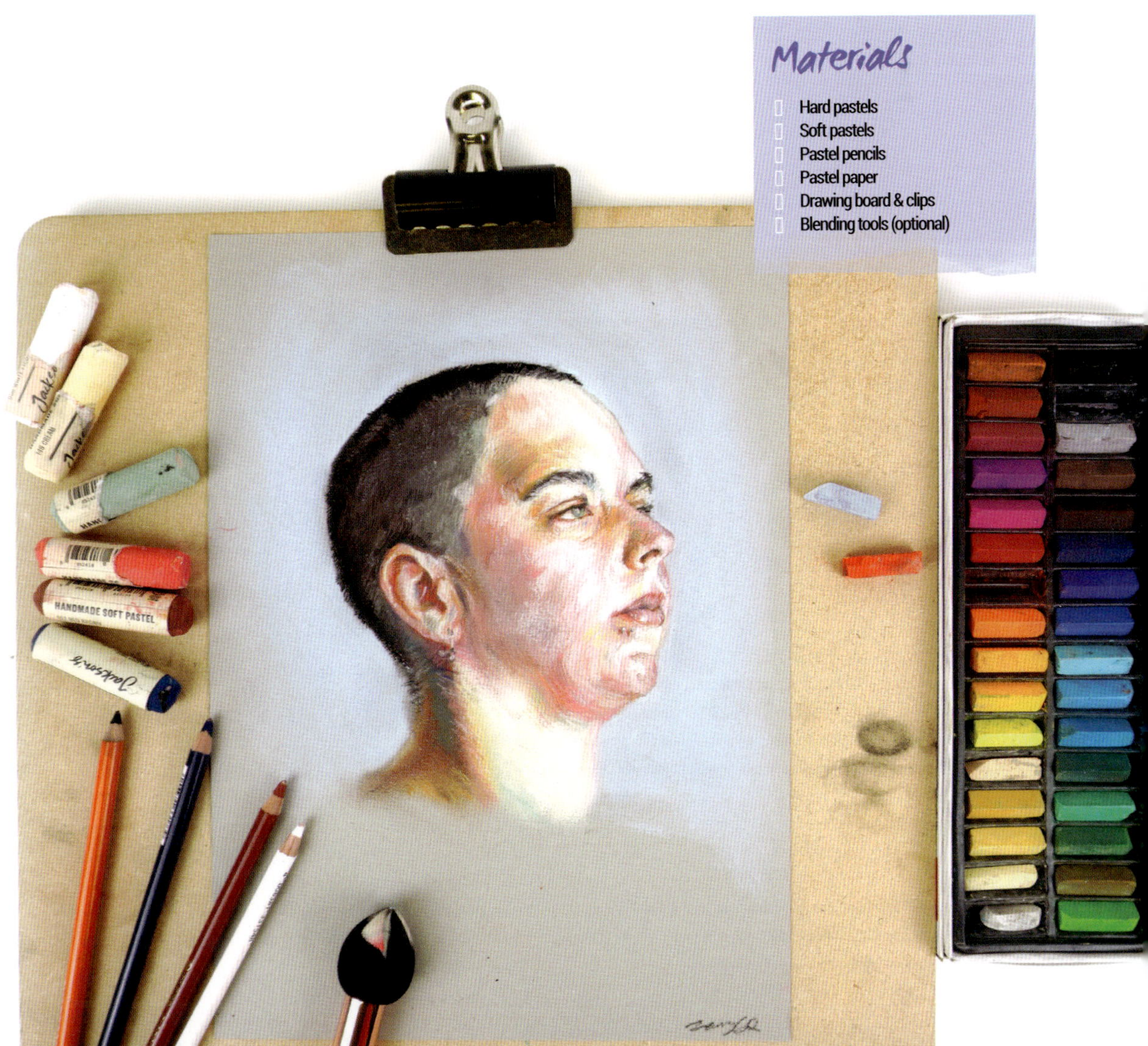

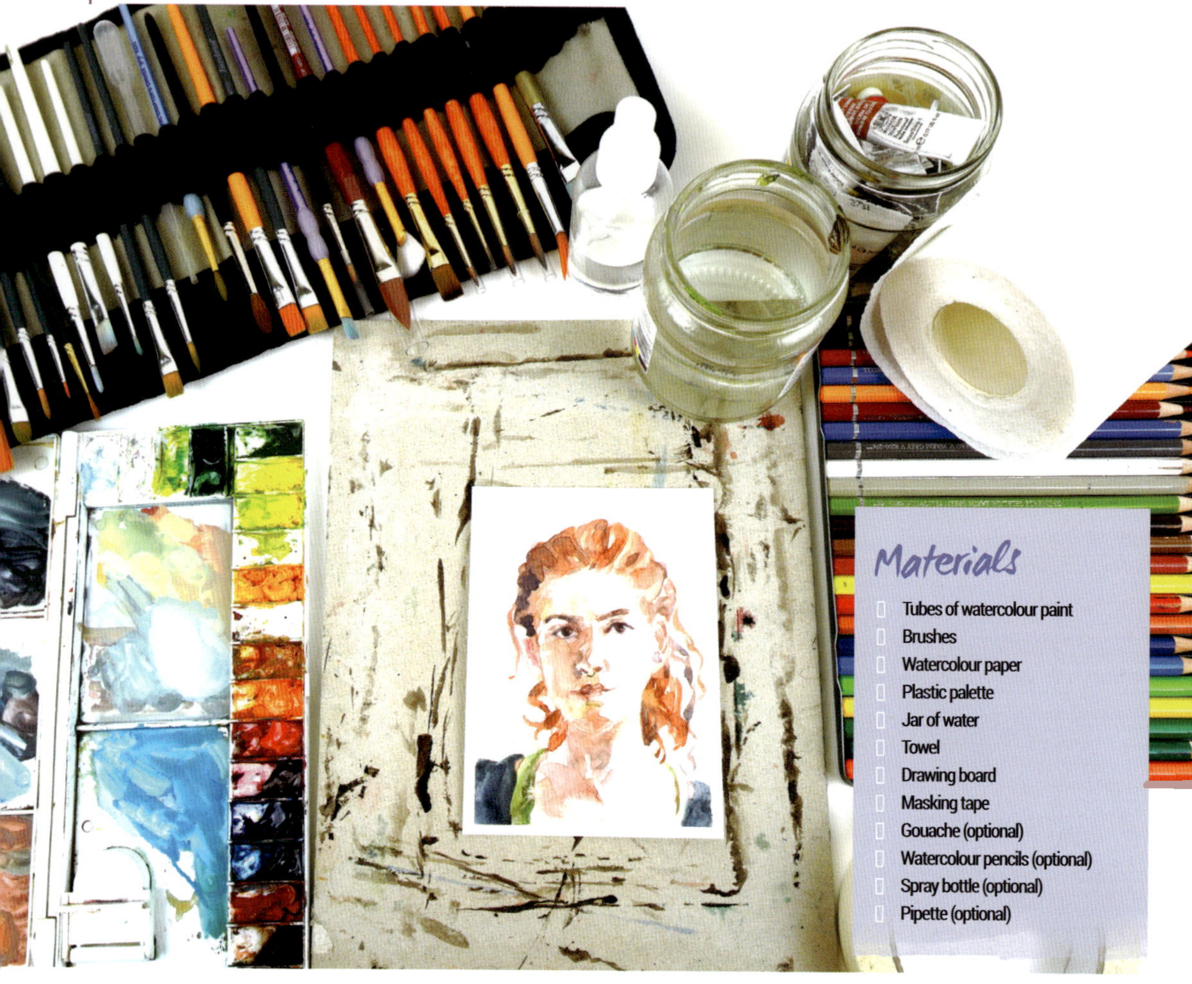

Watercolour

Con

Watercolour is an approachable medium, as it is fairly compact – a minimalist set can fit in a coat pocket – and easy to use, with fast drying times. However, it has a surprisingly challenging learning curve as it can be unpredictable and unforgiving, owing to the difficulty of correcting mistakes. Combining watercolour with gouache makes things a little easier. Gouache is an opaque form of watercolour that can cover mistakes, though the colours are less intense.

Pro

Watercolour has unique translucent colour that produces a wide range of effects. It tends to fare best at small to medium sizes. It is also very safe, with no solvents, and good substitutes are available for more hazardous pigments.

"It is also very safe, with no solvents, and good substitutes are available for more hazardous pigments"

Pro

While beginner sets are affordable, they are frustratingly difficult to use, and put many off watercolours. Though expensive, it is much better to start with a few artist-quality paints instead. The same goes for brushes; a couple of quality brushes will do more than a whole set of cheap ones – watercolour is very easy to clean, so they should last a long time. Watercolour tubes can dry out, but should last longer if stored in an airtight container.

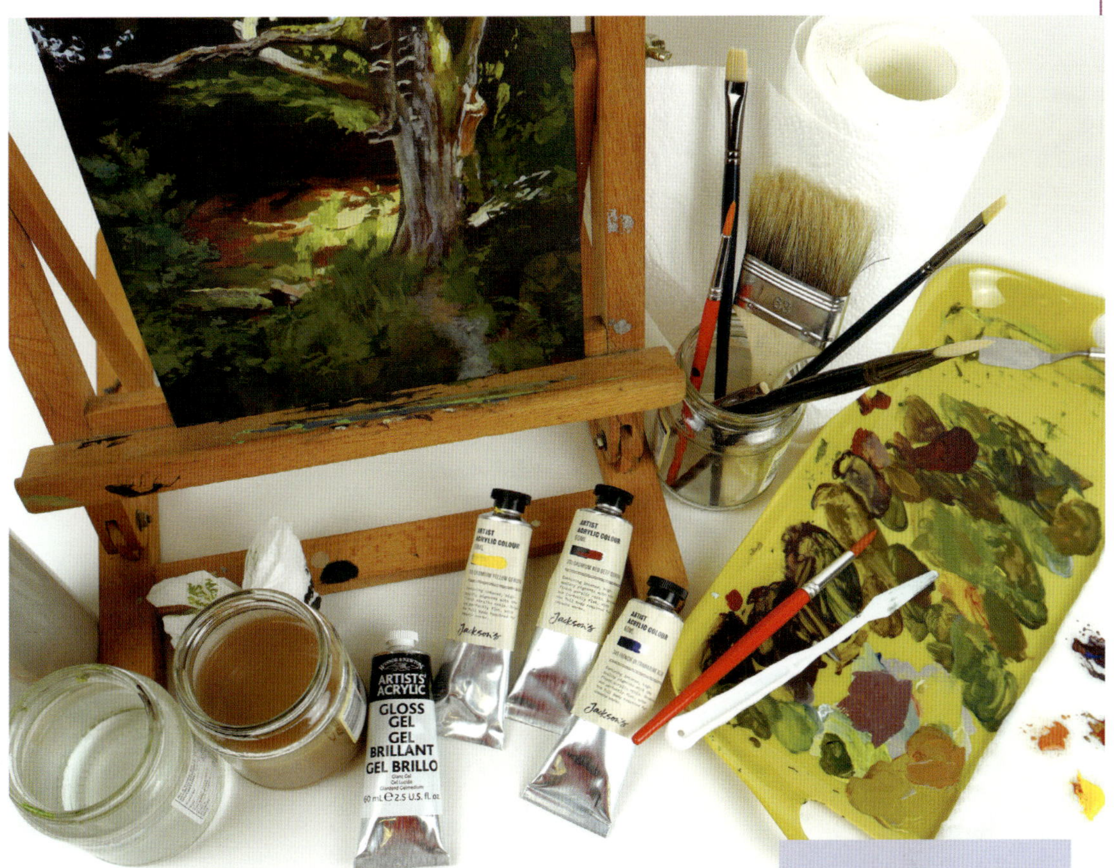

Acrylic

Pro

Acrylics have fast drying times and tremendous versatility. They can be used with water, but can also be combined with many different mediums. These are substances added to change the paint, transforming it by giving it extra body or thinning it, adding texture or gloss, extending or shortening drying times, or changing the flow. Acrylics suit any size work.

Pro

It is relatively easy to get started with acrylics, as they are water-soluble, don't produce fumes, and adhere to almost any surface strong enough to support wet mediums. Overall, they are reasonably affordable to start with as they don't require many specialised accessories; any pots and trays work fine as brush washers and palettes. Beginner sets of acrylics are affordable, but fall far short of artist-quality paints. Like watercolours, it is better to select a few artist-quality tubes to avoid frustration. Cheap acrylics tend to have sunken, dull colours when dry.

Con

Fast drying times make them excellent for layered approaches but prevent any reworking. The paint must be kept wet when in use, and readily dries on equipment, which can be hard on brushes. It is important to clean up while wet. Tubes tend to dry out faster than oils, but should last years. when stored properly.

Materials

- Tubes of acrylic paint
- Brushes
- Wet palette
- Plastic palette
- Easel
- Illustration board
- Jar of water
- Spray bottle
- Plastic palette knife
- Paint scraper
- Acrylic gloss medium (optional)

sketching for painting

Lancelot Richardson covers different ways to use drawing to develop ideas and support the painting process

Drawing is an important tool to aid our painting as a way of recording reference, thinking about ideas on paper, or planning a more finished piece. Having a clear vision builds a foundation for creating more successful work, and it saves time on the painting process by leaving less room for error.

There are lots of different ways to use drawing alongside painting. Sketchbook drawings, for example, may serve as potential painting ideas that can be expanded upon with directed studies that solve problems with more complex subjects, such as figures. Thumbnail drawing, meanwhile, serves as a more linear route to a painting, starting with simple compositional ideas before refining them into a more detailed plan. Other elements of drawing might be transferred to paintings too, such as how mark-making can influence brushstrokes.

It is easy to get tied up with details when painting. Sketching can help this problem by exploring a simpler overall idea, but don't worry if your painting starts to deviate from this either. Sometimes this is because there are genuinely ways to improve on the sketch, or it may be treated more like a guideline in order to keep the painting spontaneous and free.

A number of techniques are covered here, but it is fine to use any combination. It may only be necessary to do some quick thumbnails to establish a composition, or perhaps a more invested project calls for a thorough planning of multiple elements. There is no strict sketching process – instead, sketches can be used to explore the subject and answer any questions about it before you start painting.

Develop a sketch

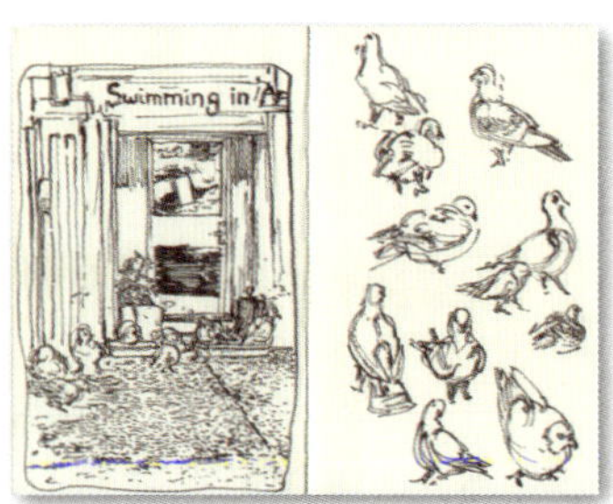

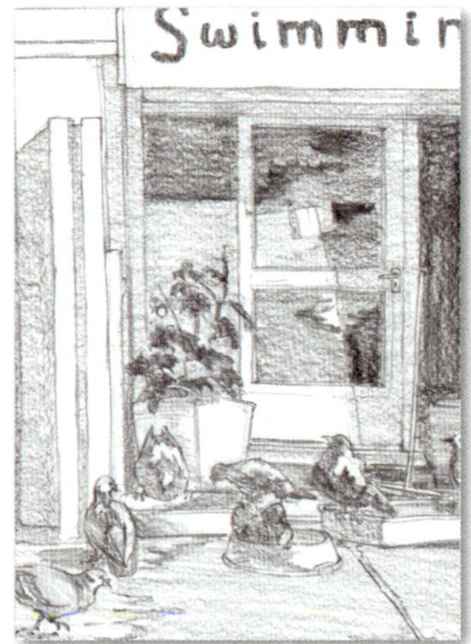

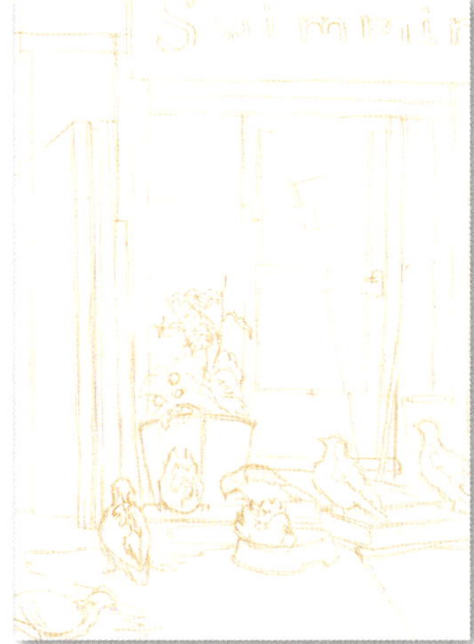

1 In the sketchbook
I tend to use a sketchbook to draw from life and explore the subject. Here is a rough sketch of a scene, with some quick sketches of the pigeons in different poses. Drawing from live subjects is a good way to record natural poses, even if the drawings are simple.

2 Refining the idea
Here the sketchbook drawing is tightened up so the placement of the different elements works, with a rough indication of tone. I've also adjusted it to fit the proportions of the paper I'll be using. This is a useful reference, and it helps a lot if the initial sketch is painted over.

3 Laying out the painting
The painting's layout is sketched with yellow ochre watercolour pencil – a hard graphite pencil works fine, too. The major elements of the composition are placed, but the sketch is kept light and simple so it doesn't interfere with the painting. The previous drawing will help with more complex elements.

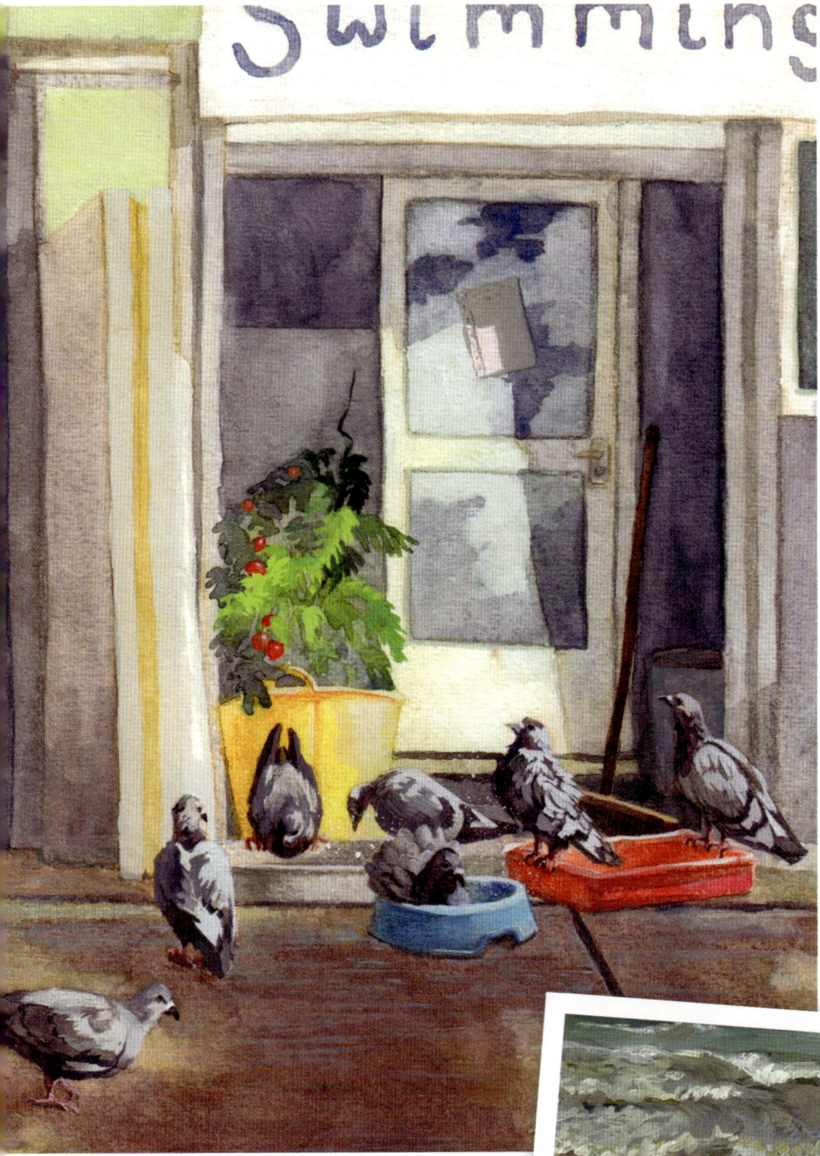

4 Final painting
The final painting is broadly the same as the sketches, though the sign is cropped a bit to de-emphasise it, and the placement of the pigeons is adjusted to improve the composition. The detail on the pigeons was solved using extra sketches, in order to get the right shadow shapes for the plumage.

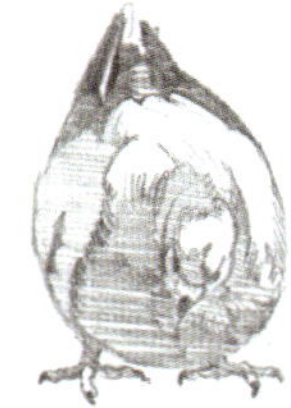

Exploring a subject

Doing detailed studies can help with exploring a subject and understanding challenging aspects, like poses or structure. These sketches of pigeons were done to get a better feel for their overall body shapes, and the tonal shapes created by their feathers. Some of the poses were reused in the final piece.

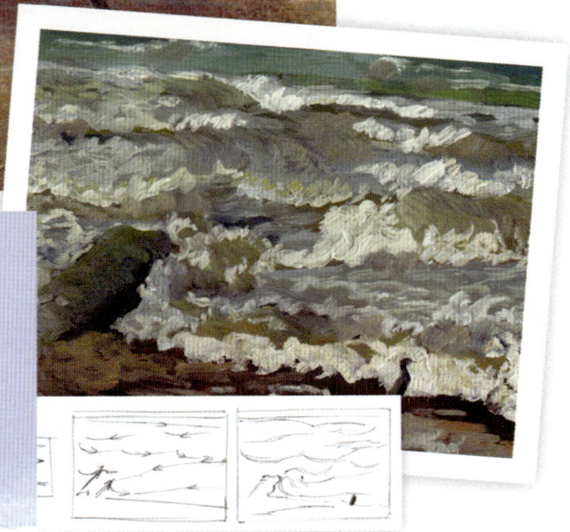

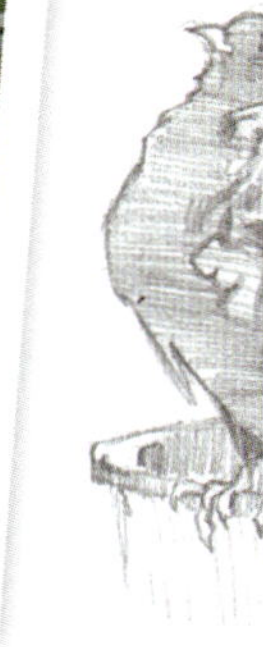

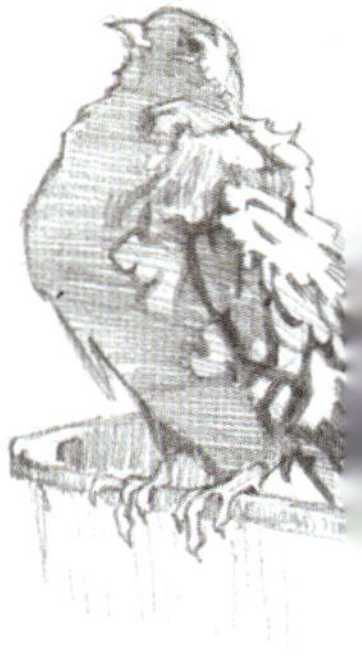

Gestural compositions

Gestural studies are useful for determining the underlying structure of a painting, and give it a sense of continuity or 'flow'. This example shows how the waves create a zig-zag pattern down the painting to the shore. One way to think of this is as the imaginary path a viewer's eye should take through a painting.

Develop a plan with thumbnails

Using thumbnails is an effective way to plan out the composition for a painting and test out different ideas

Thumbnails are quick, disposable drawings that are used to plan out more complex work. In this context, they are used to plan the composition of a painting. They can save time and trouble further down the line with regards to reworking tricky compositional issues.

Since thumbnails are quick to draw, try to do lots and get as many ideas out on paper as possible. Seeing a sketch on the page, even a really simple one, can make it easier to tell if an idea will work, and doing a lot introduces new possibilities to choose from. They don't need to be perfect; the best thumbnails are small and simple, so the overall idea of a composition is clear.

Here I go through different stages of experimenting with compositions. It may be fine to only do some of these things, or go through everything depending on how clear the idea is, or the scope of the project.

1 Tiny compositions

These thumbnails are very tiny at only a few centimetres across. I've experimented with shifting the proportions of the dark and light areas of the image by cropping it differently. Some show a larger foreground, while others emphasise the building. If an idea works at a small size, it will likely scale up well.

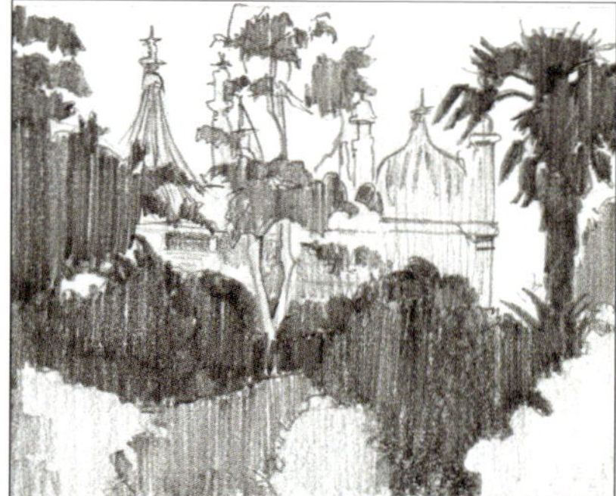

2 Tonal plans

From the first thumbnails, I take three and work them up with more tonal values. It is useful to draw tonal values as clear, simple shapes, as it unifies the scene. This give a better sense of the composition as a whole and helps the painting read better.

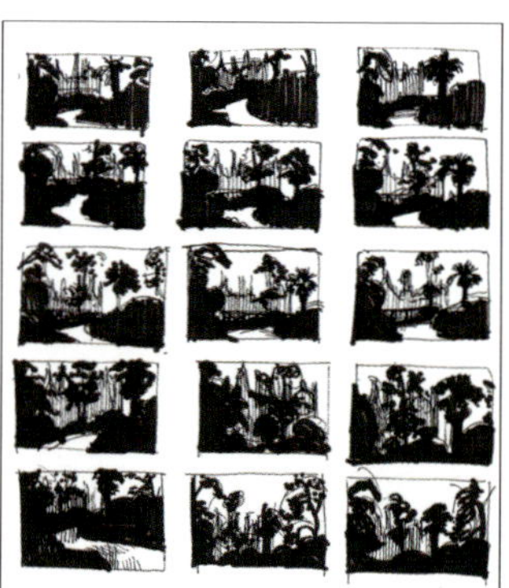

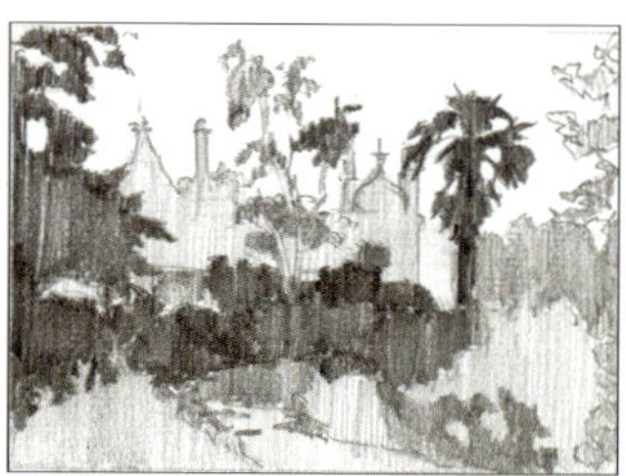

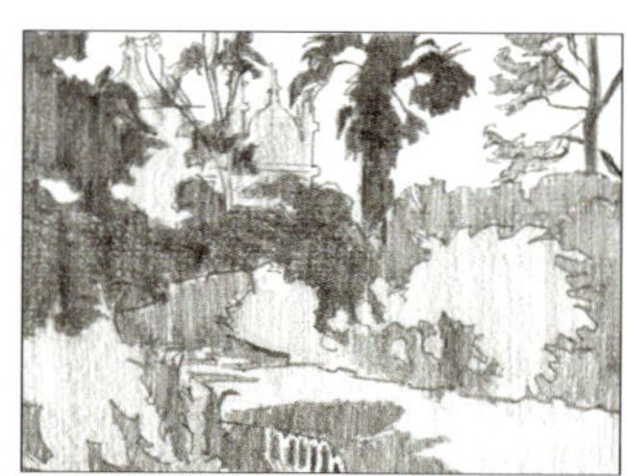

3 Tight thumbnail

This final thumbnail progresses one from the previous stage by scaling it up to add detail and shows how the light and shadow areas interact. The trees are spaced out for a better composition, and the division between the plants and sky has been made just a little more uneven to add visual interest.

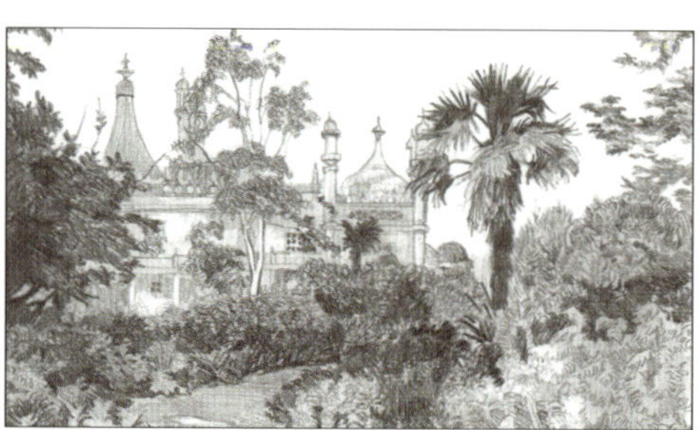

Developing ideas with preparatory drawings

Preparatory drawings are done to research ideas for paintings, especially larger compositions containing lots of complex elements

Preparatory drawings are created to help an artist plan for a painting. For example, it may include sketching out a composition or solving problems with challenging subjects, such as posed figures.

Being able to think on paper makes it easier to see what something might look like in a more finished form, and gives artists material to refer to as they paint. Creating drawings also allows artists to rework ideas. The example below by Degas has numerous drawings supporting it that show how the concept evolved, and how the figures' poses were considered.

When working through ideas with drawings, don't be afraid to deviate from the original plan if something isn't working out, or if a major improvement can be made. Letting go of something can be painful, but it is well worth it if it will improve the final piece.

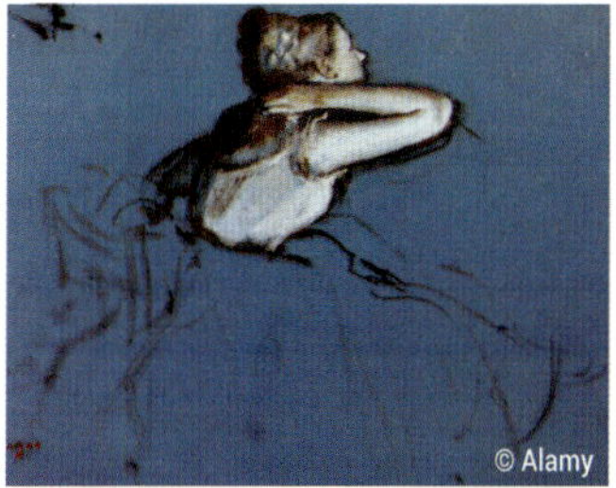

Detail studies

Sketches can be used to tackle specific problems like difficult poses. Different sketches were made of this pose to achieve a more convincing action.

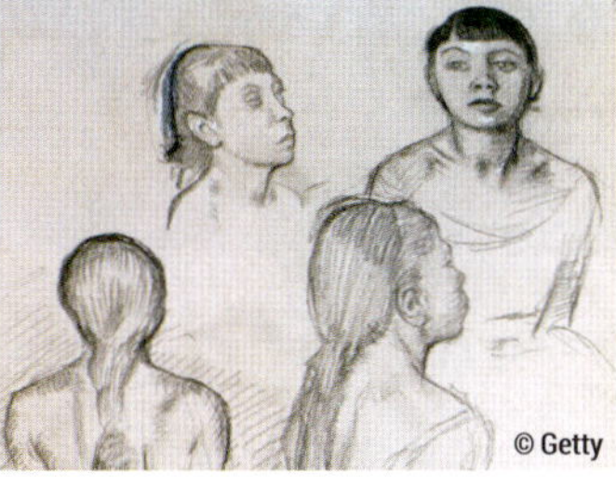

Letting go of ideas

Preparatory sketches can be relatively simple as they explore subject matter. This figure appears in the far left of the grissaile, but not in the final painting.

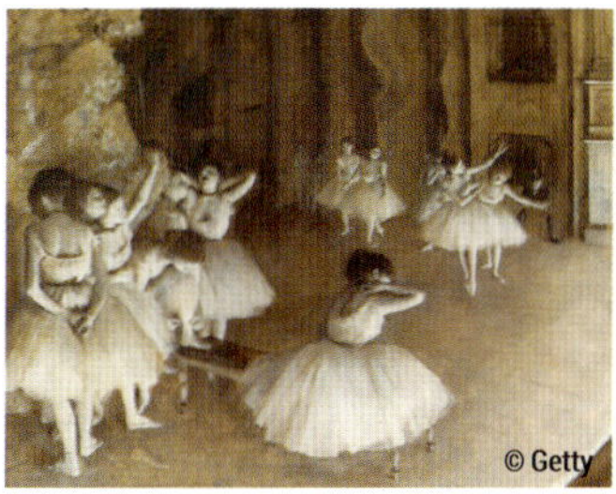

Oil grissaile

This grissaile – a monochrome oil paint sketch – was likely done before the final painting. A lot of detail is established, with the figures clearly posed.

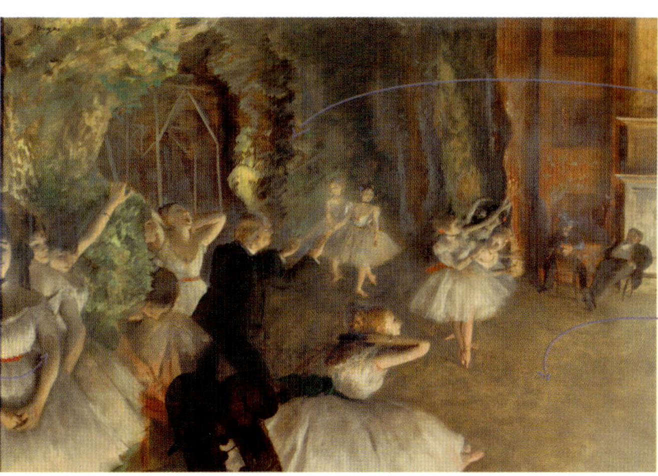

The line of figures is adjusted to create a stronger diagonal. Some are removed entirely, like the figure on the left, while others are added, along with the violins.

Another major element of the composition dropped from the drawings is the cropping of the stage, which gives it a free, more open feel.

The final painting has a considerably looser, more energetic handling than many of the sketches. The knowledge gained from drawing makes it easier to paint complex subjects freely.

Sketching in colour

Colour sketches are quick studies for planning colour compositions, or taking quick notes about observed colour. These can be quite abstract, as they are focused on looking at how certain colours interact in a composition, rather than details. Often these are done at a fairly small scale in order to simplify the image into major areas of colour.

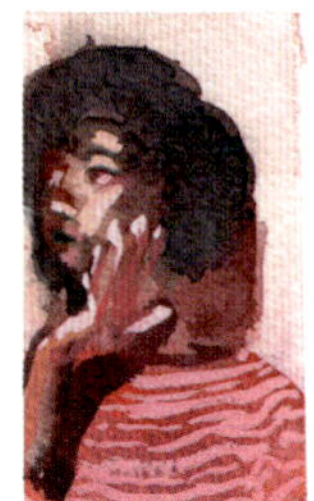
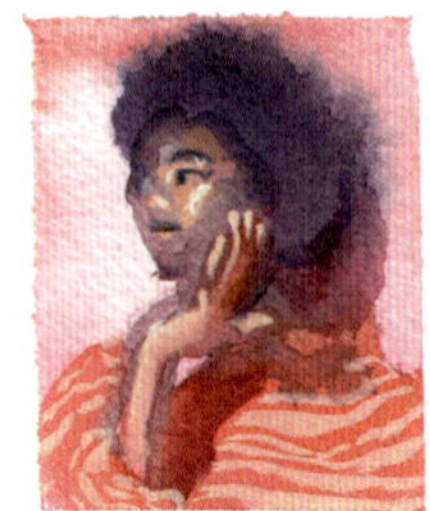
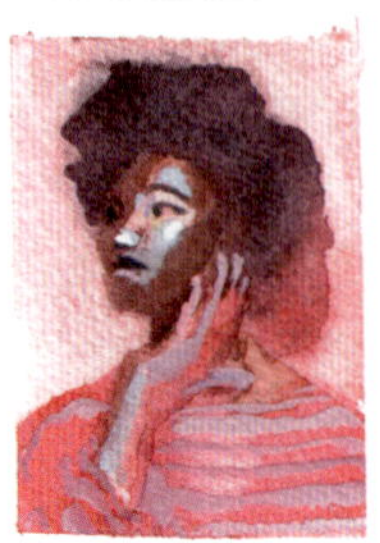

1 Experimenting with colour schemes

These small-scale studies are of the same subject, but offer different takes on it utilising three different colour schemes; two complementary colour schemes of red and green, and blue and orange, as well as a purple-blue analogous scheme. Colours can be pushed in different directions by focusing on specific combinations.

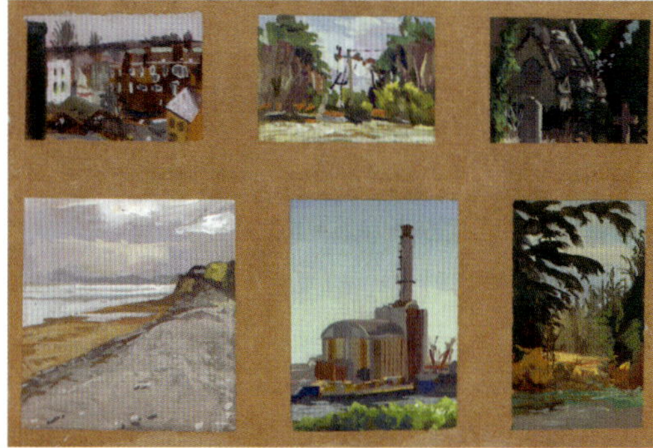

2 Colour notes from life

This page shows a selection of quick gouache sketches done from life. Portable watercolour or gouache sets are a great way to take colour notes to back up photo reference, which may not capture the intensity of colour, or the personal response. These can help dictate the colour in a more developed painting.

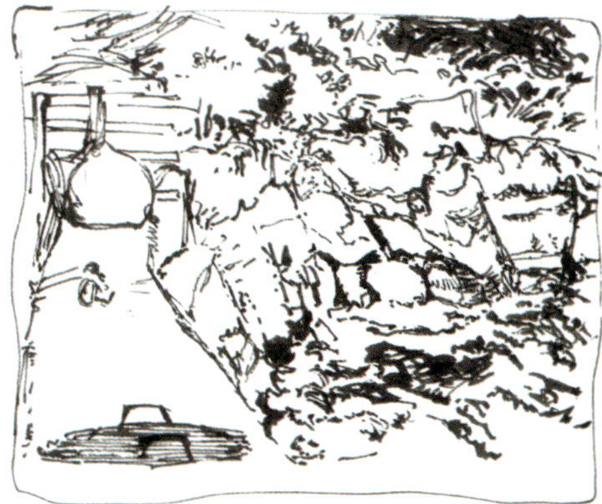

3 Digital colour

Digital software is a handy tool for testing colour. Here a sketchbook drawing is scanned in and painted over to compare different potential colour schemes. It needn't be perfect, just a quick sketch of what different combinations would look like. Editing tools are useful for adjusting colour or cropping images as well.

Look to the masters

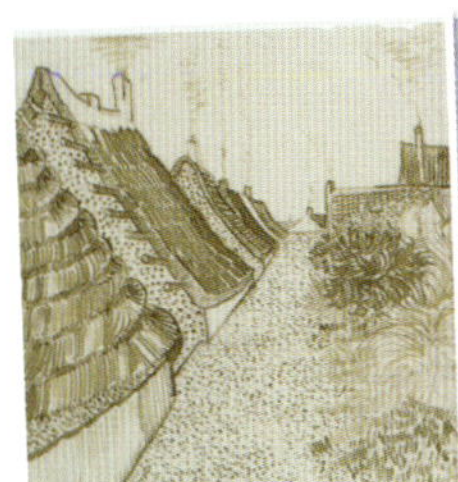

Van Gogh's drawings tell us a lot about how he interpreted his observations into paintings. They show the textures, patterns and rhythms underpinning his characteristic brushstrokes, and give his work a tactile sense of surface direction.

Here they're especially noticeable on the rooftops, translating almost directly from the drawing to the painting. The smoke from the chimneys is expressed with marks that track its motion, giving the impression that it is swirling up into the sky.

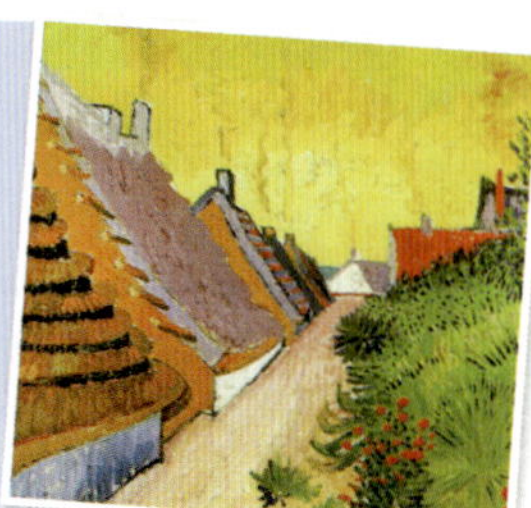

Mark-making for painting

Applying the marks made in a drawing to the painting process can add variety and energy to static brushstrokes

Mark making is one element of drawing that is about the different range of marks made with our tools. It is easy to get trapped in the habit of making the same marks in drawing, or brushstrokes in painting, so exploring ways to vary these can help make our artwork more visually interesting.

Consciously building a wider 'vocabulary' of different marks can help with developing a more distinctive style. Drawing is a good way to develop this, as it offers lots of tools to experiment with, and a low-stakes space to practise, as drawing is typically cheaper and less time-consuming.

Another way to find new marks is to copy a variety other artists' drawings and combine their marks in different ways. The marks developed in drawing can be carried into painting by emulating them with brush strokes and shapes.

This process is just one possible way to have a more mark-driven approach. It is a good idea to keep drawings to hand while painting as a reference – this helps with breaking away from directly copying photos or getting over invested in details that just don't matter.

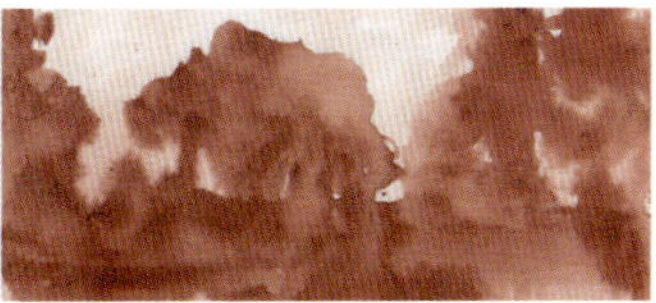

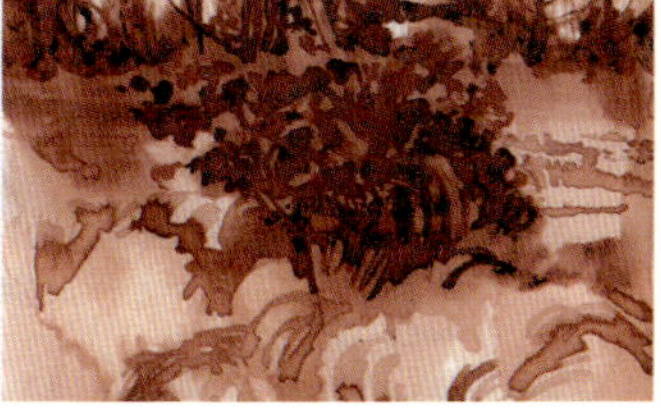

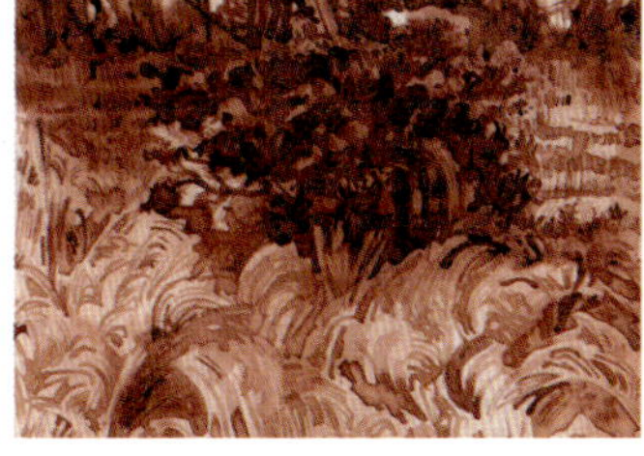

1 Broad sweeps
This drawing is done in ink with a brush and red pens. First I apply broad sweeps of diluted ink to lay in the dark tonal shapes of the gorse bush and trees. Where the ink bleeds, the tonal boundaries are softer and there is an added element of randomness.

2 Marks as shapes
When painting, a mark might be a line or shape, or multiple marks can collectively form a shape. Here, a broad-tipped reed pen is used to build the tonal shapes of the trees. The thickness of the marks was changed by twisting the pen like a flat or filbert brush.

3 Showing direction and texture
The grass is visually complex, as each stalk is too thin to draw with these tools. Instead, thin, sweeping marks track the overall direction and texture. Different sized marks imply perspective.

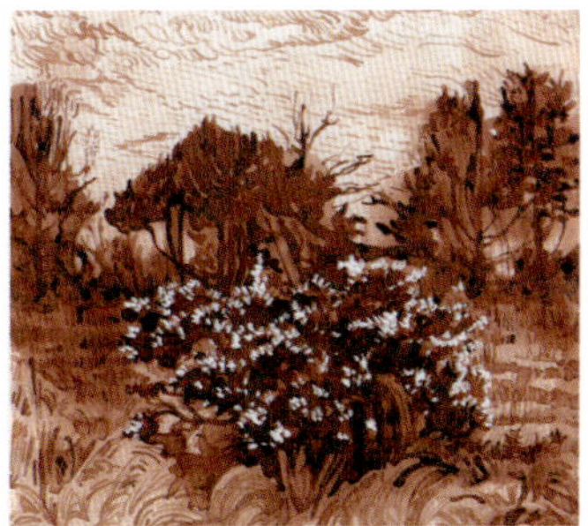

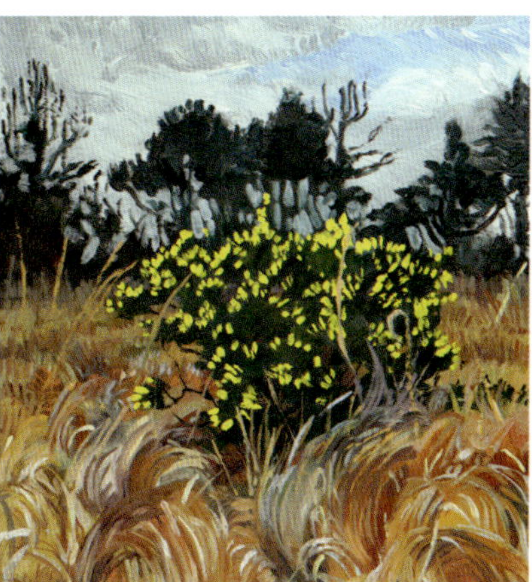

5 Final painting
The brushstrokes in this painting are influenced by the marks from the drawing. The clouds, though using thicker brushstrokes, follow the direction of the marks, and the grass also does this, but combines light and dark brushstrokes using a round brush. The flowers are dabbed on with a smaller brush.

4 Adding clouds and flowers
The sky and flowers utilise some more expressive ideas. The volume of the clouds is implied with the directional marks. The flowers are added with correction fluid by using quick, dabbing motions and following the underlying structure of the gorse bush.

colour theory for watercolour

Lancelot Richardson introduces the fundamentals of colour theory, and shows how it can be applied to a watercolour painting process

The relationships between different colours are broken down using colour theory. This guide will look at how colours are arranged on a spectrum around a colour wheel and how they form groups depending on their relative positions on it. It also looks at how colours are made up of the fundamental elements of hue, saturation and tone, and shows how to use these ideas to assist in the painting process.

Colour theory is especially useful when composing images and mixing colour. Different colour combinations can form compositions with different moods and harmonies. There are many ways to achieve harmonious colour compositions; certain placements of colours on a colour wheel and their combinations is one way to do this. The balance of light and dark in an image – its key – is also important.

Mixing colour can feel rather like a shot in the dark when you don't know how different colours behave and interact. When mixing colour, the colour wheel can guide us to mixing better neutral colours or understand what paints are needed to make more intense mixes.

These ideas are a guideline with which to get started. Colour is a diverse and subjective topic, with multiple interpretations that may vary depending on how it is used, the science of colour and light, and the language we use. This guide focuses on how painters typically use colour, but it is well worth digging deeper into this topic and learning more about the science of colour, and how it is used in other settings, such as printed media.

Understanding the colour wheel

THE COLOUR WHEEL is an essential part of understanding the spectrum of colours we see. Even though colours exist on a continuous spectrum, artists typically break them down into individual blocks that can be named. This forms the outermost ring of the colour wheel.

In painting, the conventional primary colours are red, yellow and blue. These form the basis of an artists' colour wheel and are evenly spaced around it. Secondary colours are created by mixing two primary colours – if red, blue and yellow are the primary colours, the secondary colours are green, orange and violet. Tertiary colours are created by mixing a primary with a secondary colour – for instance, vermilion is an orange-red.

Using red, yellow and blue as primary colours is not entirely accurate, as greens and blues take up more of the colour spectrum than this covers. Sometimes alternative colour wheels are used, such as red, blue and green, or cyan, magenta and yellow. It is possible to mix traditional primary colours with these alternative colour wheels, though they will not be as intense as pure pigments. The idea of primary colours is that any colour can be mixed from them – however, again, these secondary mixtures are less vivid than pure pigments. The closer two colours are on the colour wheel, the more intense their mixture is. The farther apart two colours are, the duller the mixture.

Colour groups

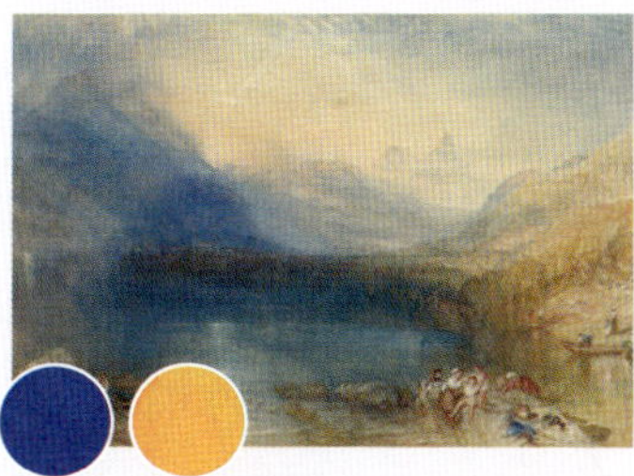

1 ⊙ Complementary colours

Complementary colours sit opposite each other on the wheel. They have the highest colour contrast, often looking very intense when placed next to each other in a composition. Two saturated complementary colours may clash and strain a viewer's eyes, especially in close proximity. One way to use them effectively is to ensure one colour is more neutral – in this example by Turner, the oranges are pushed into lighter, more neutral browns to balance the saturated blues. Mixing two complementary colours together produces a neutral grey, or even a black, as they cancel each other out – the greys in the centre of the colour wheel can be made this way.

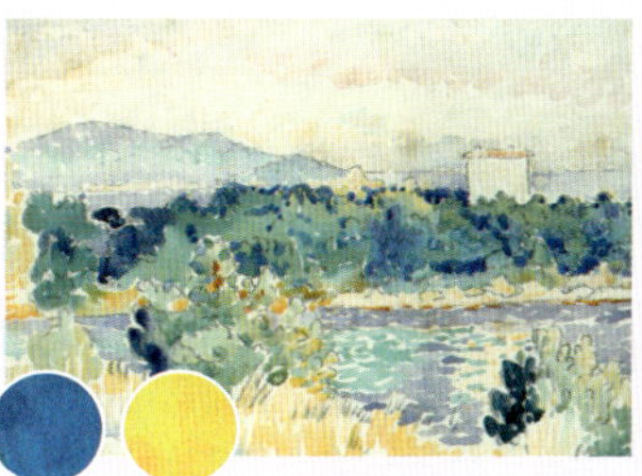

2 ⊙ Analogous colours

Analogous colours are neighbours on the colour wheel. They can span a very narrow portion of the colour wheel, or a wider section.

Because these colours neighbour each other, they have less colour contrast and harmonise easily – almost too easily. To add contrast in these sorts of colour schemes, one option is to push the tonal or saturation contrasts (or both) instead – this example by Henri-Edmond Cross uses darker blues to contrast lighter yellows.

When mixed, analogous colours produce bright intermediary hues. The closer two colours are on the colour wheel, the more saturated their mixture.

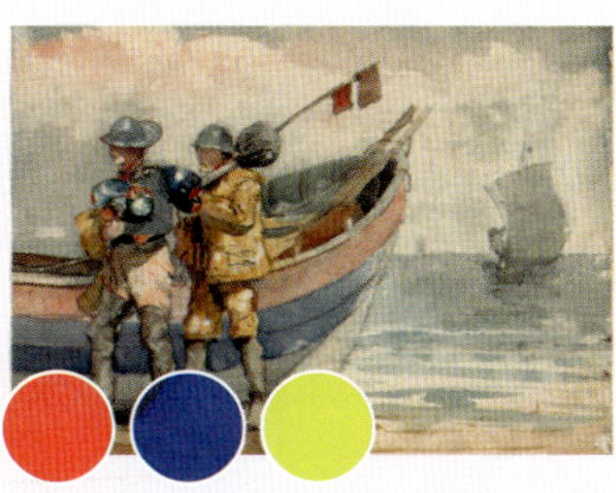

3 ⊙ Triadic colours

Triadic colours schemes are comprised of three colours evenly spaced around the colour wheel.

This can be challenging with saturated colours, as a large area of the wheel is included in these schemes, making colour contrast hard to manage. One option is to pick a dominant colour and let the other two support it as more subdued tones. Another strategy, used in this example by Winslow Homer, is to tie a triad of saturated colours together with whites, which give the eye a break, and reflects subtle indications of the triad, tying the composition together. Alternatively, triad colours can be used in small amounts to 'spice up' neutral arrangements.

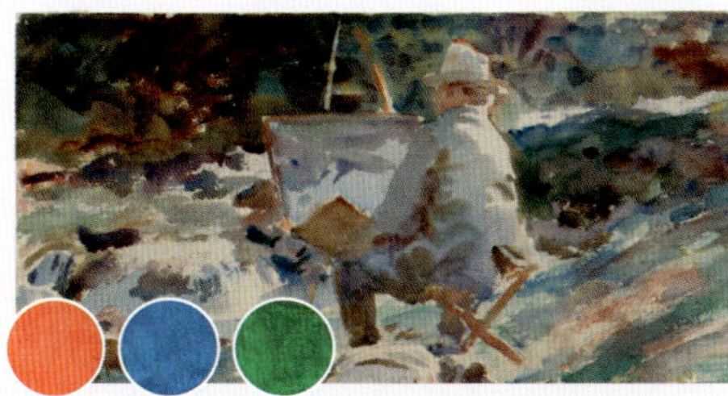

4 ⊙ Split complementary colours

Split complementary colour schemes are like complementary schemes, but one colour is split into two. The other colour sits opposite the centre point of this pair. The separation between the split pair can be narrow, like in this example by Sargent that splits across the blue-green colours, or can expand until it transforms into a triadic scheme. This is a great set-up for a limited palette, as it has the harmony of a complementary colour scheme, but covers more ground on the colour wheel and includes a wider range of colours in the composition. Some complementary schemes split both colours – sometimes called a tetradic scheme. They work especially well if the range of each pair is limited.

The emotions of colour

COLOUR CAN PLAY a key role in the mood of an image, depending on the dominant hues and how they are used, such as how grey or saturated they are, or the key of the image.

Colour can be associated with certain emotions. There are many complex reasons why a colour creates a psychological reaction in a viewer, and this depends on context, societal influences and other colour interactions as much as a colour's inherent properties. A field of yellow flowers would be a bright, uplifting scene, but yellow is also associated with danger as it appears on warning signs and wasps. Therefore, some of these associations may seem contradictory.

RED = excitement, aggression, romance
YELLOW = warmth, friendliness, danger
GREEN = nature, sickliness, envy
BLUE = relaxation, coldness, grief
WHITE = cleanliness, innocence, emptiness
BLACK = oppressive, calm, powerful

Tonal value

TONAL VALUE is how light or dark a colour is on a scale that ranges from white to black.

Monochrome colour schemes are purely tonal – they only use one colour, and only change its tonal value. As colours get lighter or darker, their saturation changes as well. Different colours have different tonal values – yellow is very light, red and green are in the middle, and blues and purples are quite dark.

Tints and shades are light and dark forms of a colour. Lightening a colour creates tints, whilst darkening it creates shades. This can be done by adding white or black paint, though this may give 'flat' results. In watercolour, lightening colours can be done by diluting them so the white of the paper shows more. Darkening colours is best done by mixing them with a chromatic black – a black made from mixing colours.

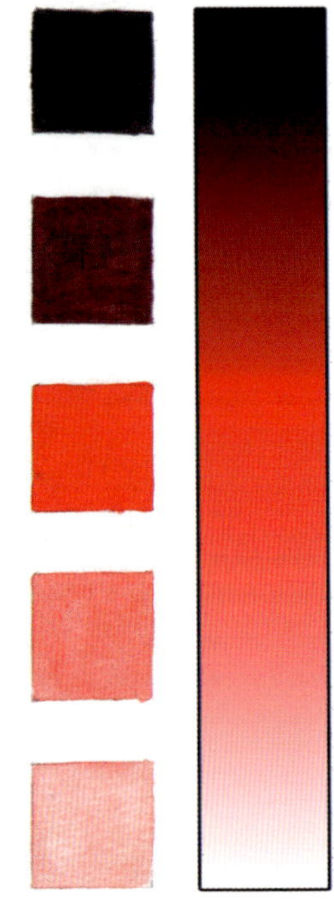

Saturation

SATURATION is how intense or 'vivid' a colour is, on a scale that ranges from grey to a pure colour. This is also called chroma, or purity.

It is tempting to use saturated colours exclusively – after all, they look colourful! However, if all the colours in a composition are saturated, none of them look especially vivid. To use saturation effectively, employ its full range and use some duller colours – a saturated red will stand out dramatically on a dull green background. Most of what surrounds us is made of duller colours – human skin, for instance, is largely comprised of warm greys.

The farther apart two colours are on the colour wheel, the less saturated their mixture is. This is why if you mix an orange-ish yellow with a blue, the resulting green will look dull.

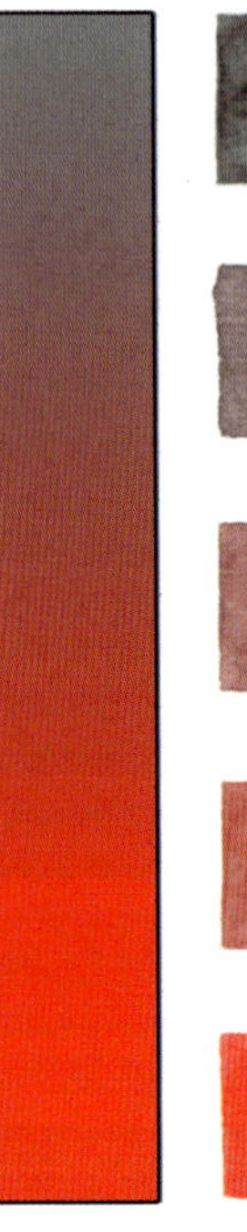

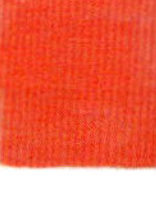

Hue

HUE IS A COLOUR'S place on the outer ring of the colour wheel, or on a spectrum of colours. Though we often identify certain hues with specific names – such as red or blue – it is actually a continuous spectrum resulting from the wavelengths of light reflected off a subject.

Hue is often used as synonym for colour, but is a little different as it refers purely to a colour's position around the colour wheel or in the light spectrum. It is combined with saturation and tonal value to create individual colours. For instance, brown colours are often oranges with a lower saturation and darker tonal value.

Colour schemes in painting tend to look at hue contrasts. Because hue loops back on itself in a circle (unlike saturation or tonal value), these relationships are easier to visualise on a wheel.

High key versus low key

THE KEY OF an image is the dominant tonal value it has overall, and how it limits its tonal values to a certain range.

High key compositions are dominated by light tonal values, and omit or minimally use dark tonal values. This creates a dominance of more pastel colours, and allows saturated colours to act as colourful shadows. In the example by Rosa Bonheur below, whites and light colours dominate, and a lot of the shadows are limited to middle greys. High key compositions often have a light, airy feel – here, it helps showcase the movement of the horses.

Low key compositions have a predominance of dark tonal values, and omit or minimally use light tones. This is good for showing atmospheric and weather effects, as well as night scenes. The addition of small touches of light values creates dramatic tonal contrast. This example by Whistler (right) is full of atmosphere. The tonal contrast draws immediate attention up to the sitter's face.

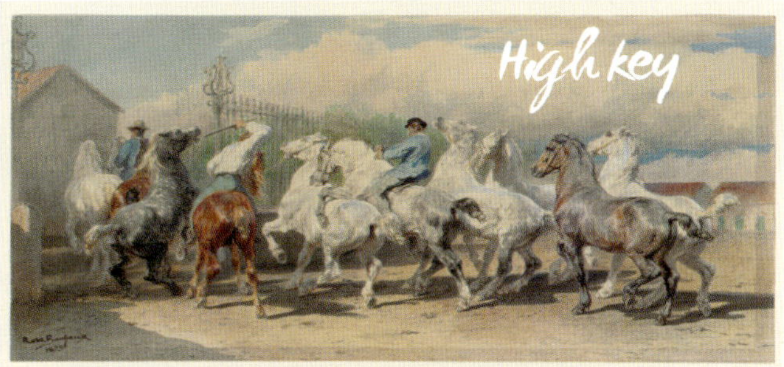

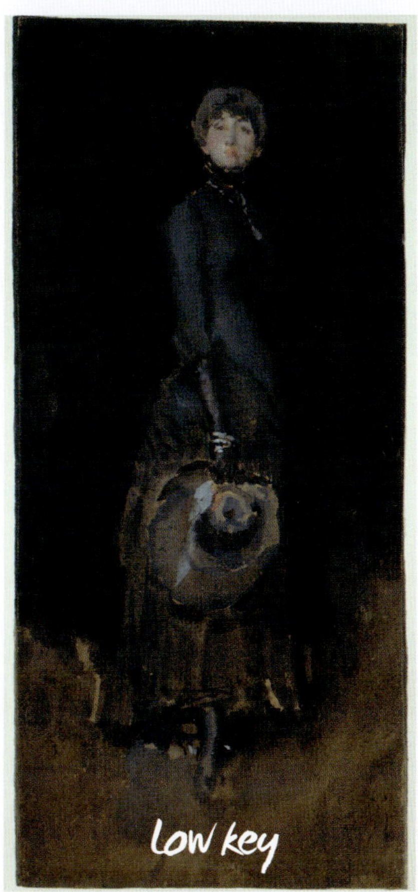

Warm, neutral & cool tones

COLOUR TEMPERATE is how 'warm' or 'cool' a colour is perceived to be. Blues, greens and violets are typically considered cool colours, whilst reds, oranges and yellows are considered warms. Neutral colours are less saturated colours that don't show colour temperature as strongly, with greys being completely neutral. Neutrals can lean towards being warm or cool.

Temperature is a relative property that is used to compare hue – for instance, magenta is near red on the colour wheel, but is a comparatively cooler hue, whilst orange has a warmer hue than red. It is also used specificity variants on a colour – for instance, a warm-leaning red would be approaching orange – like vermilion – whilst a cool-leaning red would approach purple – such as crimson.

Like many aspects of colour, temperature can be quite subjective. It can be tricky to decide what the coolest and warmest colours are precisely, or where warm colours stop and cool ones start.

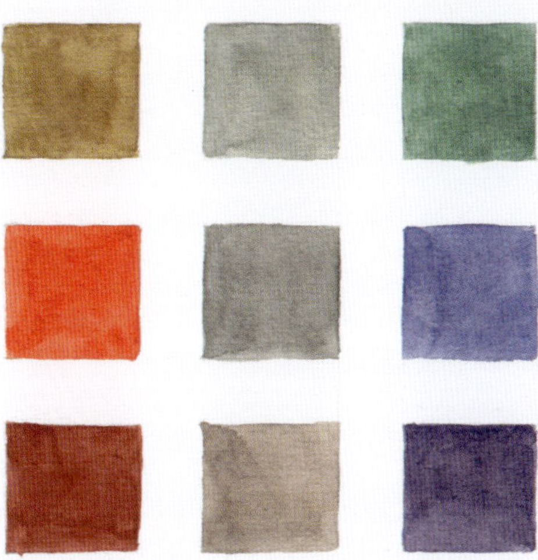

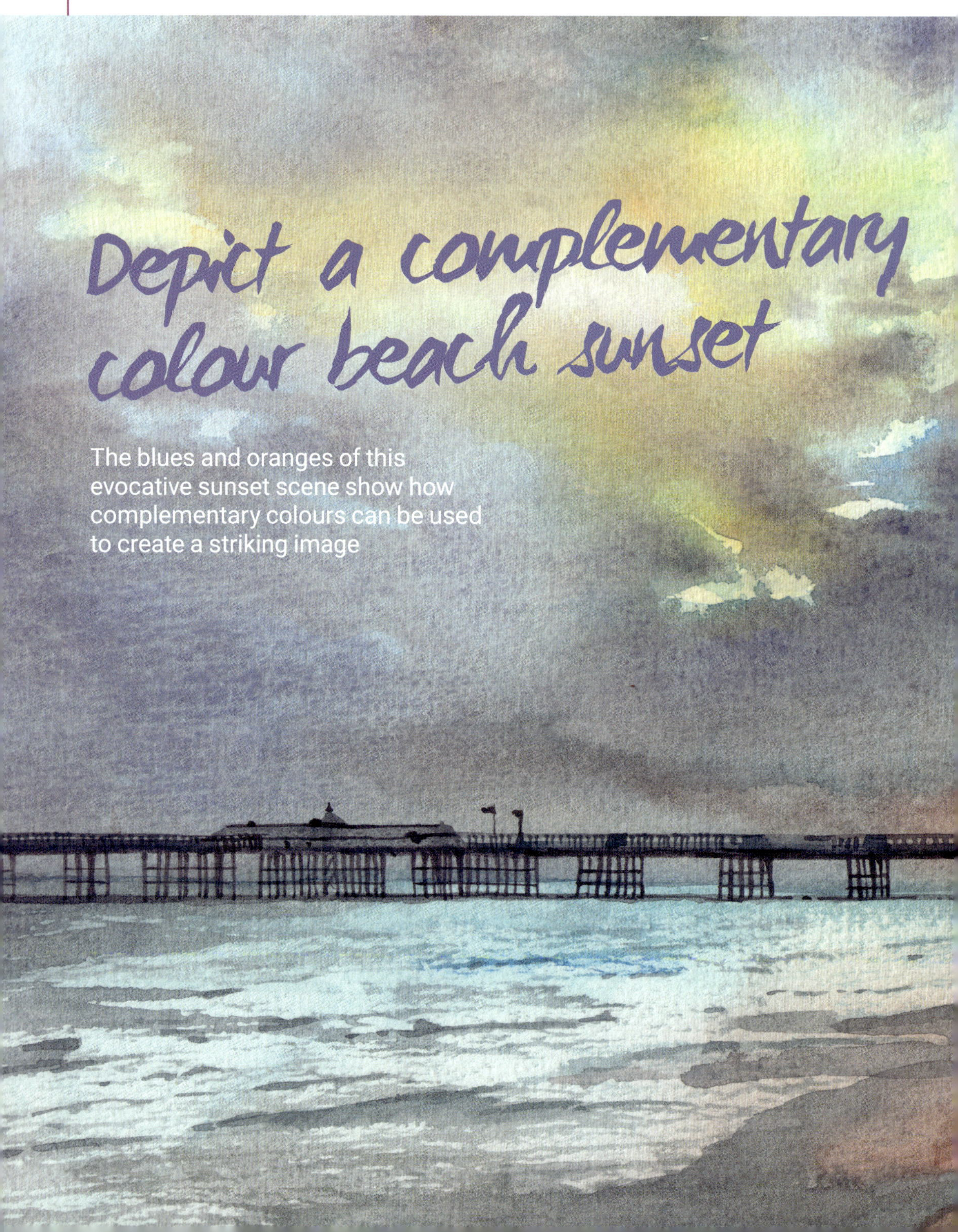

Depict a complementary colour beach sunset

The blues and oranges of this evocative sunset scene show how complementary colours can be used to create a striking image

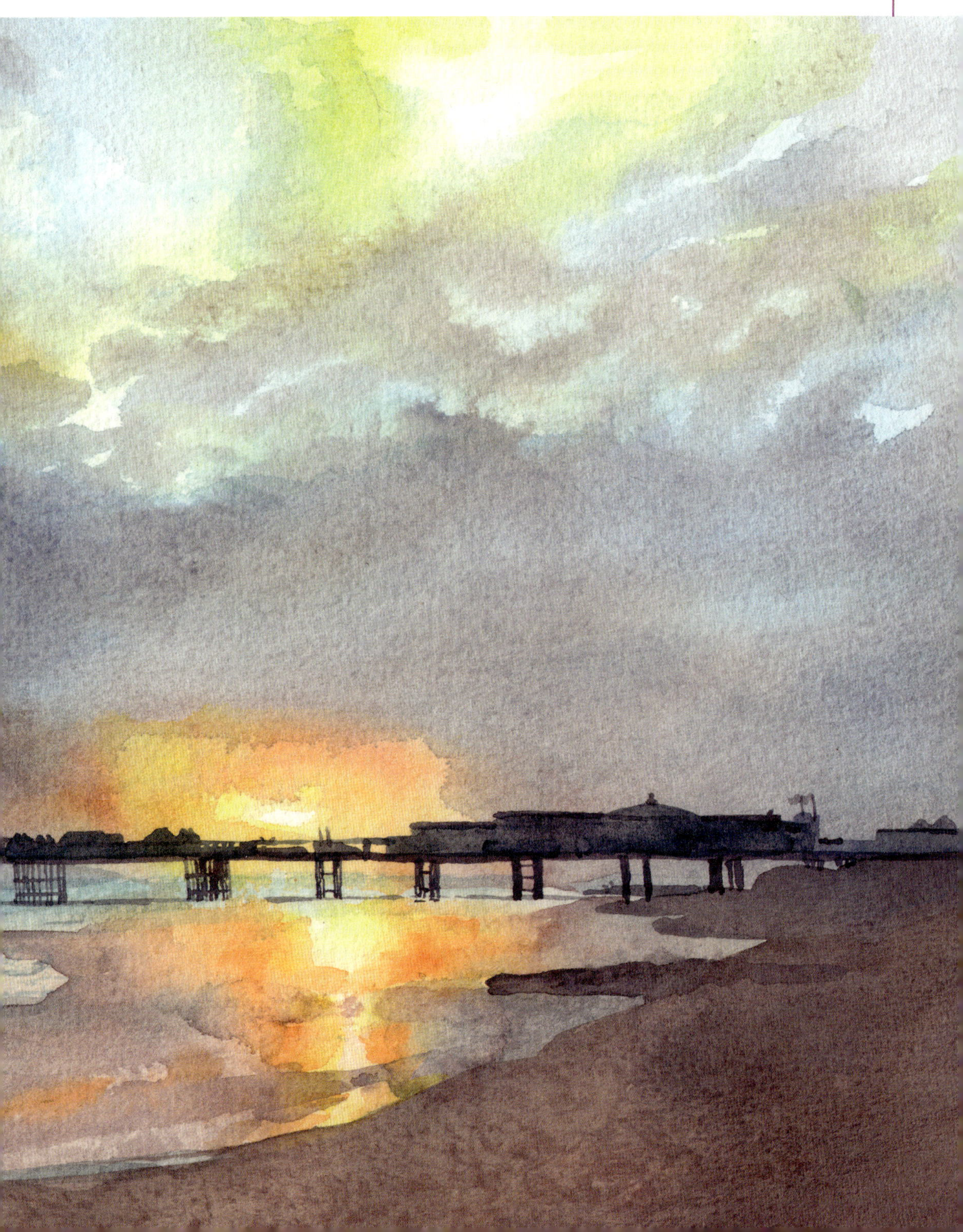

Materials

- Winsor and Newton Artists tube watercolours: Lemon (Winsor) Yellow, Cadmium Yellow, Pyrrole (Winsor) Red, Permanent Alizarin Crimson, French Ultramarine, Phthalo Blue, Venetian Red
- Brushes: 1 inch flat wash, 3/8 inch medium flat, round sable #8
- Seawhites cold press watercolour paper
- 2H graphite pencil
- Spray bottle

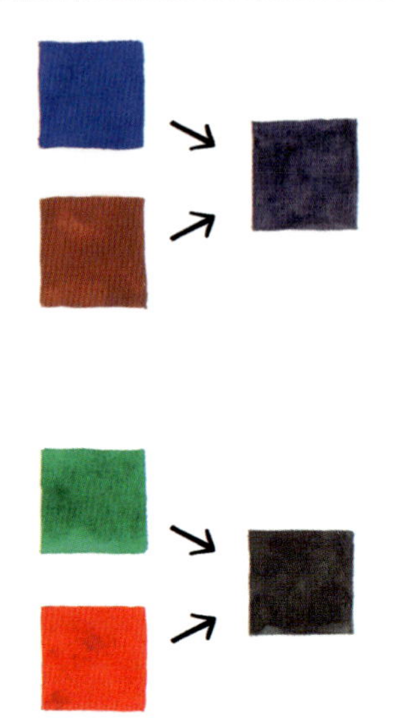

Mixing shadows

It is tempting to use black when mixing shadows. However, tube black can result in 'flat' shadows, so it is best to use chromatic blacks. Chromatic blacks are shadows mixed using colours, such as red and green, or blue and brown. These are usually complementary, though mixing a triad of colours can work too. Add these to colour mixes to make richer shadows.

Follow these steps...

1 ◐ Wet-in-Wet: initial wash

To start, I create a loose sketch in pencil and apply broad washes using the flat wash brush.

The colour scheme for this image is going to be a roughly split complementary of blue with a yellow and orange pair, so I start with these colours. After laying in the blue wash first, I add the oranges and yellows while it is still wet to create soft edges as they bleed together.

The paint in this stage is very watered down to keep things light, and the very lightest areas still keep the white of the paper.

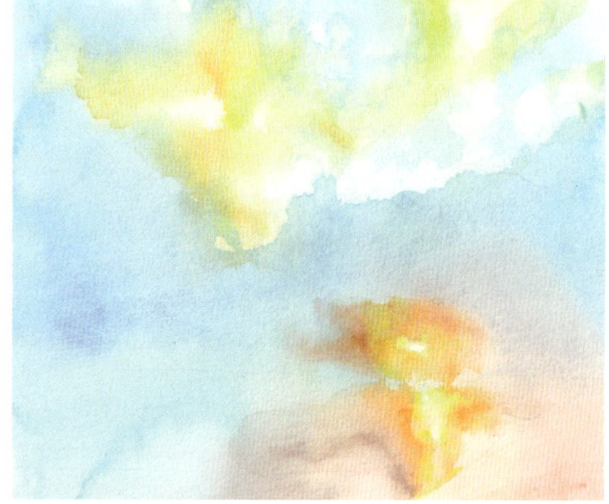

2 ◐ Intensify colour

In this image, the yellow and orange are going to be the most saturated colours, while the blues are going to be duller and darker, and other colours will be much more neutral.

After allowing the blues to dry completely, I add more intense yellows and oranges to push the saturation of these areas up. To achieve the soft blooms of colour, I gently brush a little water onto the paper and let the paint bleed into it as I apply it – this is a bit easier to control than a spray.

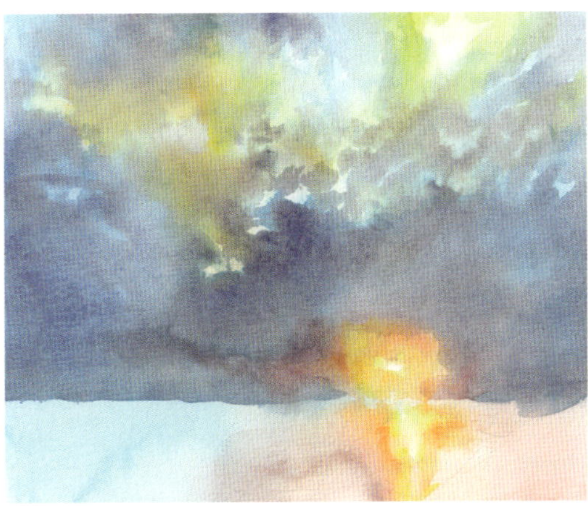

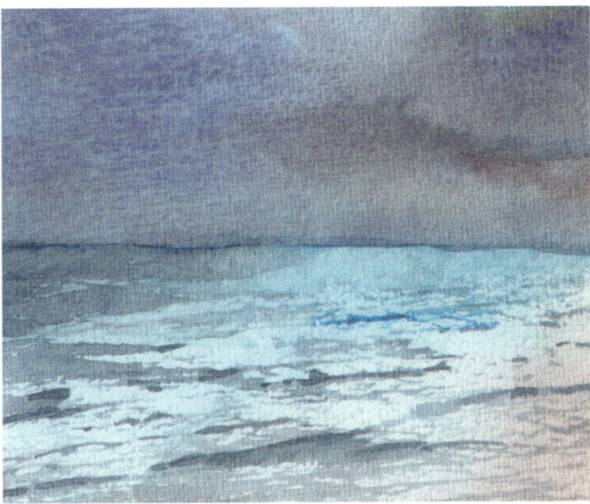

3 ⬤ Add clouds

The clouds cover a large area with fairly neutral blues. This colour may not seem exciting, but it provides a backdrop for the vivid sunset colours.

For the neutral blue, I mix Ultramarine with a tiny bit of Phthalo Blue and some Venetian Red to dull it. The mixture is kept quite diluted to keep it pale enough, and around the sunset I add extra Alizarin Crimson where the red light glows through the clouds. To soften the clouds, some parts of the sky were wetted with a spray bottle to allow the paint to run.

4 ⬤ Add sea texture

The sea is in a couple of layers. It is more saturated and slightly green-leaning near the horizon line and sun, so I use a little wash of Phthalo Blue with a tiny bit of Lemon Yellow to push it greener and with Ultramarine to dull the saturation a touch.

For the second layer, there is a bit more Ultramarine and touch of Venetian Red in the mixture to make a more neutral grey-blue colour. This is applied with a fairly dry brush, dragged over the grain of the paper to make the broken-up texture of the waves.

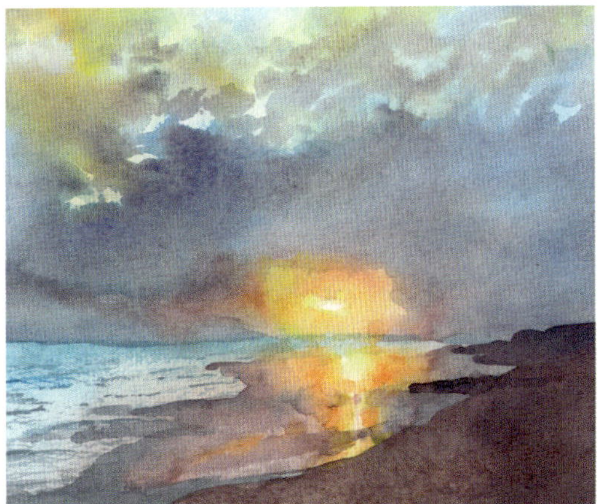

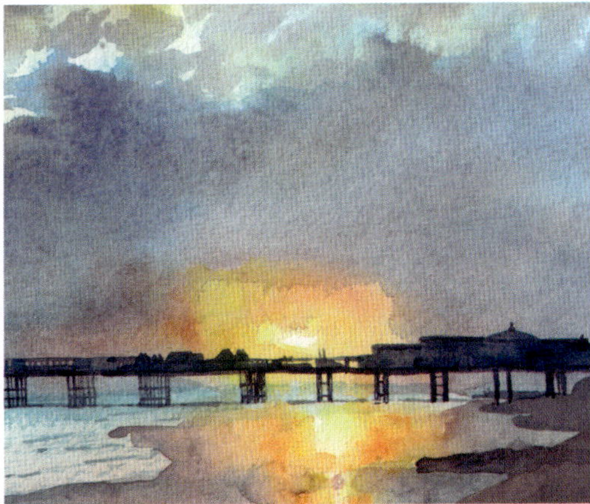

5 ⬤ Dark neutral tones

The sand and beach seem almost purple due to contrast from the blues and yellows, even though these areas are dark, neutral colours. Dull blues are used for the wet sand – these are blended into the reflection of the sunset with a little Alizarin Crimson. I brush water on the paper first so the paint will bleed.

To get the colour of the shadowy beach, I mix Ultramarine Blue and Venetian Red to get a dark neutral colour, then add a little Alizarin Crimson to warm it up. The texture of the beach is scumbled in using a dry, round brush, making twisting motions.

6 ⬤ Add the pier

The colour for the pier is Venetian Red and Ultramarine Blue – using a little water this time – with a touch of Phthalo Blue to cool it down. Because a lot of the other elements have been painted with more water, they are relatively light in tone and allow the pier to stand out.

The pier is added using a medium round sable brush – a good natural hair brush should hold a fine point well. I draw the boardwalk first, then add the structures on top and below. The reflection around the struts is added at the end using a more dilute shadow colour.

Analogous portraits

This portrait demonstration shows an analogous colour scheme at work and looks at mixing warm neutral skin tones

Materials

- Winsor and Newton tube paints: Cadmium Yellow, Winsor Orange, Pyrrole (Winsor) Red, Permanent Alizarin Crimson, French Ultramarine, Yellow Ochre, Venetian Red
- Faber Castel watercolour pencils – Yellow Ochre
- Brushes: 1 inch flat wash, 3/8 inch medium flat, round sable #8, round synthetic #7, fan
- Seawhites cold press watercolour paper

Mixing skin tones

In most situations, skin is largely made up of warm, neutral tones. When mixing colour for darker skin, I'd use a similar palette to this demonstration, but may incorporate more reds, blues and browns to mixtures to warm and darken it. Lighter skin uses more dilute paint and is sometimes more red-leaning.

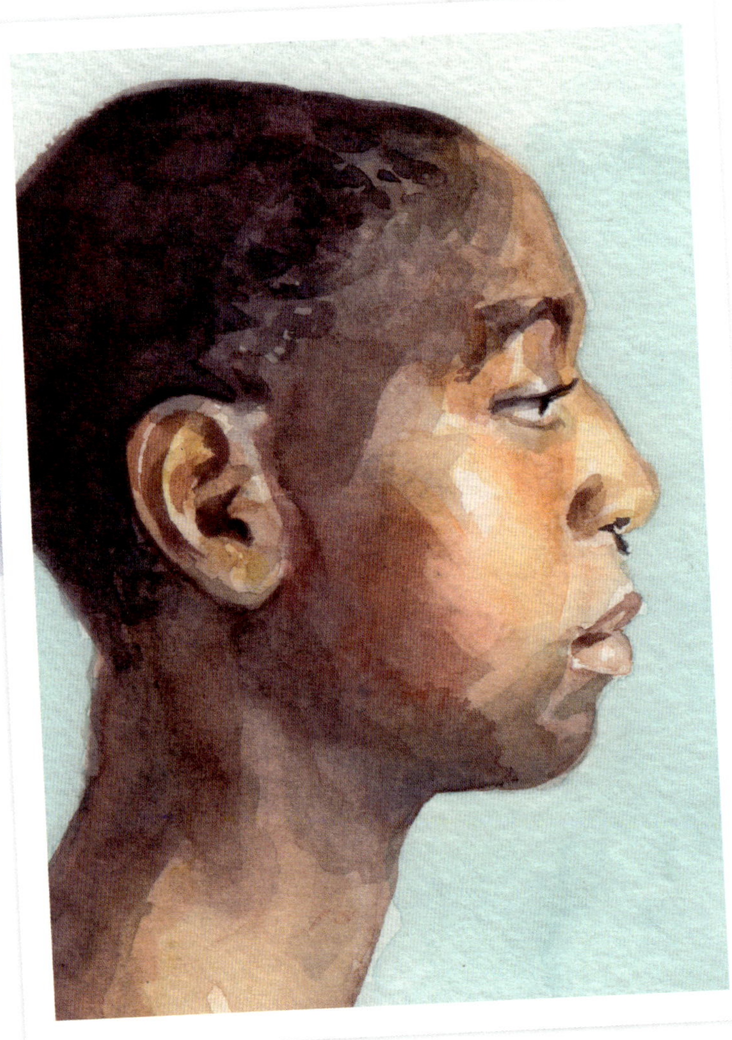

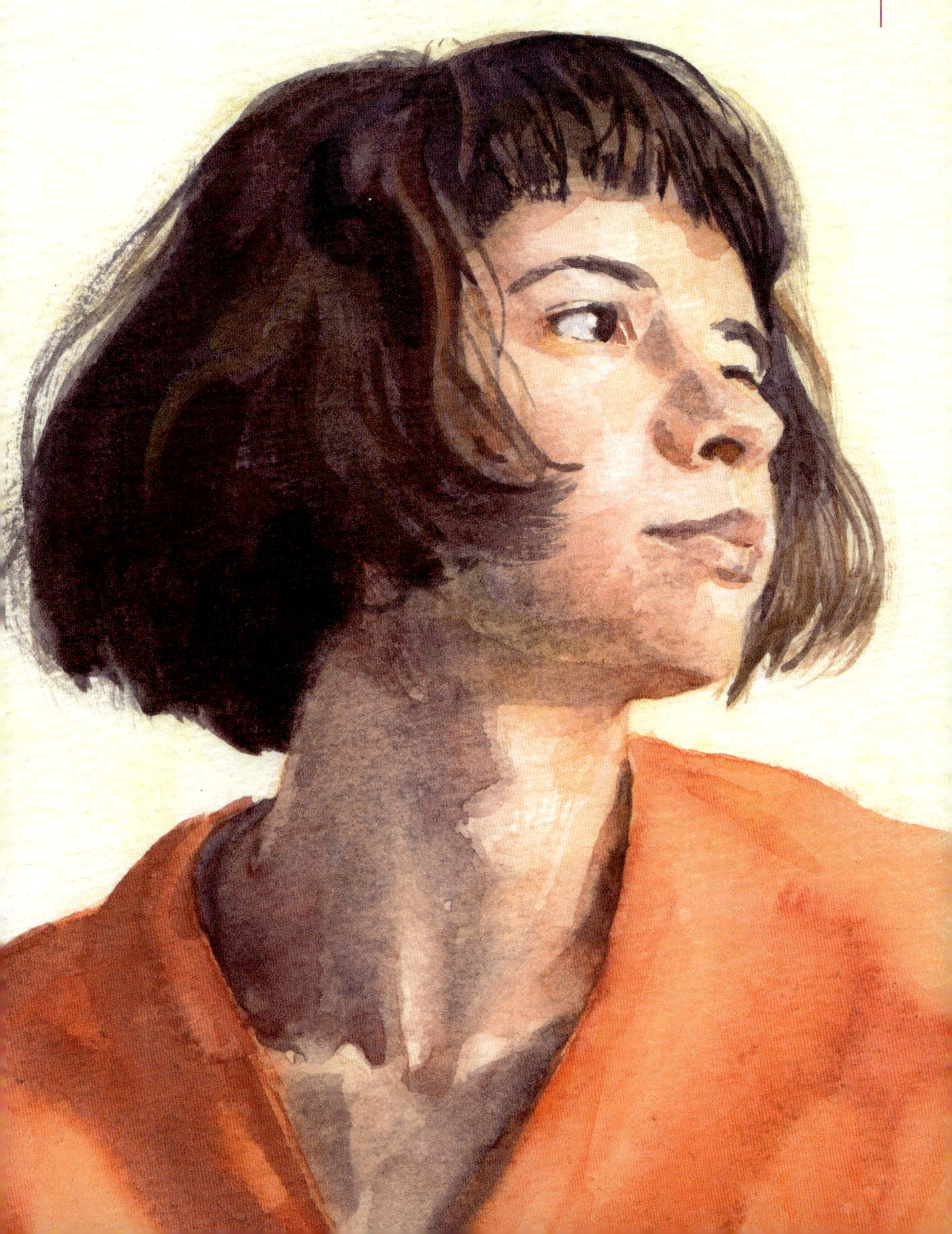

Follow these steps...

1 ▽ Lay in base colours

To start this portrait, I sketch out the face as a simple line drawing in water-soluble pencil. Then, using fairly dilute paint, I apply some warm neutrals to the skin and background. The colour scheme for this portrait is going to be analogous, with the warmest yellows and oranges for the lighter areas, and cooler reds and purples for the darker areas.

The sketch is done in a Yellow Ochre pencil to complement the colour scheme. When selecting paints, I need a lot of freedom in mixing warm colours here, so my palette has multiple reds and yellows.

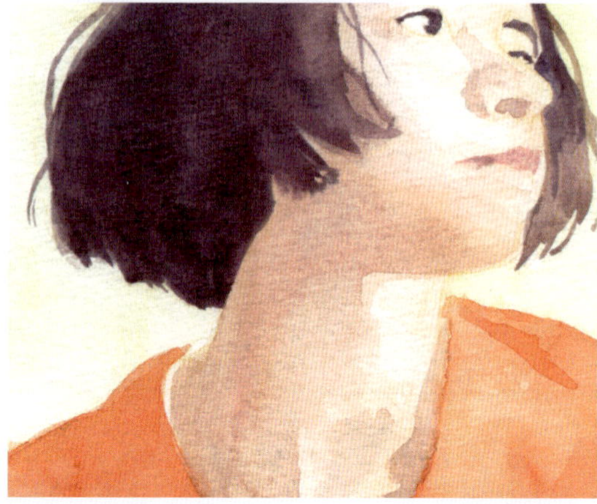

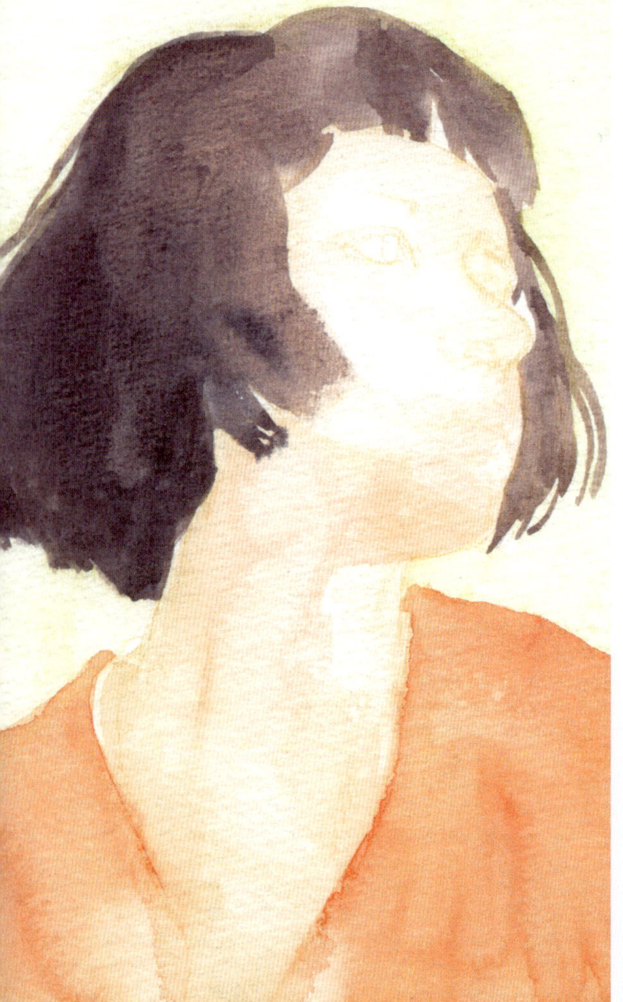

2 ▲ Establish shadows

Using broad areas of colour, I establish the major shadow shapes. For the skin, I place a roughly average, warm neutral that is starting to lean towards purples in the cooler places. Typically this is done by mixing skin tones from Cadmium Yellow and Pyrrole Red, then neutralising them by adding Ultramarine Blue and a little Venetian Red, and nudging the hue with other colours. Try to avoid saturated colours for now, and instead keep the colours fairly neutral at this stage.

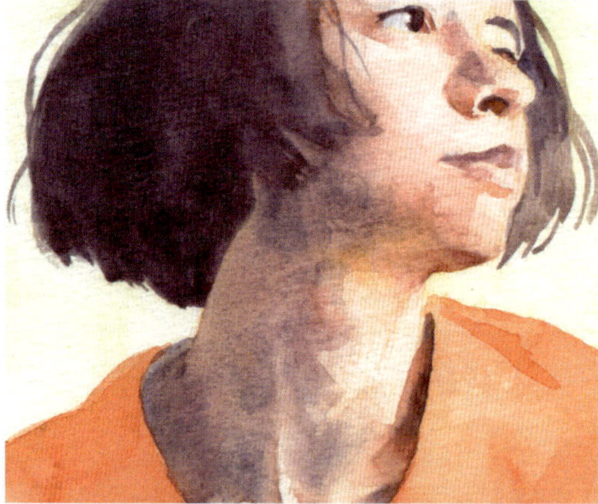

3 ▲ Shadow variations

Skin has subtle variations, leaning warmer or cooler in different areas. Here, I've intensified the shadows. Under the chin, the reflection of light from the dress nudges them warmer – these are mixed with Winsor Orange and Pyrrole Red. On the other side of the neck and the cheek, cool tones are added – Ultramarine Blue and sometimes Alizarin Crimson. Some of the deepest shadow areas (e.g. the nostril) are rendered with more red. They tend to have warm shadows and this avoids making them too dark.

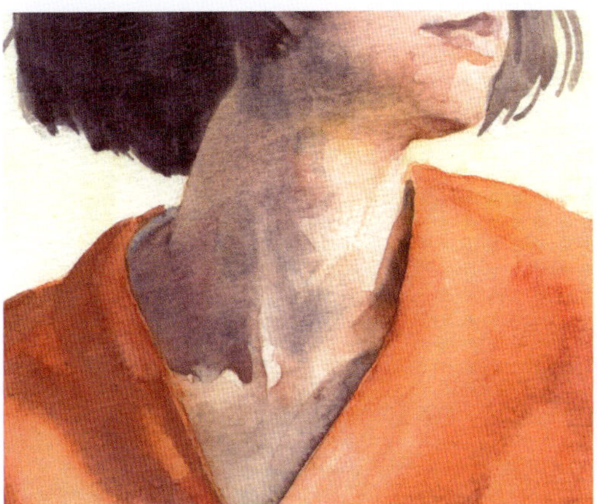

4 ⬤ Mix bright colours

The dress is the most saturated part of this portrait. To produce such a vivid colour, I mix Winsor Orange and Pyrrole Red, close neighbours on the wheel. I then add some Alizarin and Ultramarine to the cooler shadow areas.

Another thing that helps the dress colour 'pop' is the contrast in saturation it has with its surroundings – the skin tones are fairly neutral, making it appear more vivid in comparison. The best way to make a colour appear bright and saturated is to surround it by less-saturated neighbours.

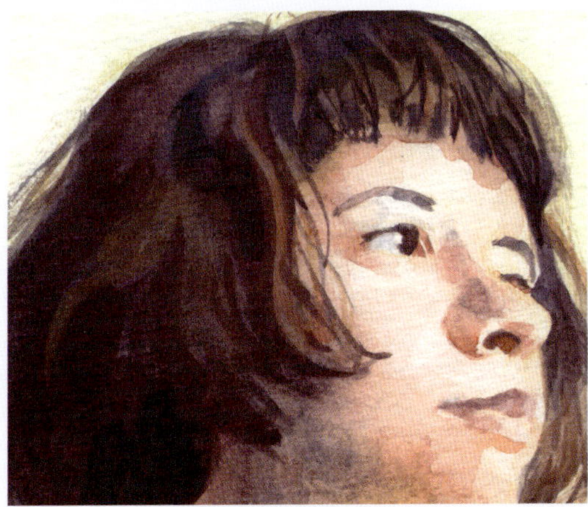

5 ⬤ Build darks for the hair

The initial layer for the hair is mixed using Ultramarine Blue and Venetian Red to make a chromatic black, with some Permanent Alizarin Crimson to warm it up.

Here, I add another layer, working with more highly pigmented paint to make it darker. The shadows are more of the same, with a lean towards Venetian Red to warm them up at the back of the head. In the light locks, a few colours peek out – these were created using thinner mixtures based around Yellow Ochre, which is opaque and can sit 'on top' of darker colours somewhat.

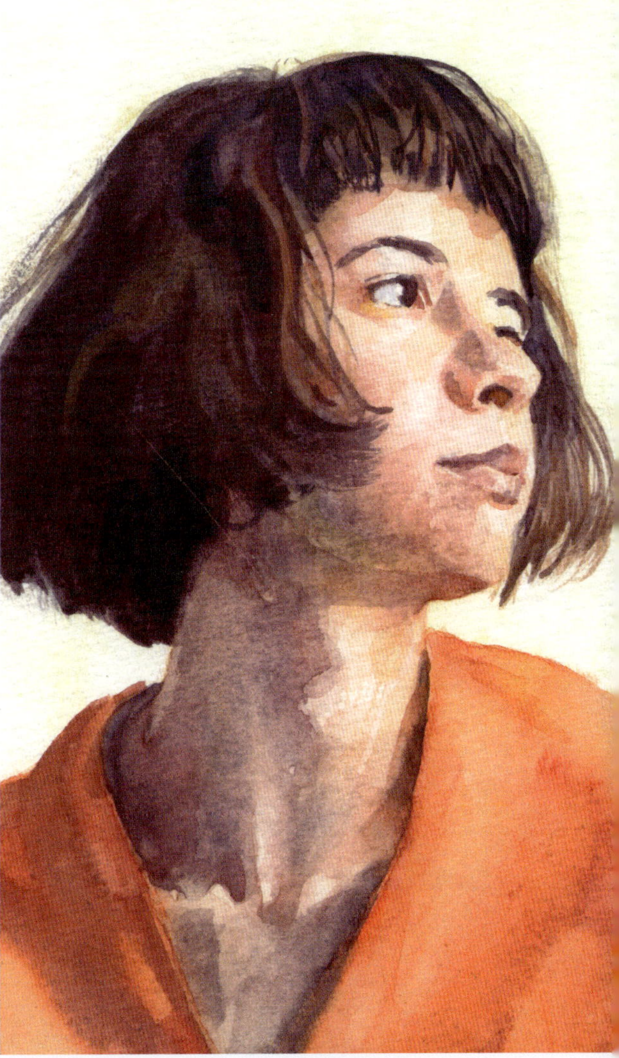

6 ⬤ Finish the face

In this stage I tighten up the details around the facial features and warm up the light colours on the face. Typically, if the shadows are relatively cool, the light is warmer (and vice versa – warm shadows have relatively cool light) so I clarify this by warming the lit skin tones with thin washes of Cadmium Yellow mixed with Pyrrole Red or Alizarin Crimson. These are very translucent, as I do not want to darken these areas.

I add a reddish neutral to the shadow shapes around the cheek and neck, and use thin washes to soften the cheek.

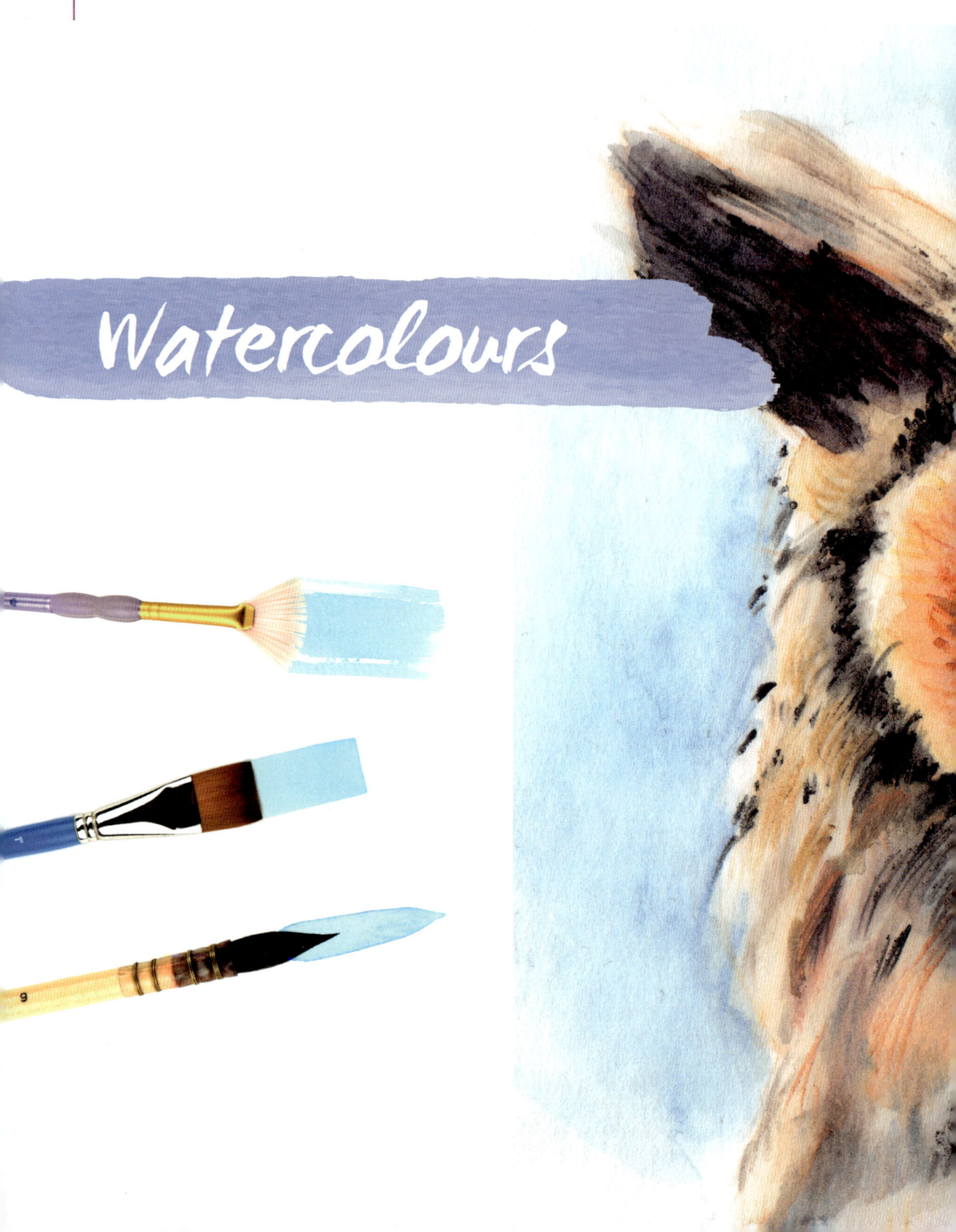

Watercolours

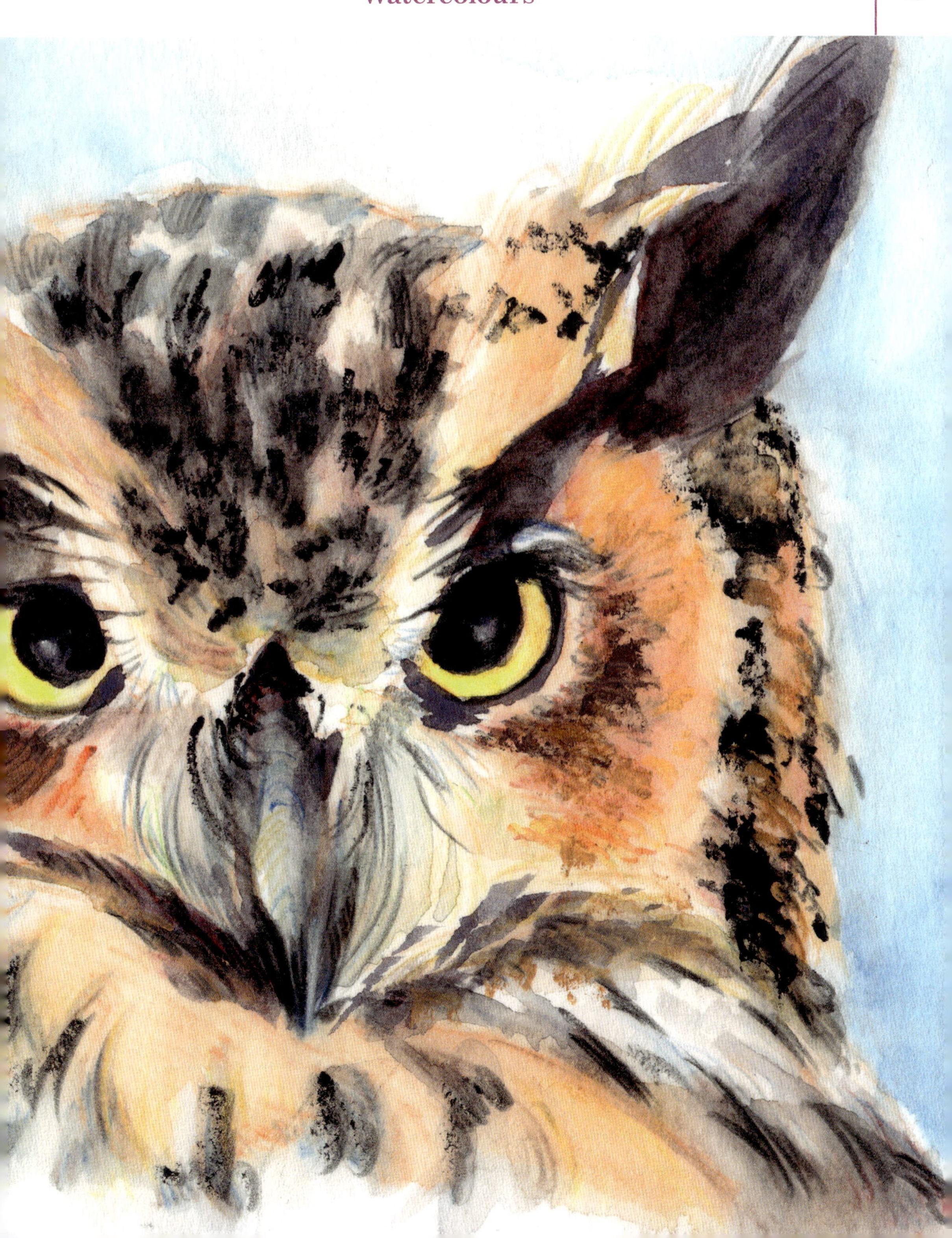

Essential kit for watercolour

This guide from **Lancelot Richardson** introduces common watercolour materials, explains what they are and gives suggestions for building your own watercolour kit

Watercolour is a diverse medium, with lots of different options for paints, brushes and papers, as well as extra tools for applying and manipulating colour. This introduction covers a range of materials available on the market, highlighting what they are used for and how they may fit into certain working processes.

There is an awful lot to choose from, and most artists won't need everything shown in this guide. Focus on picking materials that suit your process and sensibilities. For instance, if you are interested in producing large-scale work, consider choosing paint that offers wide coverage and brushes that make larger marks. If you are interested in tight details, however, it might be better to select materials more suited for producing fine brushstrokes. If you are unsure, consider selecting a few versatile materials instead of specialist ones, and expand your kit over time.

Quality of materials wins out over quantity, more so for watercolour than almost any other medium; a few tubes of good paint will create a better result than an entire set of cheap ones, and a single good brush will serve you better than a vast kit that cannot hold a point.

Below I've listed my go-to tools for painting watercolour, but bear in mind that you'll want to start small.

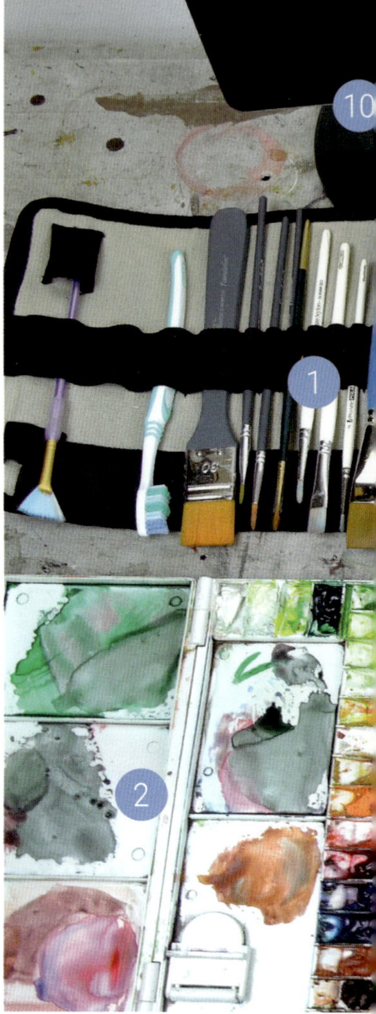

1 Brush roll

A selection of brushes in a roll covering a range of shapes and sizes useful for day-to-day painting. Keeping them in a roll protects them and keeps them together.

2 Palette with paints

I prefer to paint from tube paints squeezed into a palette, since it is convenient and suitable for the sizes I work at. Tube paints are allowed to dry in the palette – if fresh paint is needed, I can squeeze out more.

3 Watercolour paper and board

Here I use a board as a support for the watercolour paper and hold it down with masking tape so the paper doesn't buckle while I'm painting. If I'm working with more washes, I'll use stronger, gummed tape instead.

4 Pipette

Pipettes are handy tools to have around. I use them for squirting water into mixtures to help thin out washes, and they are also useful for dripping a little water onto dry paints in order to reactivate them.

5 Watercolour pencils

Often I use watercolour pencils for the initial sketch of a painting I am working on, as they add a little colour to the initial stages, and the lines melt away to something softer.

6 Watercolour tube paints

I like to store my tube paints in a jar to keep them fresher for longer. It also keeps them from getting lost! I keep a tube of gouache handy for occasional opaque highlights, too.

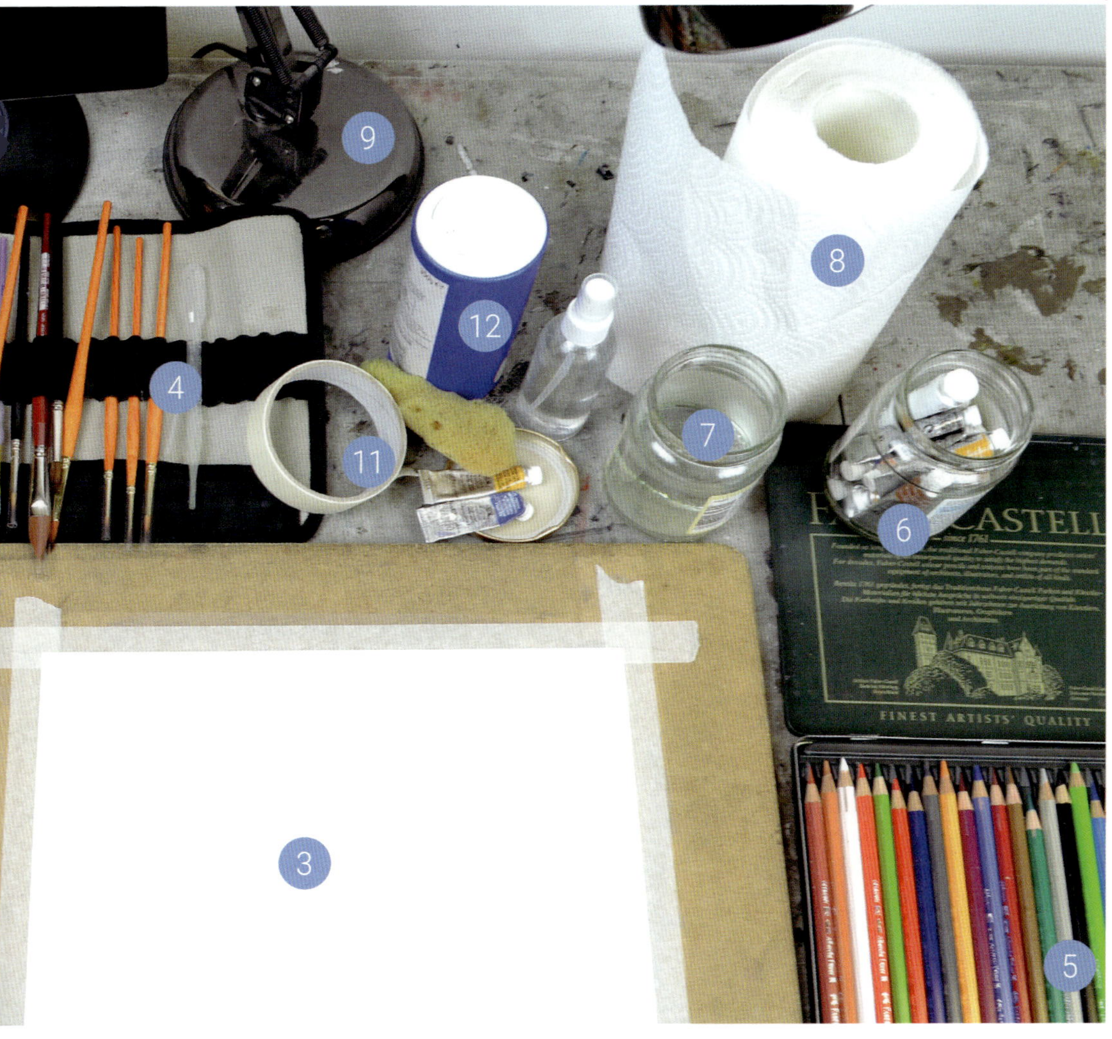

7
Jar of water

I always try to keep my water fresh, as dirty water can contaminate paint. I prefer old jars – they are clean and heavy enough to not knock over easily, or be mistaken for a cup of tea!

8
Paper towels

Paper towels are useful for mopping up excess water, cleaning palettes quickly and soaking water out of overloaded brushes. They can also leave interesting 'daubed' textures in wet areas. Cloths can also be used like this.

9
Lamp

I tend to have plenty of natural light in my space, but during evenings or cloudy weather it is useful to have extra lighting to top up any overhead lights, especially when avoiding cast shadows whilst working.

10
Tablet

When working from reference, I use a tablet or screen rather than paper printouts. This is partly for convenience, though I do find that the picture colour on a screen is better than on printouts.

11
Masking tape

Masking tape is useful for holding paper down if you haven't stretched it, and it can deal with a little cockling (wrinkling). Try to pick a fairly low-tack tape to avoid damaging the paper. And most importantly, when removing it, always peel away from the page!

12
Extra kit

These items tend to change depending on what I am working on. The salt and sponge are used for creating textures and gradients, while the spray bottle is useful for creating wet areas to work into.

Picking your paints

Watercolours can come in a variety of different forms that make them suitable for many working styles

Different forms of watercolour play different key roles in any working process due to their individual strengths and limitations. Are vibrant colours an essential requirement? Is it important to have a portable set-up for plein air sketching? Or is tight detail a high priority? Some paints will serve these needs better than others.

Watercolour paint comes in many forms, including tube paints, pans and as water-soluble pencils. There are many different brands that produce each of these, often with their own traditional formulations that provide slightly different results. Some provide cheaper options aimed at students, too.

Pigments are an ingredient that gives paint its colour, and good brands usually list the pigment numbers on their products. These are recognisable as a P plus a letter for the colour (such as R for red) and number for the pigment – for instance, PR108 is Cadmium Red. Look these up when buying paints, as different brands often give similar pigments different names, and may pad out paints with cheap pigments. Even expensive ranges may include the occasional poor-quality pigment that fades quickly – watercolour washes are particularly vulnerable to this, so be sure to select paints with excellent or very good lightfastness. It is usually better to pick paints with single pigments, as they mix more predictably.

Student versus artist quality

Paint is made of a formulation of ingredients including pigment to give it colour, flow enhancers, and binders to stabilise it. Many brands offer student-quality ranges of paint, which are cheaper for various reasons; they have more fillers to pad them out, they lack more expensive pigments, or they lack ingredients that help the paint perform better – or sometimes a combination of all three.

Overall, student paints are fine for sketching and learning, but will disappoint when intense colours and longevity is required. More expensive artist-quality paints will typically produce brighter colours, perform more consistently, and are less likely to fade over time. One mid-ground between the two is to swap out student paints that perform poorly or have bad pigments with artist-quality ones, such as replacing cadmium hues with real cadmium. Some cheaper pigments are perfectly good, such as earths like Yellow Ochre, so the student paint may work well enough.

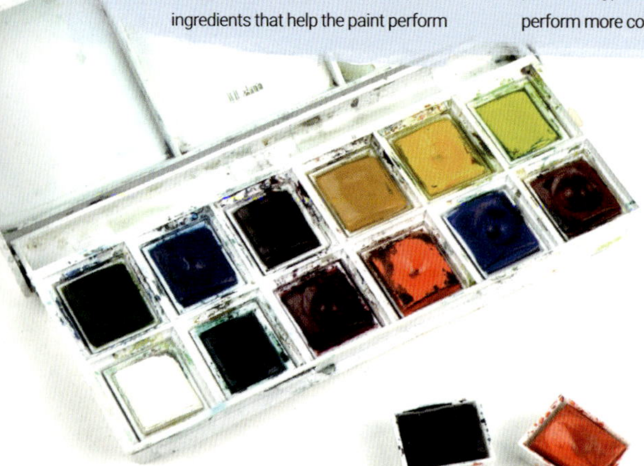

Watercolour Pans

Watercolour pans are small containers of solid paint that are activated with water. Usually they come in rectangular full or half pans, though some sets use circular ones.

The big advantage of pans is that they can be held in a portable set. Small sets are easily held in one hand, making them useful for sketching on the move. They also last a long time compared to tube paints.

The downside is pans are not as vivid as tube paints, and it is more difficult to get large amounts of colour out of them for washes. Always keep a lid on them when they are not in use to keep dust off.

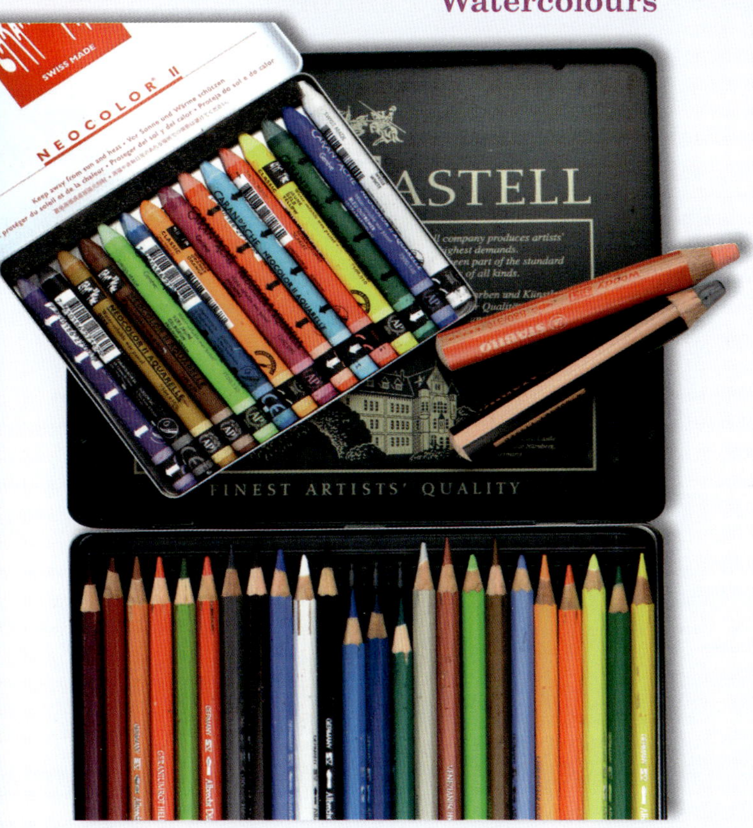

Watercolour pencils

Watercolour pencils comprise a variety of pencils and crayons that use a water-soluble binder. These work like normal crayons, but once the marks get wet they dissolve and behave like watercolour paint. If used on a wet surface, they leave marks of intensely coloured pigment.

This form of watercolour is excellent for handling details, textures and small areas of intense colour. Their solubility and colour also make them useful for sketching under watercolour washes.

Because of their fine points, they are generally not suitable for producing washes, although the pigment can be pushed around using excess water. Water-soluble crayons can cover large areas if used on their side, forming unique textures in the process.

Get the most from watercolour pencils

Follow these steps...

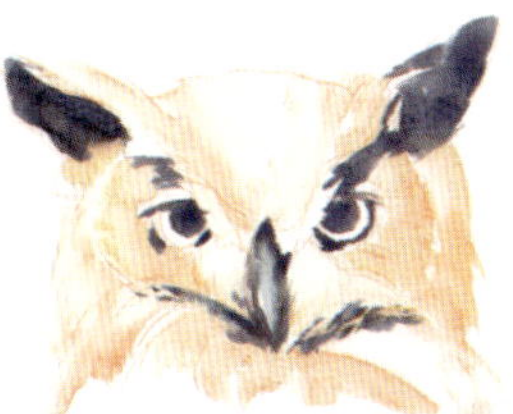

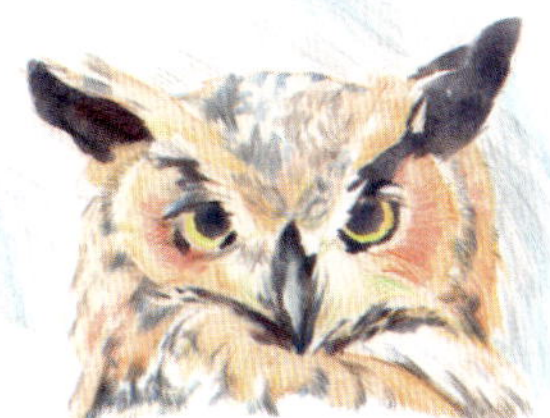

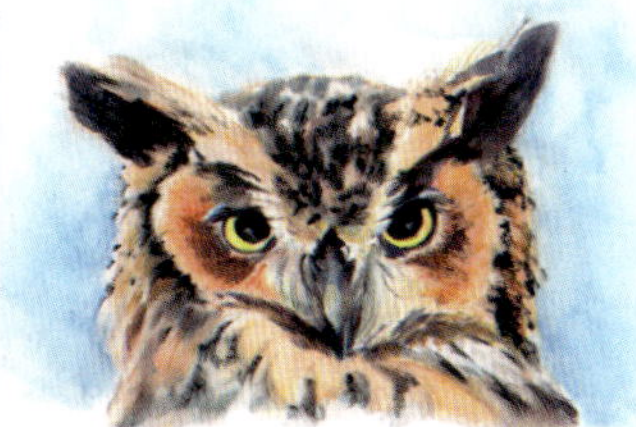

1 ● Under drawing

Watercolour pencils are great for sketching out an image, as they don't muddy watercolours and dissolve readily without leaving harsh lines. Here I sketched an outline of the owl's head with a bit of hatching for shading, then wetted it with a brush and clean water to create a simple wash.

2 ● Building colour

One way to 'mix' watercolour pencils is by layering them on top of each other and wetting them with clean water. Here some of the black feathers are sketched in with the brown and black pencils, while different combinations of browns, reds and oranges build up the other plumage.

3 ● Add texture and detail

Most of these final details were added by dipping the pencil tip into water, or by lightly brushing water into an area before drawing on it. When wet, watercolour pencils leave more richly pigmented marks. A white watercolour pencil is used for the final touches.

Essential colours

1. Lemon Yellow (PY175)

An excellent green-leaning yellow that is especially useful in landscape painting. It quite translucent and mixes vivid greens. It is also suitable for glazing, and combines well with phthalo colours. It's less effective for mixing with reds, but still retains some luminescence.

2. Cadmium Yellow (PY35)

Comes in varying shades. This is a versatile red-leaning yellow with a lot of uses – if you pick just one yellow, make it this one. It is quite opaque and mixes excellent warm lights as well as oranges, making it useful for colourful subjects and skin tones.

3. Yellow Ochre (PY43)

Yellow ochre, a warm yellow, is a useful earth pigment, used for skin tones, dull greens and a wide variety of neutral colours. It is very opaque, like most earth pigments – this means it isn't very good in glazes, but it does mix well into light colours.

4. Pyrrole Red (PR254)

Also known as Ferrari red. A modern alternative to Cadmium Red with good light fastness and high intensity – a little goes a long way. It is very versatile, mixing well into skin tones, oranges, shadows and lights. If you buy just one red, go with this one.

5. Permanent Alizarin Crimson (PR206)

A more lightfast alternative to Alizarin Crimson, which can fade quite quickly. Permanent Alizarin Crimson is very translucent, making it a great colour to mix into shadows. It mixes an excellent chromatic black with Phthalo Green, and is also useful for painting cool shadows in skin tones.

6. French Ultramarine (PB29)

A staple of artists' palettes, this is a slightly red-leaning blue with a dark tone. It mixes a good chromatic black with Venetian Red – these two colours can form a limited palette together. It is versatile, mixing into shadows and neutrals well. If you only have one blue, this is the one you need.

7. Phthalo Blue (green) (PB15)

An intense blue – handle this with care as it goes a long way (this also makes it excellent value for money!). Some artists don't like phthalos as they can overwhelm colour mixes, but when handled with care they are excellent for mixing greys and greens.

8. Phthalo Green (yellow) (PG36)

Like Phthalo Blue, this is a really strong colour. It's useful for landscapes, though it is also handy for mixing greys and cool neutrals, as it behaves a lot like Phthalo Blue. Phthalo paints are very translucent, making them useful for glazing and mixing shadows.

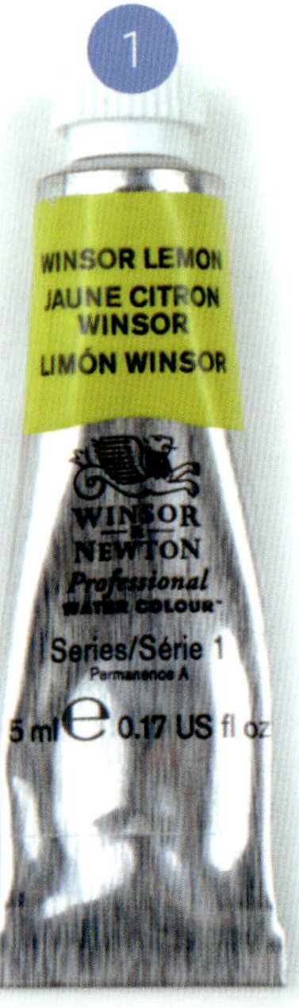

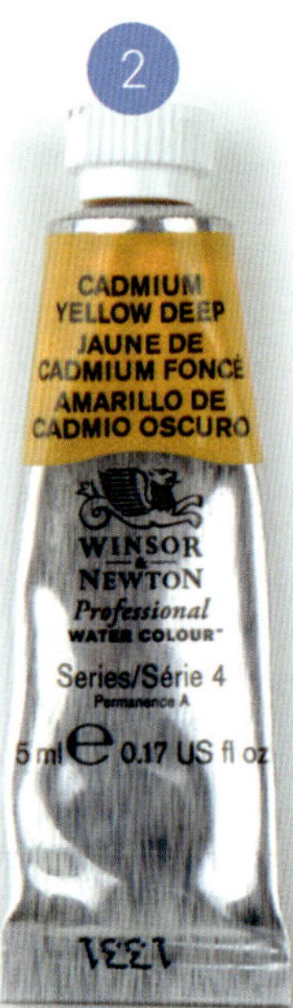

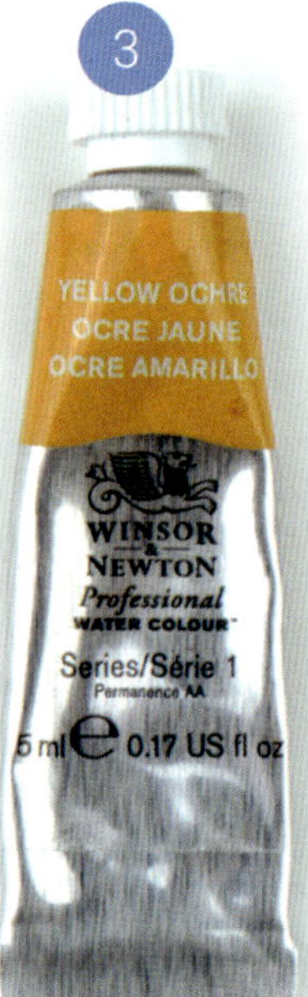

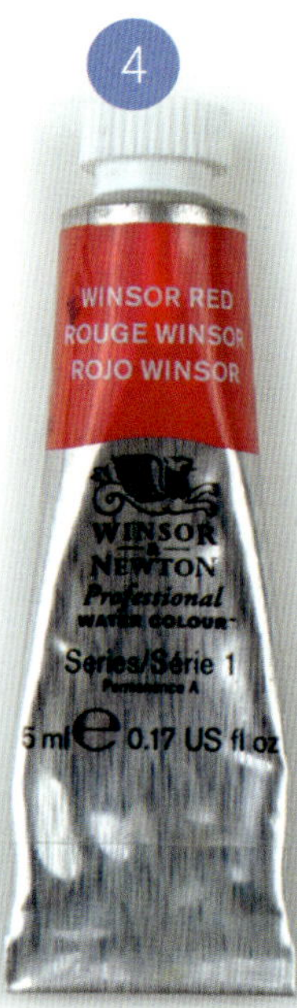

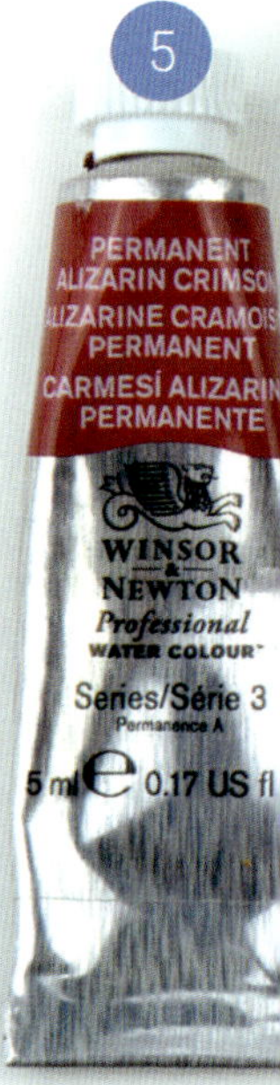

9 Venetian Red (PR101)

There are lots of names for this pigment and it varies between manufacturers. It is a strong, reddish-brown earth pigment and is fairly opaque. It is very useful for mixing lots of brown and neutral colours. If you pick only one brown, go with this one.

10 Burnt Umber (PBr7 and others)

This colour varies between manufacturers, but should be a dark, slightly yellow-leaning, opaque brown made from earth pigments. It is handy for mixing neutrals, skin tones and warm shadows, generally being more useful with natural subjects. It is less versatile than Venetian Red, but more suited to subtle shifts in colour.

11 Ivory Black (Pbk9)

This is a traditional black (thankfully no longer made with ivory!), which is fairly opaque. It's useful for dulling colours and is especially good for mixing dull greens. Generally, it doesn't mix great shadows, as it tends to look a bit flat, but it's occasionally handy for deep, opaque blacks.

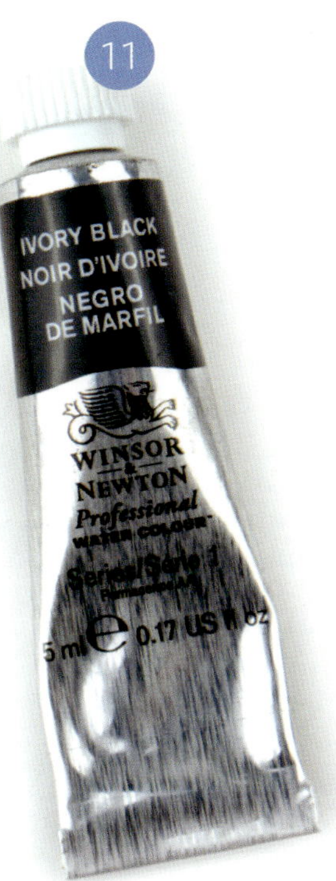

Tube paints

Tube watercolours are liquid forms of watercolour paint. They are designed to be used fresh from the tube and watered down – this is the best way to achieve high-intensity colours. Because of this, they are less portable than other forms of watercolours.

Many artists squirt them into palettes and let them dry out for later use, but dry tube paints tend not to work quite as well as fresh ones.

Tube paints are the best option for more developed work, as they're easier to mix, are better-quality colours, and they excel at creating larger washes of colour.

The colours shown on this page are staples of my palette. As manufacturers may rename colours, I have provided pigment numbers.

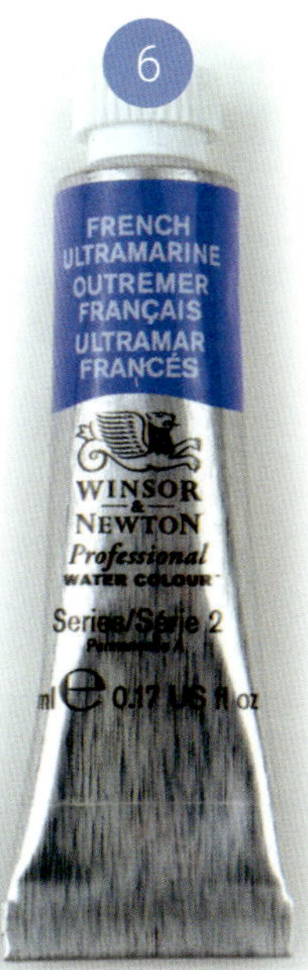

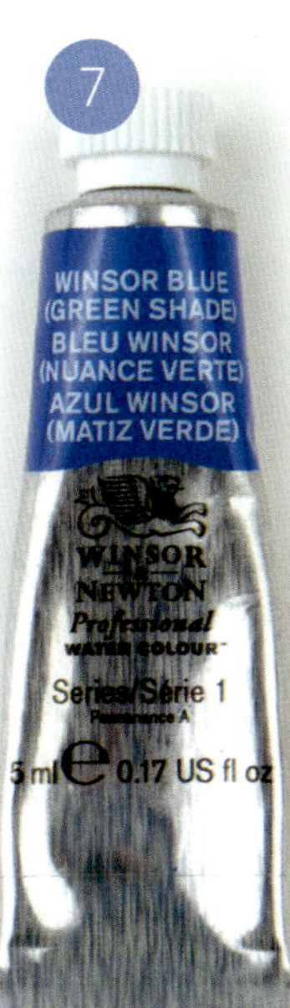

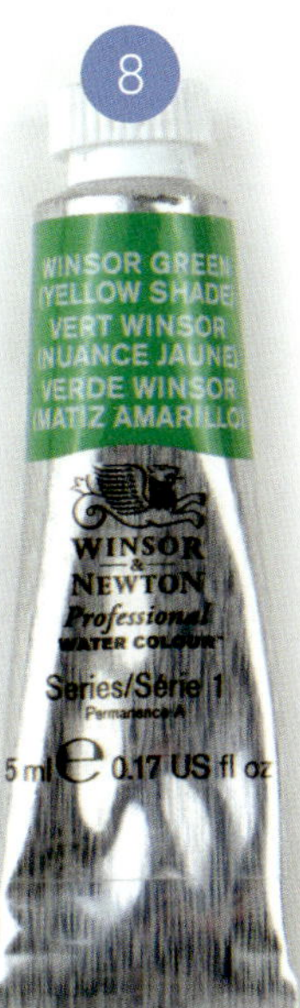

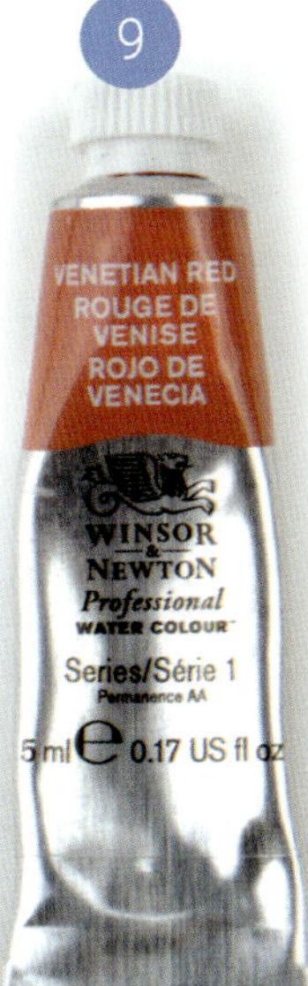

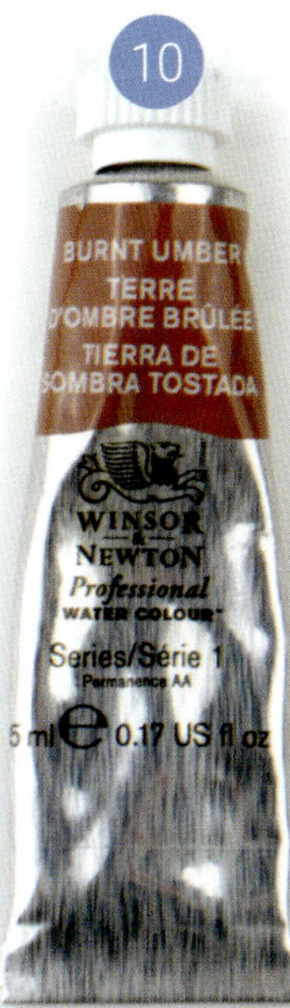

Brush up on brushes

Brushes are an essential element of your kit. This guide introduces some common brush types and explains their different uses

There are many brushes to use with watercolour, and picking suitable ones will make painting significantly more enjoyable. A big part of this is personal inclination – the brushes should suit our working processes and individual styles. Different brush shapes make unique sets of marks, making them more or less suitable for different jobs.

With watercolour it is best to opt for quality over quantity in brushes. Brushes should hold their point when wet and not 'split' or deform, and should not drop bristles when used – cheaper brushes tend to do both of these things. Good brushes often look 'denser', as they have more bristles.

It is usually best to have some bigger brushes, as they can make a wider range of marks and hold more water – try to avoid starter packs padded out with cheap, tiny brushes! A good starting point for your kit is a large flat for washes, a medium-large round, another medium-sized flat, and possibly a small round or rigger for details. Add brushes as needed – for instance, a hake brush for big washes, or a fan for textures.

Good brushes aren't cheap, but will last for years when well cared for. Don't let paint dry in them, as it will damage the shape – be sure to wash them thoroughly with a mild soap after use.

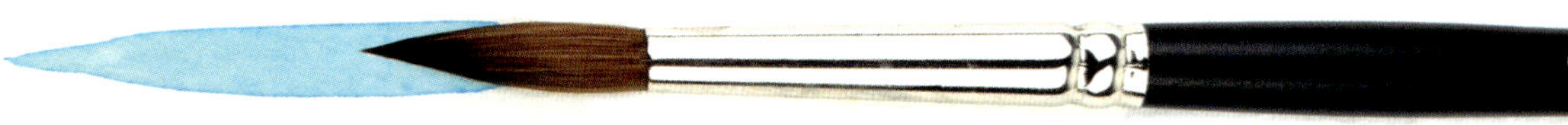

Round

Round brushes are a versatile option, capable of doing a lot of different jobs. A good round will hold its point, and make thin enough lines to draw with, but with increased pressure creates a wide variety of thicker marks. Bigger sizes hold water well and can make small washes. Round brushes tend to make more 'organic' feeling marks.

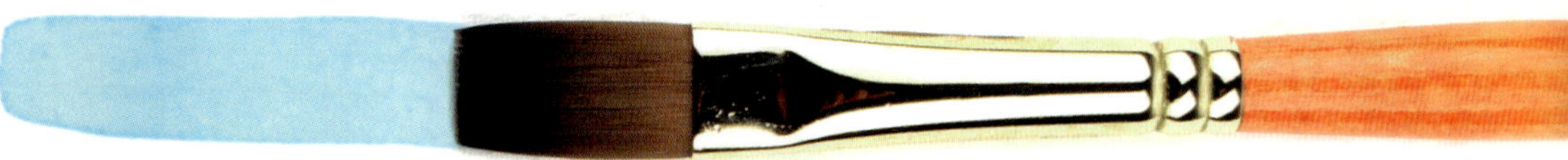

Flat

Flat brushes are good for laying down even areas of colour, but are also very versatile. When turned on their edge, they can make thin, straight lines, making them useful for details. The body of the brush can also be dragged along at a shallow angle for dry-brush effects that work well on cold and rough papers. They are good for small-medium washes, painting man-made structures and adding rough, random textures.

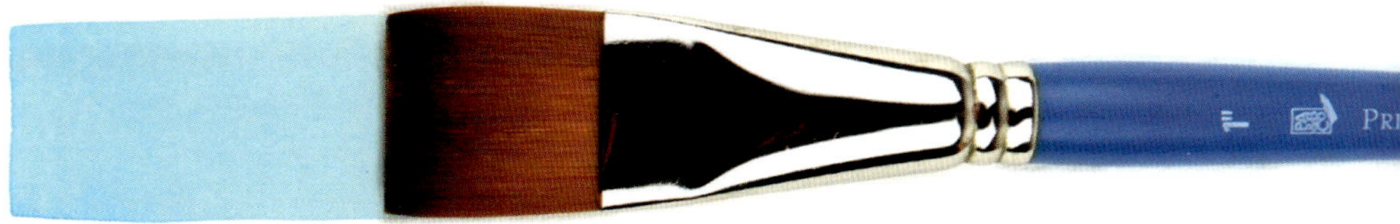

Flat Wash

🔺 Flat wash brushes tend to be larger, thicker flat brushes – ones that are an inch or more wide are most useful. They are used for laying in large areas of colour, applying water and creating broad brush strokes. By using large brushes like this, washes don't get streaky from drying part way through.

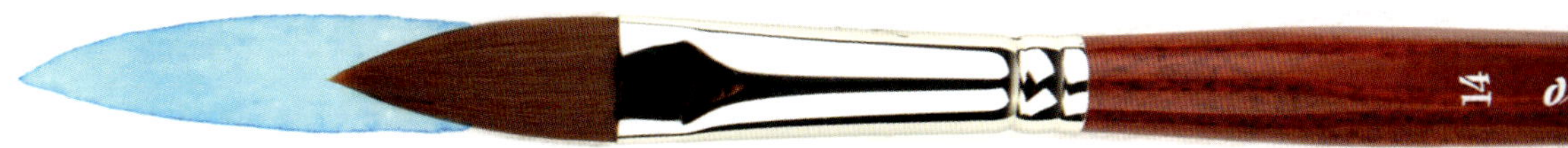

Cat's Tongue

🔺 Also sometimes referred to as an oval brush. This is a more unusual brush shape with a pointed tip that can produce fine lines and a flat belly for holding lots of liquid to produce thick marks and washes. Changing the pressure means it can go from thin to thick and back again within one brush stroke, opening up a wide variety of different marks.

Mop

🔺 Often used interchangeably with quill brushes. Mop brushes have a bigger belly than a round that is great for holding lots of water, and are good for working wet-in-wet in particular. They are very soft and tend to be far less 'springy' than round brushes, so while they can make thin lines, they are not as good at it as a round and can be harder to control.

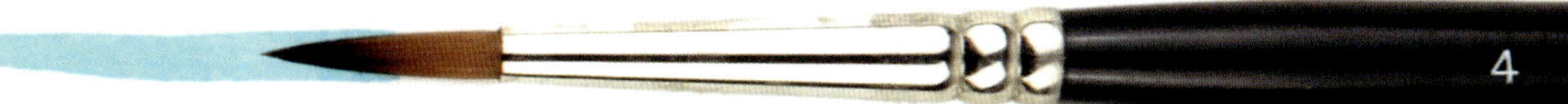

Small Round

🔺 Small rounds are used in different ways to larger round brushes. They tend not to hold much water, so are not suitable for any kind of coverage or long line. However, they are useful for fine, isolated details, especially if extra precision is needed, and for painting very tiny things. Another unique use of this brush is stippling, a type of painting that involves creating many closely packed dots of colour.

Rigger

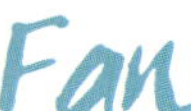 Rigger brushes are a specialised brush used for painting long, thin lines of a consistent width. The clue is in the name – they were used to paint ships' rigging! However, they can be useful in many situations; they hold more liquid than a small round brush and make longer lines. Ensure the hairs are filled up with paint to achieve this. The brush length can accommodate a slight tremor, as the hair cushions movement.

Fan

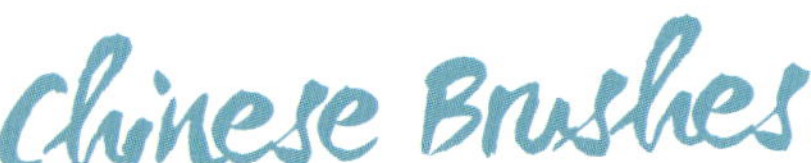

Fan brushes are fairly specialised brushes that are good at generating random textures. Dragging or flicking the brush creates lots of thin, stringy marks, pulling it sideways creates thin, slightly uneven lines, using the edge creates random organic textures, and tapping it generates a stippled effect. The unusual shape means changes in direction, angle and application can produce a wide variety of marks, which is especially useful for landscape work.

Chinese Brushes

Chinese brushes are typically used with ink in calligraphy, but work well with watercolour too. They tend to be medium to large round brushes made with a variety of different natural hairs, and sometimes combine two different types. This means they are quite soft, but generally good at holding a point. These are a great option for big, loose brushstrokes.

Types of brush hair

There are many different kinds of brush hair in use that can be broadly categorised as synthetic or natural.

Natural bristles are made with hair from a variety of different animals, such as sable, squirrel, goat and many others. Typically, natural brushes are softer and more flexible than synthetics, hold more water, and form better points.

Synthetic brushes have become very diverse, ranging from quite firm to almost as soft as the hair they are trying to emulate. They tend to be more hard-wearing, though they can lose their shape faster than natural brushes. It is better to go with more expensive synthetics – their firmness is particularly good for flats.

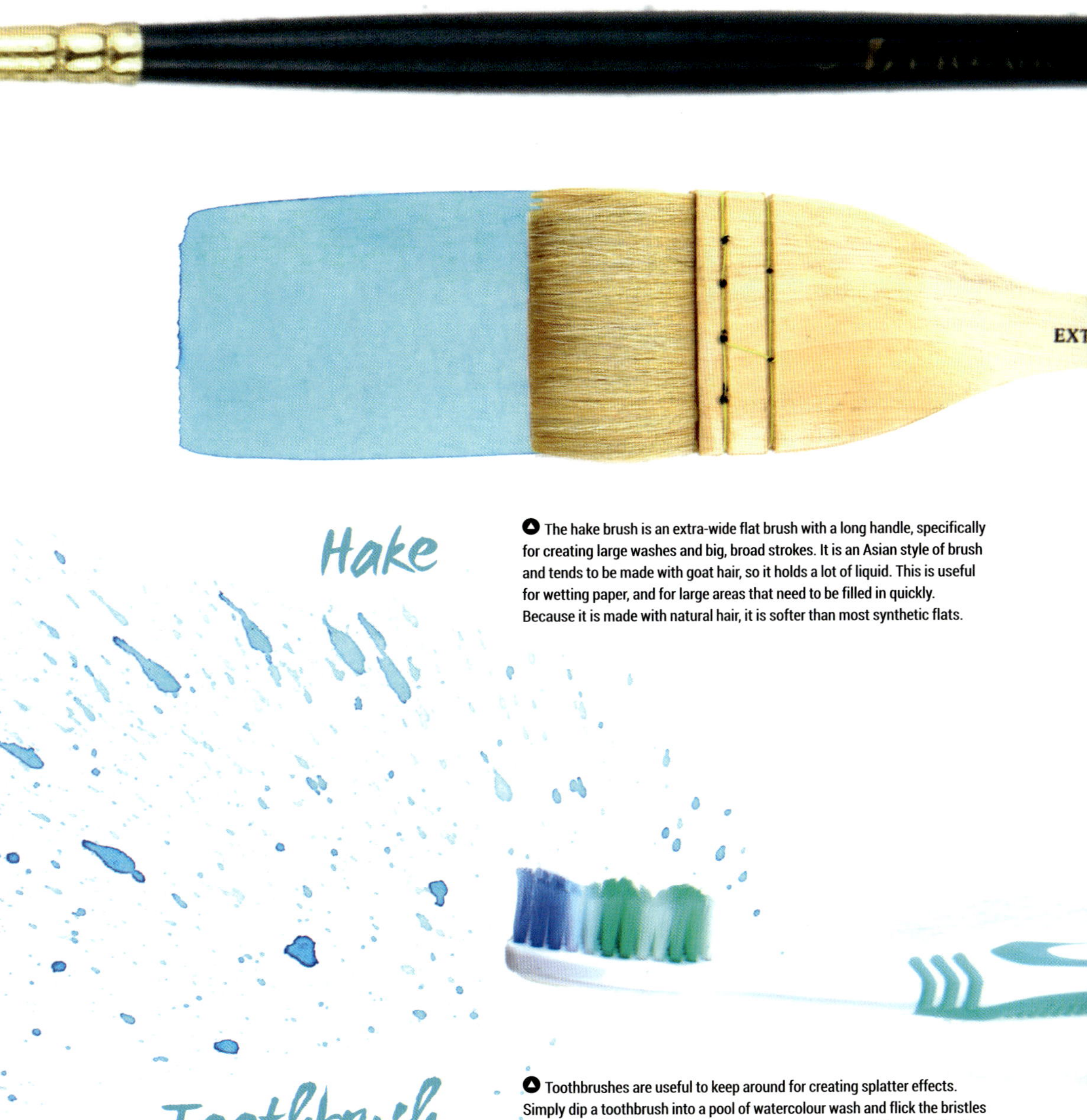

Hake

The hake brush is an extra-wide flat brush with a long handle, specifically for creating large washes and big, broad strokes. It is an Asian style of brush and tends to be made with goat hair, so it holds a lot of liquid. This is useful for wetting paper, and for large areas that need to be filled in quickly. Because it is made with natural hair, it is softer than most synthetic flats.

Toothbrush

Toothbrushes are useful to keep around for creating splatter effects. Simply dip a toothbrush into a pool of watercolour wash and flick the bristles with your thumb or a piece of stiff card to create a spray of droplets. This is effective for creating random textures. It can be hard to control, so use loose sheets of scrap paper or card to guard other areas from this effect.

clean your brushes

Watercolour brushes are more delicate than brushes designed for acrylic and oils, and should be treated accordingly, explains **Rob Lunn**

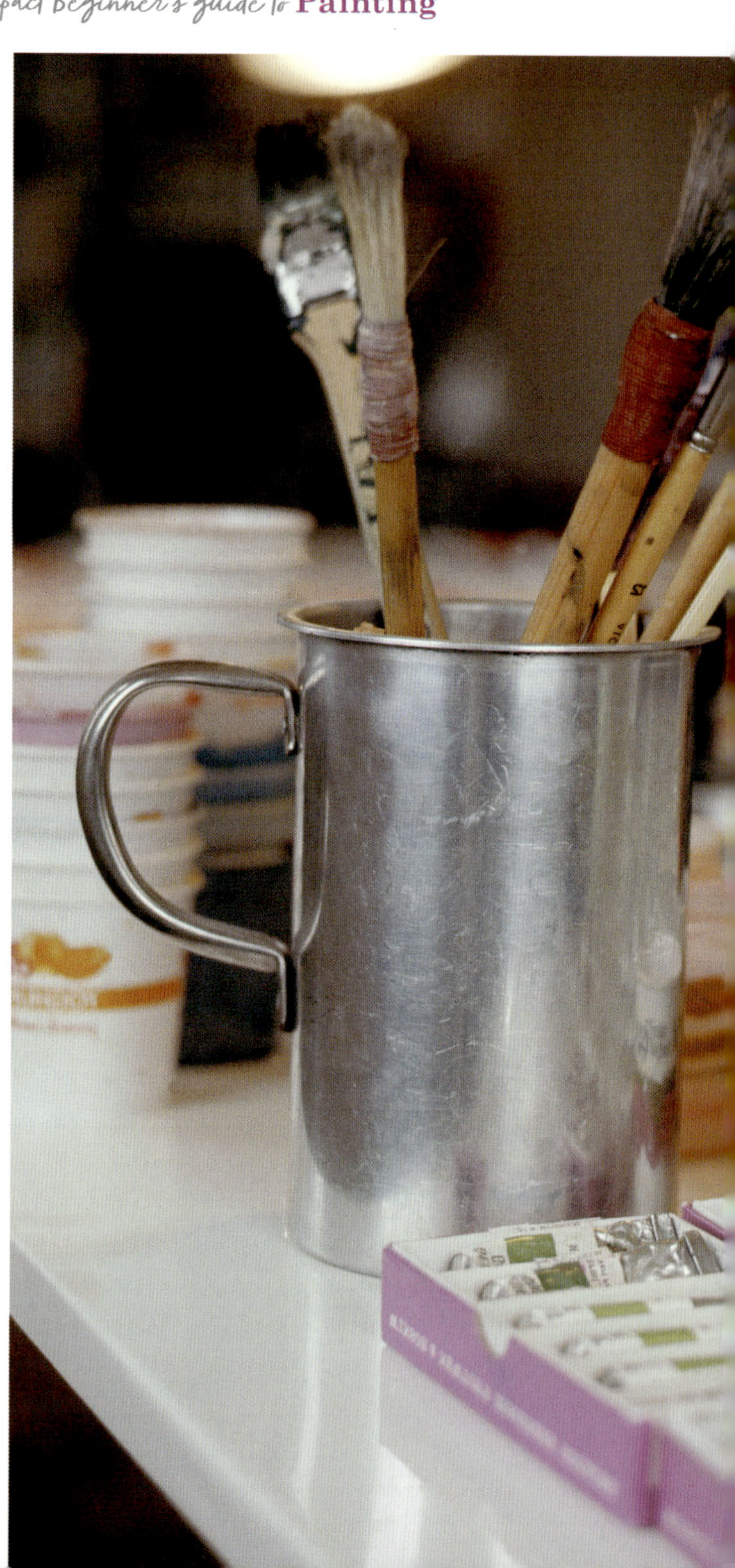

Learning how to clean your paintbrushes properly is an important skill. As the old saying goes: If you look after your tools, your tools will look after you. When you start painting, a good set of brushes is one of the most important investments you will make – and they can set you back a fair amount of money, too. So it makes sense to give them a bit of TLC.

The golden rule when it comes to looking after paintbrushes is to keep them wet while in use and give them a good clean when they're not. This approach will help keep your brushes in good nick for a long time. But cleaning paintbrushes is easier said than done – there are some techniques you need to know if you're going to get the paint out effectively.

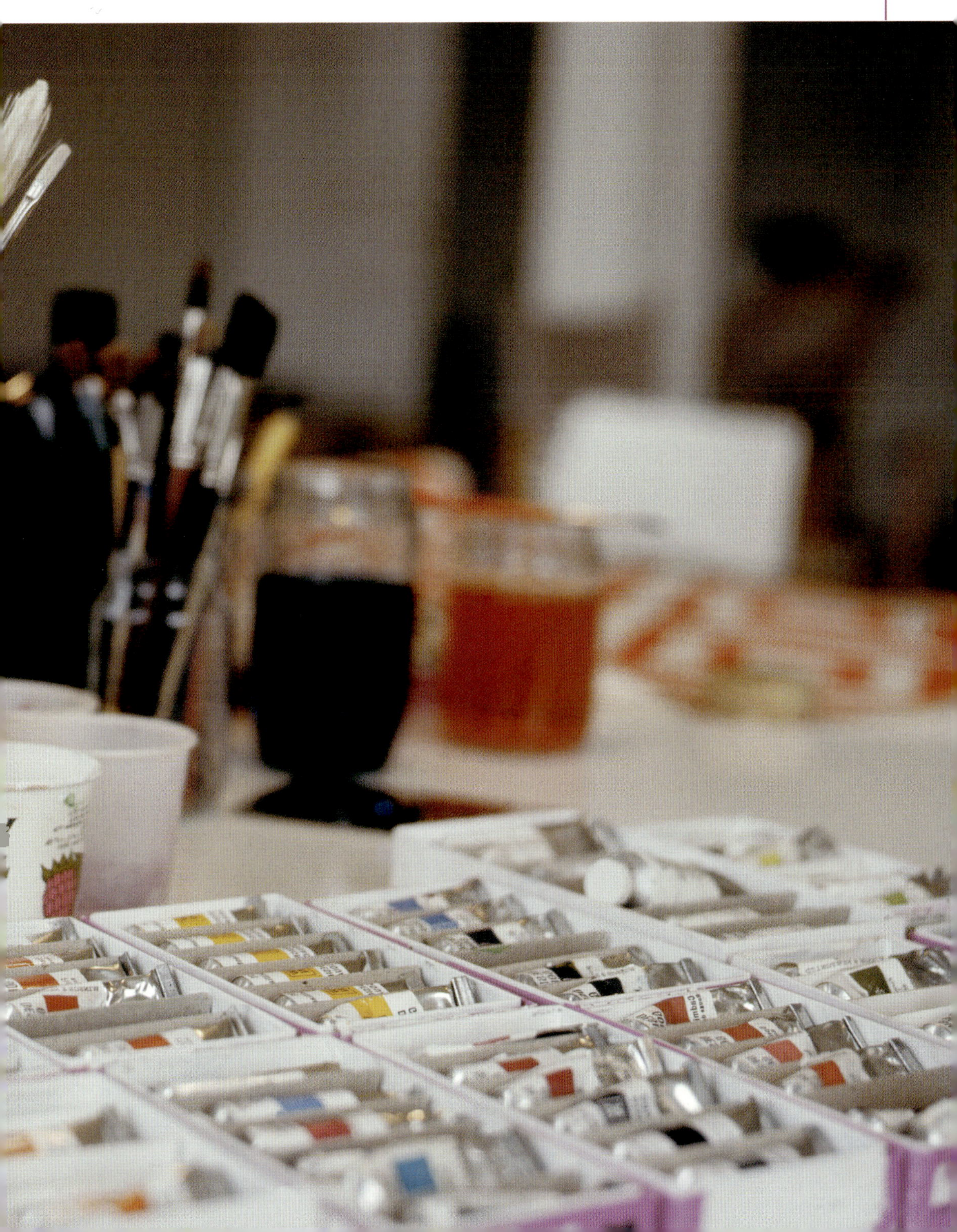

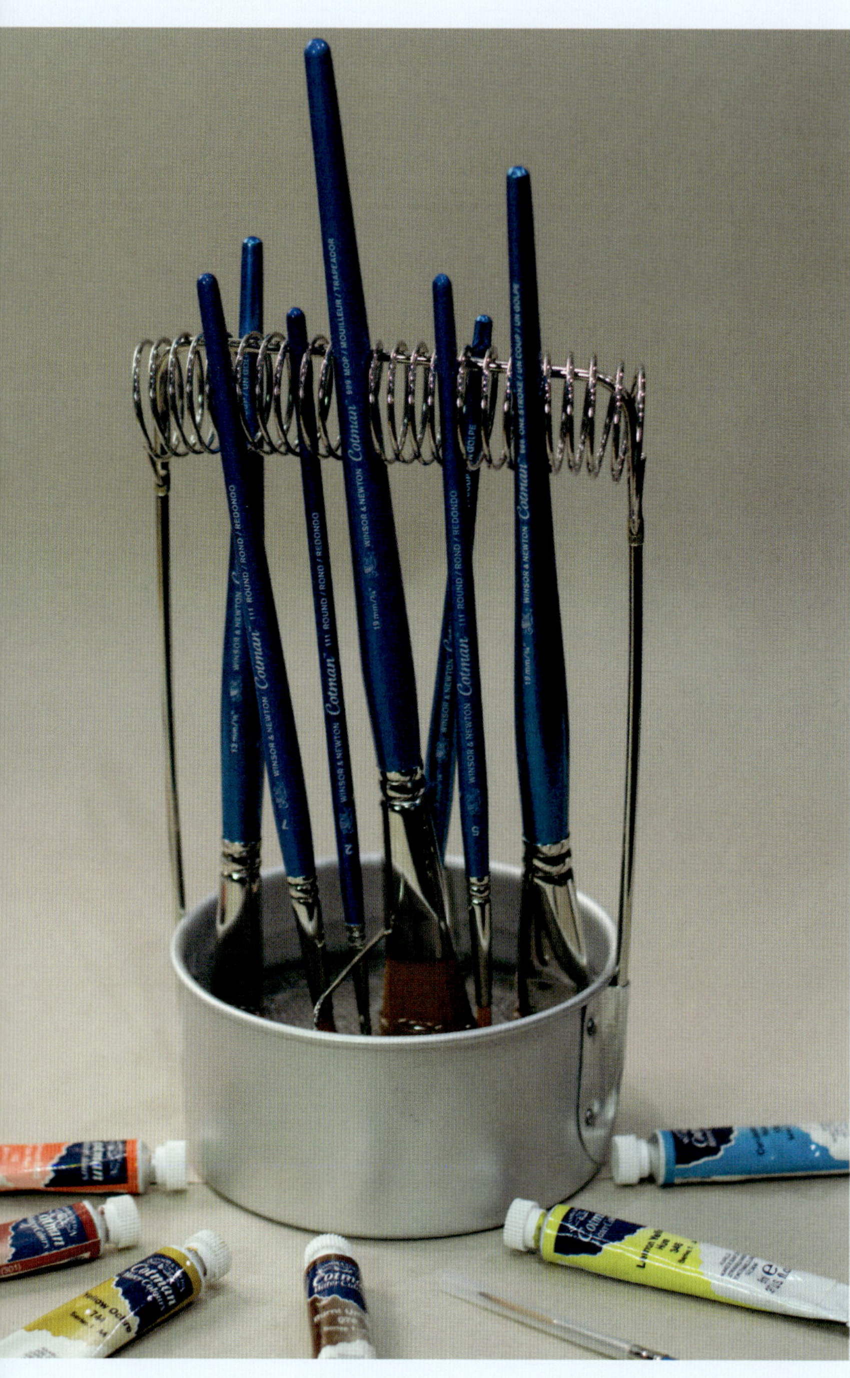

1 ○ Clean with water as you go

As a lot of watercolour paint is used in highly diluted 'washes', it should take less work to remove the pigment from the bristles. Instead of cleaning with a cloth, keep a vessel of water close to hand at all times, swilling the brushes between washes. One tip is to use a brush washer with a holder so you can suspend the bristles in water when not in use.

2 ○ Dry with a cloth and store

Using water in a jar or brush washer, clean as much paint as you can from your bristles. Use a clean cloth to make sure you've removed the paint. Repeat if necessary.

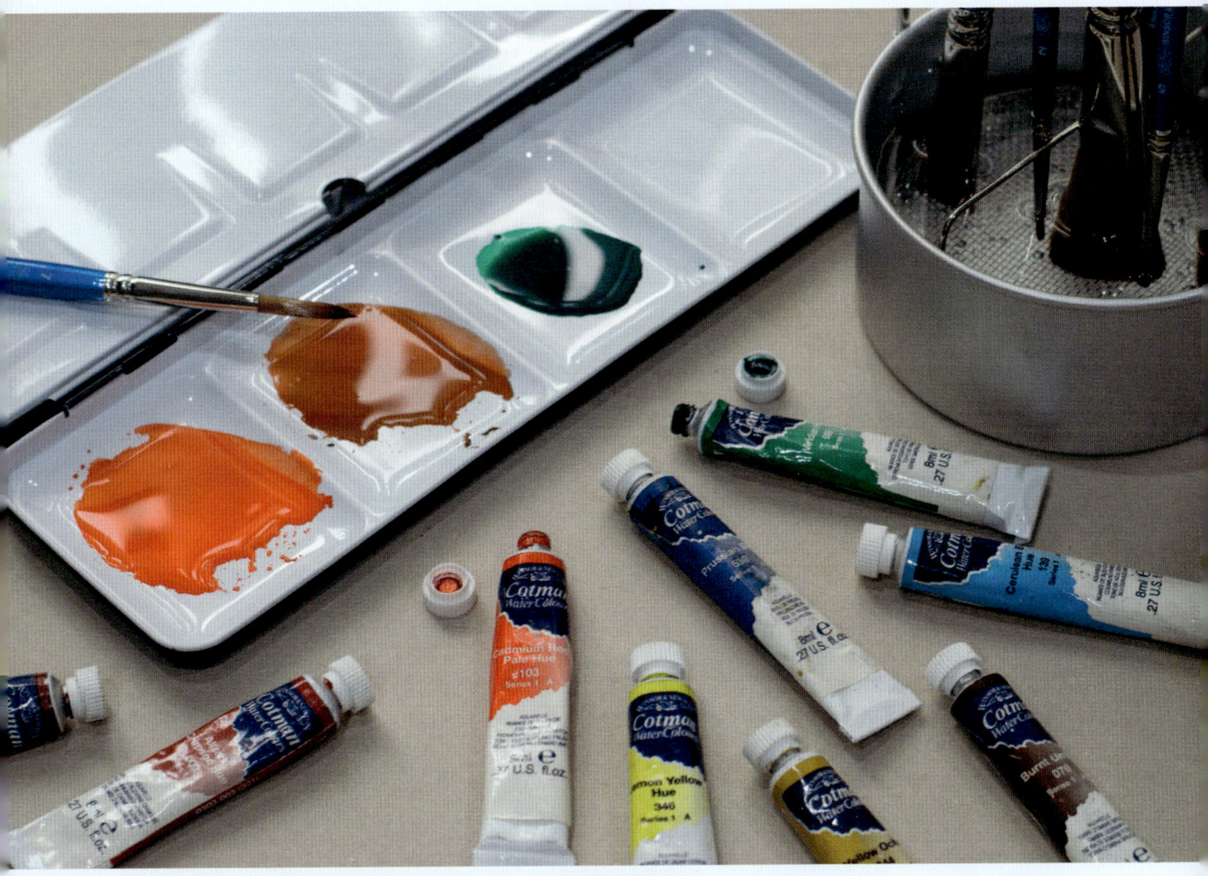

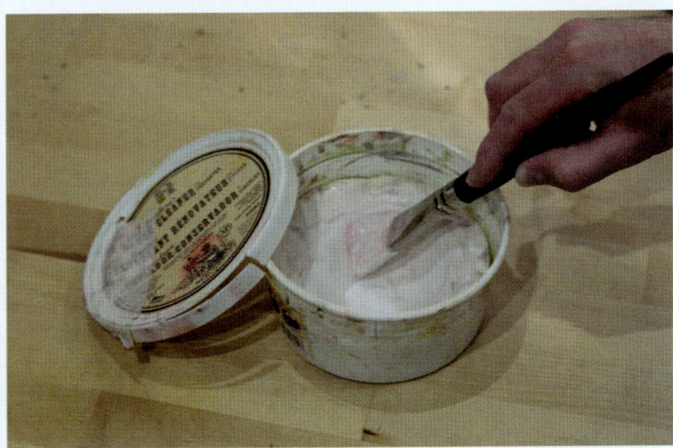

3 ◐ Reshape the bristles

For a final clean, consider using a paintbrush cleaning soap. We recommend The Masters Brush Cleaner and Preserver (available in 2.4oz pots or industrial-sized pots). Using a little water, work up a lather with your brush in the centre of the soap. Work the lather through the bristles with your thumb and forefinger, always working from the ferrule out towards the ends of the bristles. Continue until no pigment can be seen in the lather. Note that some pigments will stain bristles permanently.

Dirty 'wash' water should be collected and disposed of responsibly. It is also possible to allow dirty wash water from watercolour paint to settle naturally in larger containers. The golden rule is: never chuck it down the sink!

Paper choices

The surface we work on plays a pivotal role in the process and end result of our artwork

Choosing the right paper depends on preference and working style, so it is important to consider what is needed of the paper before buying it.

Watercolour paper is broadly split into three main types: hot press, cold press and rough. Each type of paper performs differently, resulting in different marks and textures, but they can all be good quality. Different types of paper have their own strengths and limitations; for instance, a rough paper would make detailed botanical illustration very difficult, whereas textured effects would not show up well on a hot press paper.

Paper is usually made from wood pulp (also labelled 'woodfree') or cotton. Cotton papers are considerably more hard wearing and longer lasting, but also more expensive. Mould-made papers tend to be of superior quality to machine-made papers, as they come in heavier weights and have a stronger surface, but machine-made papers may have a more uniform surface. It is worth testing out a selection of papers with watercolours if possible, as many brands have their own formulations and may behave differently despite being a similar type of paper.

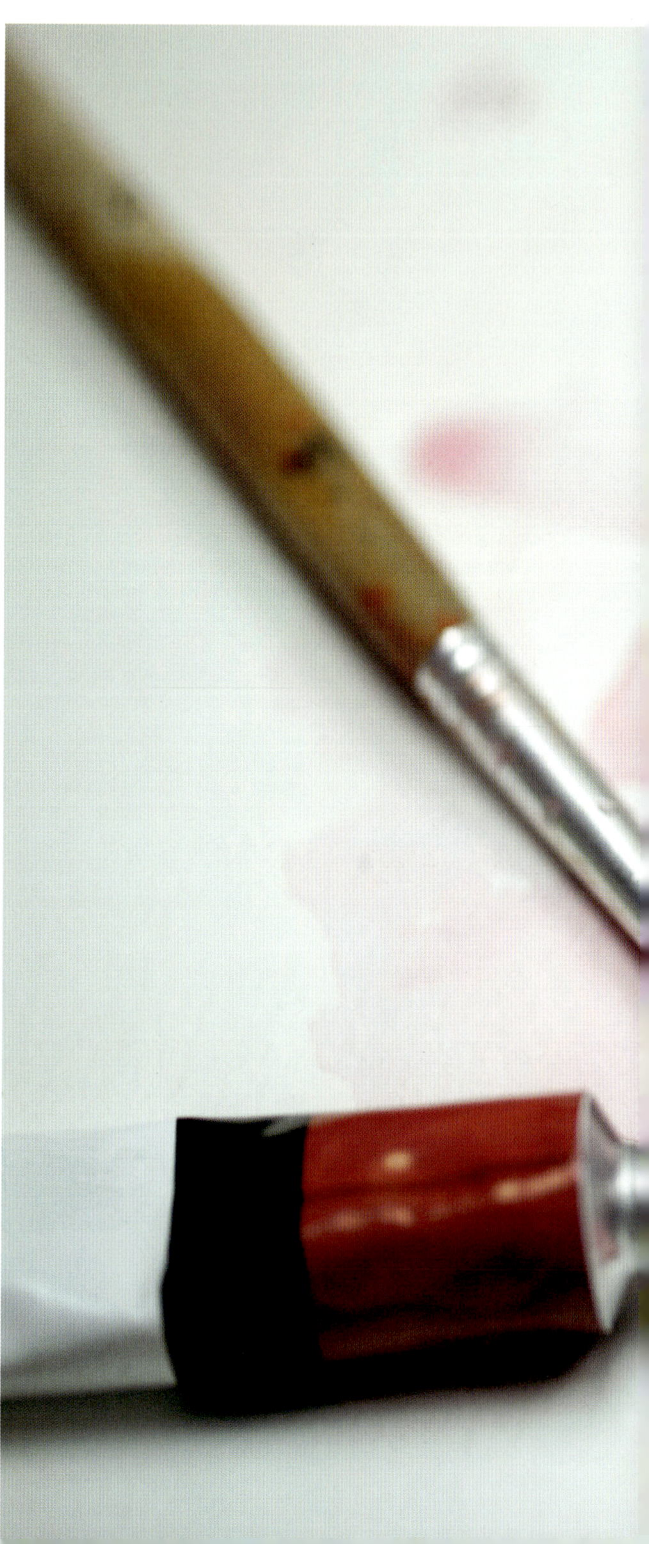

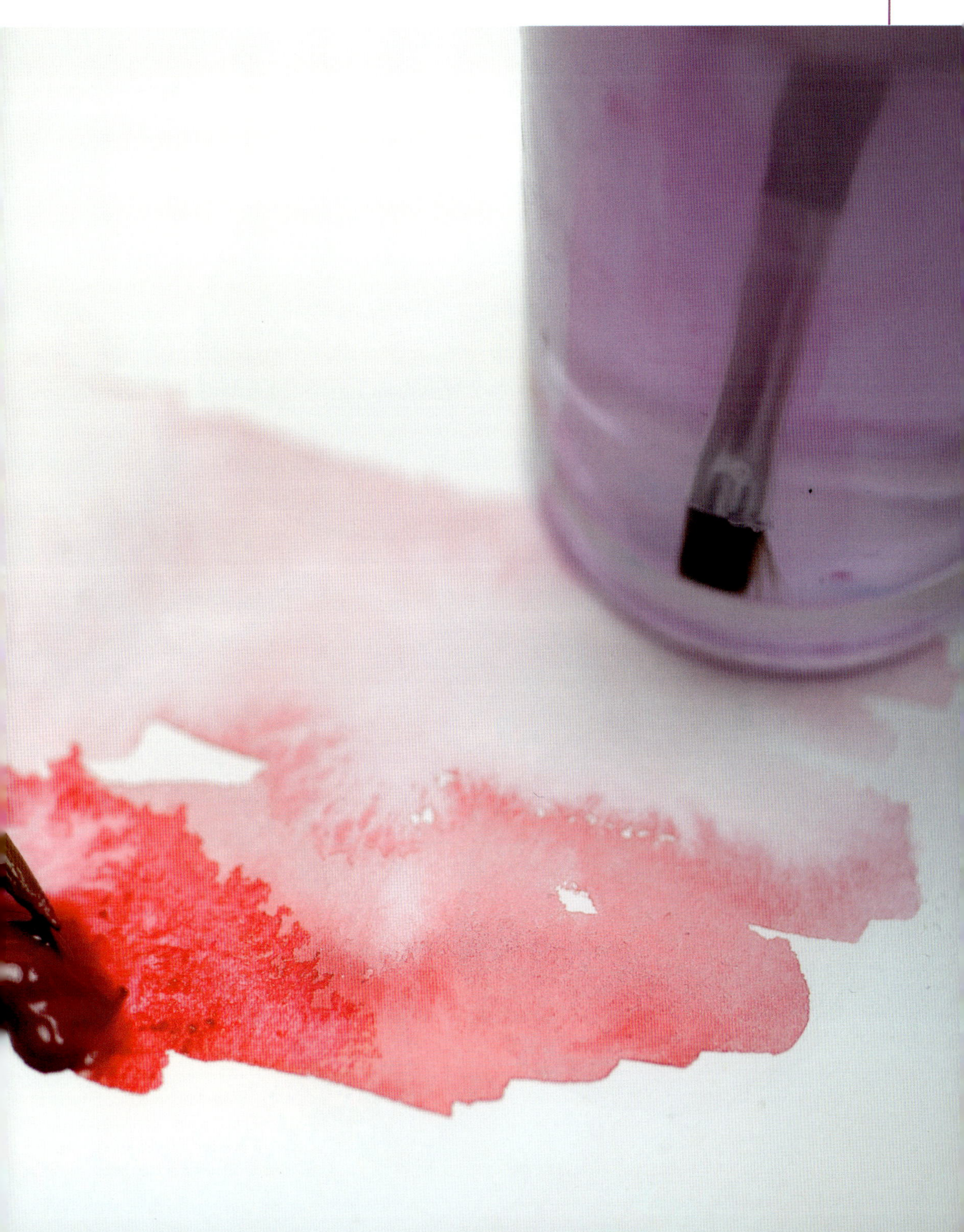

Hot press paper

Hot press paper refers to the process of making paper by flattening it between two hot rollers, resulting in a flatter, less-textured surface. This smooth surface is better suited to detailed work, and lacks the granulating behaviour of more textured papers, making it less suitable for unusual effects. This type of paper also works better with pens and pencils. Hot press paper is often made with a lot of size (a substance used to control absorbency), which means it can handle large washes well and let them dry uniformly.

Cold press paper

Also called 'NOT' paper. Cold press paper is made in a similar way to hot press, but is pressed between two cold rollers instead, resulting in a rougher surface texture. This is the most commonly used watercolour paper as it is versatile – the texture is enough to add interest but doesn't interfere with detailed work too much. Watercolour can be used with a dry brush on this type of paper to produce gritty textures, and in washes the pigment sinks between the teeth of the paper, forming a granulated effect.

Rough paper

Rough papers have the most highly textured surfaces, as the name suggests. This is great for dry brush effects, creating granulated textures within washes, and adding a naturalistic feel to paintings, though it's unsuitable for detailed work as the texture can interfere. Sometimes they also produce interesting 'bleed' effects, which are unpredictable. These papers can vary in how paint behaves on them, due to differences in textures and absorbency. Another quality of rough papers is that they tend to be tough, allowing for wetter washes and for paint to be 'lifted' out without too much damage to the surface.

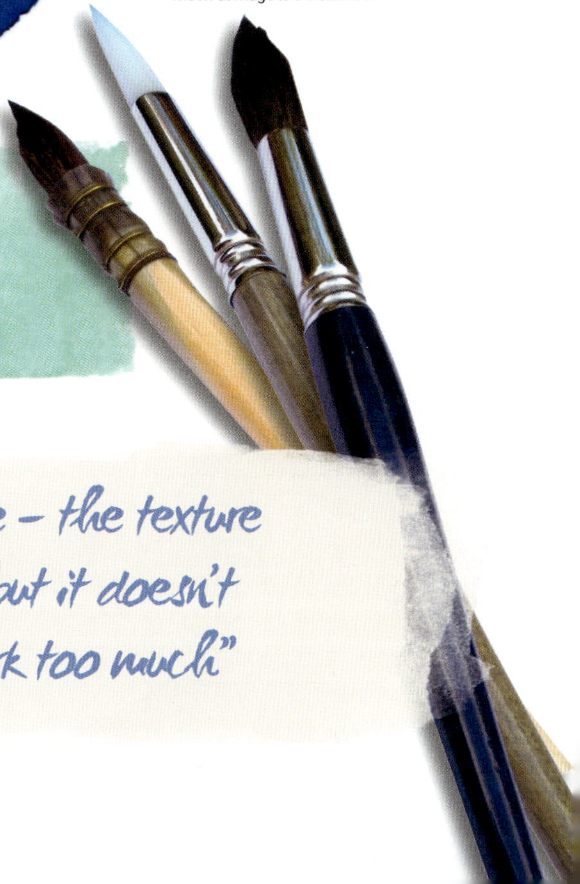

"Cold press paper is versatile – the texture is enough to add interest but it doesn't interfere with detailed work too much"

stretching paper

Stretching watercolour paper is done to prevent it from going bumpy – 'cockling' – when it gets wet. This is important when using lighter-weight papers under about 425gsm, or if your painting approach involves a lot of wet washes.

The key is to prepare everything before starting, so all the equipment is to hand. It's also a good idea to cut the tape ahead of time.

Afterwards, artists usually paint on the paper while it's taped down. Completed paintings can then be cut away, leaving the tape around the edges and covering it with a mountboard when framing. Pulling the tape off will likely damage the artwork.

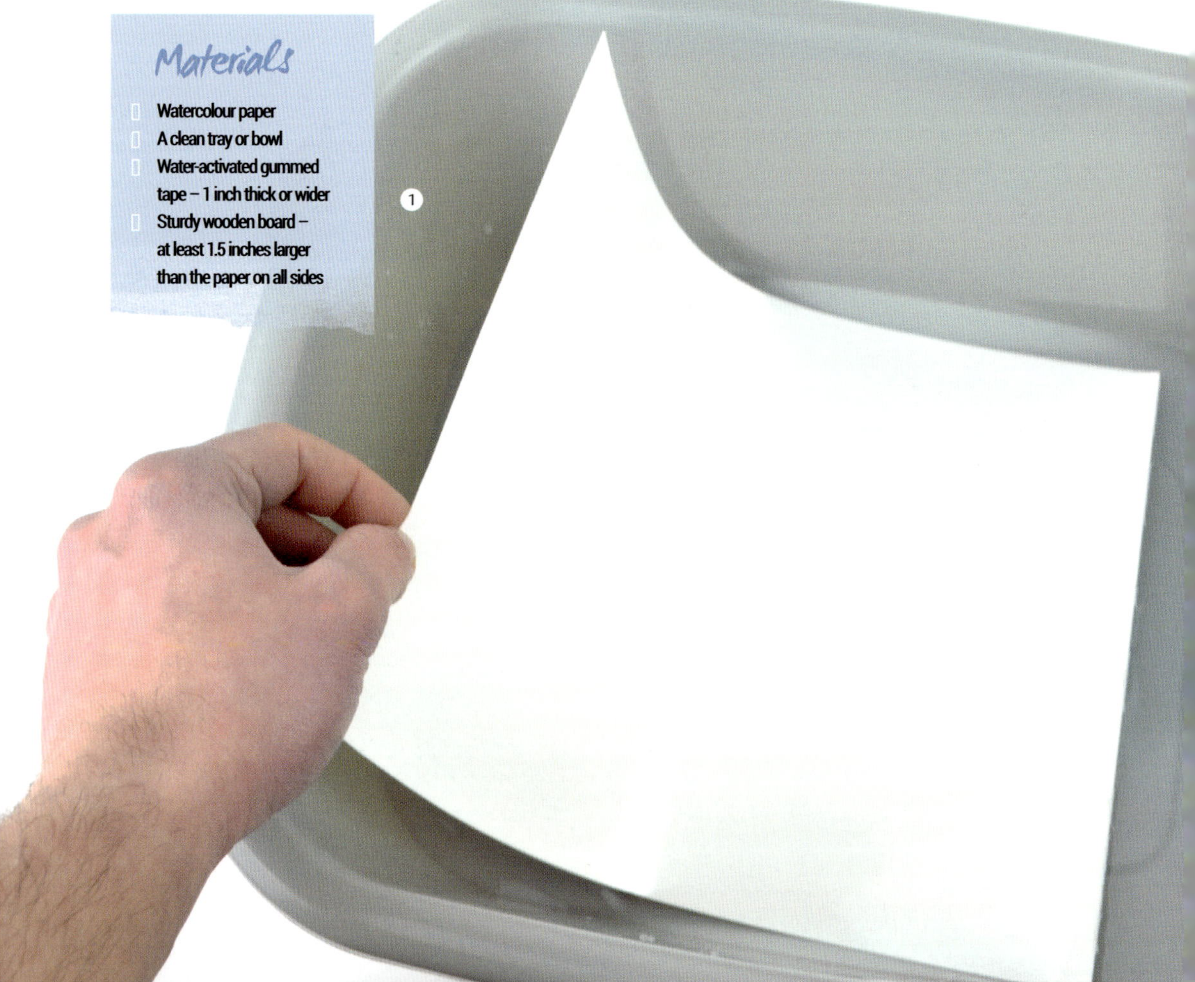

Materials

- Watercolour paper
- A clean tray or bowl
- Water-activated gummed tape – 1 inch thick or wider
- Sturdy wooden board – at least 1.5 inches larger than the paper on all sides

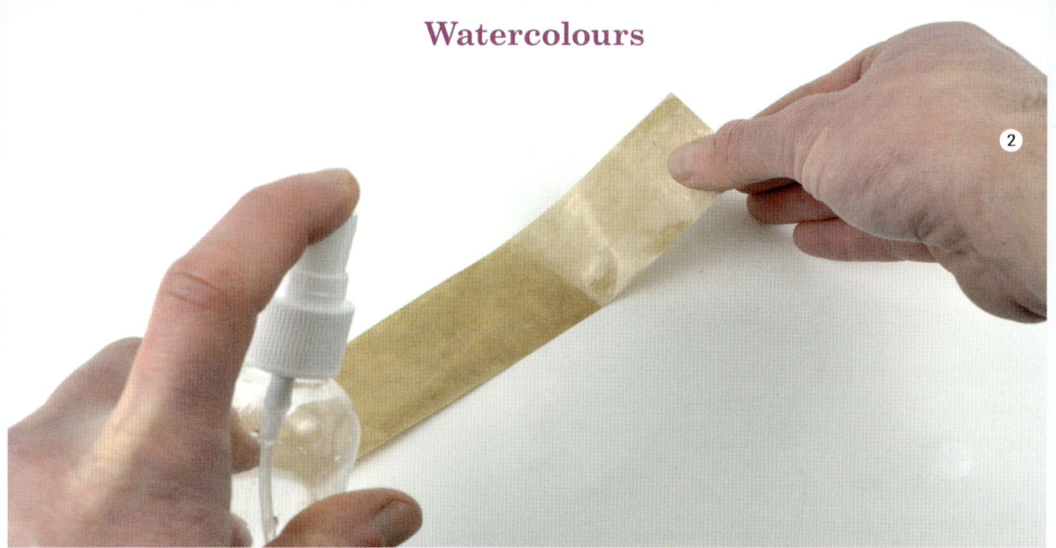

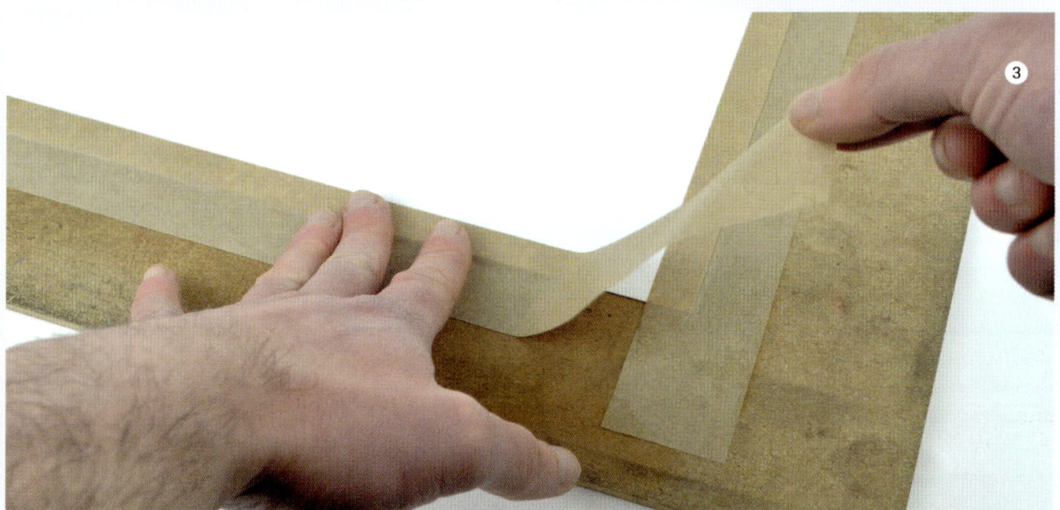

Follow these steps...

1 Soak the paper

Start by soaking the watercolour paper in clean water, in a tray or flat-bottomed basin. It should be wet enough to be saturated and 'floppy'. Try not to leave it in too long, as this can remove too much size from the paper, making it too absorbent and causing paint to 'sink'. Take it out, letting any excess water drip off, and lay it flat on the board. When picking up paper, pick it up by the corners so the oils on your hands don't affect the surface that will be painted on later.

2 Wet the tape

Cut the tape into strips, making sure there is plenty of excess at each end. The adhesive on the tape is activated by water, so here I'm spraying it with a spray bottle to wet it evenly. Another way to do this is to run a damp sponge over it. It only needs enough water to activate, so try not to saturate it or it will fail. It's very strong, so hold it at each end and avoid letting it stick to itself.

3 Tape down the paper

Tape down the paper with the gummed tape – for extra security, the tape can be long enough to wrap around the edges of the board. Try not to get the upper side of the tape wet as this can cause it to fail. Now leave the paper to dry completely, ideally overnight. Don't get tempted to use a hairdryer or heater, as this can cause the tape to fail and the paper to buckle. I find it works best when the paper is flat while drying.

Additional tools

While paint, brushes and paper are the core of our kit, other equipment can be useful or open up avenues to experimentation

Outside of paints, paper and brushes, there are a number of other tools and materials that can help with painting in watercolour. Some tools are purely practical, such as palettes and spray bottles. These are worth having on hand (for instance, spray bottles are useful for reactivating dry paint) but may also change depending on your work process, such as selecting deeper palettes if you use washes.

There are also lots of other materials that can combine well with watercolours, often to create unique effects. This is not an exhaustive list, and it is worth experimenting by combining watercolour with other materials. Anything that interacts with water, either by dissolving, absorbing or repelling it is worth considering.

When selecting other equipment, try to pick items that suit your working process and the outcomes you'd like to achieve. Watercolour has a lot of versatility as a medium and suits a wide range of artistic styles because of this.

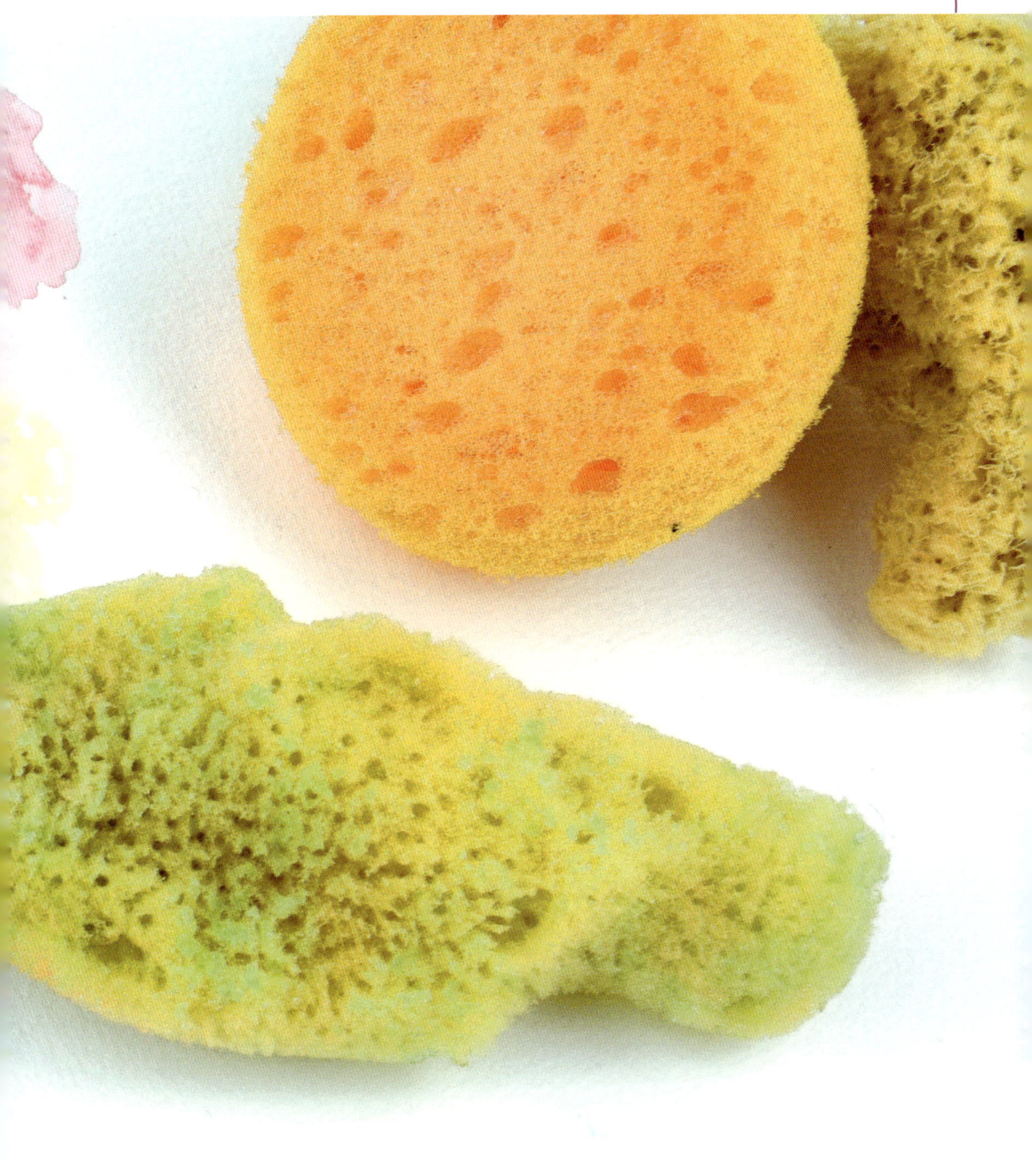

Sponges

SPONGES COME IN many forms and shapes, and work much as expected – they can suck up large amounts of wet pigment.

This is useful for two purposes; firstly, they can be used to lift out excess paint, creating a subtractive texture as they remove pigment from washes. The other way of using them is to make up a watercolour wash by mixing paint and water, and using the sponge to apply it.

Both methods are an effective way to create naturalistic, random textures, and applying paint with a sponge works well for blending two colours together, both wet-in-wet and wet-on-dry. Try experimenting with how saturated the sponge is – it tends to create grittier textures the less water it holds.

Usually, sponges work best when wetted and wrung out before use, so they are slightly damp all the way through.

Palettes

PALETTES ARE AN essential piece of kit and come in many different shapes and sizes. Typically, watercolour palettes are made from plastic, ceramics or metal, though sometimes other materials are used, such as enamel. They may have large areas to mix on, or deeper wells for holding lots of water for large washes.

For tube paints, plastic or ceramic palettes are usually used – plastic palettes are inexpensive and come in a huge range of styles, but tend to stain and can be harder to clean. Ceramic palettes have more durable surfaces and are still quite diverse in style, but can be heavy and are more fragile, making them a less portable option.

Pans tend to be held in metal or plastic palettes with a folding lid – this keeps them free of dust. Both come in lots of styles, so consider how much mixing area you need, and how many pans you want in your set. Metal palettes are more hard-wearing, but cost more. Some of these palettes are very portable, as they hold fewer paints and fold down to pocket size.

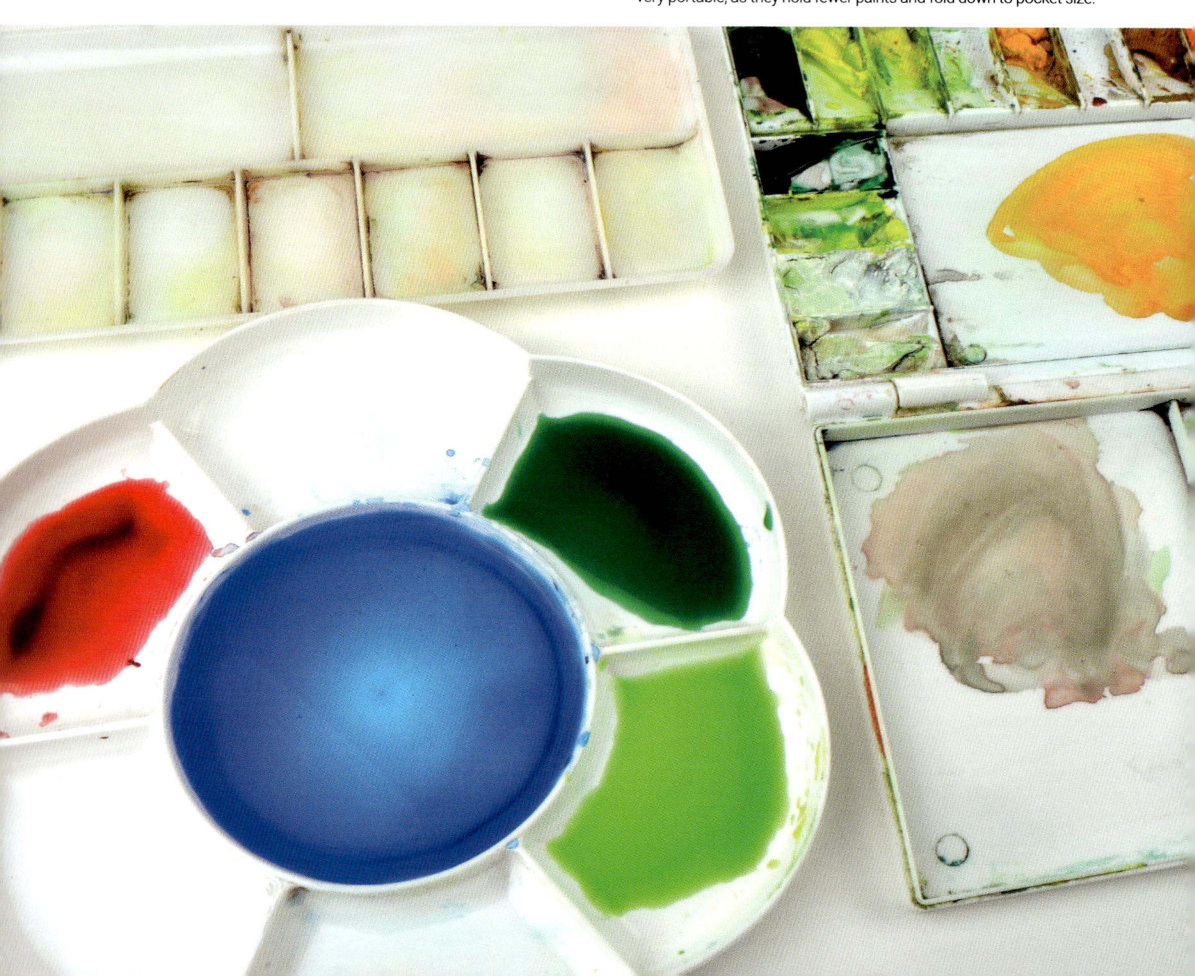

Spray bottles

A SPRAY BOTTLE is a useful and inexpensive item that is well worth including in your kit. It can be part of a working process, as it can wet paper quickly and evenly, which is handy for wet-in-wet work and laying down even washes of paint. Using watercolour pencils on wet paper like this can also produce interesting effects and more highly pigmented marks. Spraying water around applied paint can also create misty patterns and soften hard edges whilst avoiding leaving brush strokes.

More practical uses include spraying water to clean dry paint from palettes (especially when out and about), activating dry watercolour pans, and wetting gummed tape.

If you are keen on working wet-in-wet, consider trying different spray bottles. Different nozzles can produce bigger or smaller water droplets, deposit more or less water, or cover different-sized areas.

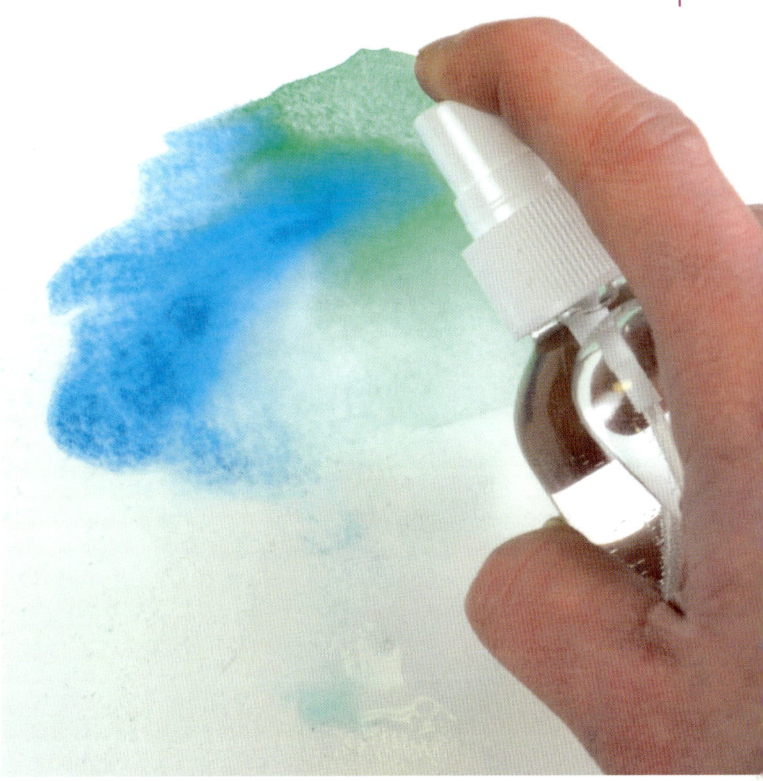

Salt

COMBINING SALT WITH watercolour washes can create interesting textures and patterns. The salt needs to be applied to a wet area of paint, where it absorbs the wet paint and leaves a pale, random, crystalline pattern. Using more pigmented paint washes tends to result in a more defined pattern due to contrast. This technique is particularly useful for abstract and landscape work, but can be incorporated into other subjects, especially when creating an underpainting in a layered approach.

All you need for this technique is regular kitchen salt or sea salt (they work the same but may produce different patterns). The random textures and patterns they produce can be controlled by the placement and quantity of the crystals, with large concentrations able to produce gradients. Be patient with this technique – the watercolour needs to dry completely before the salt is removed for the full effect.

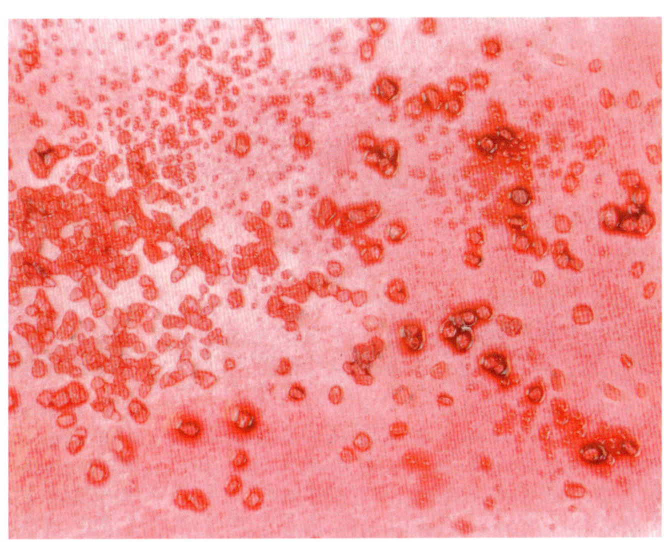

How to use salt

Follow these steps...

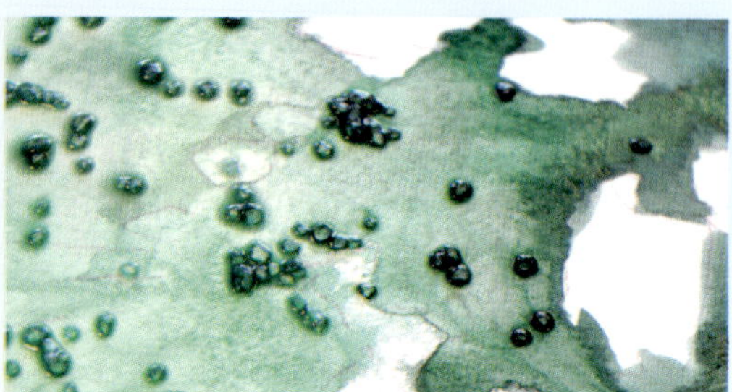

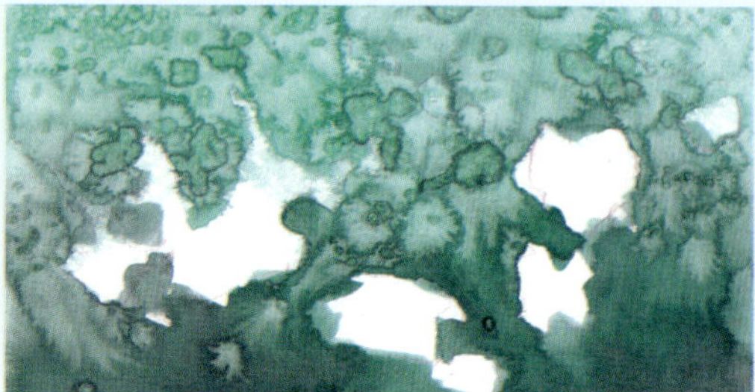

1 ⬥ The initial wash

To start, I sketch out the rough placement of the major elements of the roses and greenery, then fill the green areas with a wash. Immediately after this, the sea salt crystals are applied, with concentrations at the top of the image.

The idea is to create a random texture to imply the leaves in the distance and suck some of the pigment from the wash to lighten the area, forming a gradient. The salt needs to be applied as quickly as possible for the maximum effect, before the water starts to sink into the paper.

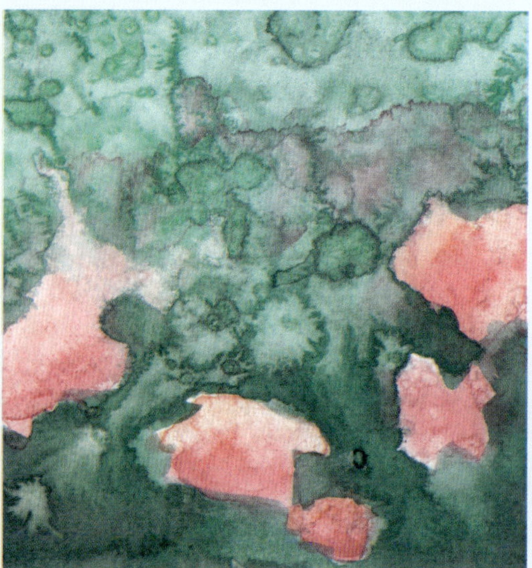

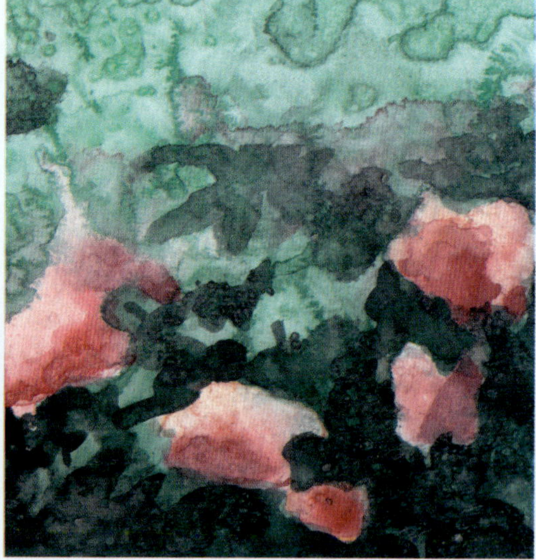

2 ⬥ Building colour

In this step I follow a similar process with the roses, applying a pinkish wash with a round brush after letting the first one dry. The salt is carefully scattered in the areas I want to lighten, to create a gradient that mimics the overall light and shadow on the roses.

In some places, the paint isn't as intense as I would like, so to remedy this I mix a stronger colour and apply it to the wet areas away from the salt with the round brush.

3 ⬥ Add shadow & detail

After letting everything dry, I add another layer of green for the foliage, paying more attention to the leaf shapes and working with the pre-existing patterns. I let it sit for a bit before adding salt; this allows a decent amount of pigment to sink into the paper, but produces a random, gritty texture. Once the shadows dry, I use the round brush to add extra leaves and branches, and extra detail to the roses. Salt textures are fine to paint on, though take care to remove all the salt first.

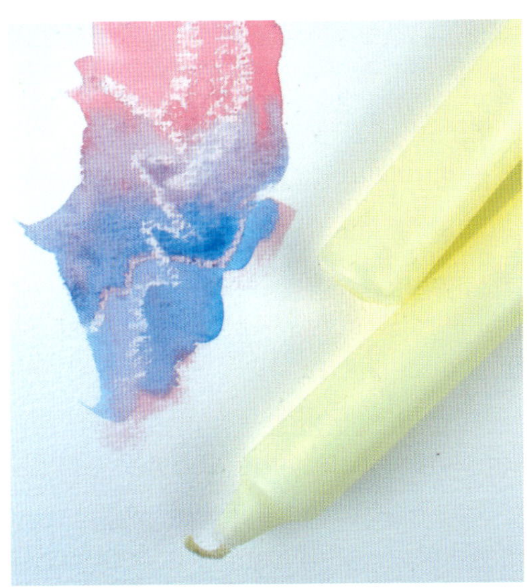

Wax

WAX NATURALLY REPELS water, which makes it a useful tool. When wax is applied to paper, the watercolour cannot adhere to it – this technique is sometimes called 'wax resist'. Regular wax candles can be used for this effect, as can wax crayons if colour is wanted. Oil pastels interact in a similar way, but tend to be a bit unpredictable and may bleed into watercolour paint.

This technique is especially useful for producing gritty natural textures such as stone, especially when done on cold press or rough papers. A wax candle can be cut into a chunk and rubbed over the paper so the grain picks it up and leaves gaps the paint can get into. Wax can also be drawn with, either to create under-drawings that repel paint, or, in the case of white wax, preserve highlights early on in a painting process.

Pens

PENS ARE GREAT to have around for sketching with watercolour. One popular way of working is by creating a pen sketch and painting it with watercolours.

A common challenge is selecting the right kind of pen, as many have inks that run when they get wet – whilst this is sometimes desirable, it can also be a nuisance. Ink is often labelled as waterproof, water-resistant and water-soluble. Water-soluble ink will, of course, run into watercolour paint and muddy it. However, water-resistant ones will also do this; the difference is that they maintain their lines whilst water-soluble inks will fade or may dissolve completely. Waterproof pens are the only ones that shouldn't do this (depending on their quality!) and can be painted over with watercolour.

This also applies to bottled inks that you may want to use with refillable pens, brushes and nibs.

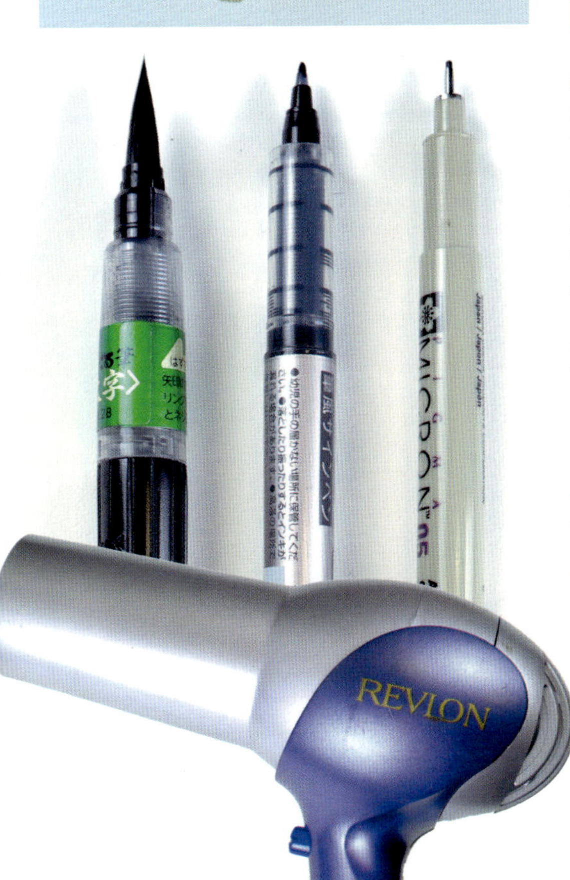

Hairdryer

A HAIRDRYER IS worth having on hand for speeding up drying times, especially if you work in a layered fashion with less water.

Do take care when you do this, as the heat can also interfere with other processes – such as melting wax and reducing the effect of salt. It may also cause tapes to become unstuck and paper to buckle more easily – this is especially true with thinner paper. To avoid disturbing wet paint, direct the hairdryer vertically down at the page.

Another use for the hairdryer is pushing around washes – turn it onto the lowest heat setting possible and use the air to direct water over the paper. This is handy for getting a little control over gradients, and can also be used to create drip effects by pushing the paint around.

Simplify painting with a strong composition

Margaret Merry demonstrates how to use watercolour to capture the charm of a summer garden, with its ephemeral light, shade and colour

Since ancient times, gardens have been a source of inspiration for artists. However, they can be tricky subjects to tackle because when the eye is confronted by a confusing array of tone, form and colour, it's difficult to know where to begin.

The answer is good composition, and the best way to compose a garden painting is to find a point of focus, such as an ornament, a chair or a fountain. Old, weathered walls are a favourite of mine. For my demonstration, I chose this quirky, painted sewing machine table, set against the plain background of a white wall. The dappled light that shines through the trees casts some interesting shadows.

For all my work, I use a limited palette comprising: Ultramarine Blue; Cobalt Blue; Yellow Ochre; Raw Sienna; Burnt Sienna; Burnt Umber; Lemon Yellow; Alizarin Crimson; Cadmium Red. However, when painting flowers or similarly colourful subjects, it's useful to have one or two extra pigments, such as the Brilliant Opera Rose and Cobalt Turquoise I've used in my painting. Transparent pigments, not opaque ones, are best for painting flowers.

Light is an important consideration when painting gardens because it is constantly changing. I painted this watercolour in strong afternoon light, shaded by trees. For a more romantic effect, early morning is the best time because all the colours are softened.

Green is the predominant colour in a garden and to maintain colour harmony, I mix my own using my basic pigments.

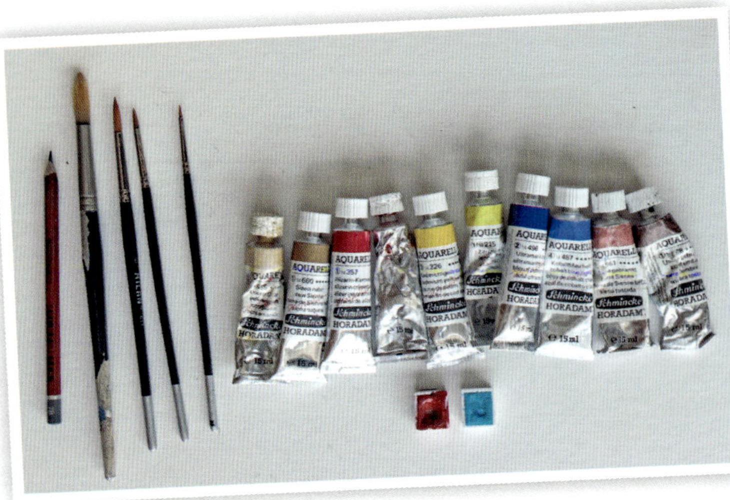

Materials

Margaret uses tubes of Schmincke watercolour paints. She likes to paint on Arches 300gsm paper, approximately 11x15in with a fine surface stretched onto a board. This is her preferred paper because the surface has just the right amount of resistance to enhance the inherent transparency and brilliance of the medium. Margaret uses synthetic round brushes.

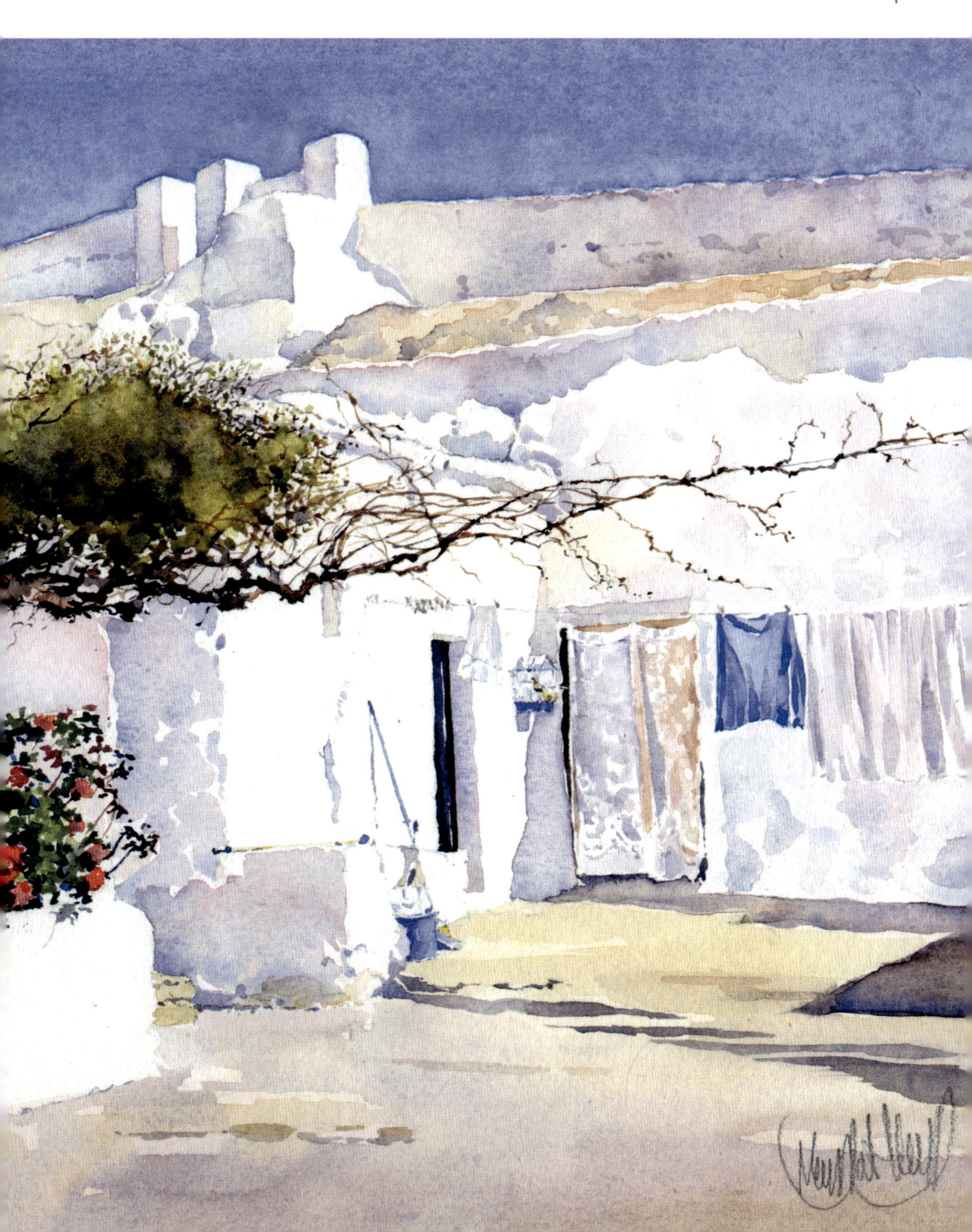

Follow these steps...

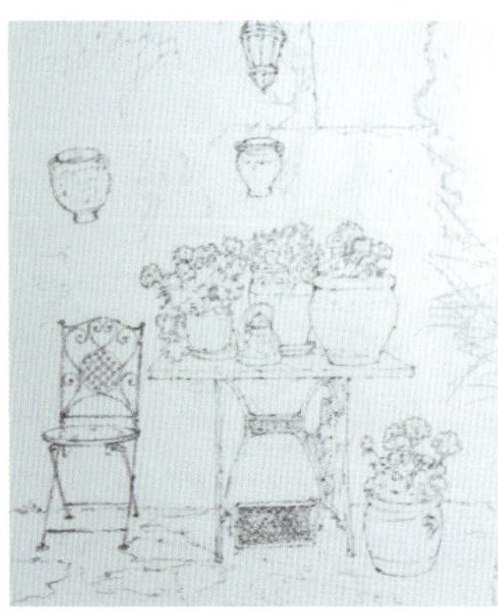

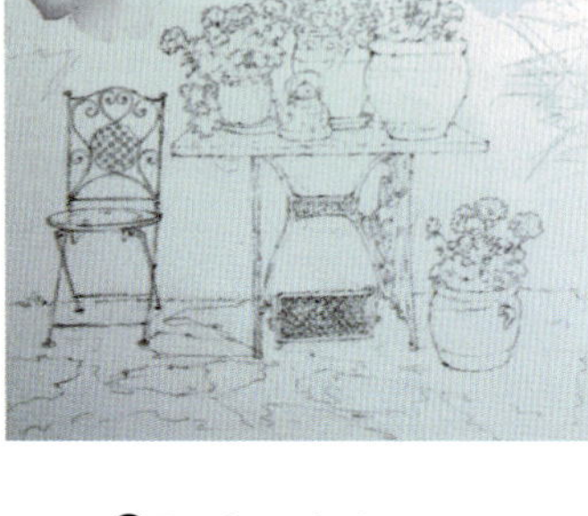

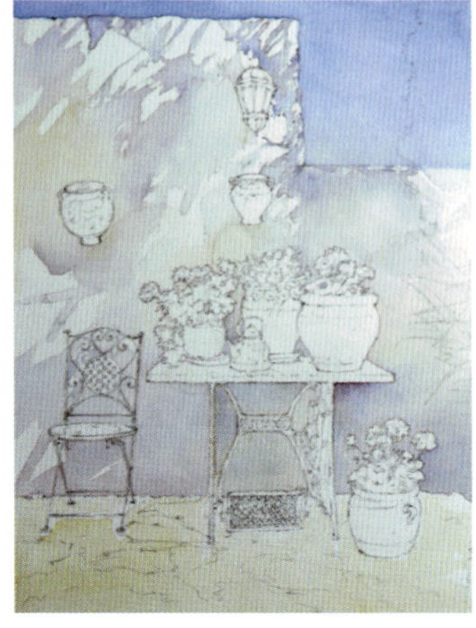

1 ⬥ Do a preliminary drawing

With well-sharpened 2B pencils, I make a fairly detailed drawing of the composition, altering things I don't like, such as the position of the chair. I have included the cypress tree on the right and a few fronds of palm leaves because I like the sense of enclosure they create. Use soft strokes for drawing and don't be tempted to use an eraser because this will mar the surface of the paper.

2 ⬥ Begin painting

I apply a transparent wash of Cobalt Blue for the sky, using a synthetic size 12 brush, extending it over the tree. With a mix of Cobalt Blue, Yellow Ochre and Rose Madder, I paint the shadows in quick, bold strokes, softening hard lines with the brush loaded with clean water. I allow the water to separate the pigments to prevent the background from being too uniform.

3 ⬥ Continue to apply background shadows

I continue painting the shadowed areas with my Cobalt mix and with a smaller synthetic brush (size 6). I carefully work around all the various objects so that the paper remains white. I paint rapidly because I want to finish this stage before the pigments dry. Lastly, I lay a transparent wash of Raw Sienna on the ground.

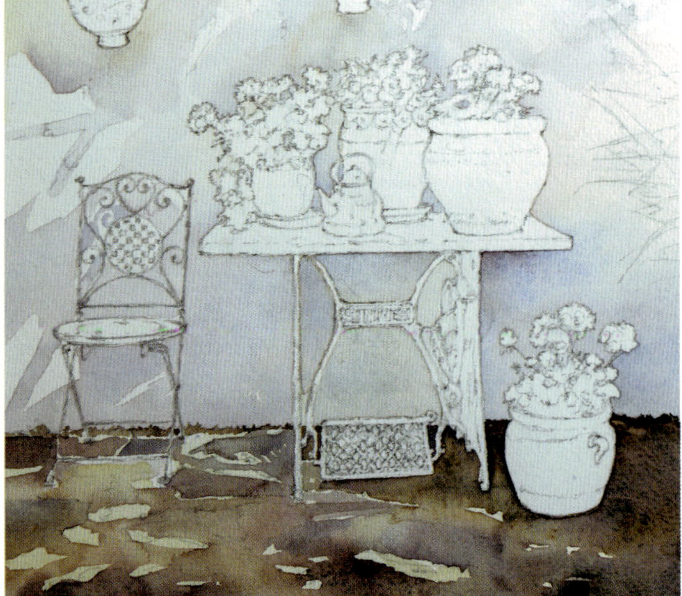

4 ⬥ Finish the background

When the Raw Sienna has dried, over-paint it with a mix of Ultramarine Blue, Raw Sienna and Alizarin Crimson. While the paper is still wet, allow some touches of Burnt Sienna to flow into the grey, giving warmth to the foreground. Again, I let the pigments separate and I use my size 2 brush to quickly draw around the various objects before the paint dries.

Know your tools

When I first began to paint with watercolour, I used it mainly to lay flat washes over pen and ink drawings or pencil sketches. In this way, I familiarised myself with the medium and developed my technique from there.

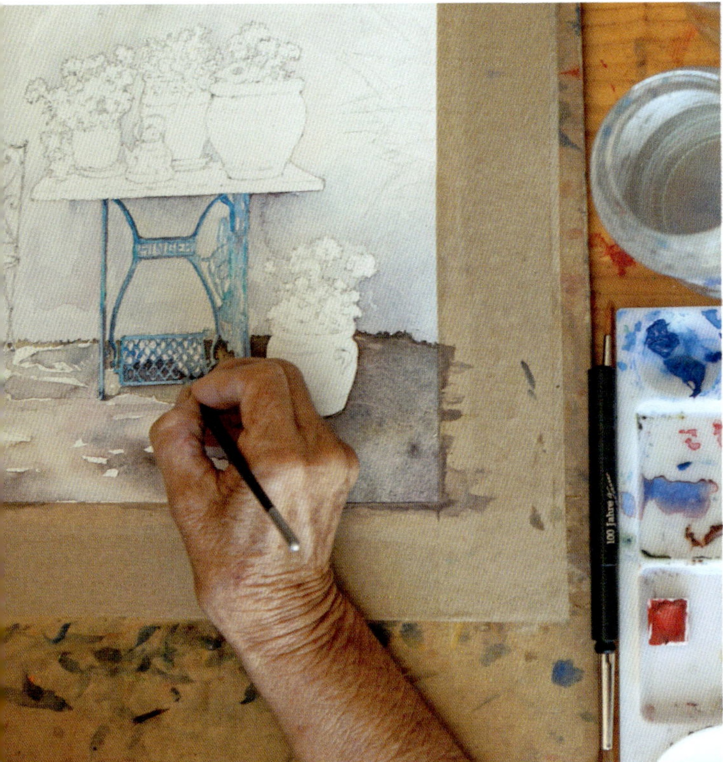

5 **◔ Draw with the brush**
Now that all the unnecessary white has been eliminated, I can begin working on the main feature: the sewing machine table. This involves detail, so I continue using my size 2 brush, which has a fine point yet is large enough to hold a reasonable amount of water. I use Cobalt Blue with a touch of Cobalt Turquoise and I vary the tones by diluting the lighter parts with water.

6 **◔ Add more detail**
Now that the table has been painted, it looks as though it's floating, so more shadow is needed. I use my dark grey Ultramarine mixture to paint around and below the table and add more definition where the blue tends to merge into the background. The marble top is painted with a very diluted grey and I add some dabs of Yellow Ochre to the wet paint.

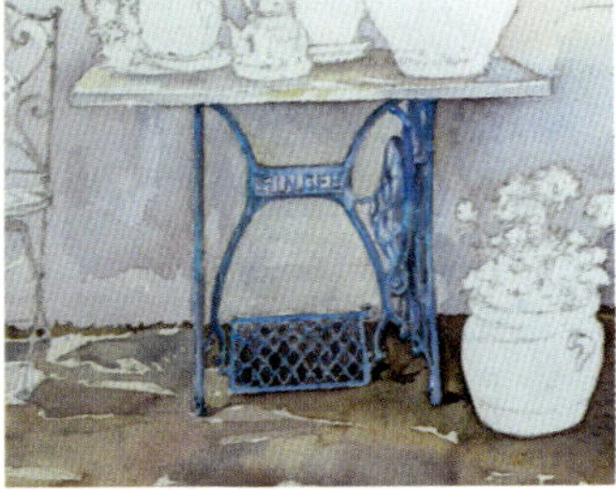

7 **◔ Draw with a fine brush**
The little metalwork chair is relatively simple to paint as it involves mostly drawing. For this I use my finest synthetic brush, size 0. The chair is painted black but I never use black pigment because it contaminates other pigments. I mix, as an alternative, Ultramarine Blue with Burnt Umber. I use less water than before and with a steady hand, draw the details. With the Ultramarine grey mix, I add more shadow around and below the chair.

8 **◔ Paint the flowerpots and lamp**
I return to my size 2 brush to paint the lamp and the flowerpots on the wall. In order to avoid overworking them, I use plenty of clean water to soften the outlines and give just an impression of detail. I introduce more colour by adding Burnt Sienna and Cadmium Orange for the terracotta pot and the lamp, and Cadmium Red for the decoration on the ceramic pot. I paint the shadows on the pots with a watery grey, using circular brushstrokes for a rounded effect.

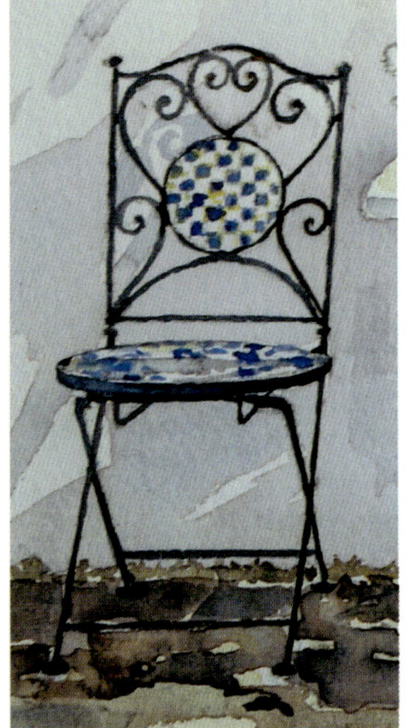

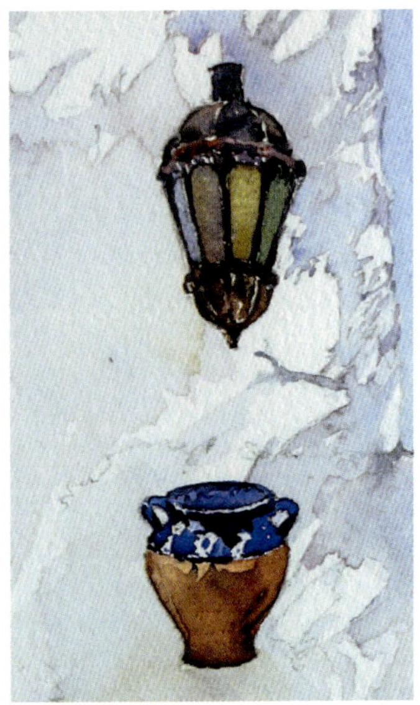

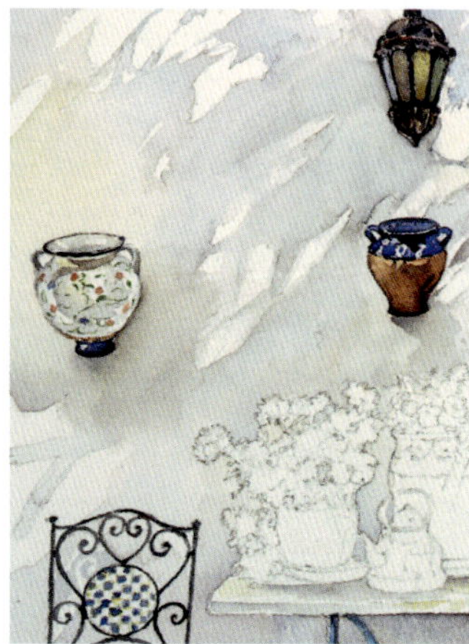

9　⏶ Embed with shadows

As was initially the case with the table, the lamp and the pots look as though they're floating. This is fixed by adding shadows around and underneath them. For this, I use the subtle Cobalt Blue mix with which I began painting the background. Again, I soften some of the hard lines with a brush loaded with clean water.

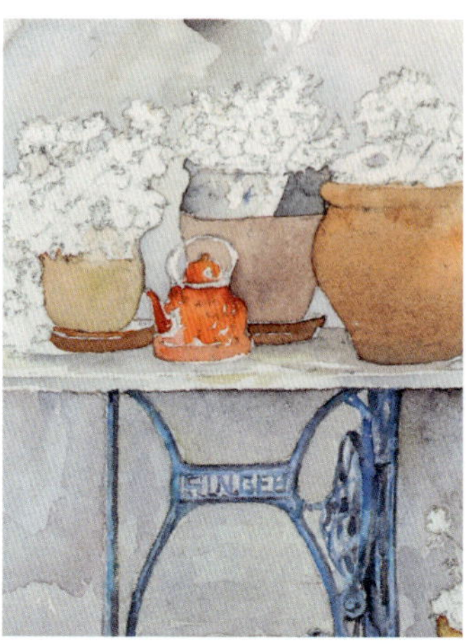

10　⏶ Work on the terracotta pots

My method for tackling terracotta flowerpots is to paint a transparent base coat using Cadmium Orange, Burnt Sienna and Raw Sienna. The shiny kettle has a transparent coat of Cadmium Red and where the light falls, I've left white patches. Before I continue with the second stage, I make sure the base coat is completely dry.

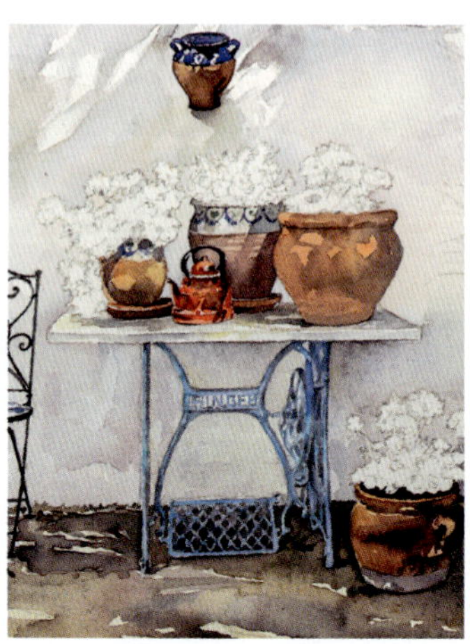

11　⏶ Create form

To create form, I paint a second coat using my Ultramarine mix and, as before, my brushstrokes are curved to follow the shape of the pots. I like the patterns cast by the shadows and so I make a feature of these, but still keeping the paint very fluid to maintain transparency. I apply the same technique to the red kettle and finish by painting the decoration on the pots.

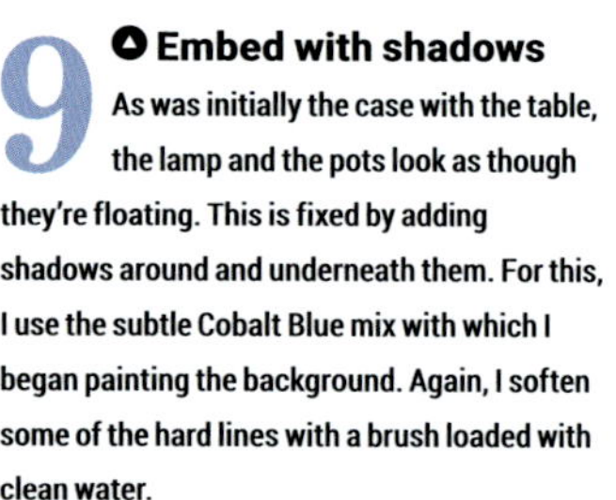
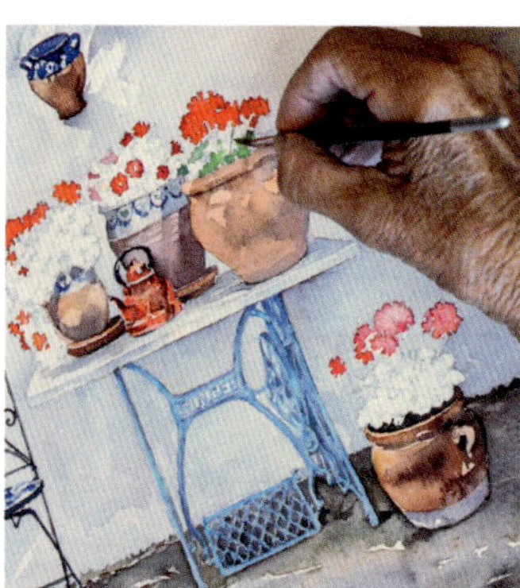

12　⏶ Paint flowers

I give the flowers and the leaves the same treatment as the pots. The first task is applying a base coat. I use Cadmium Red, well-diluted, for the flowers and a mix of Lemon Yellow and Ultramarine Blue for the leaves. The pink geraniums in the foreground are painted with Brilliant Opera Rose mixed with Cadmium Orange. I use two brushes, size 2 and size 4.

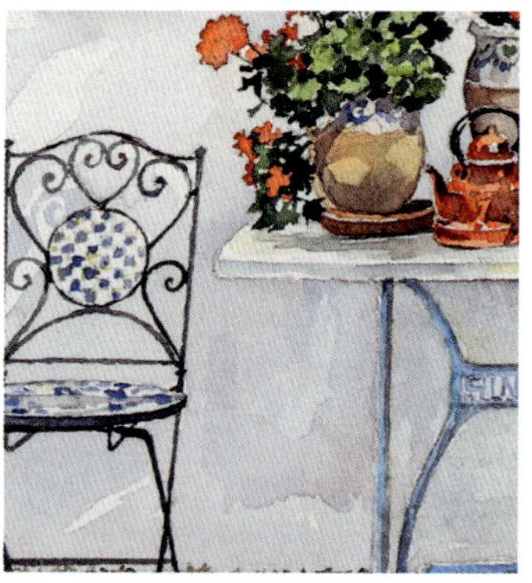

13　⏶ Add definition

I begin with the leaves, adding a touch of Raw Sienna to the green mixture to make it darker. I have to take care not to paint too much detail, but, at the same time, I want to make a feature of the leaves. Knowing what to paint and what to leave out comes with experience! Again, the hard lines are softened with water and it's the latter, rather than the brush, that works to blend the greens into each other.

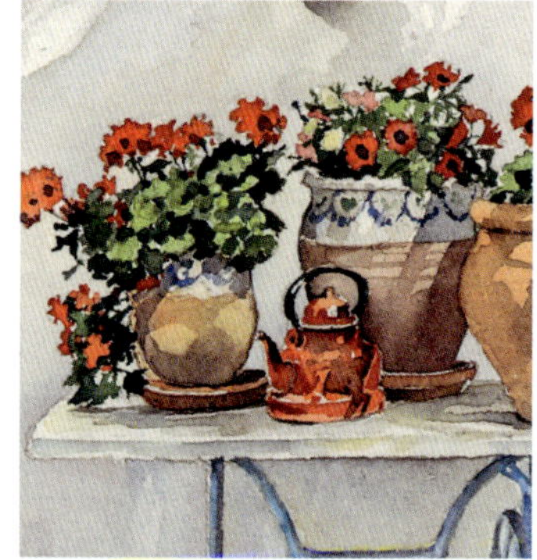

14　⏶ Finish the flowers

I paint the darker tones on the flowers as I did with the leaves, using just a hint of Ultramarine to define the shaded parts. When painting flowers, it can be very easy to lose the freshness and transparency of the medium if they are overworked and for this reason, I keep the pigments as pure as possible, bearing in mind that it is difficult to rectify mistakes when painting flowers in watercolour.

15 ◑ **Complete it**

As the painting nears completion, it's time to paint the cypress tree and the palm fronds to form a frame. For these, I use my basic green mixture (Ultramarine Blue and Lemon Yellow) darkened with Raw Sienna and Burnt Sienna. For the lightest areas, I drop pure Lemon Yellow into the wet paint and with a fine brush, I draw the pointed leaves, from base to tip, using a flicking movement. A few last touches of shadow complete the painting.

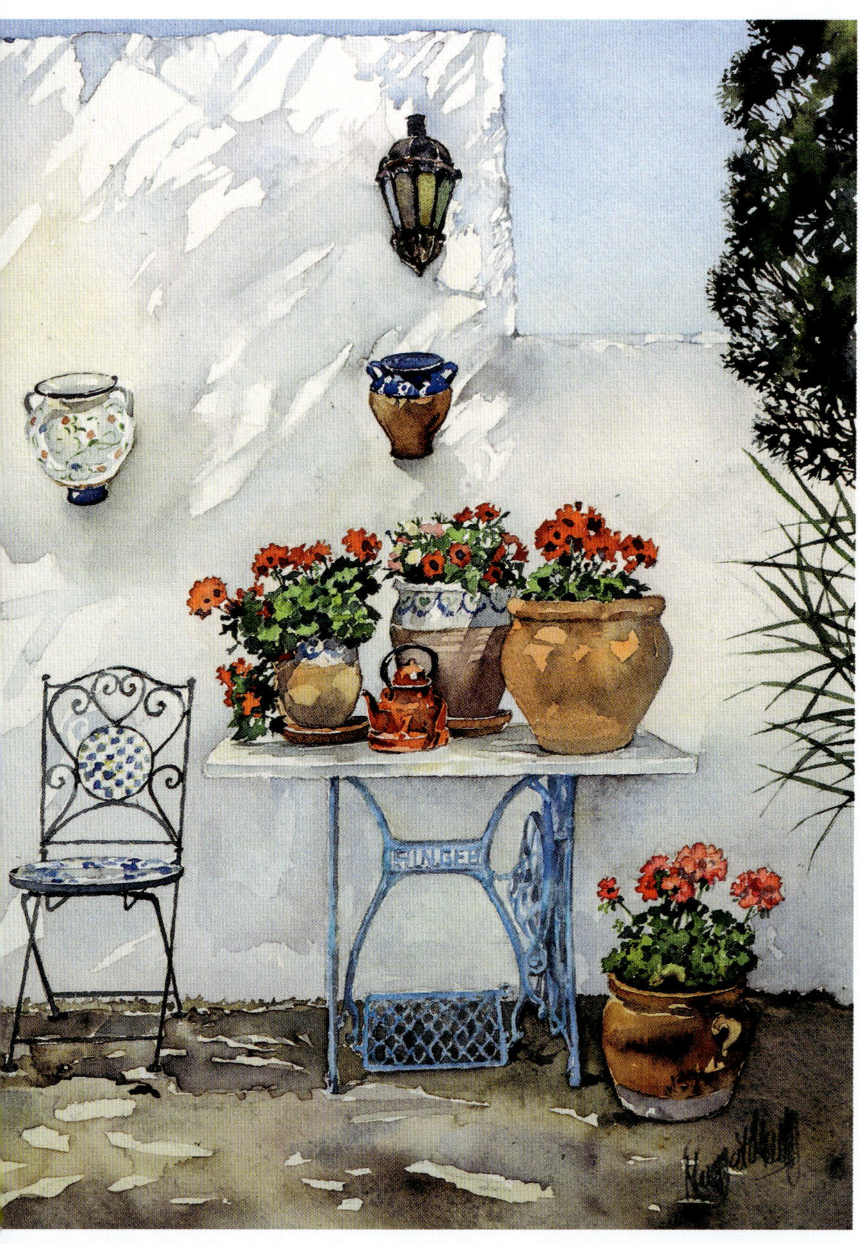

Speed painting

Watercolour is a medium best suited to rapid, spontaneous painting. I find that if I spend too long on a work, inspiration wanes and I'm invariably dissatisfied with the result.

lesson learned!

When I was an art student, we once spent an entire session painting vertical stripes in oils, using just Cobalt Blue, Yellow Ochre and Alizarin Crimson. The point was to demonstrate the wide range of greys that were possible using just these colours – and it's a lesson I've never forgotten.

Capture a winter farm

Using his unique '5 Cs of Painting', **Robert Newcombe** demonstrates how to paint a snow scene in watercolour from a sketch

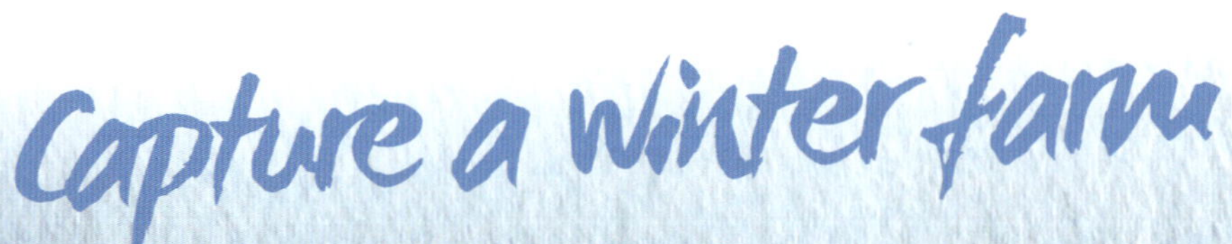

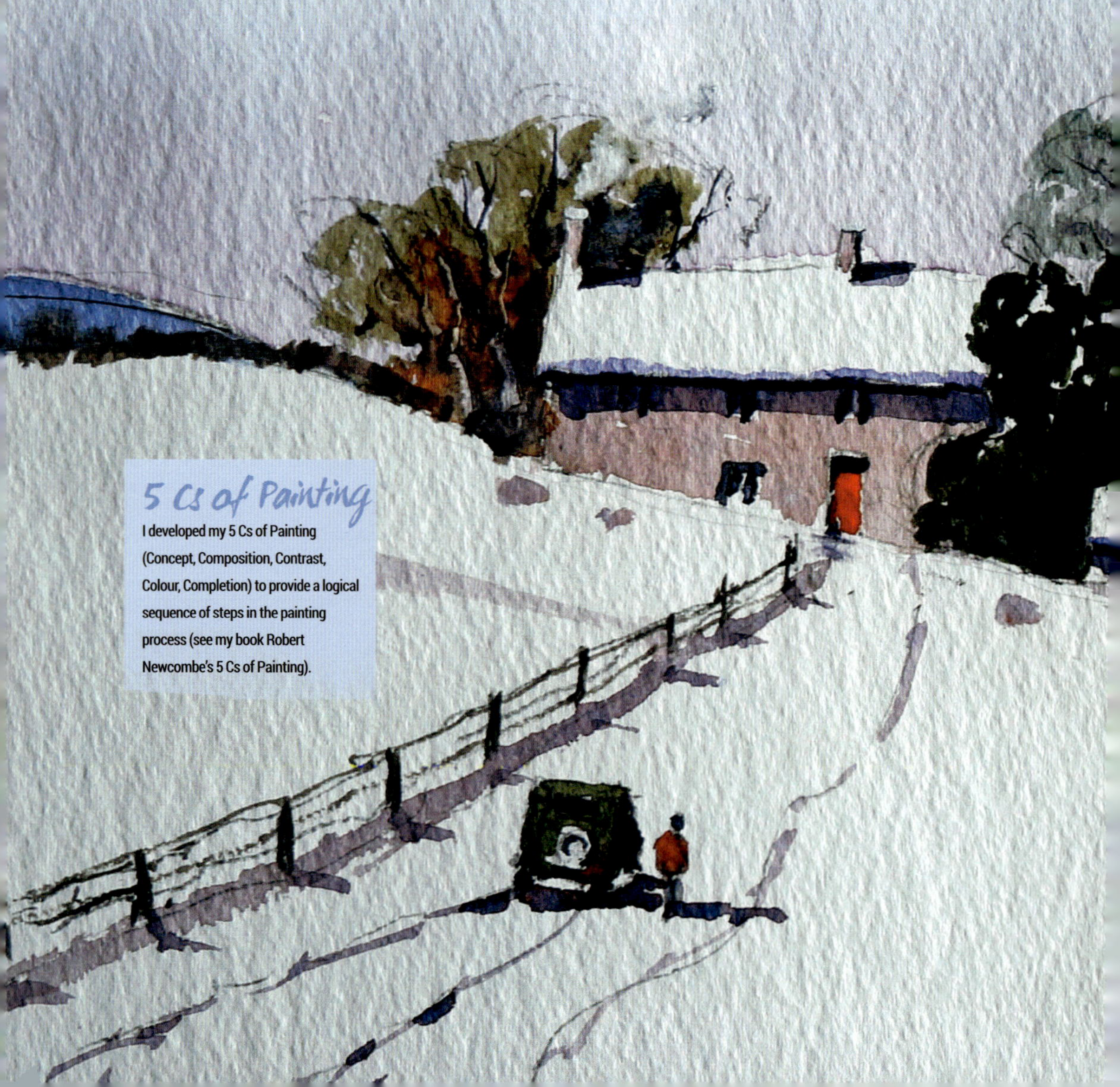

5 Cs of Painting

I developed my 5 Cs of Painting (Concept, Composition, Contrast, Colour, Completion) to provide a logical sequence of steps in the painting process (see my book Robert Newcombe's 5 Cs of Painting).

Iwas in the English Lake District in the early 1980s just after I had taken up watercolour painting as a hobby. It was late November and there had been a fresh fall of snow. Taking the road towards Derwent Water I came across this magnificent view of Skelgill Farm; it was too cold to paint but I did a ten-minute sketch of the scene shown in step 1 with a felt-tip pen, using a soft pencil to shade in the reddish-grey stone walls of the farmhouse and assortment of barns. I added some colour notes. I didn't realise until many years later that Skelgill Farm is mentioned in Beatrix Potter's The Tale of Mrs Tiggy-Winkle, with a drawing of part of the farm by the author as an illustration.

I will now use my '5 Cs of Painting' to show you how I develop a unique interpretation of this subject.

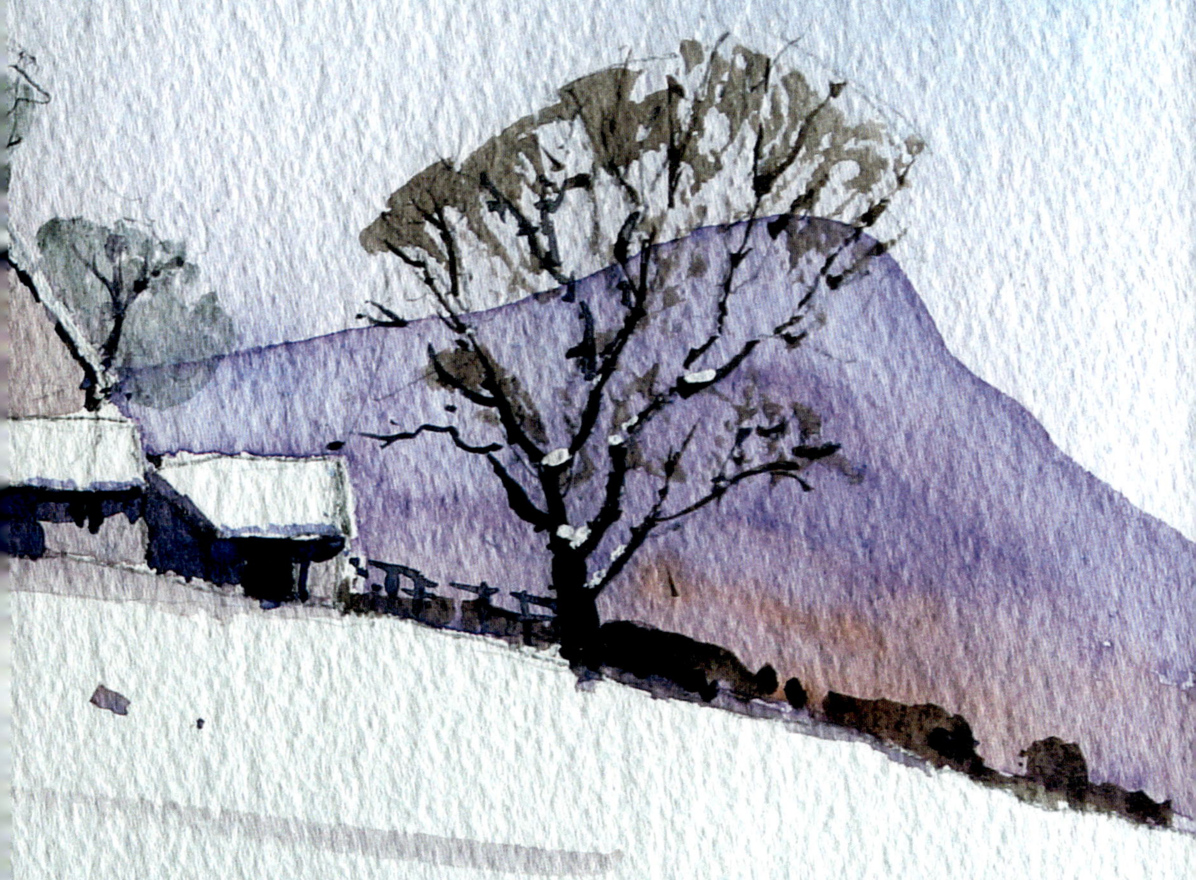

Materials

- Winsor and Newton (Professional Watercolour range): Burnt Sienna, Burnt Umber, Cobalt Blue, Ultramarine Blue, Brown Madder, Light Red, Indian Red, Cadmium Red, Permanent Magenta or Alizarin Crimson and Winsor Blue (green shade)
- Brushes – a one-inch Hake brush for the broad washes and Escoda Perla (8 and 12) for the architectural details and a rigger brush for the trees
- Paper – Whatman Not 140lb (300gsm), size one-quarter Imperial (11 x 15 inches) – Whatman is whiter than some watercolour paper and is ideal for snow scenes
- 2B pencil
- Putty rubber

Snow paint

Snow paintings are a gift for watercolourists as the white of the paper represents the snow (no white paint) but the critical skill is to preserve the white paper.

Follow these steps...

1 ◔ The sketch

The concept (the first C) is a Lake District farm under snow. The subject is predominantly cool with a brilliant winter sun coming from the front-left, which lights up the front of the farmhouse and barns creating strong shadows.

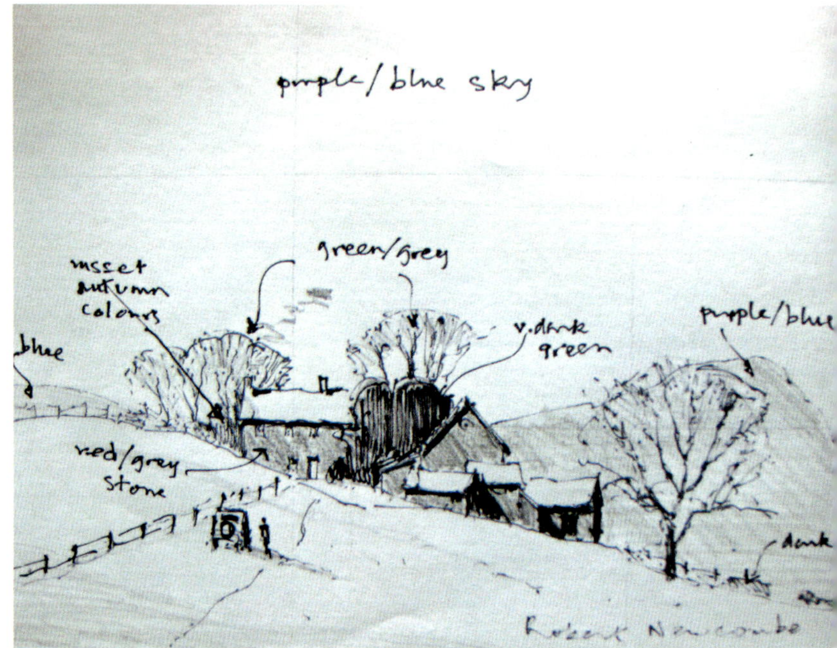

2 ◔ The pencil drawing

Composition is the next C and refers to the design of the painting. I felt it was a perfect composition. The snow-covered roof of the farmhouse contrasts with the dark yew tree at the centre of interest, there are some lovely autumn/winter trees and the sloping ground adds to the character of the subject. The mountain (Catbells), which gives distance and depth, will be put in directly with the brush. I raise the horizon in the drawing to give more prominence to the foreground snow.

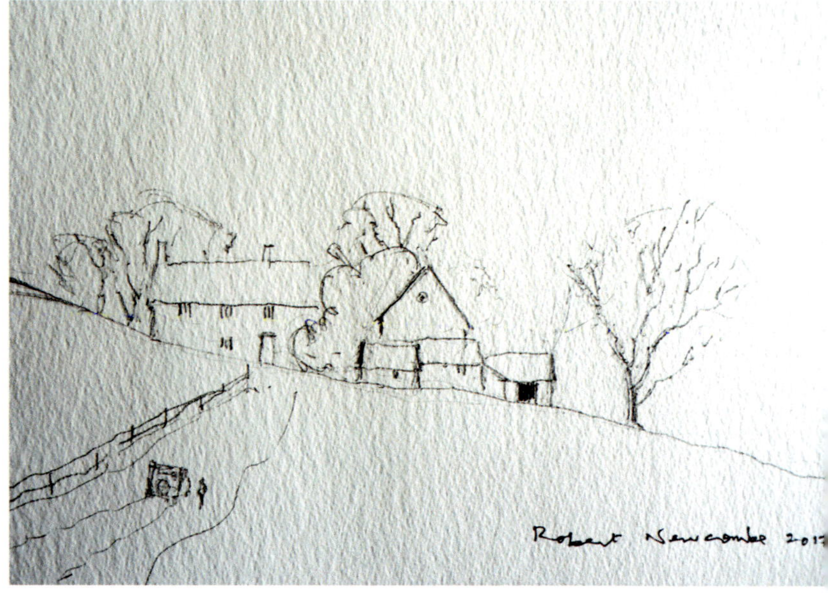

3 ❏ The tonal scale

The next C is 'contrast' or tone values. On the left of a fresh sheet of watercolour paper I create a five-value tonal scale using squares, numbering the squares from 1 to 5. Tone 1 is the white of the paper; Tone 5 is the darkest tone I can get with Ultramarine Blue. I add water to achieve tone 4 and more water again to achieve tones 3 and 2, creating a gradual transition from the dark to light. The space to the right is for checking the tones of the colours I'll use in the painting.

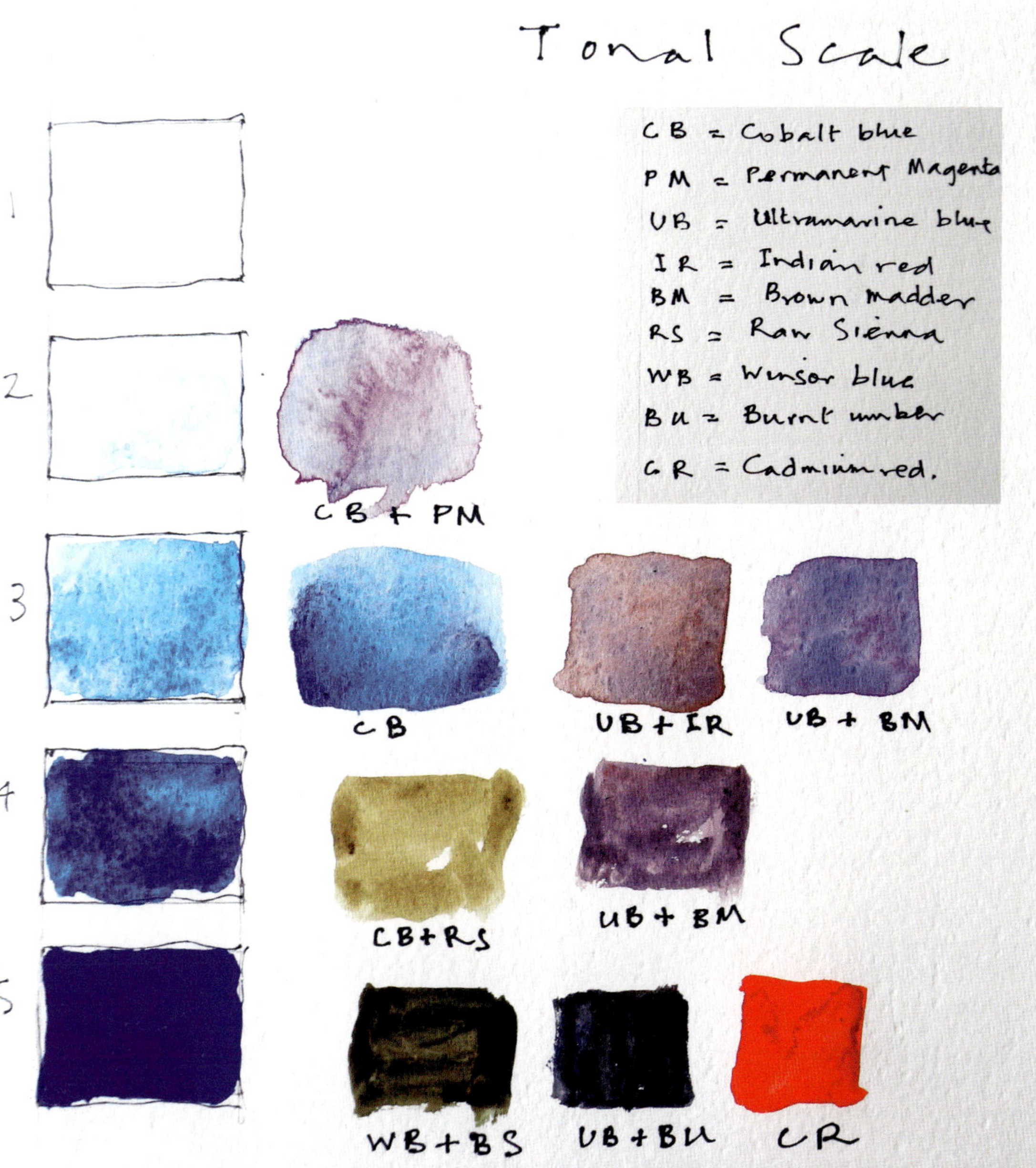

4 ▶ The tonal plan

Referring to my five-value tonal scale and using Ultramarine Blue again I produce a small tonal plan for the painting to enable me to see colours as tones. The white of the paper is the lightest tone (Tone 1 – the snow) with almost neat ultramarine blue for the darkest tone (Tone 5 – the yew tree) and the intermediate tones shown as per numbers on the tonal plan. As we paint from light to dark in watercolour this tonal plan will also give me my painting sequence.

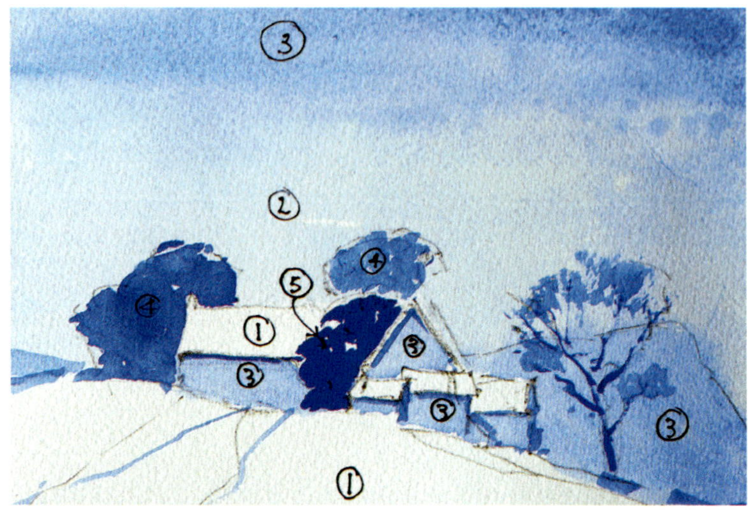

5 ▶ Paint the sky (tones 2 and 3)

I turn the paper upside down to paint the sky to prevent dribbles running down the white paper representing the snow. After checking my colours on my tonal scale sheet I use my Hake brush to paint a tone 2 purple wash (Ultramarine Blue and Permanent Magenta) starting at the snow-covered roof of the farmhouse and barns and taking the wash down to ground level elsewhere, then gradually changing this to a Tone 3 wash of Cobalt Blue at the zenith of the sky. The paper cockles slightly at this stage but will dry flat.

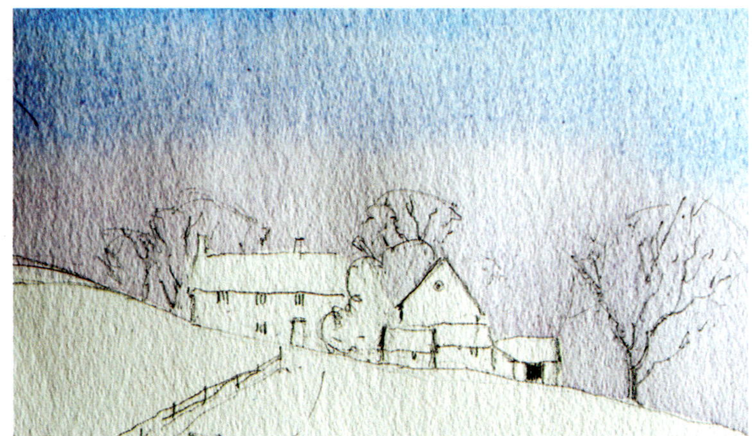

6 ▶ Paint buildings (tone 3)

Following my tonal painting sequence I paint the stone walls of the farmhouse and barns with a tone 3 mix of Ultramarine Blue and a little Indian Red to achieve the warm colour of Cumbrian stone. I use my Escoda Perla 12 brush having checked the mix on my tonal scale.

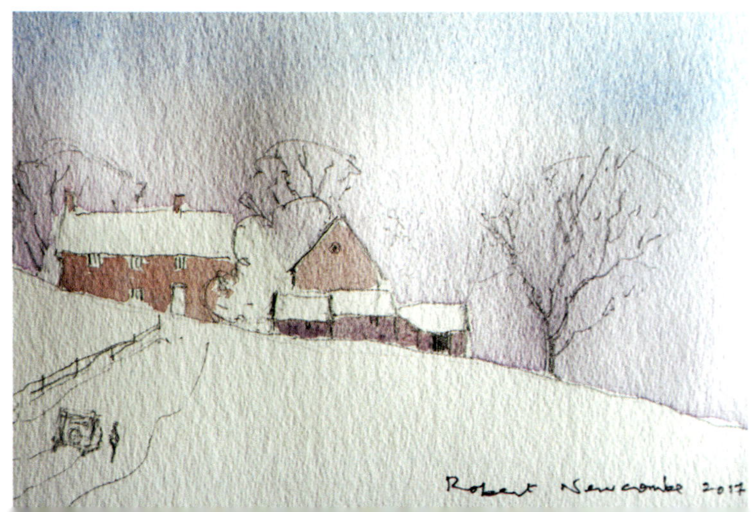

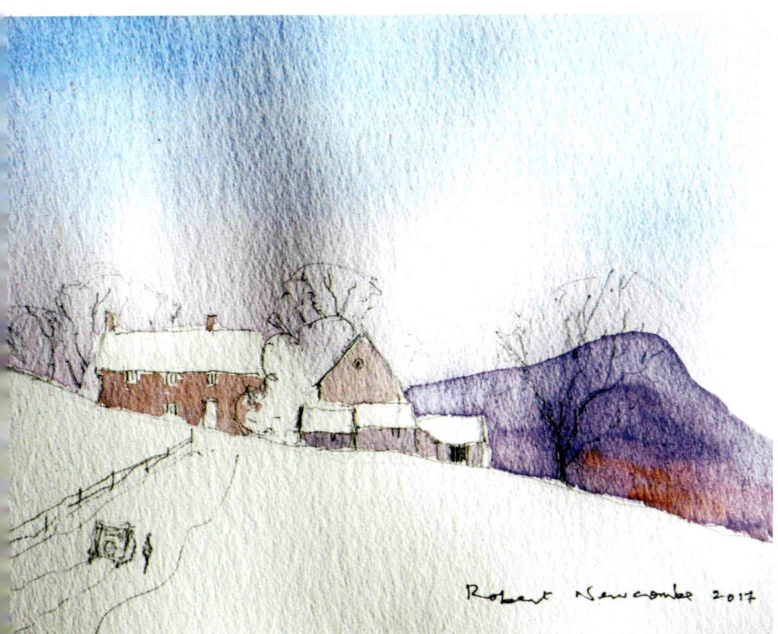

7 **◔ Paint the mountain (tone 3)**

The simple mountain shape is now painted in directly with the same brush with a mix of Ultramarine Blue plus a little Permanent Magenta to give a purplish tinge. I check the tone against my tonal scale. It may look too dark at this stage but watercolour dries lighter and I know the tone 5 oak tree I'll be adding later will push it back into the distance of the scene.

8 **◔ The background trees (tone 4)**

The tone 4 winter trees to the left of the farmhouse still had some warm autumn colours so are painted a cool green-grey with Burnt Sienna dropped in at the base. The trees behind yew tree and the big barn are painted with the same cool green-grey wash. While the washes are still damp I paint in the trunks and branches with a dark brown mix of Ultramarine Blue and Burnt Sienna, then scrape out some lighter tree trunks with my pen knife.

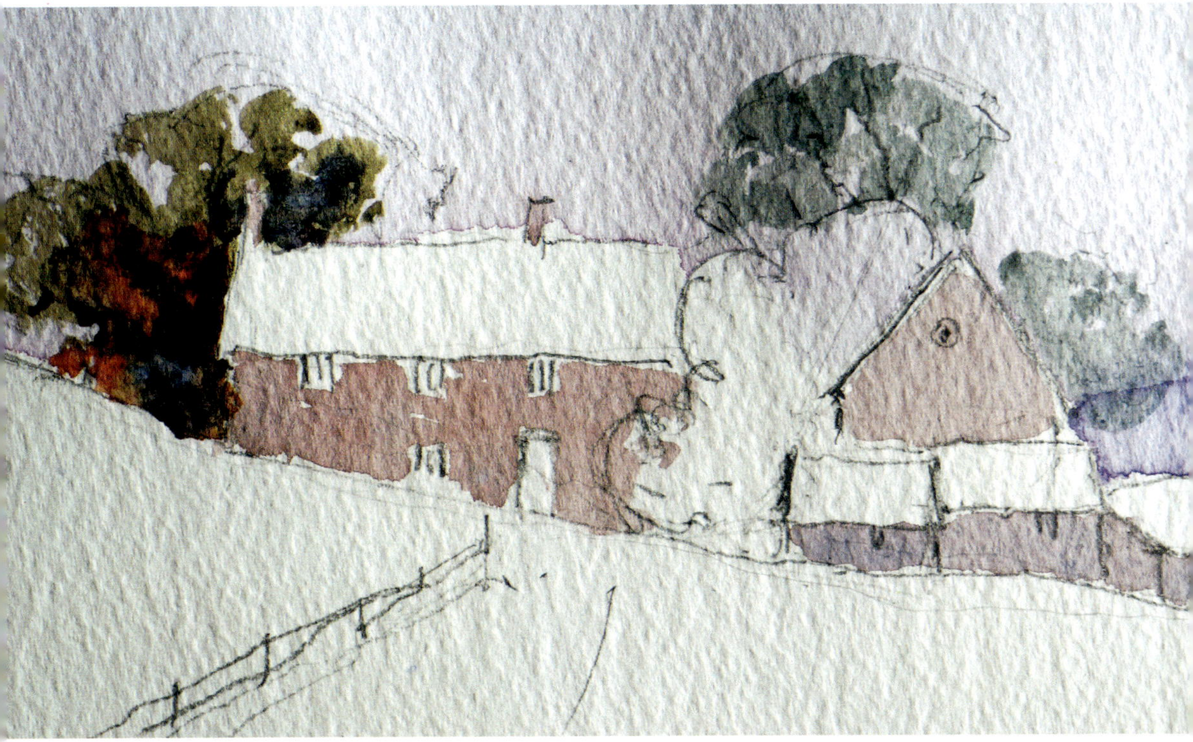

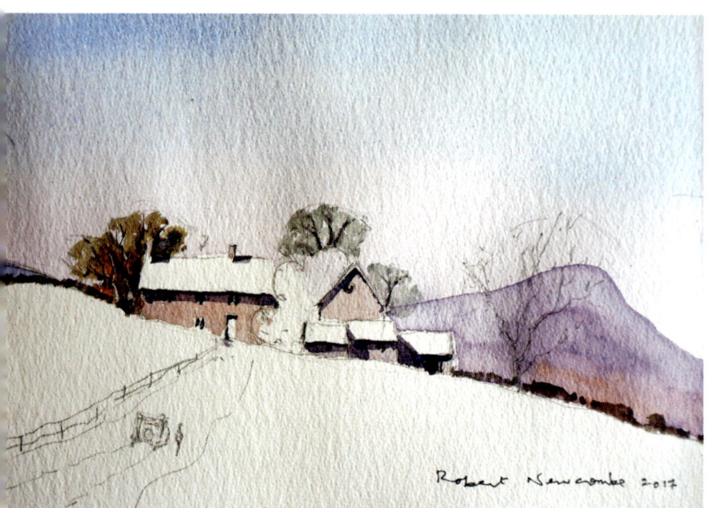

9 ◐ The shadow wash (tone 4)

Switching to my Escoda Perla 8 brush, I use a transparent mix of Ultramarine Blue and Brown Madder to paint the shadows on the buildings. The sun is coming from the front-left so there will be shadows under the eaves of the farmhouse and barns where the roofs overhang and the barns will cast some attractive raking shadows on other barns.

10 ◑ The yew tree and the oak tree (tone 5)

Next the darkest tones in the picture using tone 5 mixes. The dark-green yew tree is painted with Winsor Blue (green shade) and Burnt Sienna to create the impact of the darkest dark against the lightest light at the centre of interest. The oak tree in front of the mountain is a mix of Ultramarine Blue and Burnt Umber painted with my rigger brush. I then establish the outline of the tree with quick downward strokes of diluted Burnt Umber.

Importance of contrast

I had a major painting breakthrough when I realised the importance of tone values (contrast) in creating paintings with impact. I spent three months painting only monochrome paintings using different dark colours that enabled me to capture a full tonal range, e.g. Ultramarine Blue, Burnt Sienna, Light Red, Indigo etc (see steps 3 and 4), after which I was able to see colour in terms of tone. Try it.

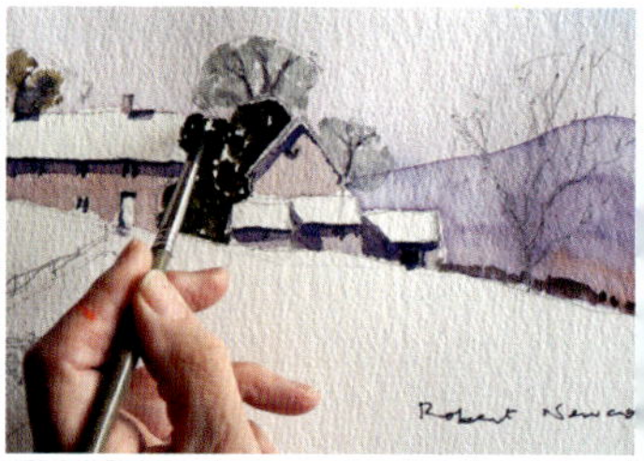

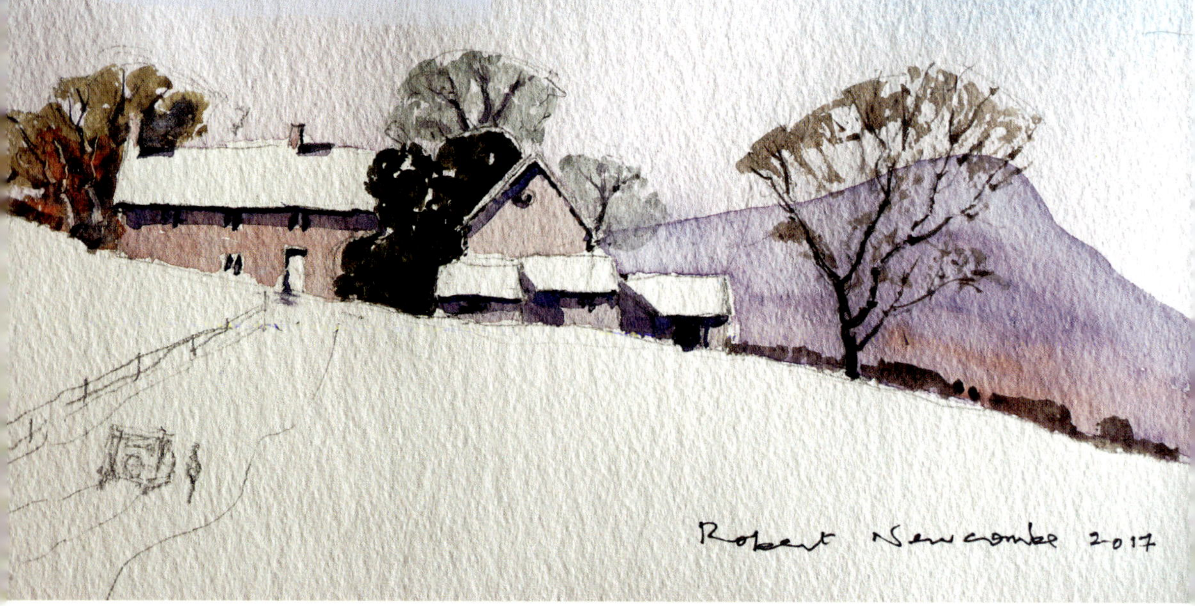

11 ▶ Make the final touches (tone 5)

I'm nearing the Completion stage of the painting where there is a danger of adding too much. Using the same mix as for the oak tree I paint the fence leading the eye to the centre of interest together with its attendant shadows, then the Land Rover and the figure talking to the driver. The last touch is to paint the front door of the farmhouse in bold Cadmium Red to attract the viewer's eye to the centre of interest.

12 ▼ The finished painting

At this point I refer back to my concept, Lake District farm under snow. Have I achieved my concept? I feel like turning up my coat collar so I think I have and the painting is finished.

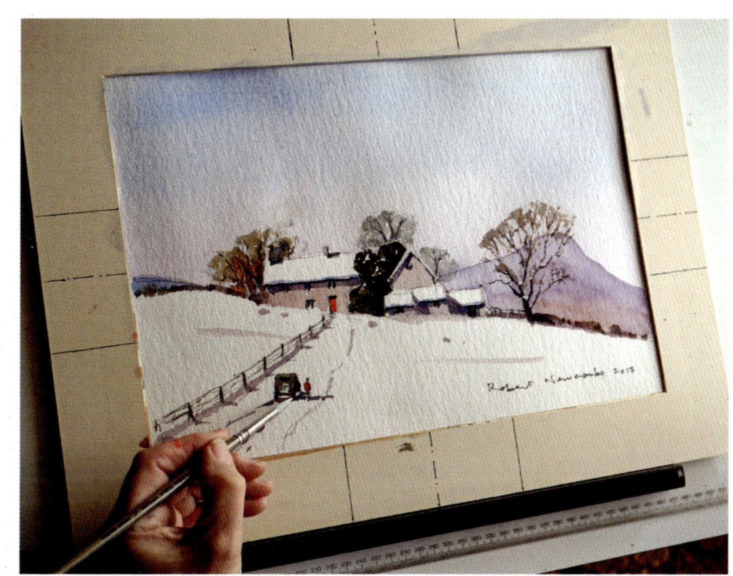

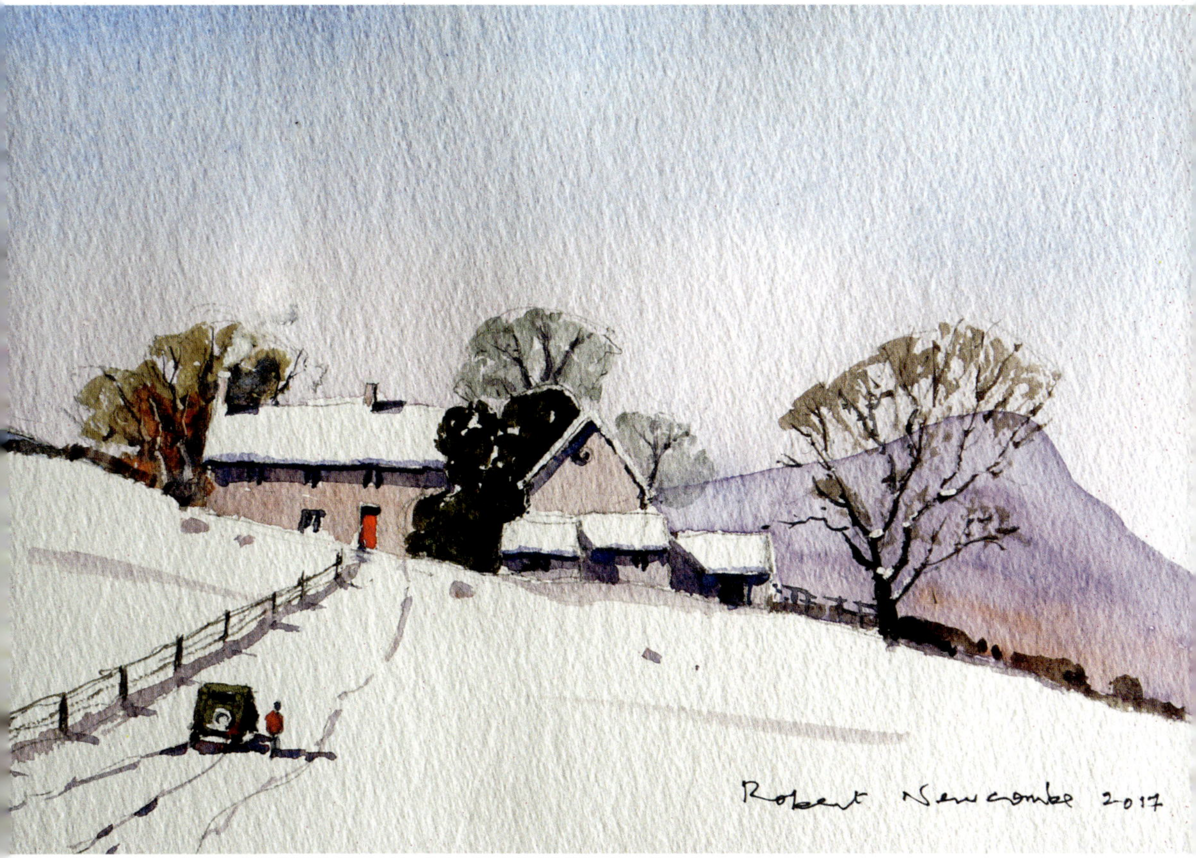

Pastels

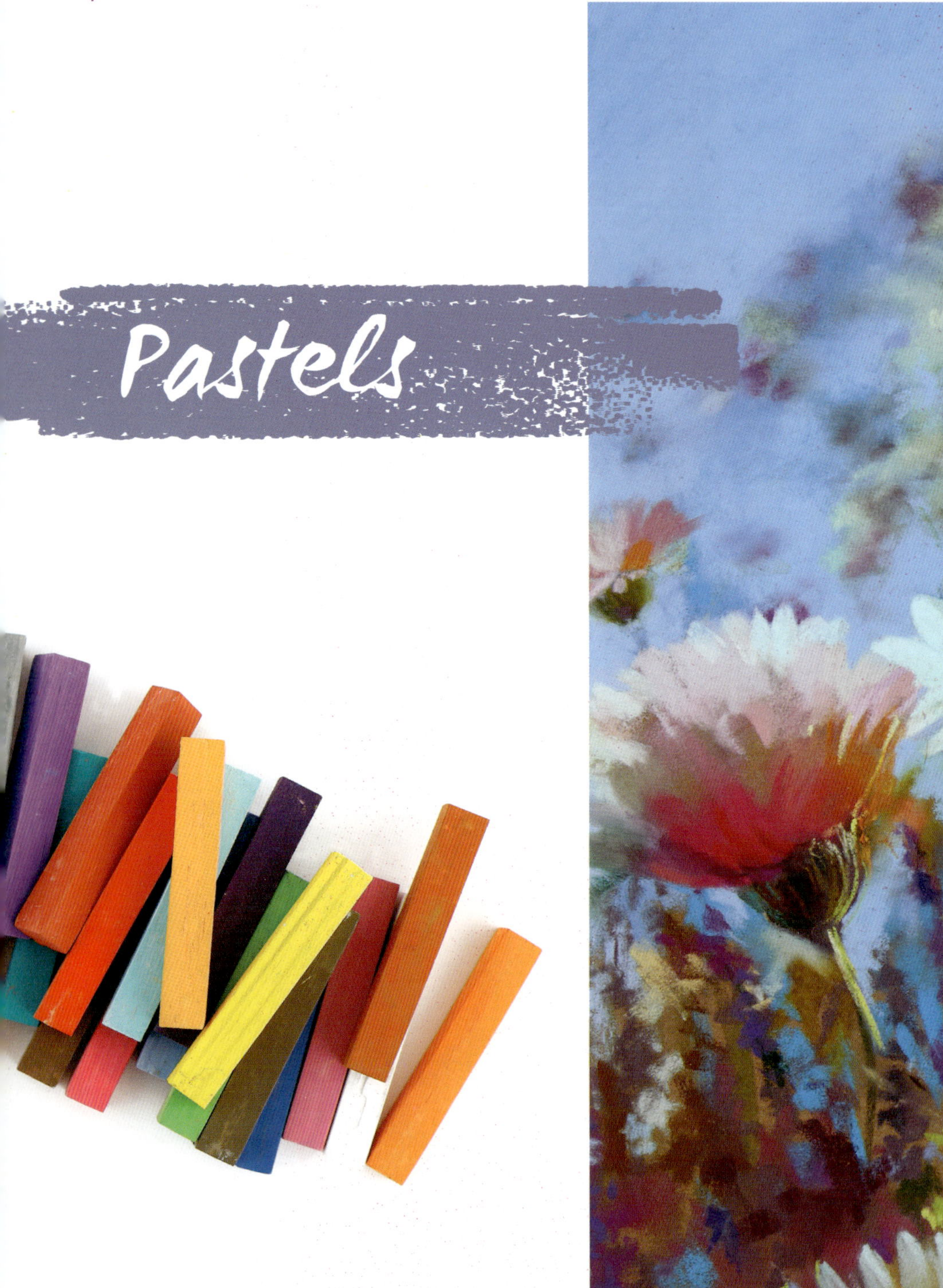

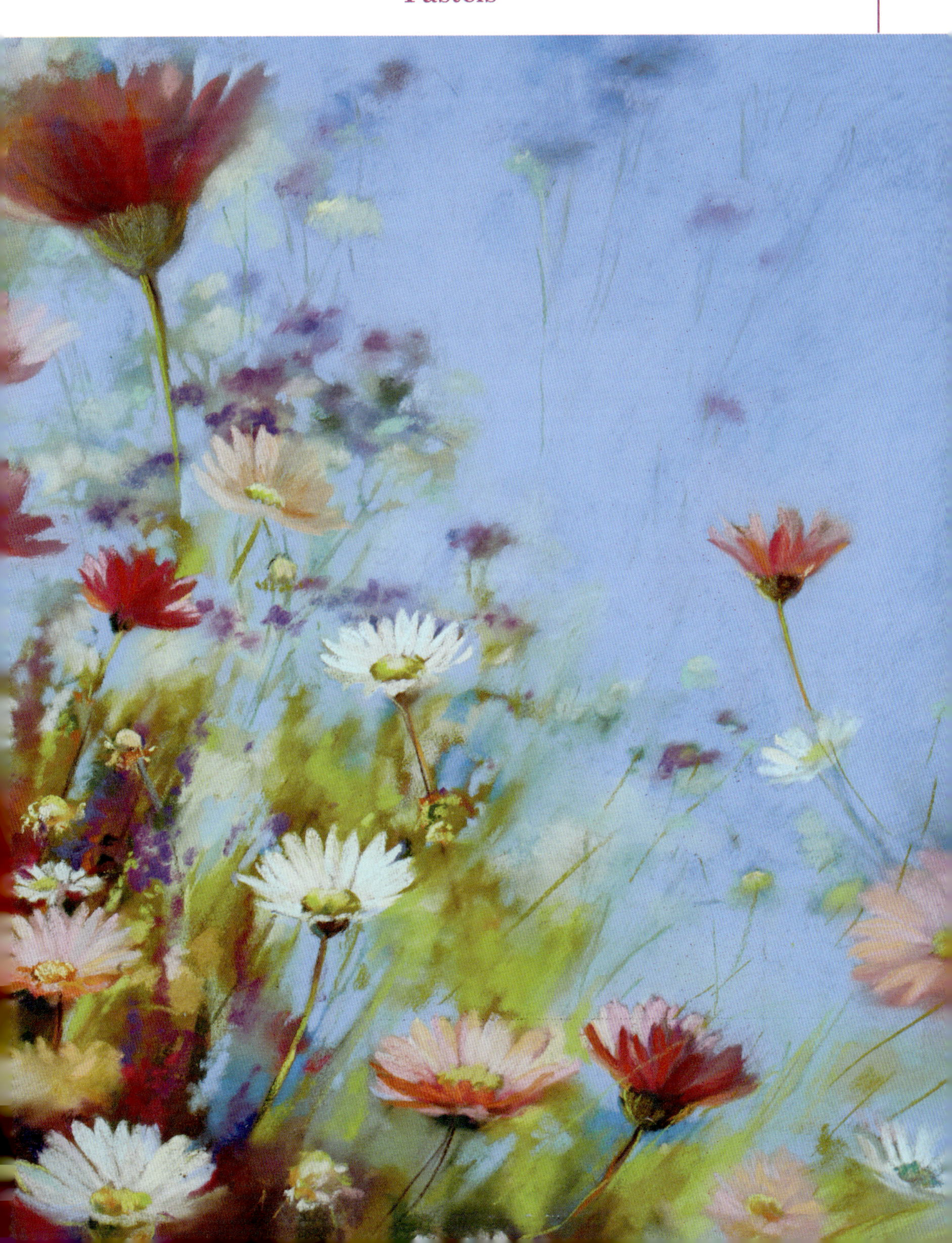

An introduction to pastels

Nel Whatmore has had a lifetime of loving pastels and encourages you to explore this wonderful medium

The advantages of working in pastels are manifold, but first and foremost, for me at least, is the beautiful range of colours that are available.

Secondly, it's a very tactile medium, which can be applied in so many different ways, and it has been further expanded by the development of pastel primers. Thirdly, there is a huge array of different surfaces to choose from, which can be overwhelming for beginners. Each has its own particular properties, and so there are endless opportunities to experiment and explore. It is a very forgiving and expressive medium, and you can be vibrant yet subtle. Pastels can come in five different forms – soft, hard, pastel, pan and oil. For this tutorial, we will be predominantly using soft pastels. Even by using just one or two types of pastel, you can create a very wide range of marks.

Over the next few pages, I will introduce you to the different forms that pastels can take and we will briefly discuss a few of the surfaces that are available. I'll cover a few techniques to get you started and some pit falls that people often fall into. Each surface has its pros and cons, but that is part of the journey to find out which surface suits you best as an artist.

Part 1: Which pastels do I choose?

1 Soft pastel beauty

Soft pastels have a very high concentration of pigment that is held together by the least amount of binder possible. This often means they can crumble very easily, but their colours are wonderfully intense. There are 'artist' quality pastels, such as Unison, Rembrandt and Sennelier, as well as 'student' quality ones made by manufacturers such as Inscribe, which, as with most art materials, are cheaper but not of the same quality. Soft pastels come in cylindrical sticks and a range of sizes. You can buy them individually, but it's often best to get a starter set with a good range of colours and, very importantly, a good tonal range so that you have a bright, mid and saturated tone within each colour.

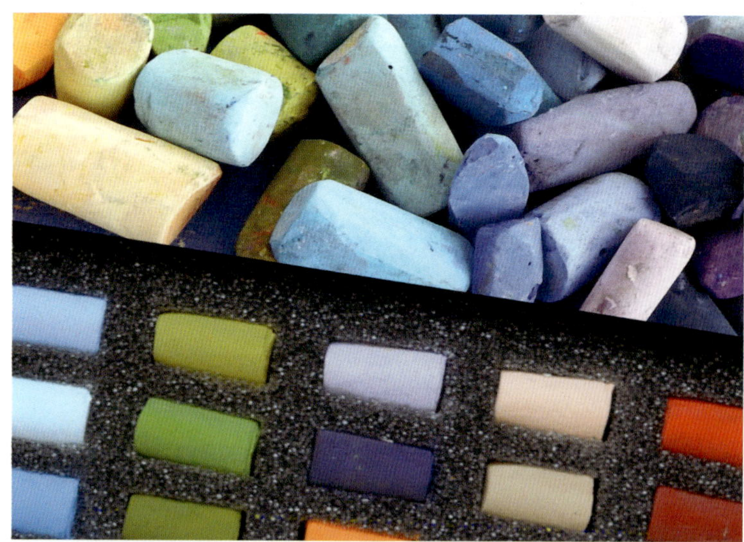

2 Why choose a hard pastel?

Hard pastels are made from the same ingredients as the soft ones, but they contain more binder and less pigment. This means that their colors are not as intense, but they don't crumble or break as easily. Hard pastels also come in artists' and students' quality. They are great for drawing out and for finer detail, as well as for fine blending and dragging one colour over another. They are easily rubbed out on certain papers.

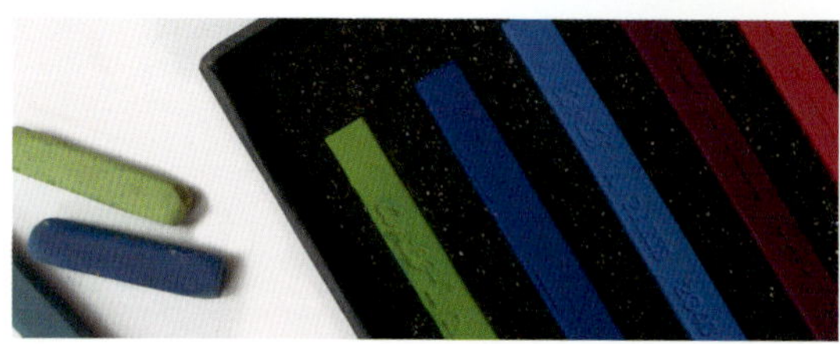

3 Pastel pencils for detail

If you like fine detail and prefer to not have dust on your hands, then pastel pencils may be the best way to go. In the 1990s, Faber Castell produced the Pitt Pastel Pencil range, which definitely features superior products. They have a much higher proportion of pigment, and they are also less susceptible to breaking when sharpened. Their use depends a little on the size you want to work and the quantity of detail you want to achieve; I don't use pastel pencils at all as I work in a more painterly way and don't particularly like holding a pencil, but I have used them on occasion for very fine detail.

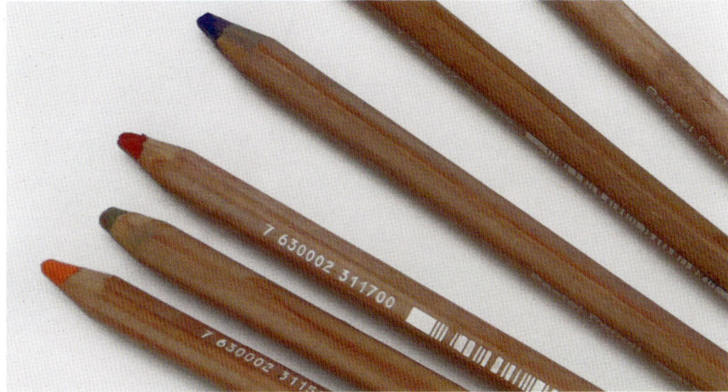

4 PanPastels, the relative newcomer

I have been using PanPastels for the past three years. What they do is create a mark that you can't make using other forms of pastel. There are 92 colours divided into 20 pure colours, 20 tones and 20 shades, plus 20 extra-darks and a few metallics and pearlescent colours. There are different applicators that you can get to apply the pastel, all of which make a different mark. I would recommend trying PanPastels as they are equivalent to buying three and half sticks of pastel – you can cover larger areas and create more movement, enabling you to almost paint.

Materials

- New Pastel School Starter Set – Unison Pastels
- Pan pastels, plus a variety of sponges to apply them
- Art Spectrum Colourfix Primer
- A range of brushes from a 2-inch flat brush to a watercolour round brush and smaller ones
- A small decorating roller with an interchangeable head. Just choose a basic foam roller to get started.

5 Oil pastels offer a different approach

Oil pastels are pigment again, but they are bound together, as the name suggests, with a non-drying oil and a wax binder. They are not generally used with soft pastels as one is a dry medium and the other oily. You can use a medium, like baby oil, to move the oil pastel around, and you can use soft pastels and oils pastels together, but only in areas that are in isolation from each other. I'll be concentrating on soft pastels over the following pages.

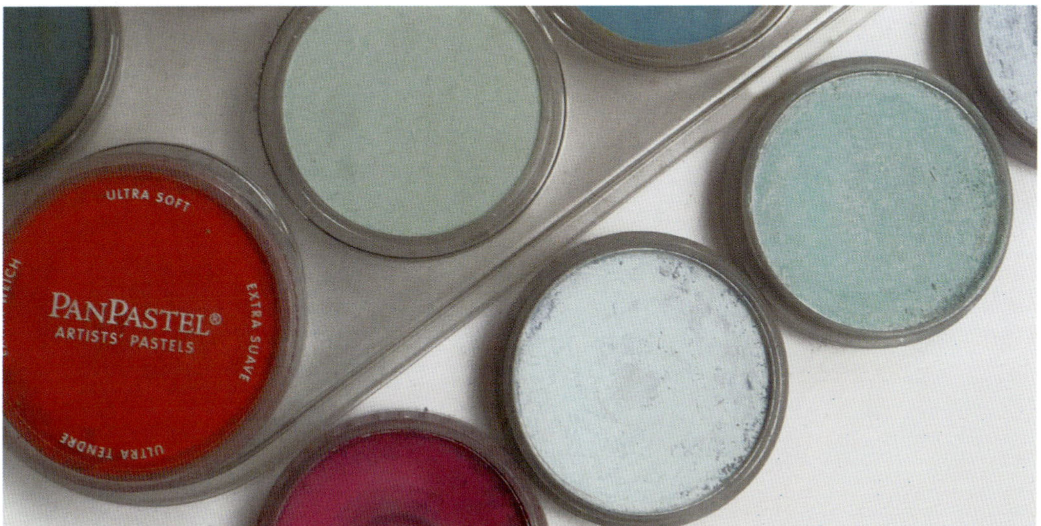

Part 2: Tools you can use for pastels

1 Blenders and rubbers

Blending colours creates certain effects and it's just one technique in our tool kit. Smudging colours together creates a smoother texture but also reduces the vibrancy of our work. Sometimes that is actually exactly what is needed, like when conveying distance in a landscape. There are many blending tools out there, the simplest and cheapest of which is your finger. However, foam blenders do have their place, like when you're working on sandpaper, which saves getting sore fingers, and also when more detailed smudging is required. I would just say be sure you know why you are blending, and don't do it everywhere! One of the best ways to rub out pastel pencils is with the Faber Castell double-ended eraser as it has a soft rubber at one end and a harder one at the other. The latter removes just a top layer of pastel, while the other gets rid of all layers. For soft pastels, a good regular rubber is fine, just not a putty one.

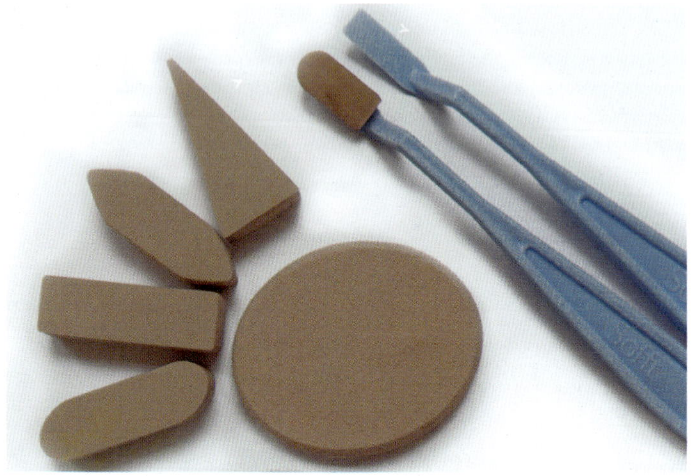

2 The importance of working vertically

The reason people find that their work can get a bit muddy is often because they are working horizontally. I know this may seem like a rather obvious thing to say, but if at all possible, work vertically using an easel or, if standing is a problem, then a table easel. Not only is it better that any excess dust falls to the floor (as long as it's covered, of course) but also – perhaps more importantly – it gives you the chance to stand back and look at your work rather than being on top of it all the time. This is invaluable.

Go BIG!

When starting to learn a new medium, the tendency is often to want to work on a smaller scale. With pastels I'd encourage you to try to work bigger as it's a medium that is easier to use on a larger scale. If you do go smaller, consider using more pastel pencils.

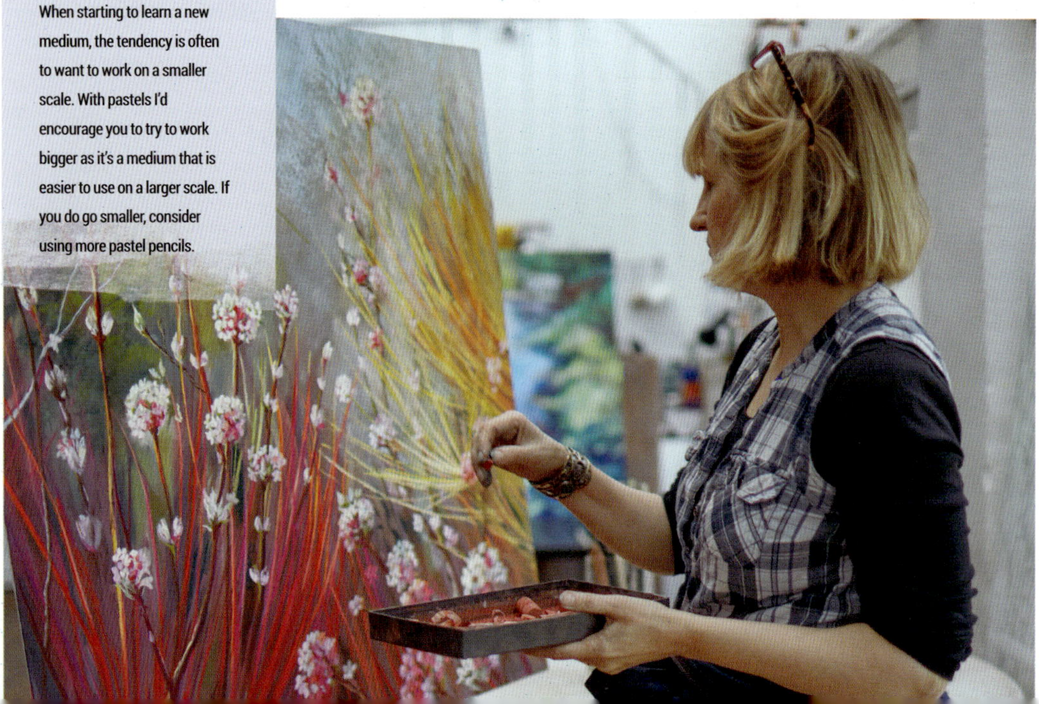

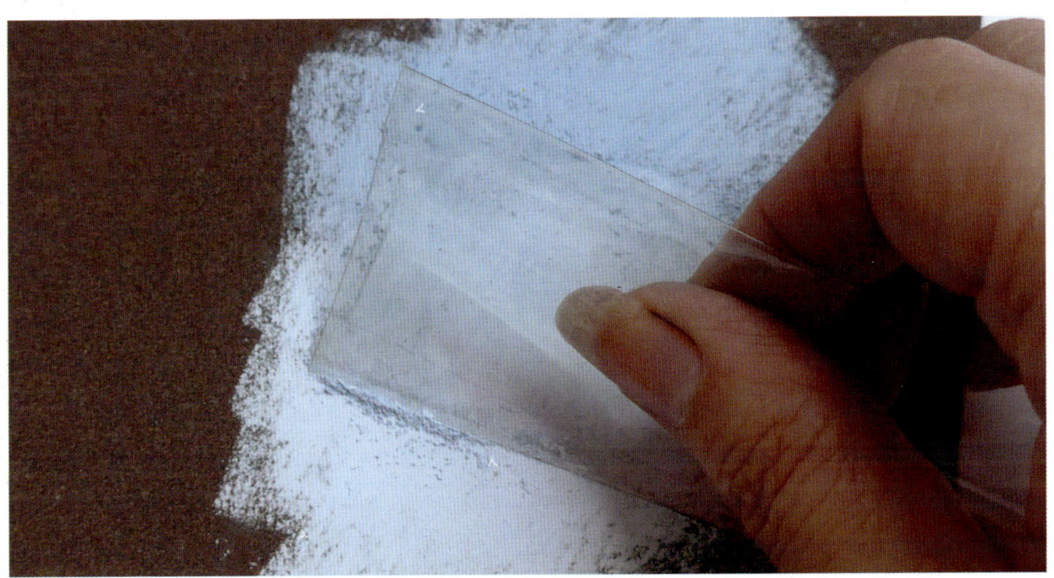

3 Refresh your surface

Most pastel papers have a tooth to them, which enables the pastel to sit in the small dips in the surface. When a lot of pastel is added, the texture of the surface becomes full of pastel and it is hard to apply anymore. One useful way of unclogging the surface and refreshing it without hugely altering your painting is by using the edge of a piece of clear acrylic to scrape across the surface. It will lift the excess pastel off and allow you to regain some of the tooth, to then reapply more pastel.

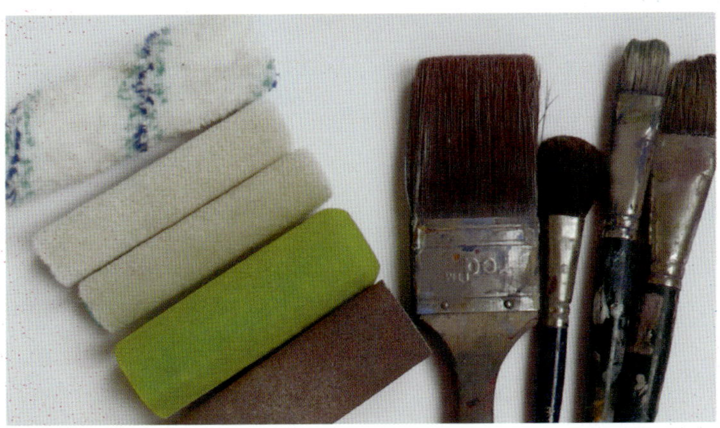

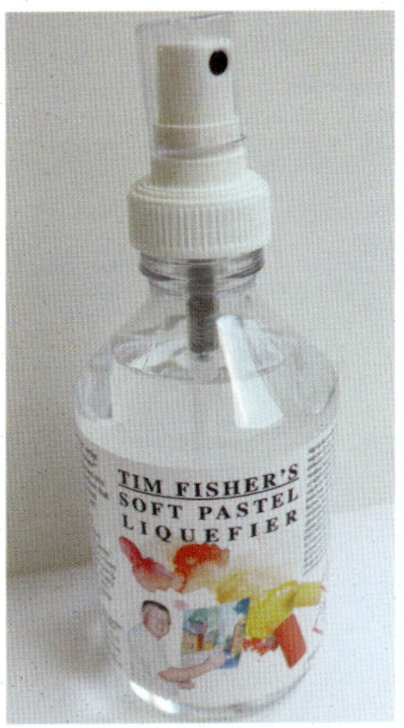

4 Brushes and rollers

It is useful to have a range of brushes and a small roller to use with pastels as it is possible to add water to it, which in effect converts the pastel into paint. It does then dry much darker, but it can create added interest to your work. Brushes and rollers are also essential for underpainting a surface first, before you even start using pastels, which I will talk about more later on. A good two-inch brush with fine bristles is ideal, as is a big round brush to create softer marks. I also use smaller ones to repair mistakes on sandpapers, but I will cover this in the next section.

5 Water and mediums

As I have already mentioned, you can add water to pastels, but you can also find various mediums that you can add to again make your pastels more fluid, like paint. One such medium is Tim Fisher's Soft Pastel Liquefier, although some people use a spirit to do the same job. There are so many things you can do with pastels – as you can see, it is not just a static medium.

Part 3: Surfaces and the advantages of each

1 Papers

There are many brands of pastel paper to choose from. If you are a beginner, I would recommend getting an A3 pad of mixed coloured pastel paper, and then buy individual single small sheets of the other brands to try them out to see if you prefer them. A good tip is to draw a simple object, like a piece of fruit, on a range of different papers so that you can make a direct comparison between them. There are several quality manufacturers, all producing papers with slightly different textures, such as Winsor & Newton, Mi-Teintes, Murano and Tiziano. It is worth noting that many pastel papers have a rough and a smooth side, so be aware of that because some subjects look better on one side than another. You'll usually find the label on the rough side of the paper.

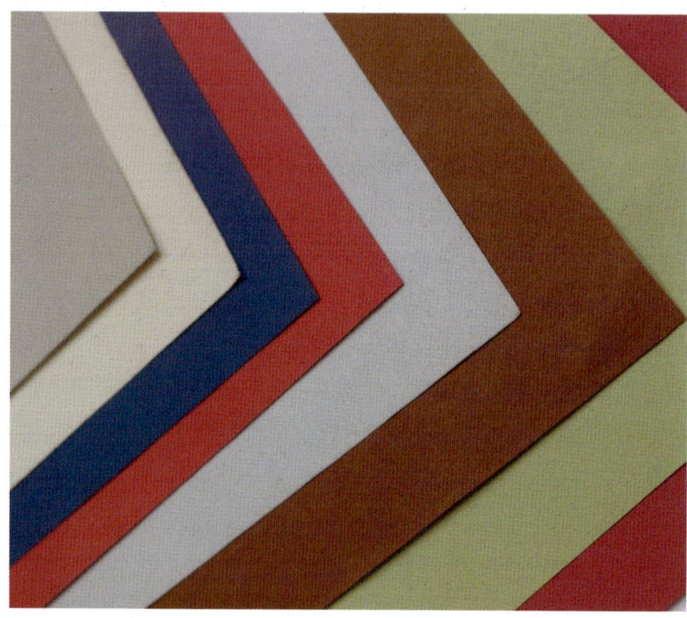

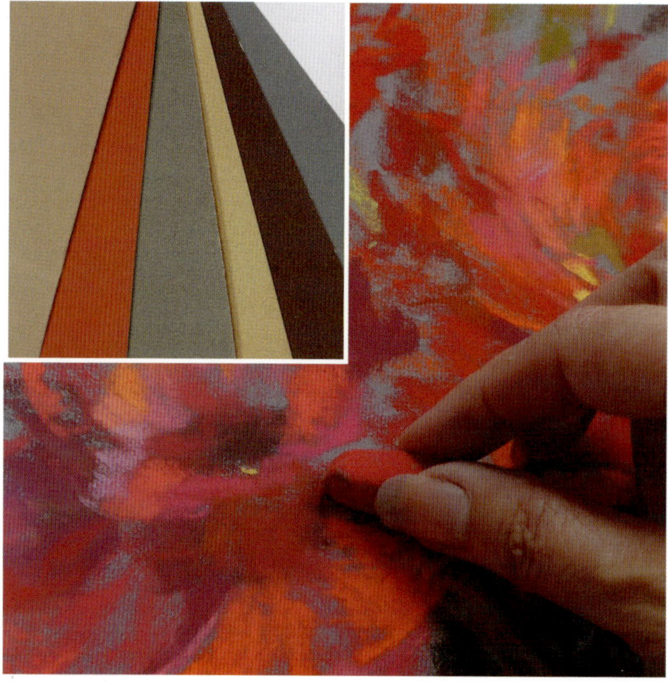

2 Sandpapers and rougher surfaces

If you are a beginner, start by working on the papers listed in the above tip, then move onto sandpapers and primers as you become more confident, because paper is more forgiving and you can rub out on it. I am a great lover of sandpapers as they do give a much greater vibrancy than pastel papers, which is very suited to painting flowers, but once you make a mark, it is hard to erase it. Sandpapers can be bought in sheets or pads, and each have their own properties. Sennelier Pastel Card is a wonderful surface, but its limitation is that it doesn't take water as it brings the surface off, and the largest sheets are 60x80cm. If you are wanting to apply water to your pastels and use a sandpaper, go for Fisher 400 Art Paper. Velour paper is as its name suggests, and you can't add water to it or rub anything out. There are many other varieties of sandpaper, the main difference between them being that some have more tooth and some don't take water.

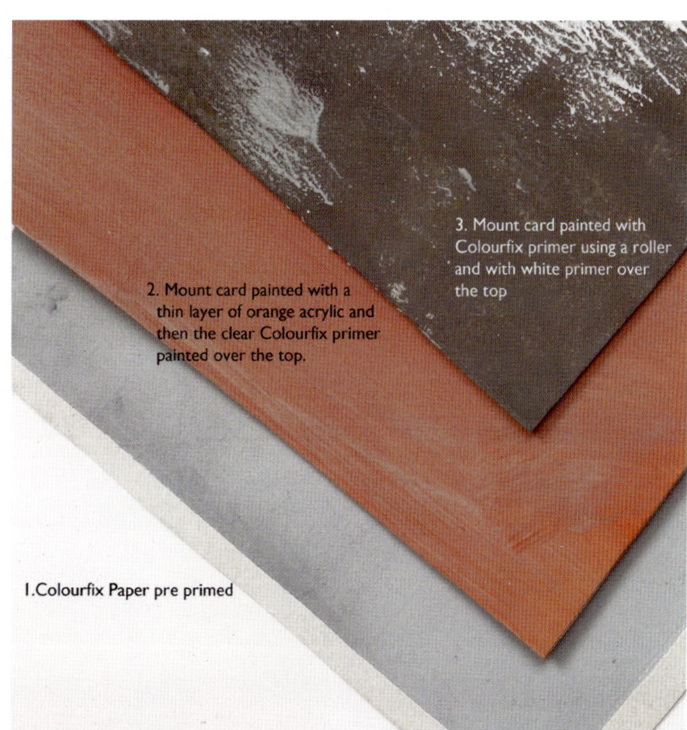

3 Colourfix paper and primers

If you want your work to have a more painterly feel, then doing an underpainting first with Art Spectrum Colourfix primer, over which you can pastel, will open up a whole new area to explore. The primers are an acrylic medium with a fine tooth that can be painted over any firm, dry surface, such as mount card or hardboard, to give it a tooth suitable for pastels. There are around 17 different colours, as well as white, black and clear. They can be applied with a brush or roller, straight from the pot, for a more textured finish, or watered down for a smoother, more transparent layer. With the clear version you can actually do an acrylic painting, paint the clear primer over the top and then pastel over it all. If you would like a greater variety of colours, acrylic paint can be added and mixed with it.

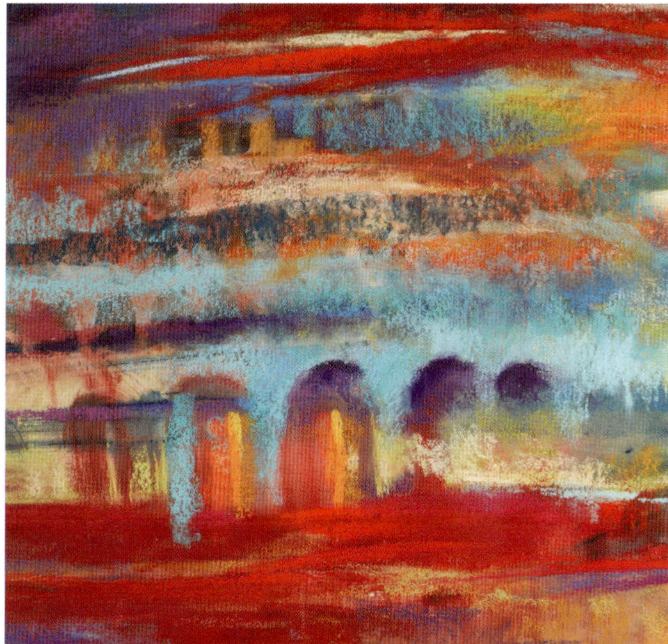

4 Can you use watercolour paper?

I have seen many beautiful pastels done on watercolour paper, particularly by Sally Strand, a truly wonderful pastel artist. So the answer is, if you already have a supply of watercolour paper, then you may as well give it a go. My only caveat is that pastels generally work better on a tinted coloured paper than on white. If you want to do a watercolour or Colourfix primer wash first, then add pastel and you may find that this works better.

If you're not sure what colour to paint the paper, then as with choosing which colour paper to use, go for a mid tone that you can see in the subject you are wanting to paint. A general rule of thumb is that the darker the paper you use, the more drama your painting will have.

Part 4: Exploring mark-making with your pastels

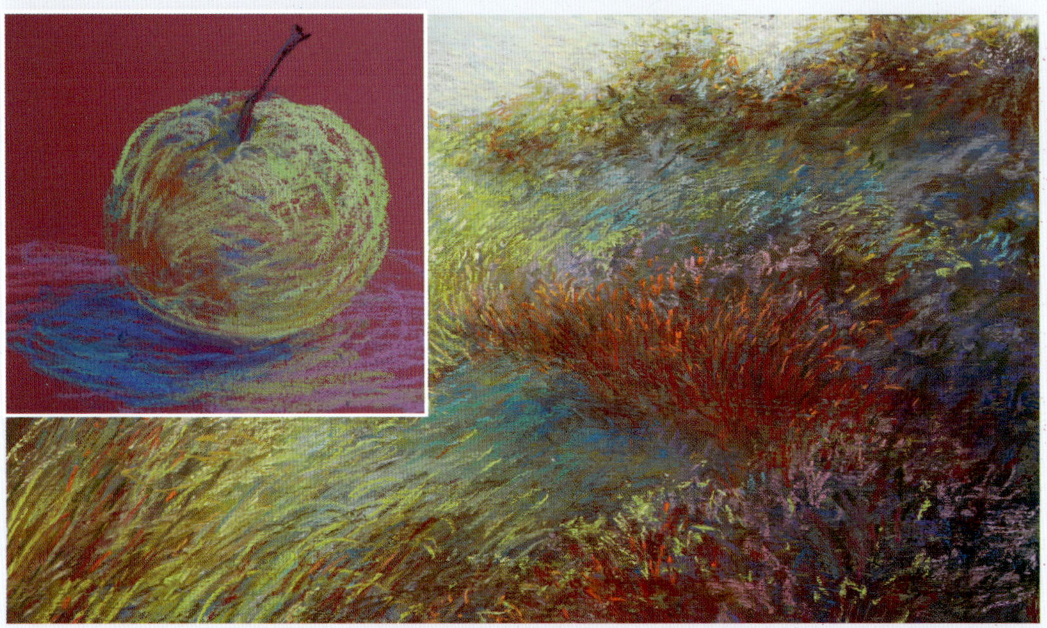

1 Hatching – don't be afraid of colour

Hatching is a technique whereby you simply use lots of lines to follow the form of an object. You can use lots of different colours and in different directions, as it's the layering of all those lines that creates energy and visual interest. You don't need to blend the colours as, rather like pointillist paintings, when seen at a distance, the viewer's eyes do the blending for you. What hatching is really useful for is leading your eye around a painting or an object. This landscape painting has many layers of different coloured marks laid over each other, creating movement.

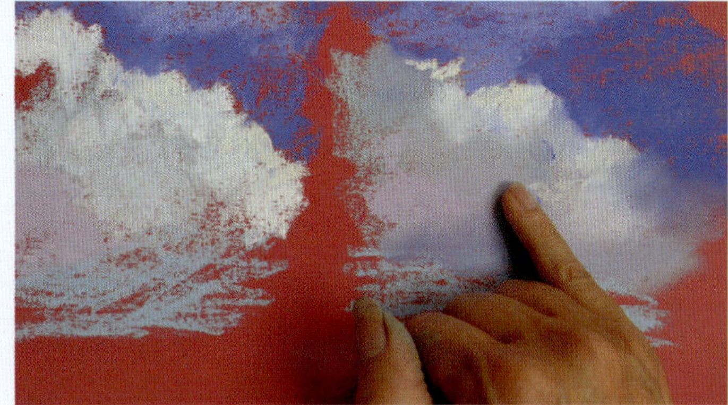

2 Smudging and blending

To blend or not to blend – that is the question! People seem to get rather worried about blending in my experience, which is really not necessary. Just view it as another technique that has a specific effect. If you are painting clouds, for example, it's a natural thing to blend the colours together as the texture of a cloud is very smooth. Alternatively, if you were painting a very shiny object, then laying down a base layer that is blended together makes perfect sense. Various tools, as I have mentioned, are available to help you blend in many different ways, and they may be more helpful if you are doing very detailed work or working on a small scale or very rough surface. I keep it simple and just have a few smaller blenders, using the palm for larger areas and fingers for smaller ones.

3 Using the pastel on its side

Always take the labels off your pastels as otherwise you end up holding them like a pencil and not being able to enjoy the full joy of the marks you can make with them. Unison produces fabulous giant pastel sticks if you want to work larger and cover wider areas quickly.

So much of using pastels is about pressure and being aware of the full range of marks your can make. One useful tip is to get six objects, all of which have very different textures, and consciously use a different technique on each. You could also choose one object and paint it several times, as I did with this satsuma, to really start to understand what pastels can do.

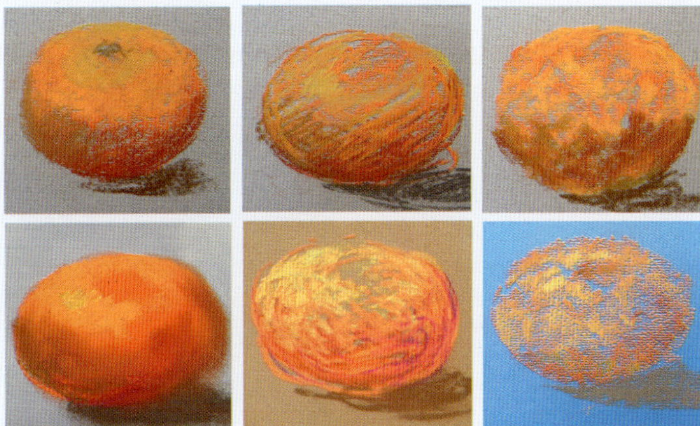

4 How to make fine lines

Being able to make fine lines is a matter of having a sharp edge to your pastel, but also of how much pressure you use. The latter is easily forgotten and many of us apply the same pressure all the time. Really try to alter how much pressure you use. A sharp edge can be achieved by breaking your pastel in two or by using smaller bits – even pieces that fall on the floor!

Alternatively for fine blending or fine animal or human hair, a harder pastel such as a Conté crayon or a pastel pencil is very useful. These are also great for sketching out a subject, so long as you choose a colour close to the paper colour so that you can then cover it up easily.

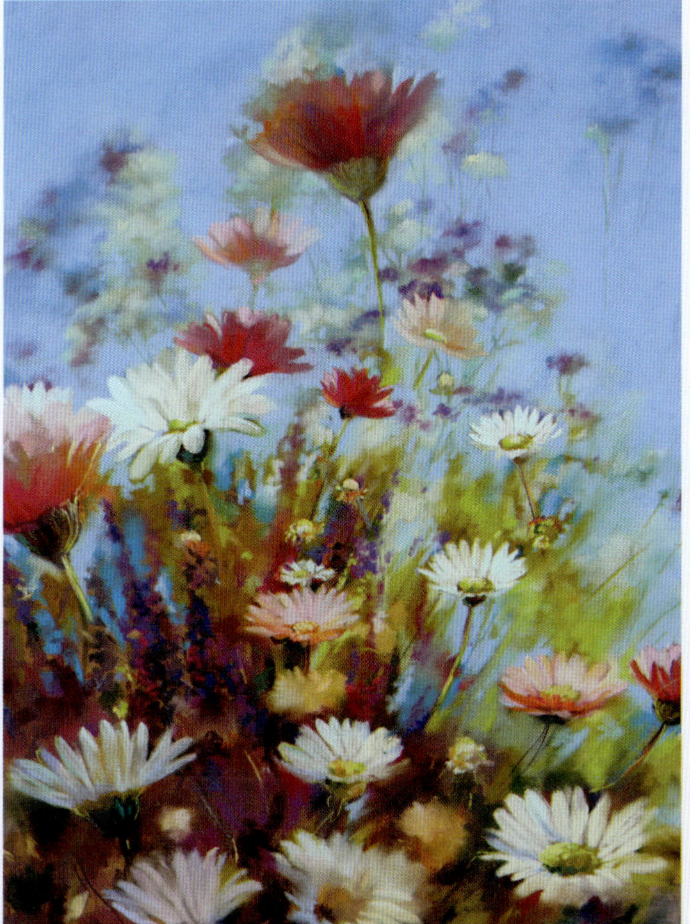

Remember tonal range

If your work is looking flat and lifeless, look at your tonal range. Usually it is because your painting doesn't have a wide enough range – for instance, all your tones are in the mid range rather than having dark darks and light lights.

Part 5: Finishing touches

1 Should you fix a pastel?

Some artists like to fix their pastels as it makes it easier for framers to handle them. In the past, fixatives always used to dull the colours of a painting and you would sometimes get unwanted darker colours coming through. Sennelier Latour fixative is a clear resin and alcohol-based fixative, and it creates a totally clear matt film.

Fixatives are actually useful for another purpose. If the surface of your painting is rather clogged, you can fix a layer and then it will allow you to continue to add more layers as it gives the surface a bit of tooth back, rather like using a refresher.

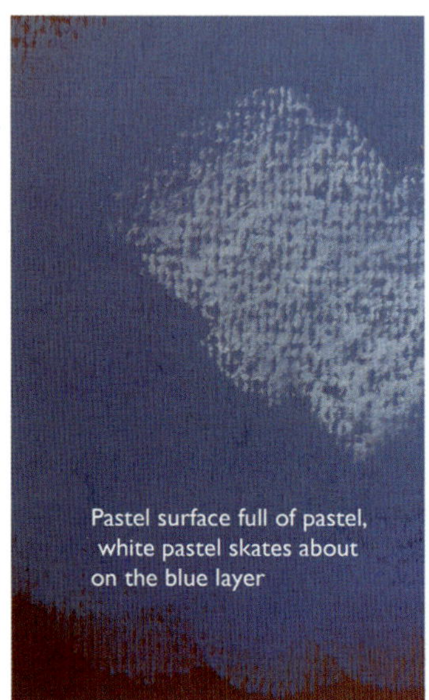

Pastel surface full of pastel, white pastel skates about on the blue layer

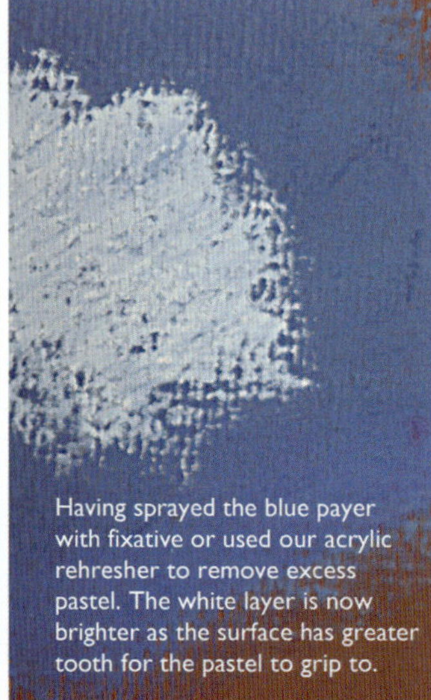

Having sprayed the blue payer with fixative or used our acrylic rehresher to remove excess pastel. The white layer is now brighter as the surface has greater tooth for the pastel to grip to.

Start to understand colour

If you want to start to understand colour, choose a very simple object or just a tree and paint it at different times of day or under different lighting conditions. Paint it about six times in bright light, on a dull day, on bright and dark surfaces. Really look carefully at how the colours alter and the contrast or range of tones changes. But, most of all, enjoy experimenting with pastels – I'm sure you'll get hooked!

2 Store your pastel works

There are several ways of storing pastel art, but I prefer to just use a piece of paper slightly larger than my piece and place it over it before folding it around the back and taping it with a small piece of paper top and bottom. That way the piece of paper stays in one place and doesn't disturb the surface. Some people use Glassine paper, but it is a lot more expensive. Alternatively you can buy a hard printing roller put a piece of glassine or tissue paper over the top and press the pastel down into the surface to reduce the amount of excess pastel that may drop from your painting when framed.

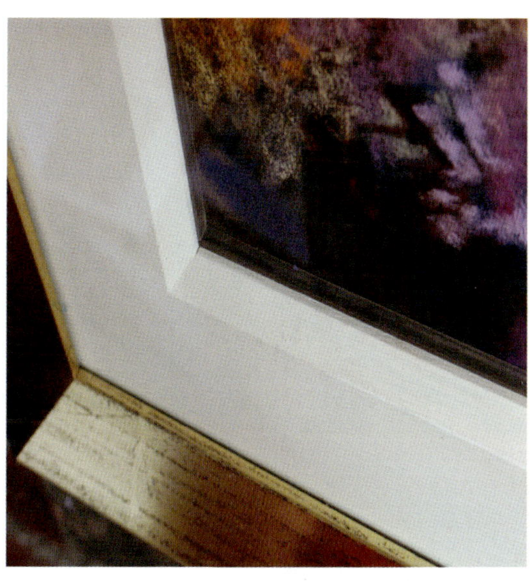

3 Frame pastels

All framers have their own methods when it comes to pastels. What they all have in common, however, is that all pastels need to be under glass to protect the surface. Don't let a framer 'fix' your painting without asking you first, as some fixatives can alter colours. In my own work I do not find the need to use fixative, but prefer to use a clear spacer between any mount or surround and the painting, leaving a three or four millimetre gap. This prevents the glass from touching the surface of the painting and any excess pastel can then fall in this thin gap, unseen behind the mount.

4 Paint in plein air

It is a great idea to make yourself up a little kit for painting outside. You don't need hundreds of pastels, just a nice selection, and some small sheets of paper on a board about the size of a placemat attached by bulldog clips. Don't worry if you find you haven't got the exact colour you need when you get outside, as that is the beauty of pastels – being forced to use what you've got, and to hatch over colours, will produce more interesting paintings.

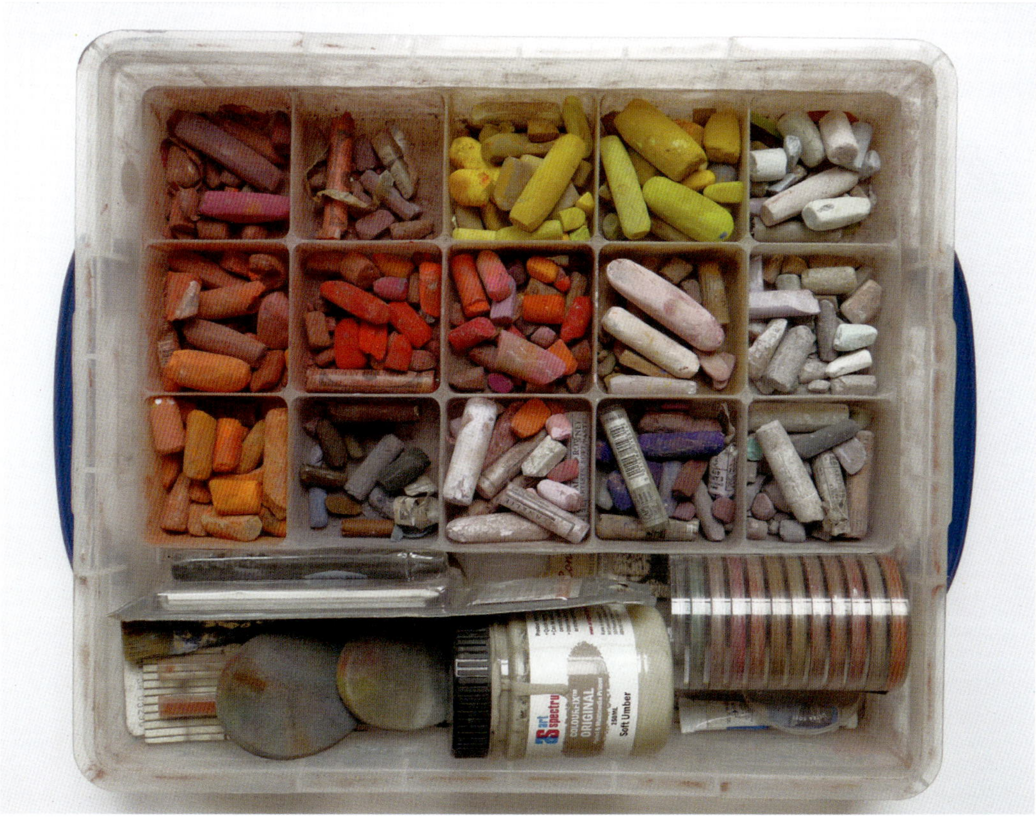

Draw a fox using pastels

Rebecca de Mendonça shows how she creates a cunning fox with a combination of soft pastels, Conté crayons and pastel pencils

In this tutorial I am going to show you how I draw a cunning and alert fox with soft pastels, charcoal, Conté crayons and pastel pencils. I want to share with you how I work on the whole piece, building up darks and lights to create the form, and then continue to refine this initial drawing and gradually work into areas of detail.

At each stage I stand back (or sit at the other side of the room with a cup of coffee) and assess how the piece is going, so I can constantly tweak it as I go along. I like to think that this results in a unified and balanced piece of work. We can create many different textures by varying our materials, from very soft Unison pastels, to hard Conté crayons and pastel pencils.

For my reference I am using a copyright-free photograph by Jiri Sifalda from the Unsplash website. I was inspired by the rich colours, and the way it captures a moment when the fox looks alert, and I want to get that feeling into my painting. I also love the variety of textures in the fur, and the cunning gleam in the eye. I decided to focus on the head so I could really enjoy the textural qualities of the fur.

I am working on mount card that I have primed with Art Spectrum Colourfix primers, but you could easily do this project on pastel paper if you don't have primers. It is a good idea before starting to have a play with your materials, trying out marks and textures for yourself on a spare piece of paper, and varying the pressure that you apply. Try flicking, smudging and using the side or end of the pastel in turn.

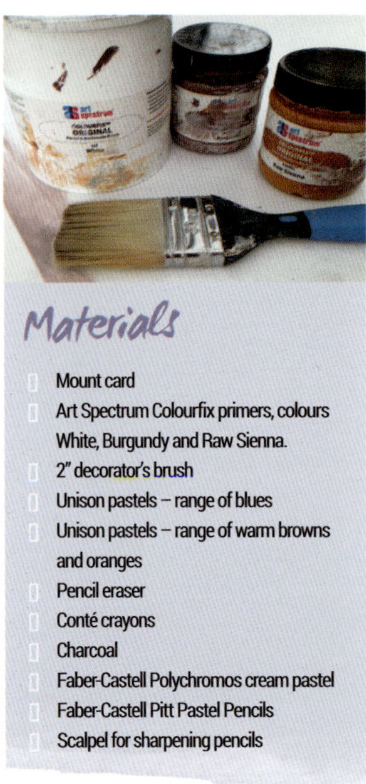

Materials

- Mount card
- Art Spectrum Colourfix primers, colours White, Burgundy and Raw Sienna.
- 2" decorator's brush
- Unison pastels – range of blues
- Unison pastels – range of warm browns and oranges
- Pencil eraser
- Conté crayons
- Charcoal
- Faber-Castell Polychromos cream pastel
- Faber-Castell Pitt Pastel Pencils
- Scalpel for sharpening pencils

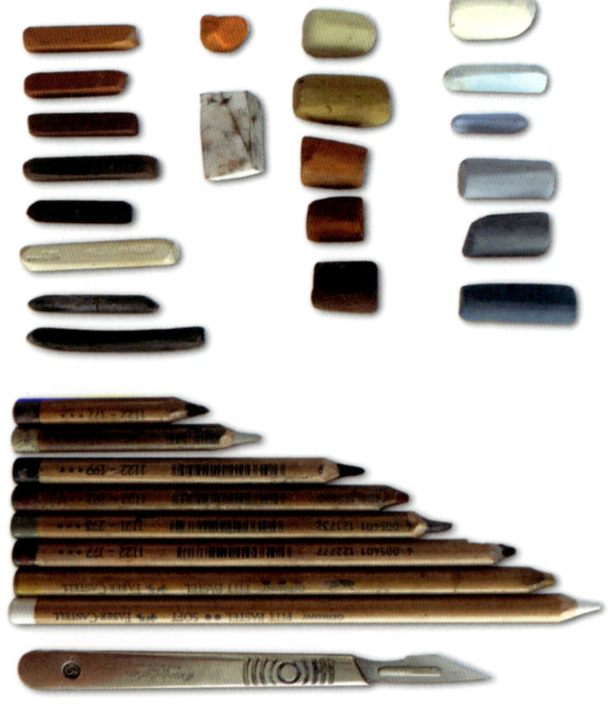

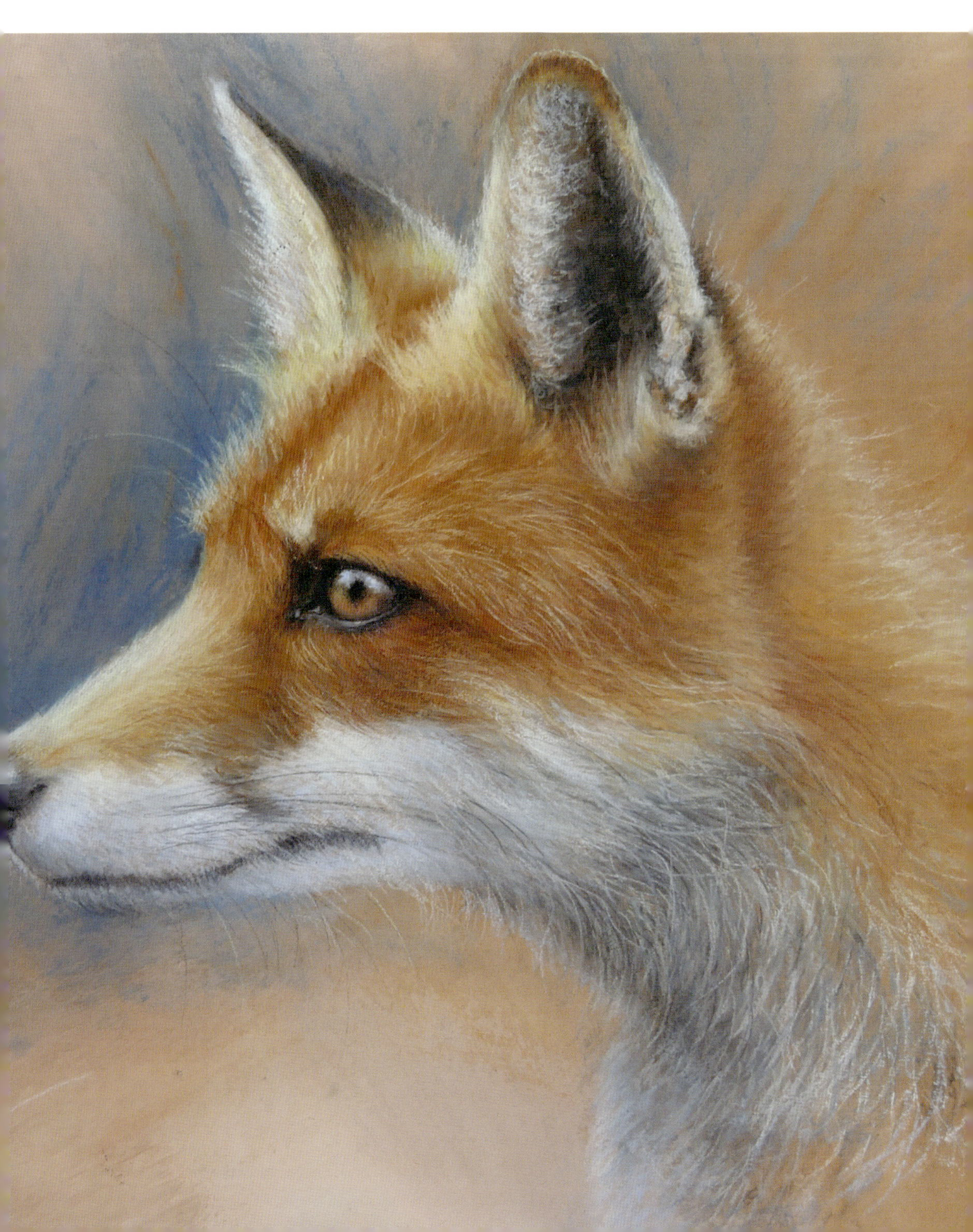

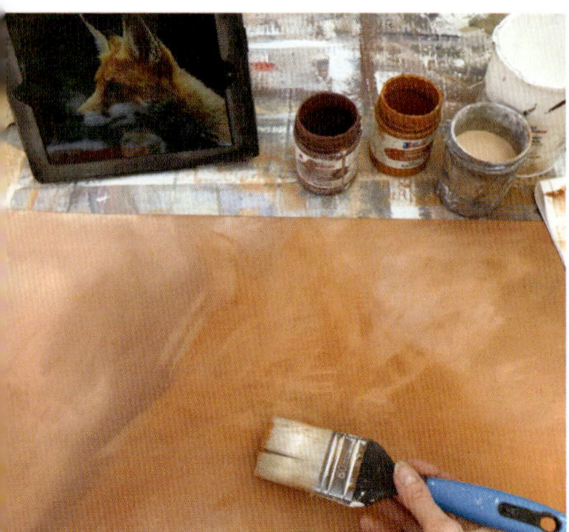

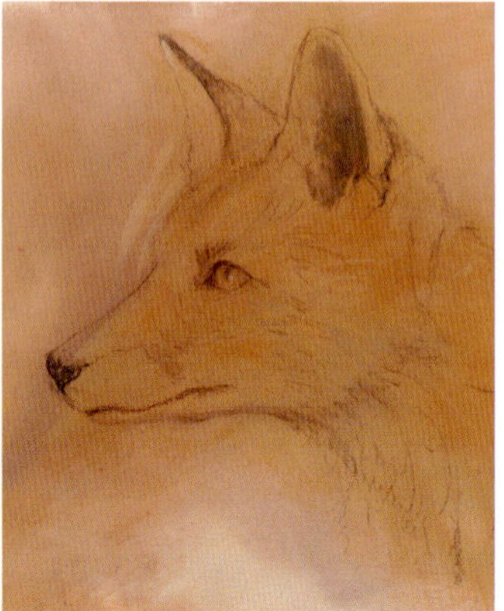

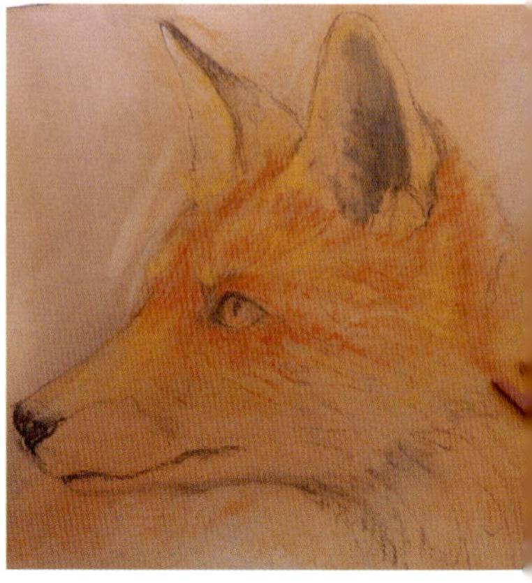

1 ◔ Priming the surface

I like to work on Art Spectrum Colourfix Primer, which I paint onto mount card with a 2" decorator's brush. This gives me a surface with two or three colours combining to create a lively surface, but again, you could easily create this artwork on pastel paper or other pastel surfaces. Here I've used White, Burgundy and Raw Sienna, and made the brush strokes follow the direction of the fox's coat. These warm browns combine to make a really 'foxy' colour, but if you're using paper, I'd choose a warm brown.

2 ◔ Charcoal sketch

I loosely sketch the fox in with charcoal. The charcoal is a soft grey, which is similar to the colour of animal's skin, so is ideal as an initial sketch. I always try to understand what it is about an image that conveys the character of the animal, and what the story is that I am telling in this picture. Here it was the intensity of that eye that really mattered, so as I draw I think about how I am going to show that. I am also looking for dark areas, as they describe the form.

3 ◔ Conté crayons for under drawing

I really love using Conté crayons for my first layer of drawing animals, as they contain less pigment than soft pastels. Because of this, they can be easily erased and smudged out if I haven't put them in quite the right place. It's a bit like a first colour sketch. These two colours, similar to Burnt Sienna and Raw Sienna, are a great base for the fox's fur. The underpainting will show through and blend with the pastel colours I lay over it.

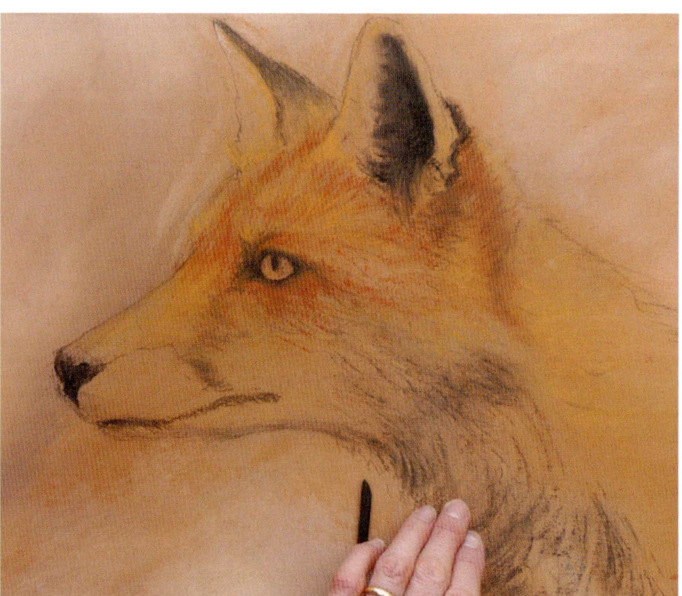

"I love the sharp edges I get with a broken black Conté crayon – they are great for details"

4 ◔ More darks, including the eye

Now I have the rich sienna colours put in, I can work into those darks a bit more, using charcoal and a black Conté crayon for emphasis. This is slightly harder than the other Conté crayons, and makes quite a permanent mark, which is why I used the more forgiving charcoal to start with. I love the sharp edges I get with a broken black Conté crayon – they are great for details such as eyes and noses.

5 ● Colour in the eye

I build the colour of the eye with a mixture of Unison pastels, in warm browns and a natural earth colour. I still use the Raw Sienna Conté crayon for its lovely golden glow. I add the colours with the end of the pastels and rub them slightly with my little finger to blend. I can then put the dark of the pupil in again in black. You have to be patient here as the layers of colour give depth, and you can use the lights and darks to create the shadows of the spherical eyeball.

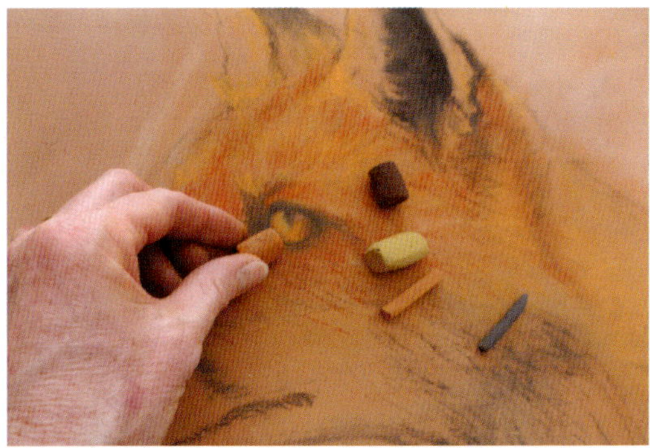

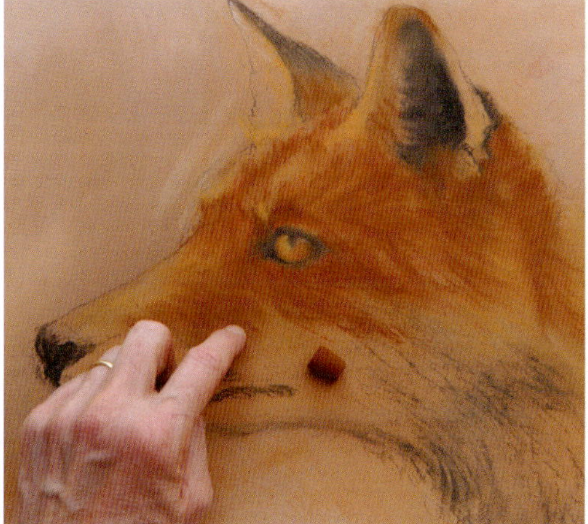

6 ● A richer red/brown on the coat

Now it's time to enrich the warm colours of the coat with Unison soft pastels. Their pure pigment creates enormous depth of colour. Having made the eye more intense in the previous stage, I need to do the same with the coat to achieve balance. I'm working on this area first as it is the focal point of the picture, and needs to be dramatic. I can work more loosely as I move away from it.

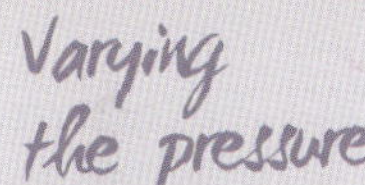

Varying the pressure

If you apply different pressure for different textures, you will get a more varied and interesting piece of work. Try strong sweeping marks, light flicks, hatching or smudging to bring in depth to your piece.

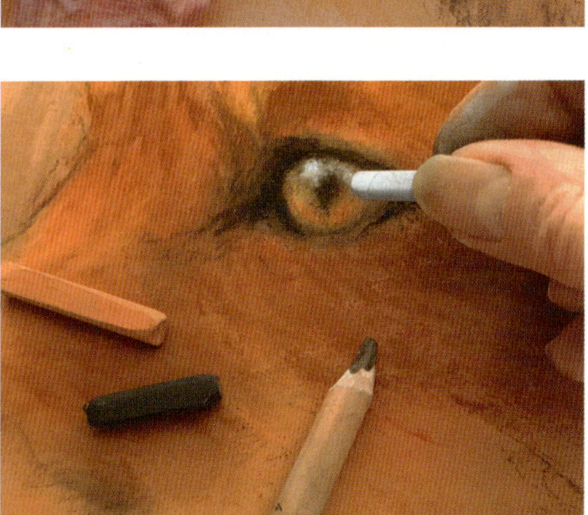

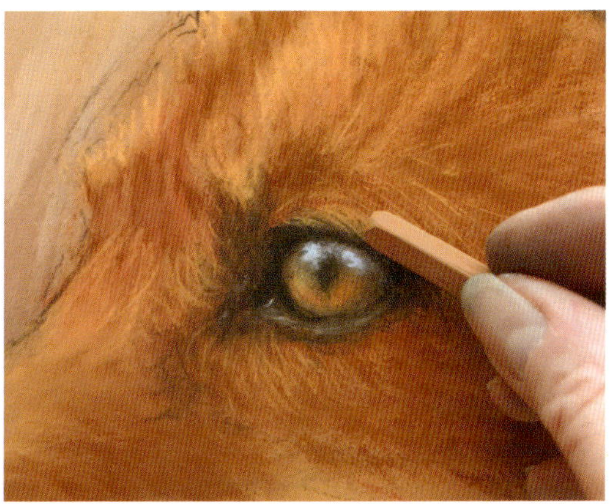

7 ● The glint in the eye

The shine of the eye is in direct contrast to the soft textures of the coat. The way to achieve shine is to have a strong tonal contrast. Much of the tone on the fur changes gradually, but with this eye, I need bright lights to jump out against the darker darks. I use a light blue soft pastel, and press quite hard with the end of it to create some bright marks, looking very carefully at the reference photo to get these marks in the right place.

8 ● Fine hairs

Now in order to blend the short fur around the eye into the rest of the fur, I use my Raw Sienna Conté crayon, making little short marks, using the sharp end. These work really well over the darker soft pastel colours already there. In places I soften the soft pastel under-layers so these new, sharper marks really show. I use this technique quite often in this piece, always paying very careful attention to the direction of the hairs.

9 ▶ Background

As the fox is a warm and vibrant red/brown, I use muted blues for the background. I want the background to make the colours of the fox jump forward, so I use a contrasting colour, and make the background darker against the light areas of the fox's head. I only put the blue around the areas I want to accentuate, and in order to make the fox look more vibrant, I use an eraser to soften and 'knock back' the blue. Rubbing and softening with my fingers, and also using an eraser, flattens and deadens the intensity of the pastels.

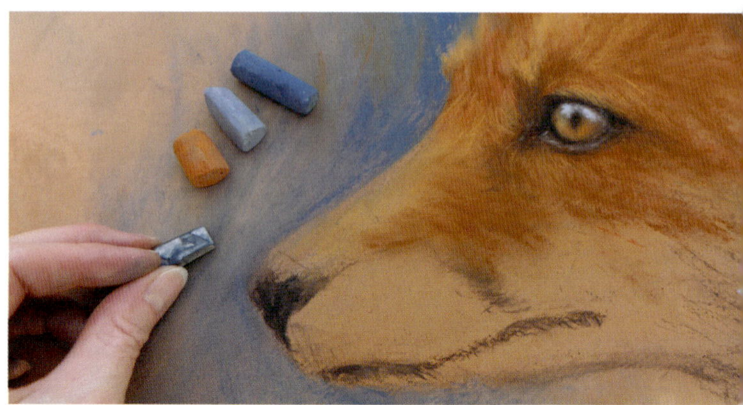

10 ▶ Light areas of coat on face and ears

I use two cream pastels: a creamy yellow Unison pastel and a Faber-Castell Polychromos one, which is harder, with which to base in the lighter areas of the fox's coat. The Polychromos pastel is good for a sketchy base, but I soften the Unison cream in to get a lovely soft surface to work over with pastel pencil later. I also put these lighter tones into the ears.

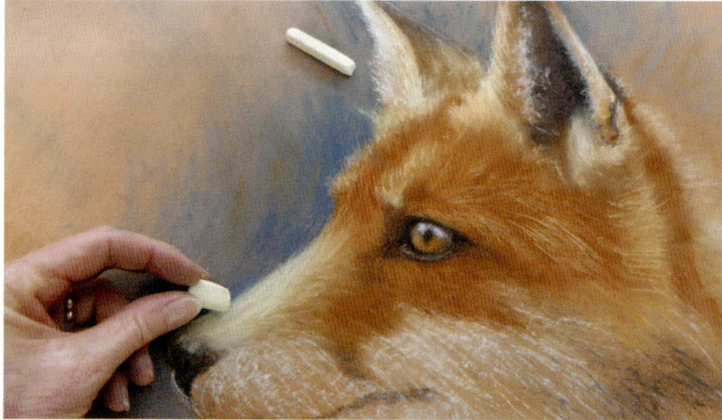

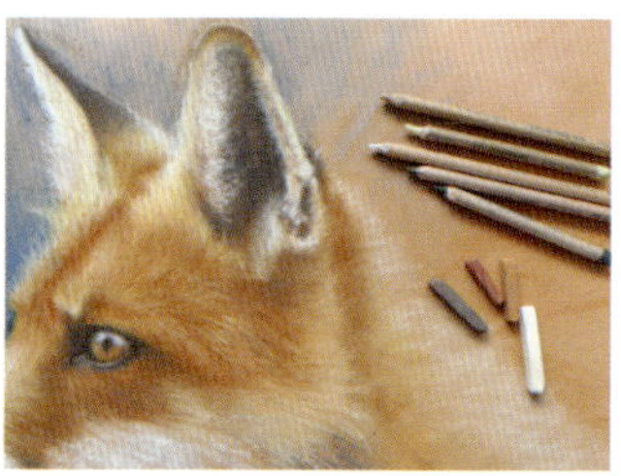

11 ▲ Detailing and refining the coat and ears

Now I have based in most of the fox, I want to soften, sculpt and refine my piece, using lightly hatched pastel pencils, a little charcoal and soft pastel, to create subtleties of tonal changes and depth. This can be a careful part of the process, but remember that you don't need to put detail in everywhere. Try to create points of interest with detail, and soften away from them with a light touch. To do this, I am constantly looking at my reference to understand exactly where to put my lights, medium and darks.

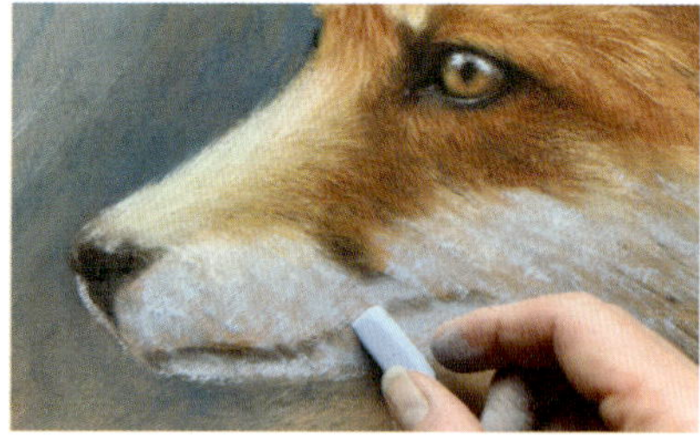

12 ▲ Light blue around the mouth

In order to paint in the soft, shorter-haired white of the fox's mouth area and lower jaw, I use a soft light blue. This is the same colour I used for the shine in the eye. I do not want to use white, as it will 'jump' out of the picture too much, so a light blue is a good starting point. I soften it on, paying attention to the direction of the fur, and then use a dark brown pastel pencil to gently draw in the curved line of the mouth.

Sharpen your pastel pencils with a craft knife or scalpel Pencils need to be sharp, otherwise they are just like pastels with no strength to them. I use a scalpel to sharpen mine, and I regularly change the blade.

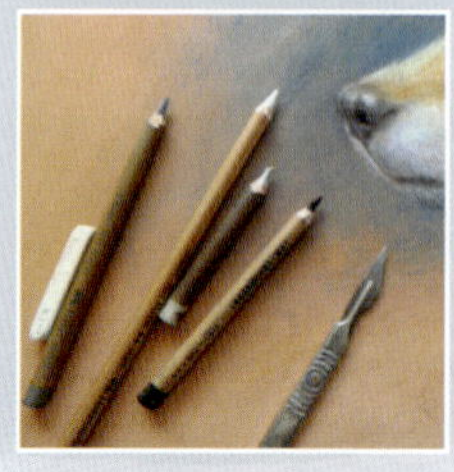

13 ▸ Subtle changes of tone

Over this light blue, I blend areas to get subtle shadows, using charcoal, Conté crayons and pastel pencils in soft greys and creams. You can draw attention to places where the colour of the coat changes, and light hairs lie over dark hairs, or vice versa. I integrate the colours using lightly hatched hair-like marks, and also blend some of the reds and browns in the white and grey areas to give the piece a unified feel.

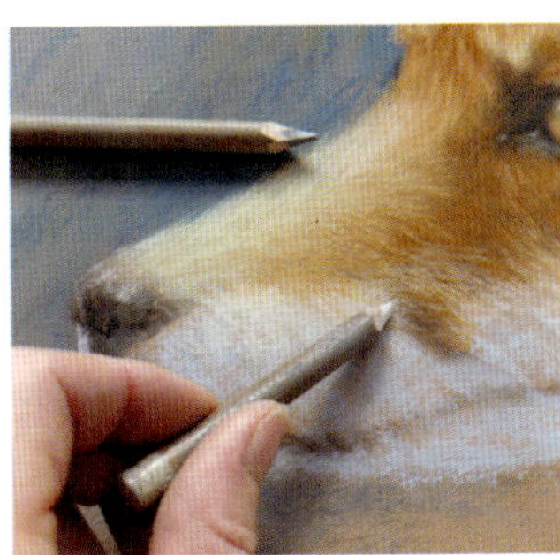

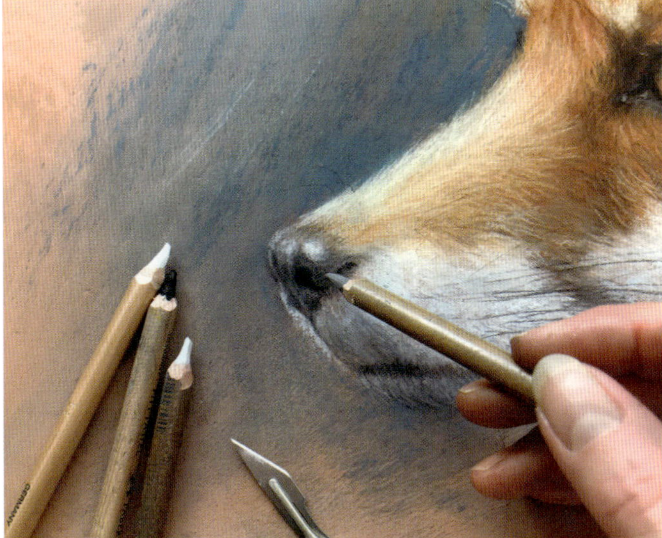

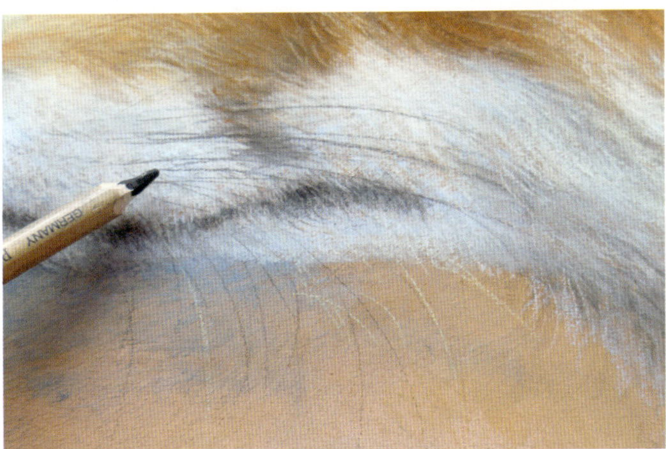

14 ▸ Long neck hairs

I love the textures of the longer, wiry hair on the neck. To create this I put on flicked marks with a lilac grey Unison pastel, charcoal and the cream/white Polychromos pastel that I used earlier. The Unison pastel can be smudged and softened with your fingers, and then the charcoal followed by the cream flicked over the top and left unsmudged. This develops depth and variety of texture.

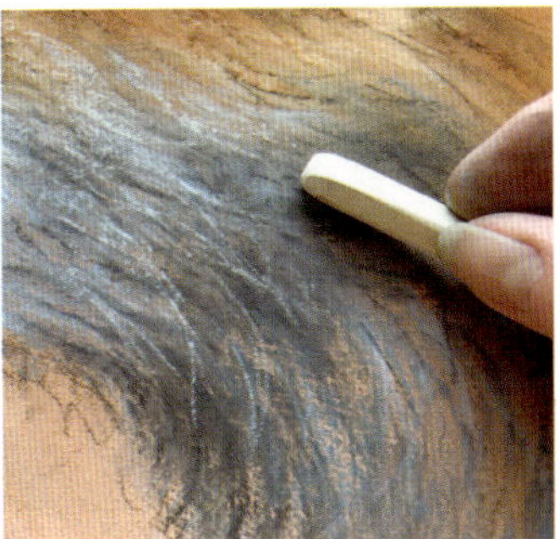

15 ◂ Nose and mouth

Using sharp grey and black pastel pencils, I refine the nose area and keep developing the subtle changes around the muzzle area. This then blends into the neck. Using flicks and very light smudges of many of the lighter colours already used, I soften the different neck areas into each other. I try to keep a light touch, as I do not want this area to dominate, but just to be hinted at.

16 ◂ Whiskers

Pastel pencils are great for whiskers, but look very carefully before you draw them in, at where they grow from, which direction they go in, and how fine they are. Then it's great to have a practice on a spare piece of paper at the light flicking movement – you need to make sure that they are thicker at the base than the end.

less is more

Don't forget that for an animal to look alive, you do not need to put in every detail. Sometimes, too much detail in the fur can make things appear flat and less lifelike.

Weather effects

Nel Whatmore invites you to explore the joys of working in pastels to discover the beauty of painting different types of weather, from long summer days to still misty mornings

When first learning about how to paint different types of weather, one of the most important things to consider is what time of day to paint, as it is often key to ending up with a successful painting. This isn't just because of the possible need to dodge rain clouds, but because the quality of the light, combined with how intense the light is, both vary hugely throughout the course of a single day. These two factors affect the tonal range of a painting and the atmosphere of it.

A very useful exercise is to choose a simple view, such as a field with one tree in it or the corner of your garden, and paint it at different times of day. I have done this on several occasions and I often chosen an early morning, midday and a late afternoon view. It is invaluable to understand how the same view alters as the Sun changes direction and weather fronts move through. Monet was the master of this approach, and he painted many series of paintings of his iconic lily pond at Giverny, the River Seine and Notre-Dame Cathedral.

In this article, I want to encourage you to look more closely at the light and how subtle variations and decisions we make will help us improve our painting of all types of weather. We will uncover how to build a painting up, exploring at how choosing your colours is key, as well as mark making and how we hold and use pastels to help us convey different weather effects.

Of course, it is impossible to cover all weathers here, so I will be concentrating on stormy landscapes, summer fields and misty autumnal mornings.

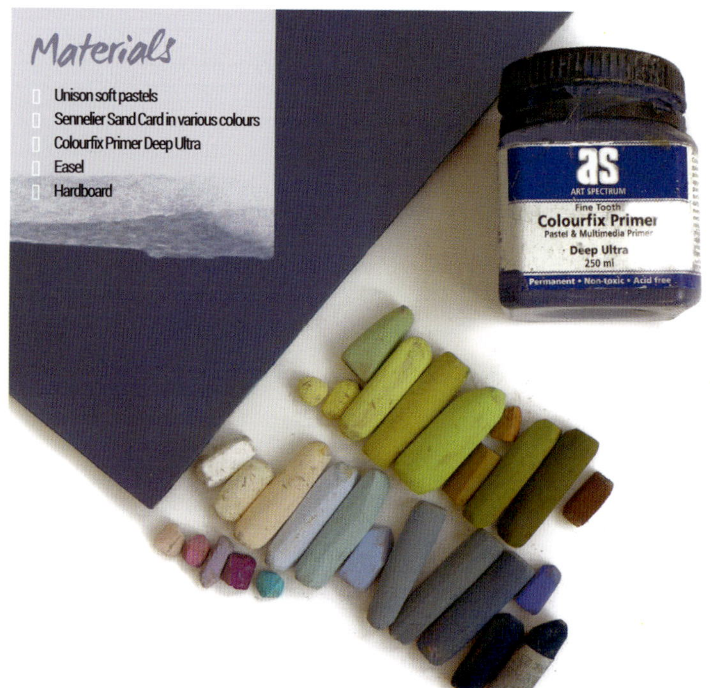

Time of day

Understand how light quality and colour intensity changes during a single day

I would like to suggest that you paint the same simple view at three different times of day, for instance morning, midday and late afternoon. In this example I had only a few hours and not the luxury of a whole day, but it was interesting to see that even if you don't have much time, there is still much to learn. These three studies were painted at 4pm, 5pm and 6.30pm in late September. Because I was working quickly, I was looking at where the light was coming from and changes in the range of colours. Painting different types of weather is always initially about understanding what colour palette to use and looking at the tonal range. Are there lots of subtle mid tones, or more dramatic extremes of darks and lights?

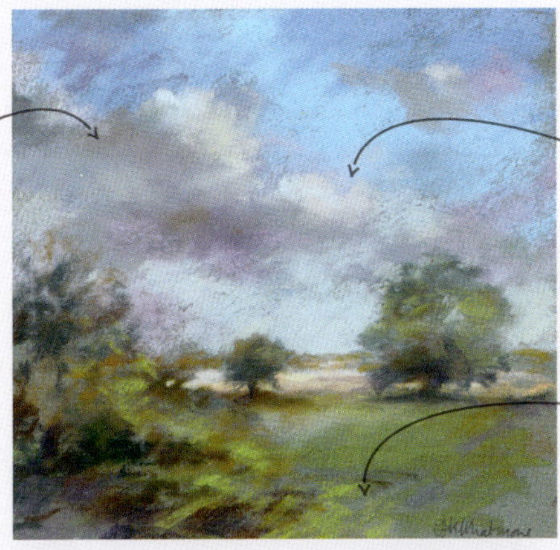

4pm Sept afternoon

Always see which way and how strongly the wind is blowing. This will affect the shape of the clouds and also the pastel strokes you make. I used the pastel on its side in order to work very quickly because of the time limit.

The first thing to note is where the light is coming from – it was behind me, but still shining down on the land, so the field in the mid distance is bright as the Sun hits it at an angle, and the tones are mostly in the mid range, with a few darks under the trees. The surface is also a mid tone Sennelier Pastel Card light blue grey.

It was not windy so the edges between the different areas are quite soft and not very distinct as it was late in the afternoon. Because the marks are soft and not very angular, it conveys a sense of late afternoon calm. I changed to a darker paper – dark blue grey – to create a richer field.

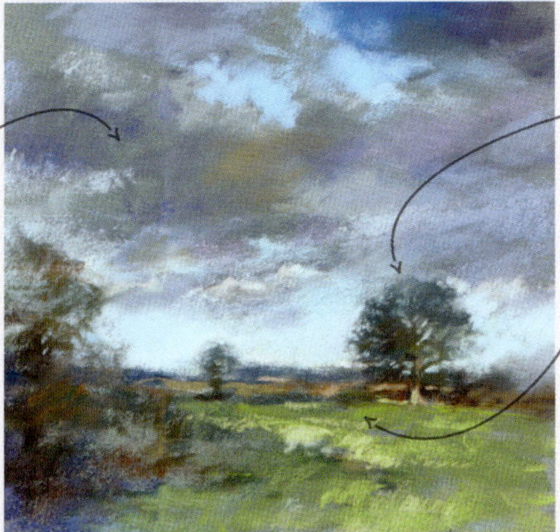

5pm Sept afternoon

The clouds are getting heavier, possibly in time for some early evening rain. There is little wind so the contrast between the blue of the sky and the edges of the clouds remains quite blurred and indistinct by blending the colours over each other.

The light is now lower in the sky. The Sun shines on the base of the tree and the tonal range of blues and greens has intensified – there are darker blues and greys, and the blue at the horizon is brighter. The range of greens makes it more dramatic.

The grass is a more yellow-green and the light is shining on it so there is more texture. Vertical short strokes haved been used, in contrast to the bottom left-hand corner, which remains in shadow and is now a darker blue-green.

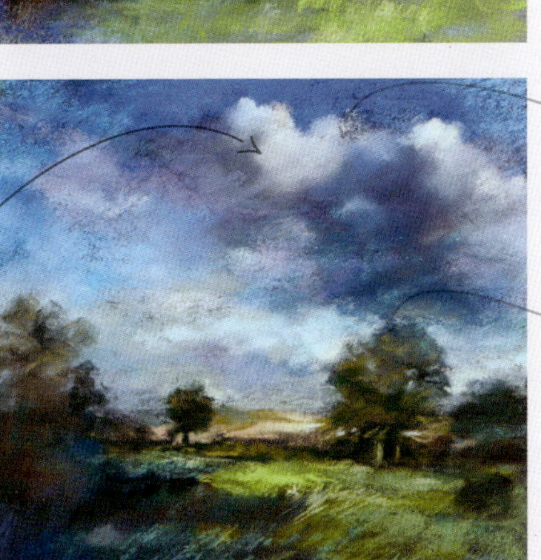

6.30pm Sept afternoon

Painting a good sky is all about the edges of the clouds and how blurred or crisp they are where they meet the surrounding blue. Look at the top edge of the cloud where it meets the now much richer blue and contrast this with its darker underside that blends into the next cloud below.

The Sun is now very low and is just catching the edges of the clouds. Notice how the tonal range has almost been compressed, making the colours more intense with brighter lights and darker darks.

The light is more dramatic and it also became more breezy, so the mark making changes. I used pastels on their ends in order to hatch colours over each other, but still in the direction that the grass is growing to lead your eye towards the tree. I have also changed to a darker paper, the Sennelier Pastel Card dark blue grey, to create a richer field.

Misty days and creating atmosphere

Creating atmosphere is essential to conveying different types of weather and is achieved by looking at colour and the balance between areas of calm and detail

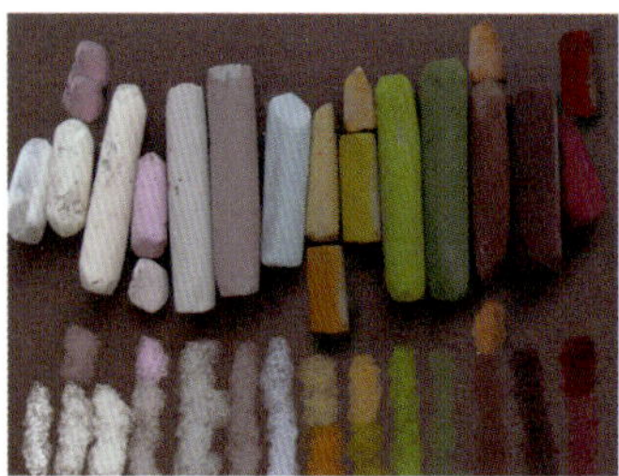

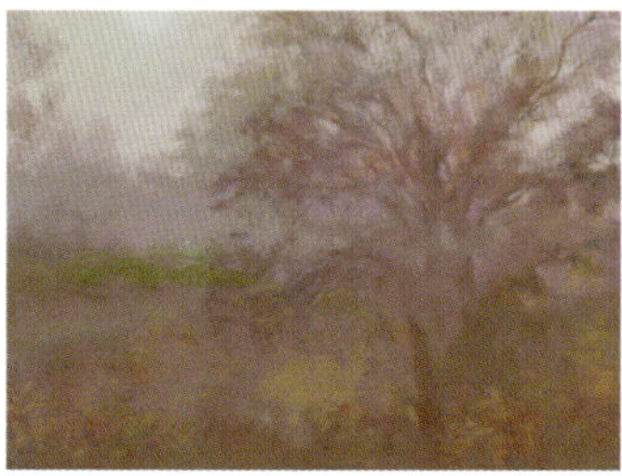

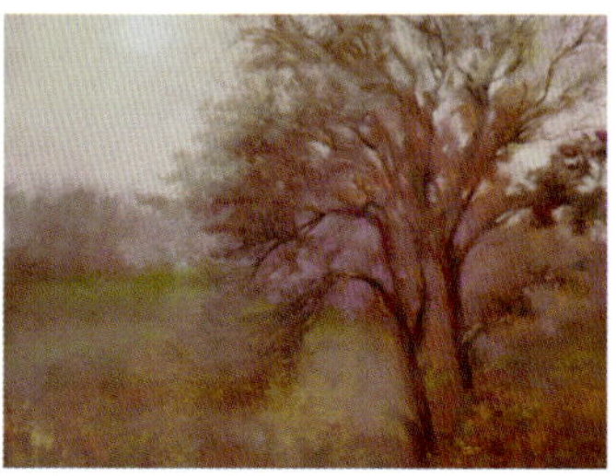

1 Choose your colours

Misty days are nearly always still, when the intensity of colours is masked by cloud cover and the light is reduced. Restrict your colour palette to a more muted range of colours, avoiding bright, saturated ones to create atmosphere. Imagine your subject is covered in layers of tissue paper, rather like looking at colours through a misty window. Ask yourself if your colour is too bright, and make sure to test them on the paper of your choice. For this example, I chose a mid-brown Sennelier Soft Pastel Card Van Dyke brown, as I wanted lots of the paper to show through and work as a colour in my painting.

2 Composition and areas of colour

Work out your rough composition by lightly applying the lighter and mid tones of pastel. It is harder on soft pastel card to go over darker colours, so start light and get darker later. Make sure the edges between the areas in your composition are soft and not hard as it creates a softness that is in keeping with it being a misty early morning. Use the pastel on its side so you can do broader stokes and cover larger areas – don't hold it like a pencil. Take the paper label off so you have the full length of the stick.

3 Soft edges

To create stillness, always have a definite area of calm where there is not much going on. Make sure your horizon, if there is one, is not a continuous hard line, but a soft interrupted one. I have pressed harder with the light pastels in the top-left corner and moved from soft pink to a light white yellow to white to lead your eye to the Sun. There are no hard lines, just a soft transition. Darker tones come into the foreground to give form very gradually. Create finer detail by breaking your pastel in two to get a sharper edge, or use pastel pencils if you prefer.

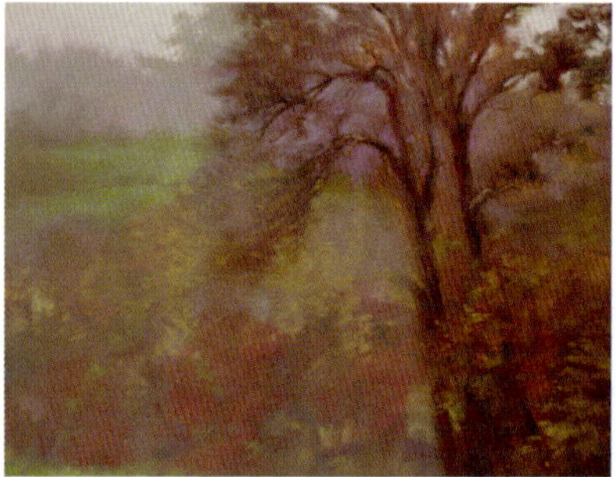

4 Introduce detail

Now building on the foundation of colours already laid down, choose small areas of your individual branches or bushes to focus on and apply more detail to give greater depth. Detail always translates into texture, which means that your eye will be drawn to wherever there is lots of it and it will become a focal point. Be selective about where you apply detail – if a painting has the same amount of detail and clarity all over, it will flatten its appearance.

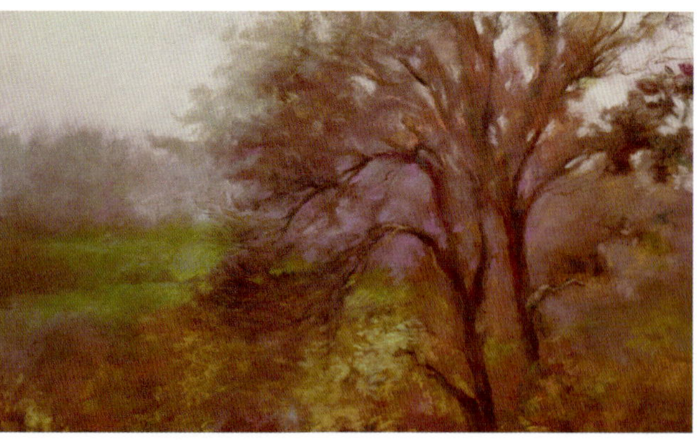

5 Use darker colours

The strength of the colours in the foreground were increased using richer or more saturated colours. To create the impression that the Sun was trying to break through from the distance, warmer greens and hints of yellow were also used to create this effect with shorter, more rapidly made marks being utilised. At this stage it is about adding highlights and deeper shades in order to give the painting more depth.

Storm clouds

Stormy skies are all about drama, composition and trying to convey the sense that the wind is blowing and the heavens are about to open

The painting I have chosen to illustrate this point is a large one called Caution to the Wind, and it concentrates very much on the sky. Getting to know different cloud formations is very useful, and when you get very large ones and torrential downpours, they can be very many hundreds of feet high. The speed and direction of the wind also affect the structure of a cloud.

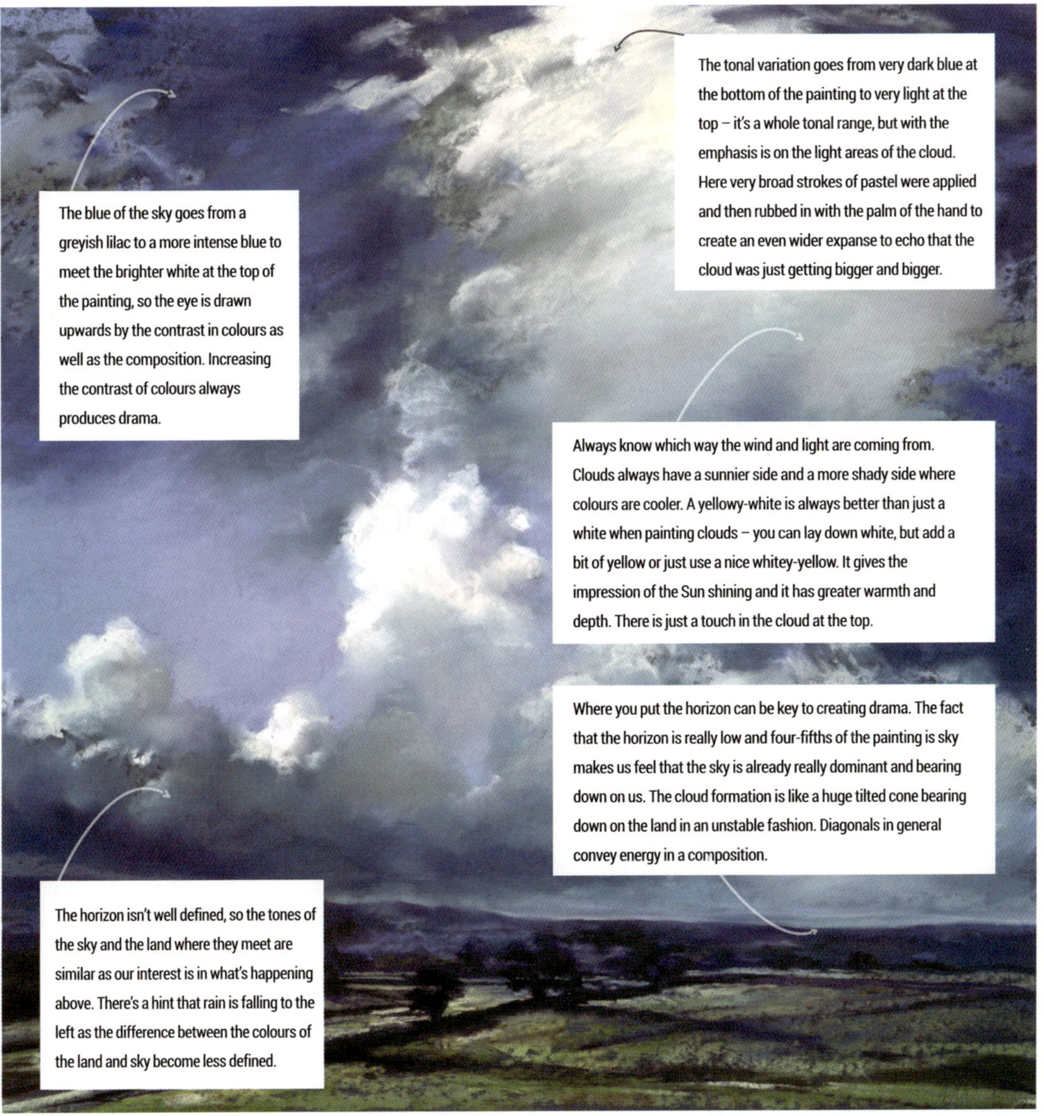

The tonal variation goes from very dark blue at the bottom of the painting to very light at the top – it's a whole tonal range, but with the emphasis is on the light areas of the cloud. Here very broad strokes of pastel were applied and then rubbed in with the palm of the hand to create an even wider expanse to echo that the cloud was just getting bigger and bigger.

The blue of the sky goes from a greyish lilac to a more intense blue to meet the brighter white at the top of the painting, so the eye is drawn upwards by the contrast in colours as well as the composition. Increasing the contrast of colours always produces drama.

Always know which way the wind and light are coming from. Clouds always have a sunnier side and a more shady side where colours are cooler. A yellowy-white is always better than just a white when painting clouds – you can lay down white, but add a bit of yellow or just use a nice whitey-yellow. It gives the impression of the Sun shining and it has greater warmth and depth. There is just a touch in the cloud at the top.

Where you put the horizon can be key to creating drama. The fact that the horizon is really low and four-fifths of the painting is sky makes us feel that the sky is already really dominant and bearing down on us. The cloud formation is like a huge tilted cone bearing down on the land in an unstable fashion. Diagonals in general convey energy in a composition.

The horizon isn't well defined, so the tones of the sky and the land where they meet are similar as our interest is in what's happening above. There's a hint that rain is falling to the left as the difference between the colours of the land and sky become less defined.

Summer days and fields

Sunshine, texture and vibrancy are all things to think about when conveying glorious summer fields – building up layers using hatching helps us do this

1 Choose your colours and surface

For paintings that need to convey warmth and have a lot of detail in them, such as a sunny cornfield, I often paint a surface like hardboard with a layer of Colourfix Primer first, then choose a range of colours from lights to darks. Using the pastels on their sides, I roughly block the areas in. As this is a very summery subject, I chose more colours with a yellow and yellow-green bias. I used Colourfix Deep Ultra to underpaint the board – you can apply this acrylic-based primer directly from the pot, but it is quite thick and is often better watered down a bit and applied with a two or three-inch brush. It has a fine pumice powder in it, which then gives the surface a tooth, suitable for pastels.

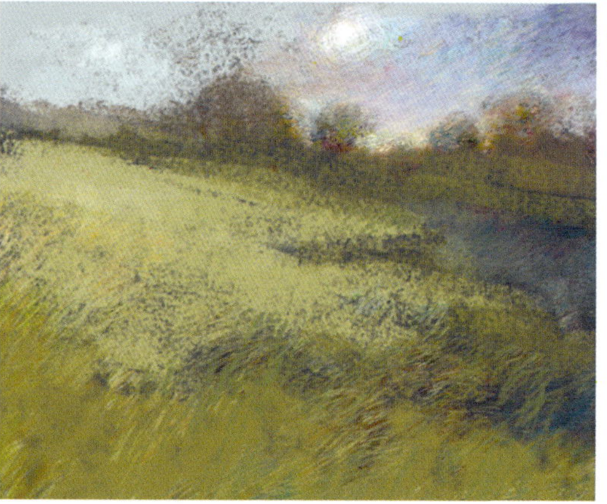

2 Decide where your focal point is

The Sun was behind the trees and it was a very warm day. To create that feeling, as if the air is almost vibrating, 'hatching' is very useful – don't blend the colours with your finger, but instead lay strokes of many colours on top of each other, usually by holding the pastel more like a pencil. I have started with the area on the top right. Degas was the master of this technique.

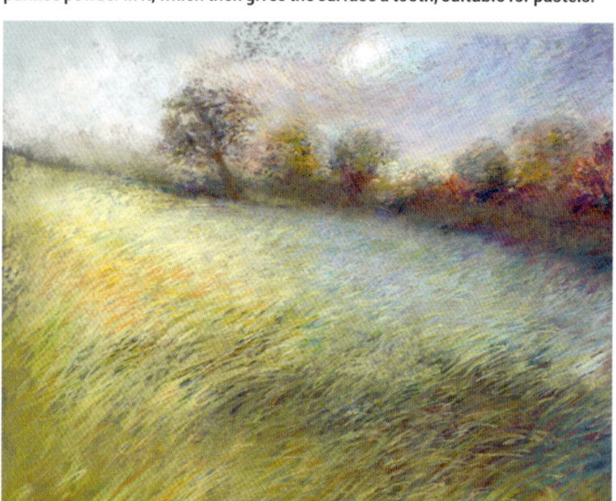

3 Use lots of colours

The beauty of hatching when done on a harder surface, like hardboard, is that you can build up more layers. Notice how there is a definite cooler area of the painting in front of the trees where the greens have a blue bias, which acts as a nice contrast to the sunnier side of the field. The vibration of all the colours together gives a sense of energy, too, as the wind was blowing across the field.

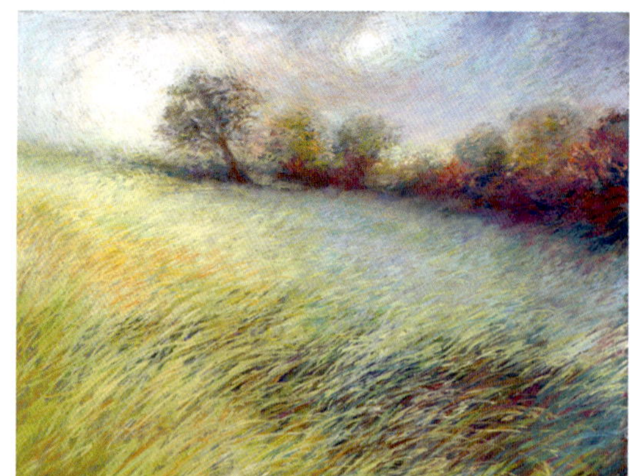

4 The direction of hatching

While you can hatch colours over each other in all directions, in landscapes it is often best to follow the contours of the land or vegetation. Lines are a strong visual indicator that can lead the viewer around your painting. See how the strokes in the sky follow the curve around the Sun to continue the feeling of movement and energy. It brings all the different areas of the painting together to give the impression of a sunny day.

The power of colour

Increasing your colour range is often the key to conveying the mood of a season or type of weather. Make yourself familiar with different seasonal colour palettes. Being bold and introducing unusual colours into landscapes often reaps rewards

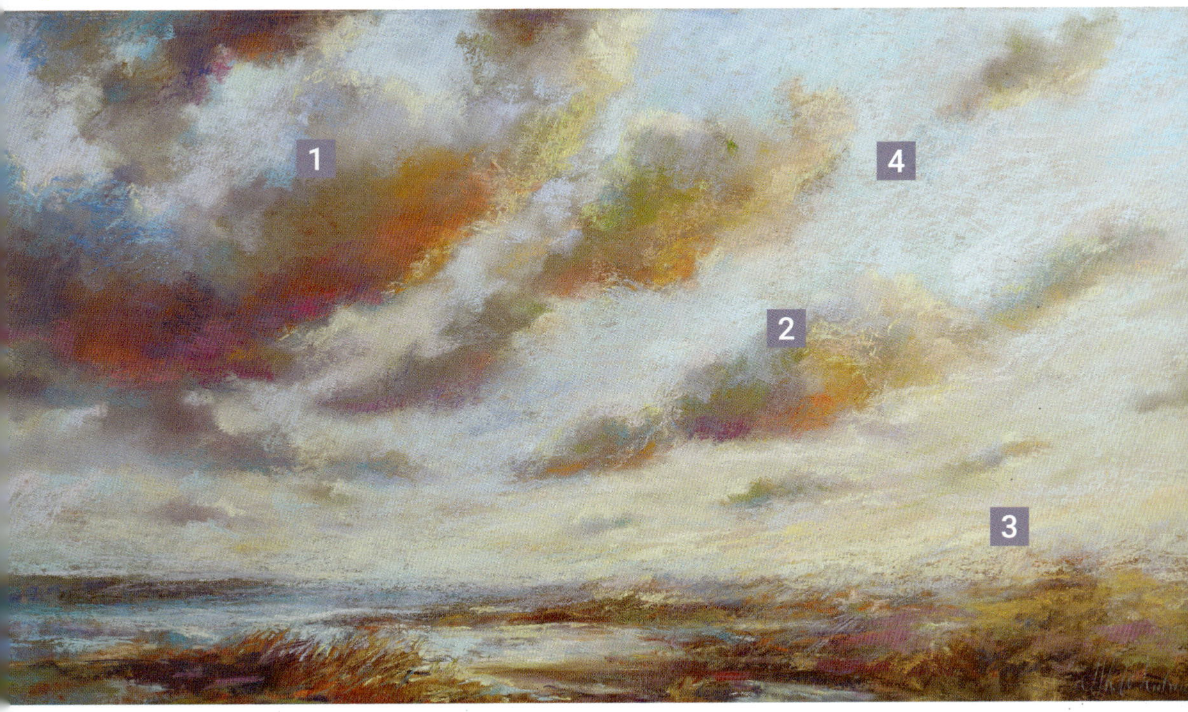

1 The importance of colour

Be brave and try using more colours in your summer skies. Stick to warmer tones and remember that the colours of the land reflect up into the sky, as well as the sky reflecting down onto water. Summer skies have wonderful colours, particularly towards the end of the day.

2 Paper or board dimensions

One of the first decisions to make is what shape paper or board you want to work on. So often people just use the piece of paper they buy without considering its proportions. Remember to think about how the shape of your paper helps you tell your story, and the weather. I chose a very long horizontal piece because I wanted to echo the fact that it was the longest day of the year and that the painting was all about the wonderful expansive Norfolk summer evening sky.

3 Warm surface colour

Choose a nice warm mid-tone colour of paper or surface, as that warmth will show through all over your painting if you don't blend your pastels and let the paper work as a colour. If you are not sure what colour to choose, cut a thin strip off one edge and test your pastel colours on it to see which one you prefer.

4 Let your layers show through

Laying down a warm tinted layer using a Colourfix primer, or smudging in your first layer then drifting another pastel over the top but not blending, gives your painting depth while increasing energy and warmth. Often when students say their work gets muddy it's because they either blend the layers of pastel together or they apply too much, clogging up the surface. If this happens to you, use the edge of a piece of acetate or even a credit card to lift some of the pastel from the surface.

Acrylics

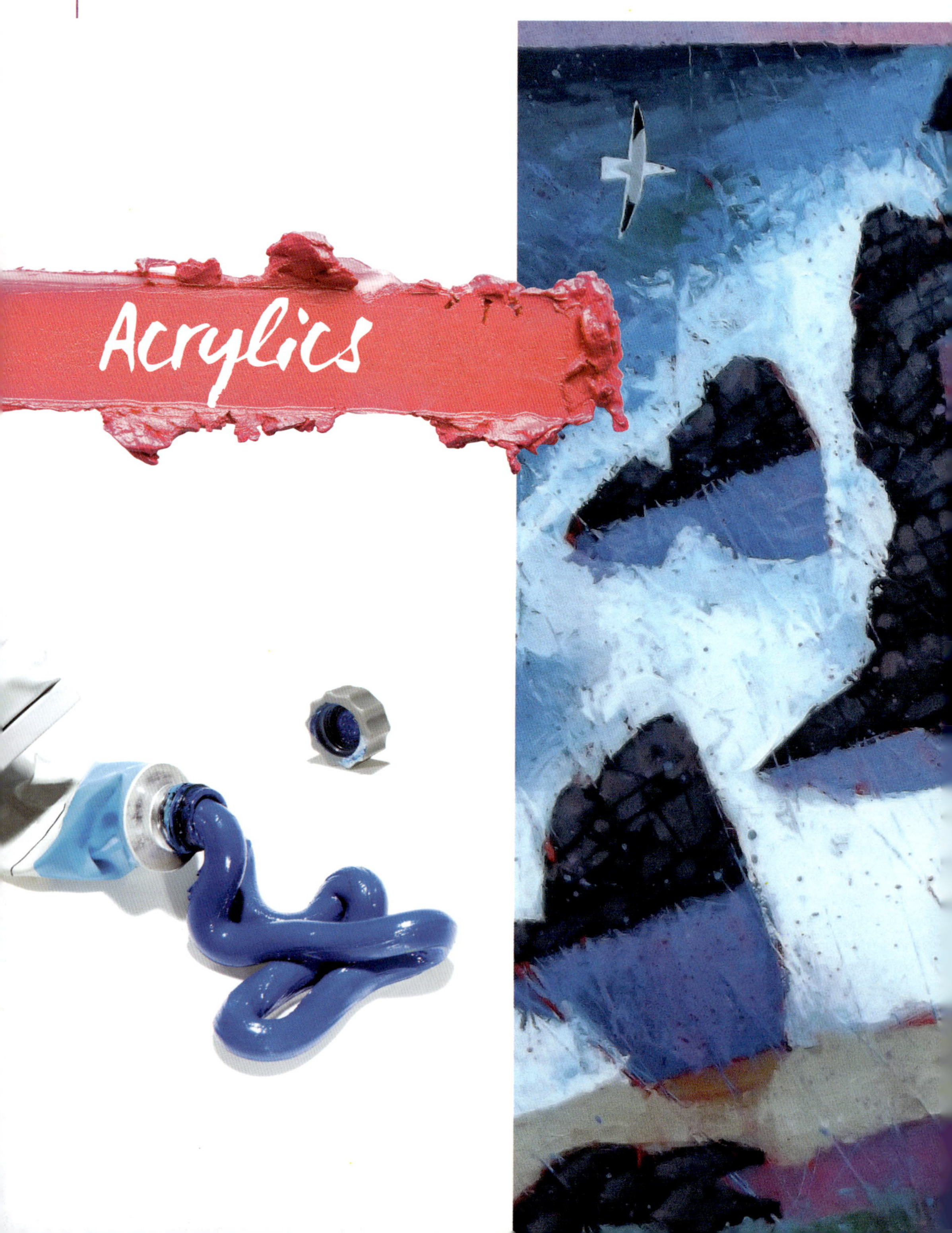

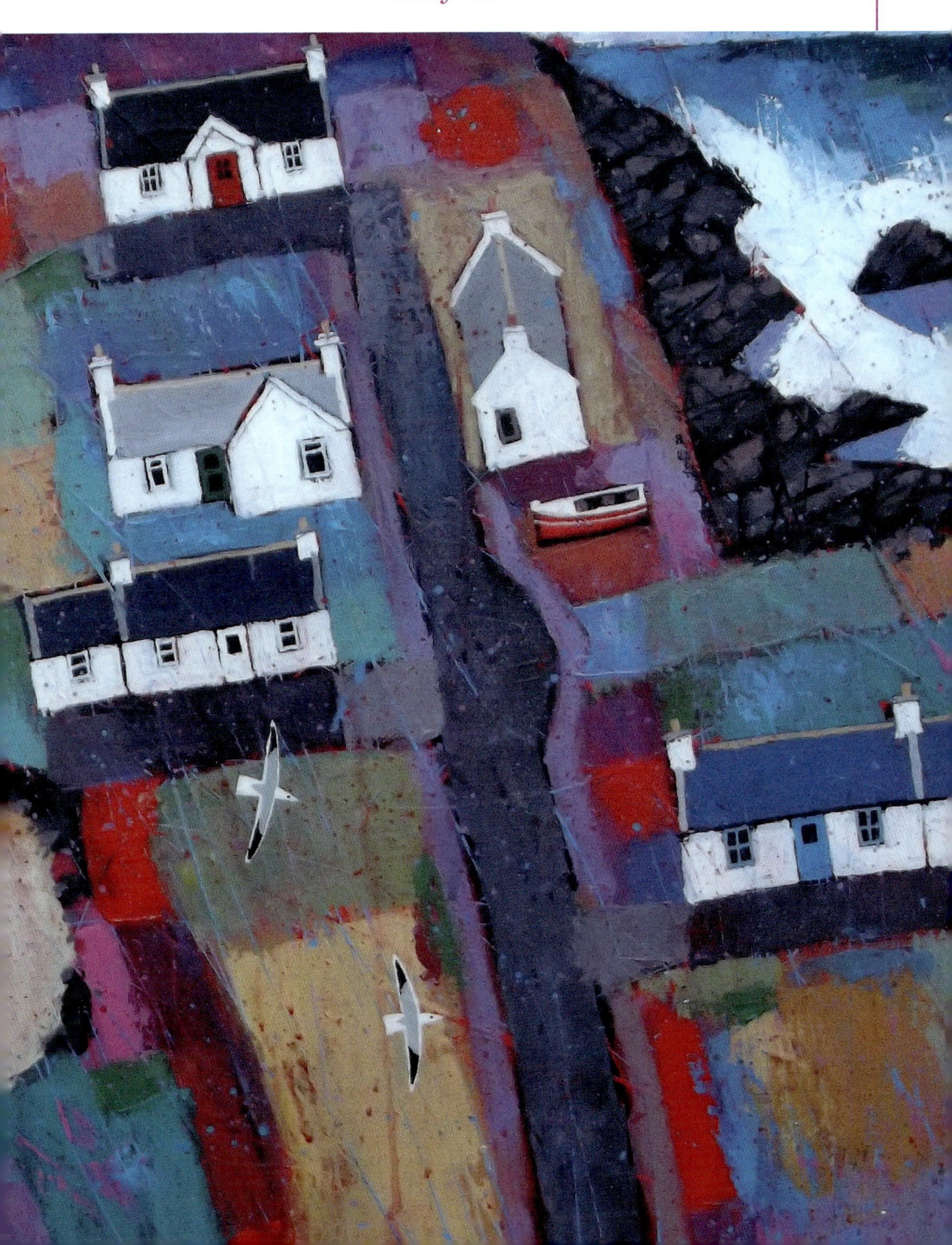

An introduction to acrylics

If you are new to acrylics, **Sylvia Paul** will inspire you to have a go with handy tips and inspiration

If you are starting with acrylics as a substitute for oils or watercolour, you may find there are disadvantages. The consistency of the paint differs from that of oils, and adding a medium doesn't give you the same thickness and texture. It also dries quickly, so some techniques, such as wet in wet, are more difficult in acrylics. However, it can provide ways of trying techniques similar to those of more traditional paints. It's perfect for applying various techniques in one painting, and excellent for mixed-media projects.

Find out about the basic paints, mediums and tools, and get tips on what supports you can work on and ways to apply the paint. Be inspired with ideas to build your confidence and discover how acrylic can be used with other media to create exciting, original paintings. Acrylic is a versatile medium that's perfect for a beginner or an improver looking for a different approach, so don't be afraid to give it a try.

1 ❯ The advantages

Acrylic does dry a lot faster than oils, but this can actually be an advantage in a painting as it allows you to build layers quickly, either in glazes or even thicker paint. I sometimes use a hairdryer to speed up the drying process even more. A painting can be dry in a day and easily transported, which is helpful if you are on holiday, painting en plein air, or part of a painting group. It can be bought quite inexpensively and used for a range of different approaches, traditional and experimental.

Materials

- Heavy body or basic acrylics
- A selection of brushes
- Canvas, board or paper
- Matte medium
- Fine texture paste
- Impasto medium
- Greaseproof paper
- Varnish for acrylics
- Palette knife
- Gesso (acrylic primer)

2 ❍ Choosing the right paint

There are many types of acrylic paint and it can be very daunting knowing which type to start with. I prefer heavy body acrylic, as this helps to build the texture, though it can also be thinned out if required. Most basic acrylics are a little thinner in consistency, but if that's what you have available you can add mediums to this to give it more body or texture. Acrylic also comes in an ink form and even in a spray can. Start with something basic and then add to this later when you know in which direction your work is going.

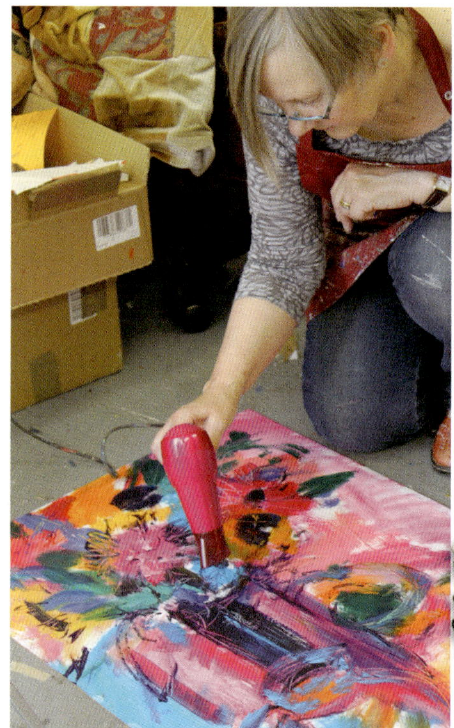

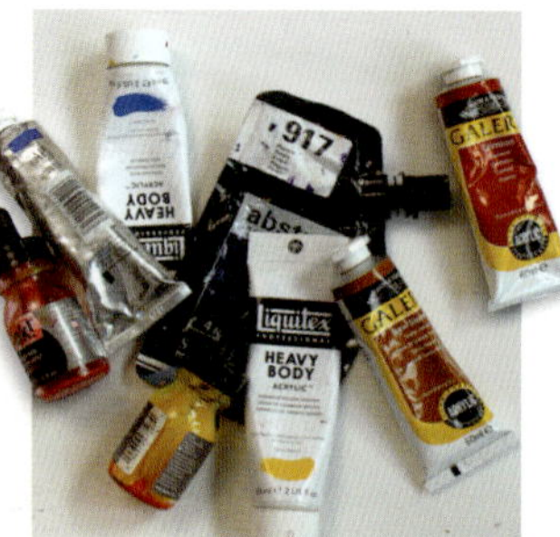

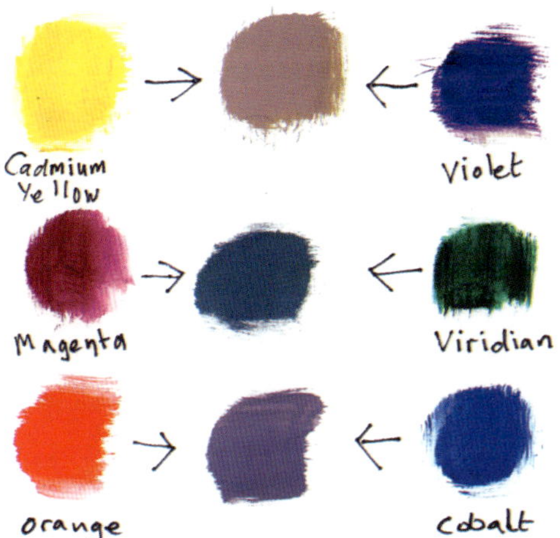

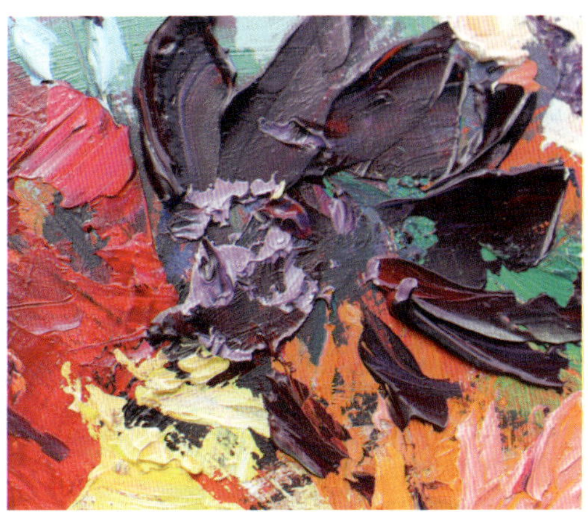

3 ◔ Colour choices

I never use paint straight from the tube, but mix basic colours to get subtle shades. If you have two reds, two blues, two yellows and white, that is a good start. My favourites are Cadmium Red, Magenta, Cobalt Blue, Ultramarine Blue, Cadmium Yellow and Lemon Yellow. Titanium White is essential and other useful colours are Violet, Cadmium Orange and Viridian Green. Try mixing opposite colours together, such as a red and a green, and adding a touch of white to get subtle greys.

4 ◔ Have a go and experiment

Think about what you want to achieve with your paintings. If you know what you want your end result to be, it will help you to decide on the techniques you should practise. However, you have nothing to lose by experimenting. If you are used to watercolours, try working with thicker paint and work on a canvas. Oil painters, have a go at working quickly and make the most of the fast drying speed. If you are new to painting, try different techniques and get to know the paint.

5 ◔ Finishing touches

Different styles of painting will need different presentation. Work on paper should be framed behind glass using a double mount to give space between the glass and the painting surface. This style of framing is best for any mixed-media work, which includes pastel, too. Varnishing will protect your work from dust and light damage, and I would recommend this for work on canvas or board that is framed without glass.

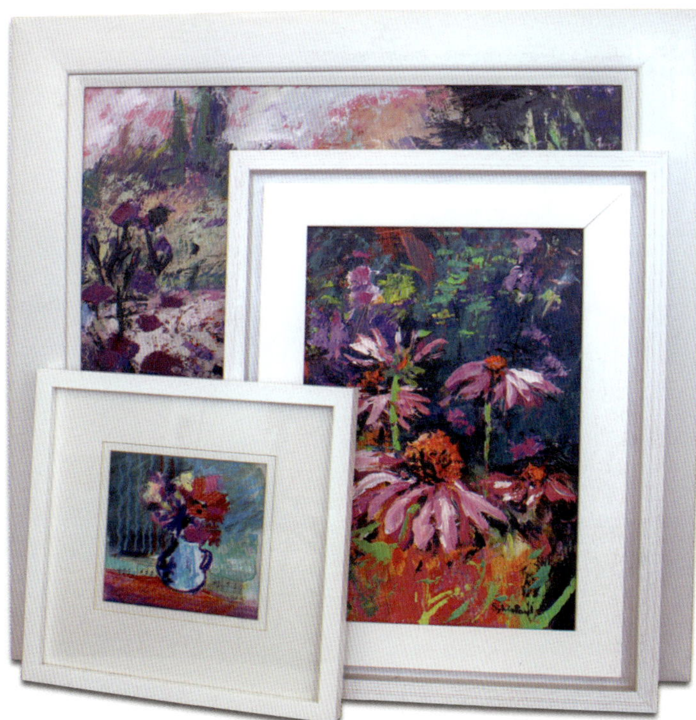

Share resources

If you are eager to try using acrylic with other media, get together with friends or an art group and share your materials. For example, some may have pastels but not pens, while others may have different texture mediums. Pool your resources as a group and purchase items that other members can try.

Tools & mediums

1 Brushes

For fine, detailed work, a selection of synthetic brushes and at least one flat, larger brush for applying washes is helpful. Bristle brushes are suitable for oil or acrylic. I tend to use less expensive ones and buy sets of these in a range of sizes. My favourite brush is a 4cm bristle decorating brush. All brushes must be washed with soap and water after use.

2 Palette knives and other tools

A palette knife is worth investing in for an impasto approach. Palette knives come in various sizes but I suggest starting with a medium-sized one, which is also useful for mixing the colours on your palette. Other useful tools for experimental work are old plastic cards, which can be used for spreading paint on the canvas, a stick for scratching in, and kitchen roll, for blending paint on the canvas. Of course, the latter is also useful for drying brushes.

3 Paper, canvas and board

Acrylic can be used on a variety of supports. Any paper or card is fine, but will give different results. Both paper and card can be given a coat of gesso to make it less absorbent and to add texture. Stretched and primed canvas can also be used for acrylics, and are especially useful for more impasto work. Ready-prepared canvas boards are available.

4 Palettes and easels

I find the best palette is a sheet of greaseproof paper, which is normally sold in a roll for cooking. To prevent the paint from drying out, place sheets of wet kitchen roll on a plastic tray and then lay the greaseproof paper on top. The advantage of a greaseproof paper roll is that you can have a large palette on which to mix your colours.

5 Mediums, gels and additives

There are numerous gels, mediums, pastes and additives for acrylics. There are retardants for slowing the drying speed and impasto gels for thickening the paint. There are mediums for thinning paint and even additives containing glitter. None of these are essential to get started but one or two could be helpful. Matte medium would be useful when thinning the paint for glazes, and an impasto medium to add body and give a thicker paint.

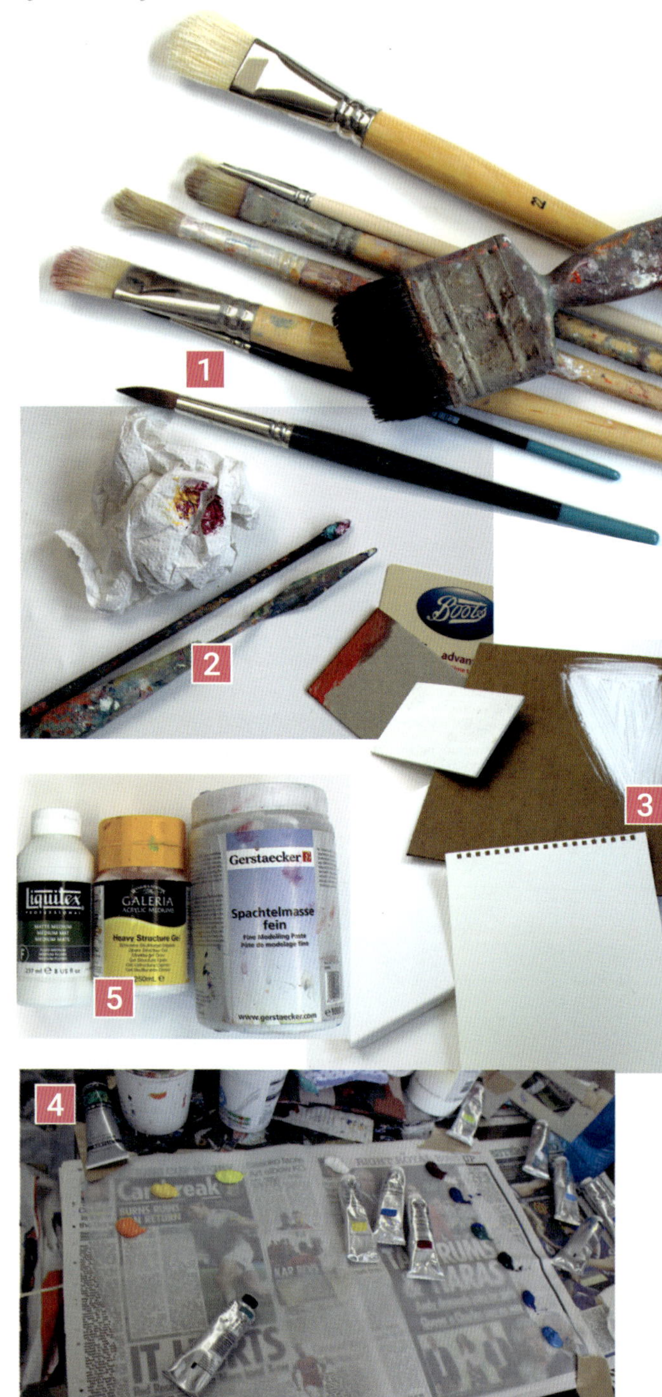

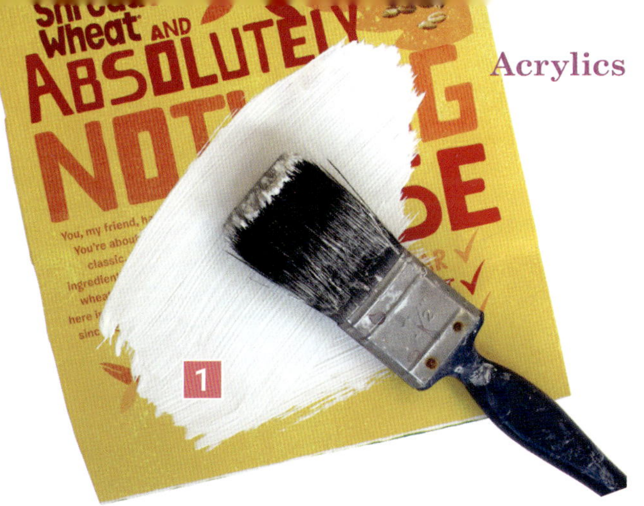

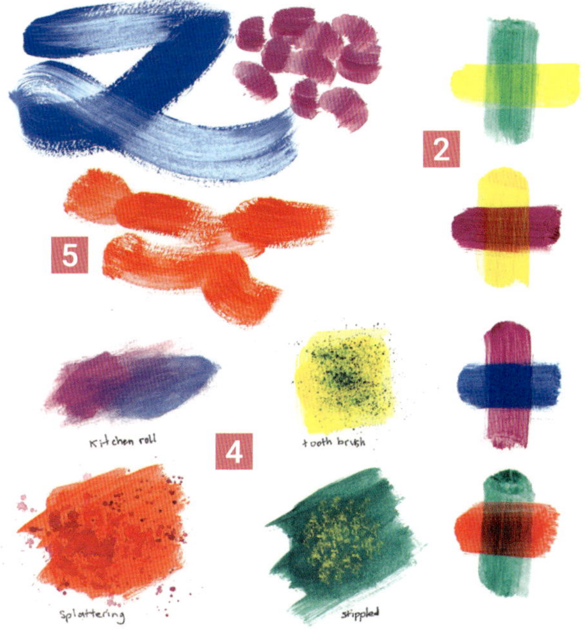

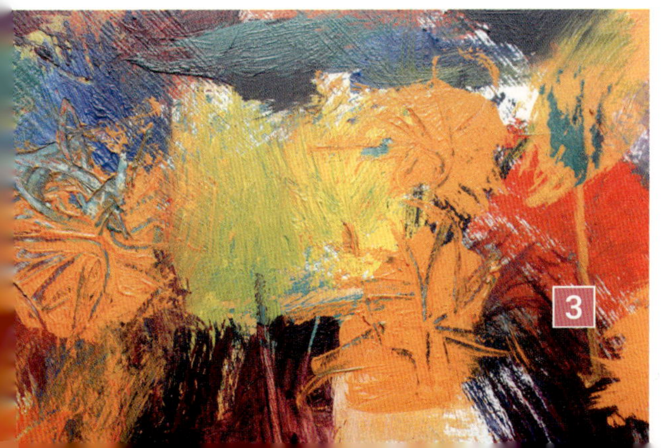

Surfaces & applying the paint

1 Choose a painting surface

The surface you choose to paint on will have a bearing on the end result and require different handling when presenting your finished painting. Paper is probably best suited to a more traditional watercolour approach, but it can also be best for any mixed-media work, which includes pastel and other drawing media. Canvas or board would suit a bold approach with impasto work, particularly for larger paintings.

2 Glazing

Glazing is a way of building layers with thin paint. Using a matte medium to thin the paint will increase the transparency and flow of the paint. You can make new hues by layering different colours, creating lovely, fresh, glowing effects. As the acrylic dries fairly quickly, you can layer the colours over each other easily. It is vital to keep your brushes clean to keep colours pure.

3 Impasto

Impasto refers to an area of thick paint and can be achieved with heavy body acrylics. Adding a structure gel or impasto gel will help to thicken paint even more. Brushes or a palette knife can be used to apply the paint thickly and, as it dries quickly, more paint can easily be applied on top. If you drag thick paint over a dry, textured surface, you can allow the colour underneath to show through.

4 Blending, splattering and stippling

With thick paint, try softening and blending an area with kitchen roll. Techniques like splattering can be useful to soften an area. You might need to mask off areas of the painting you want left untouched. Using a dry brush and fairly dry paint, dab the brush repeatedly over the surface to create a stippled effect.

5 Brush strokes

The choice of brush can transform an approach. Softer brushes create a more blended look, and for glazing you'll need a soft, flat brush. Try creating broad strokes with fluid paint and a large, flat brush for a dynamic effect. With thick paint and a bristle brush, vary the angle of the brush while applying the paint confidently then leave well alone. A painting with the brush strokes visible can be energetic and expressive. As you build in confidence, work quickly with dashes and swirls.

The basic techniques

Sue Sareen reveals how to create different effects with your acrylic paints

Acrylic paint is a delight to use; it can be used thickly, straight out of the tube, or thinly by diluting with water. Both methods are easy, clean and cost efficient. If desired, additional mediums can be added to make the paint even thicker or thinner.

Overpainting when the paint is dry is straightforward, but if you prefer, the use of slow-drying interactive acrylics can provide extra time, much in the same style as traditional oil paints.

Acrylics can also be painted straight onto any surface, whether primed or unprimed, and they are permanent when dry. Colourless or coloured glazes or other mediums can also be added later if you decide your painting needs it. So get your acrylics out, and let's get painting!

1 ❂ Don't load up on paint

Take a large, flat, coarse-haired bristle brush. Load it with just sufficient paint. Keep the brush as dry as possible and drag it across the surface of the paper. If necessary, wet the brush slightly. Using a rough, textured paper aids the process.

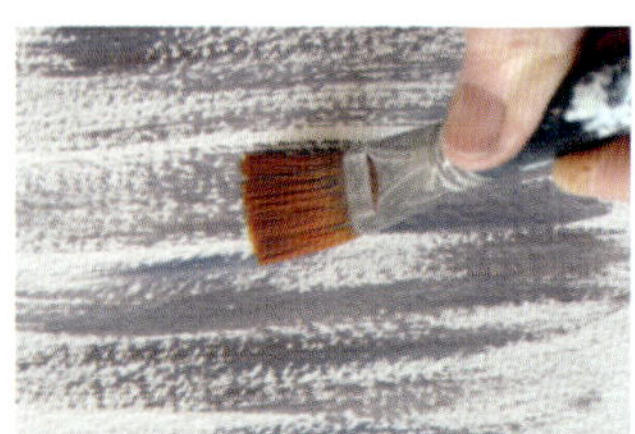

2 ❂ Perfect subjects

Use this technique to create the texture on a dry stone wall. Paint the background, then once it's dry, drag the paint in different directions across the paper using relevant colours.

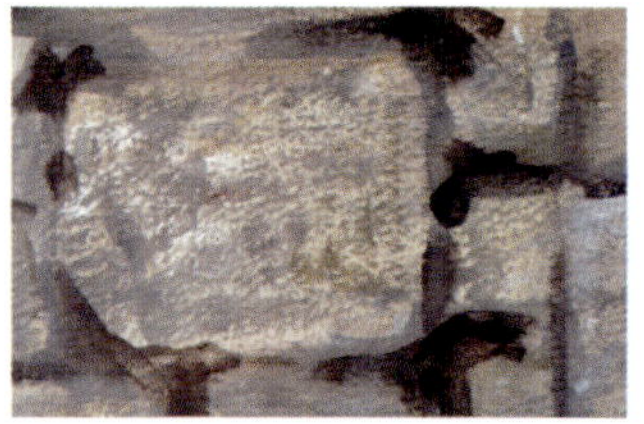

Dry brush

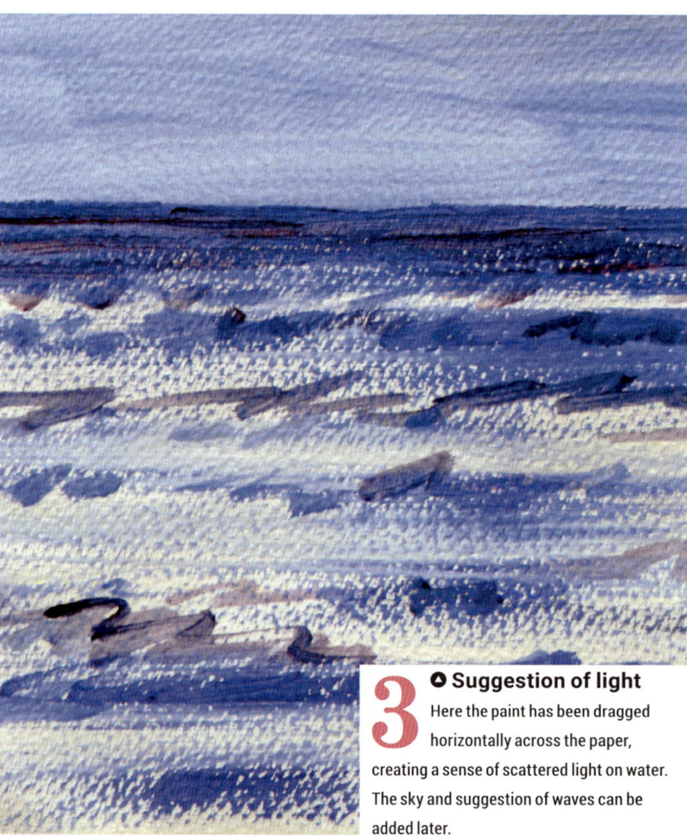

3 ❂ Suggestion of light

Here the paint has been dragged horizontally across the paper, creating a sense of scattered light on water. The sky and suggestion of waves can be added later.

Splattering

Bring a feeling of action or vibrancy to your work

1 ◉ Experiment

Take an old toothbrush or a coarse bristle brush, add the paint and flick the hair with your finger, creating a spatter on the paper. Experiment first on scrap paper, and decide what ratio of paint to water is required. Too much water tends to make big blobs.

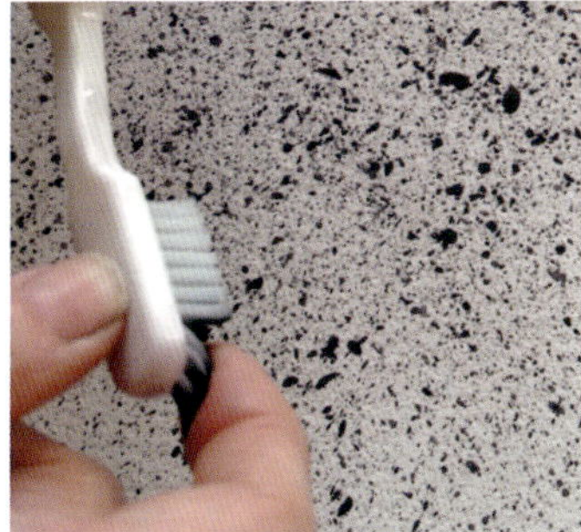

2 ◉ Sky spatter

Here the technique has been used to create the stars in a night sky. The sky was painted first, in a dark colour to make the stars contrast. When dry, the stars and skyline were added.

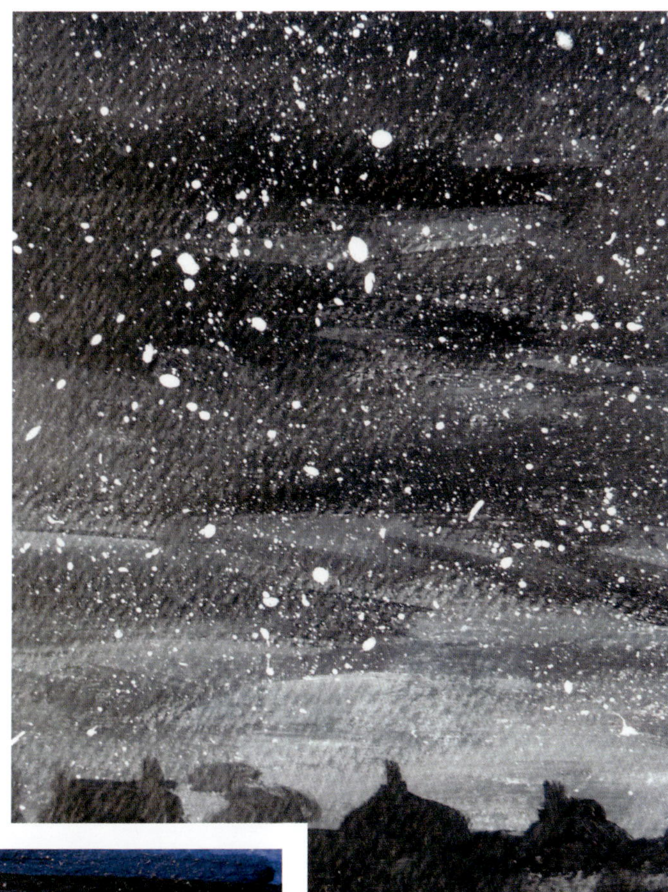

3 ◉ Spray the sea

The waves and water were painted first. When dry the white spray was splattered on. Care needs to be taken – be sure to protect vulnerable areas where you don't want the spray.

Control the position of your splatters by protecting those areas where paint is not required by covering them with scrap paper.

Dabbing and sponging

It's good to experiment. Sponges, screwed-up paper, tissue and even the ends of sticks all make interesting and different marks

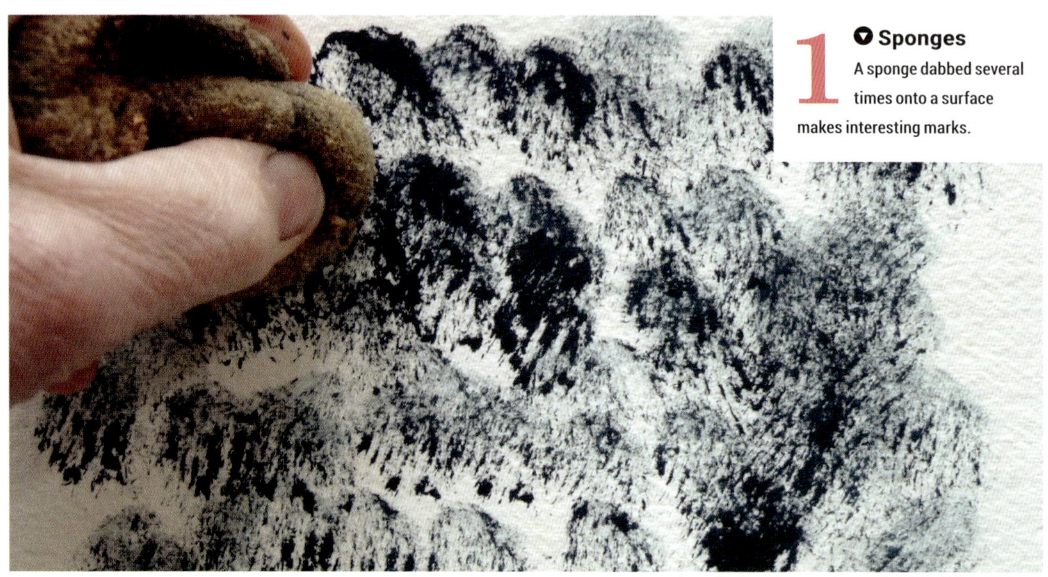

1 ❍ **Sponges**
A sponge dabbed several times onto a surface makes interesting marks.

2 ❍ **Combine for texture**
The background was painted first, in yellow and orange to represent the sky and foreground colours in the landscape. The foreground was dabbed onto the dried paper. The distant hills were added with a square, flat, acrylic brush.

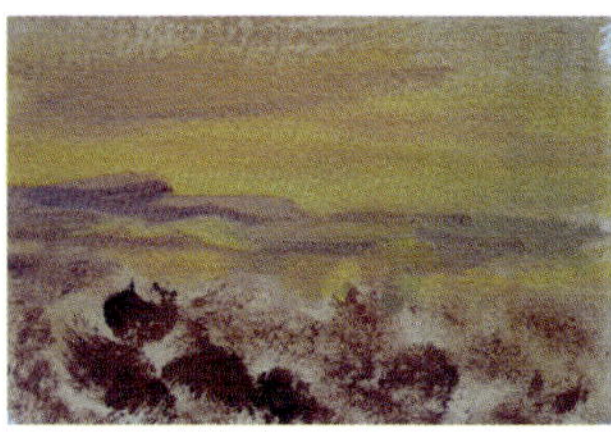

3 ❍ **Suggestive shapes**
Dabbing with the sponge onto prepainted and dried paper has been used to create the sense of flowers. Stalks were added later with a pointed acrylic brush.

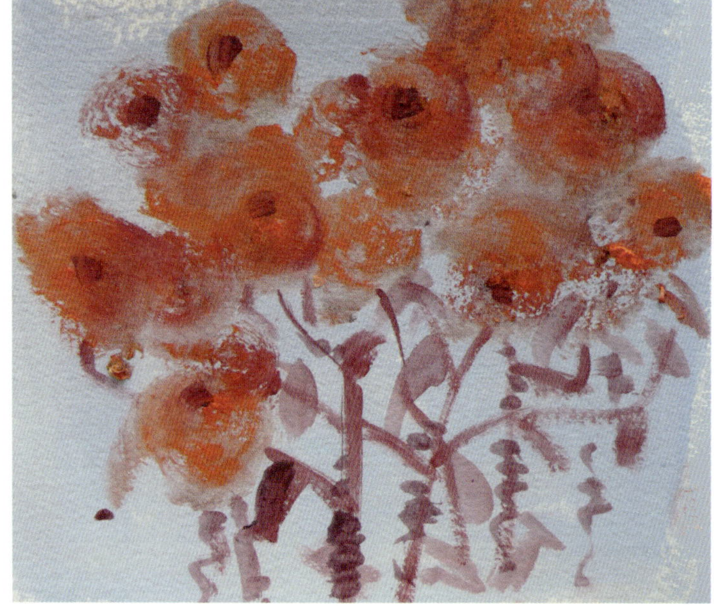

Using a palette knife

Discover how to achieve a thick, plastery impasto look

1 ⬦ **Choose your weapon**
Palette knives come in different sizes and shapes. What you use depends on the size of surface, and the marks you wish to make. It is advisable to work on primed board or canvas. These are firm and substantial, and hence won't tear with the weight of the paint. If you do work on paper, pre-priming with white or coloured acrylic or gesso reduces the absorbency.

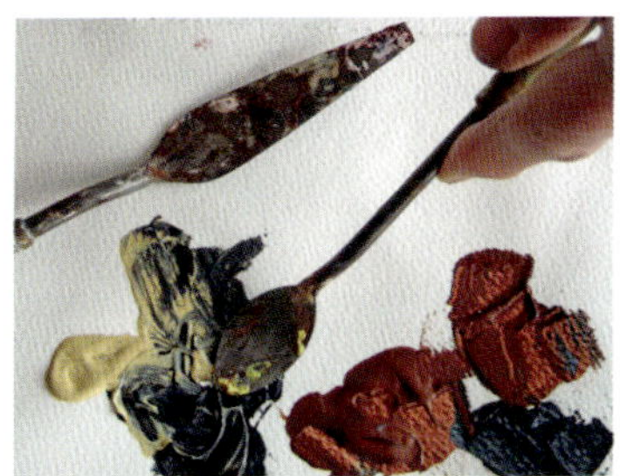

2 ⬦ **Create depth**
Using various paint mixtures of tree bark colours, an effect can be created by plastering on the paint in the appropriate directions.

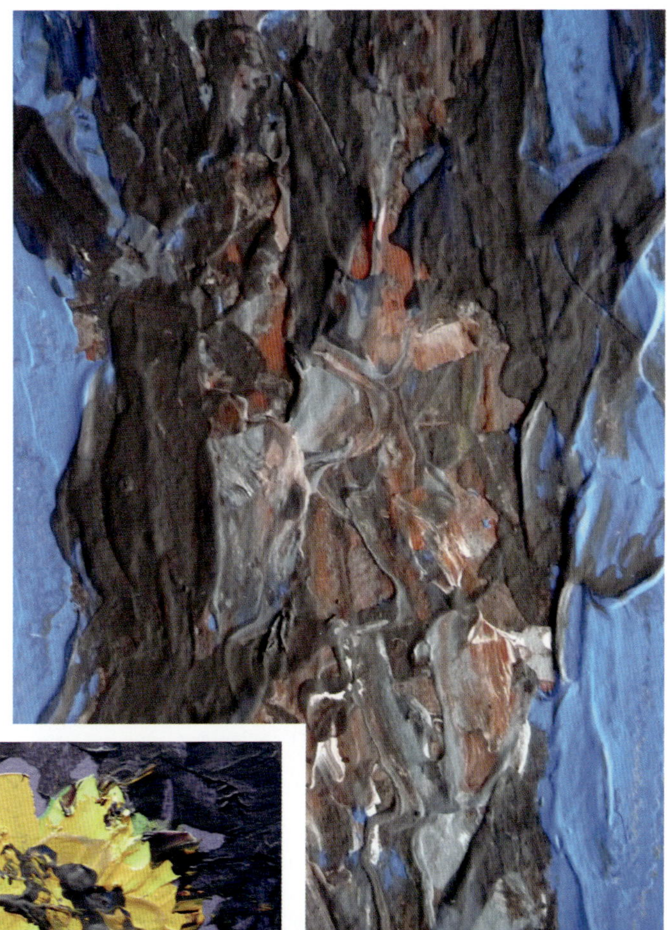

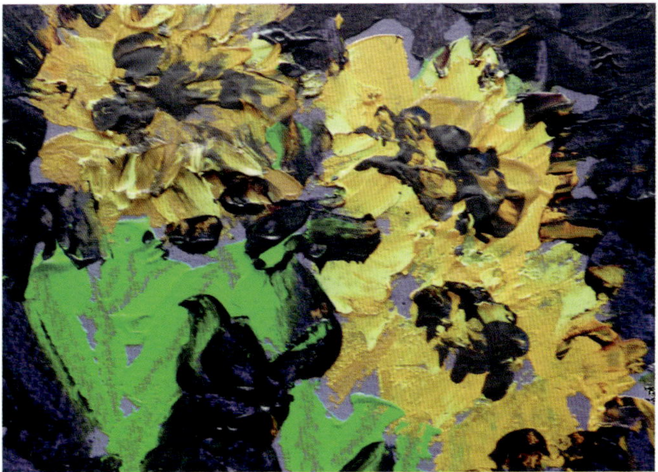

3 ⬦ **Thick application**
Using a triangular knife in the appropriate direction and with appropriate colours, a thick, impasto effect of flower petals can be achieved in a few swift movements.

Detailing

There are different ways to add detail to your painting

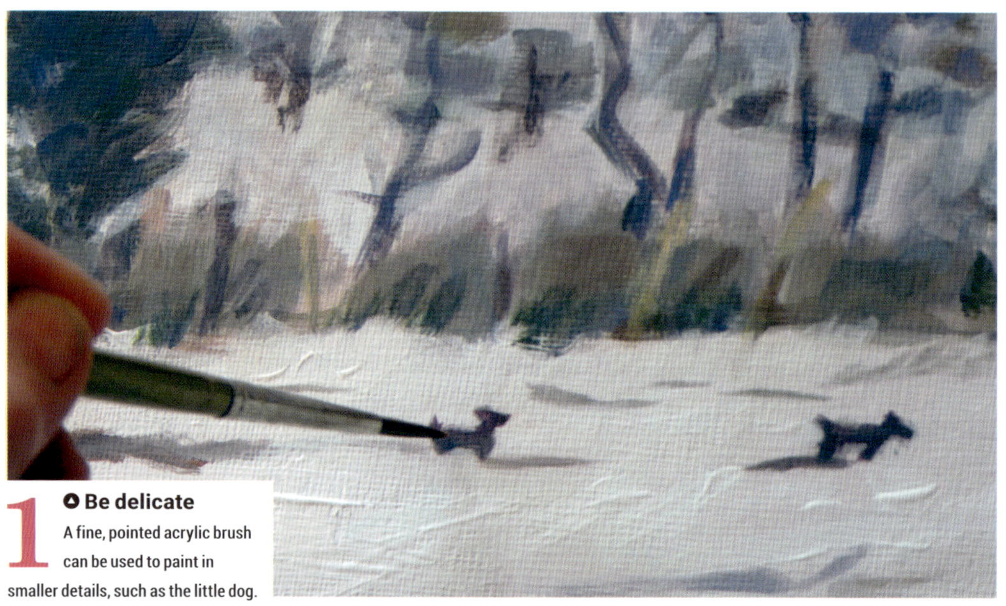

1 ⚬ Be delicate

A fine, pointed acrylic brush can be used to paint in smaller details, such as the little dog.

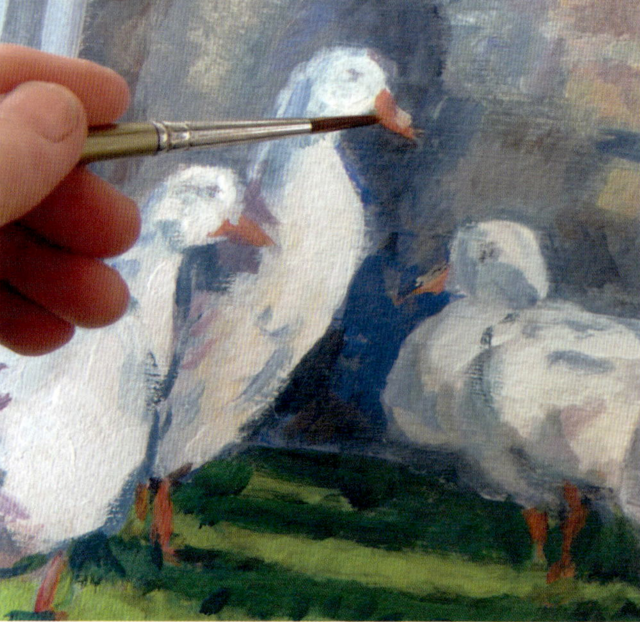

2 ⚬ Soft touches

Here the geese beaks are added with a similar small, pointed brush.

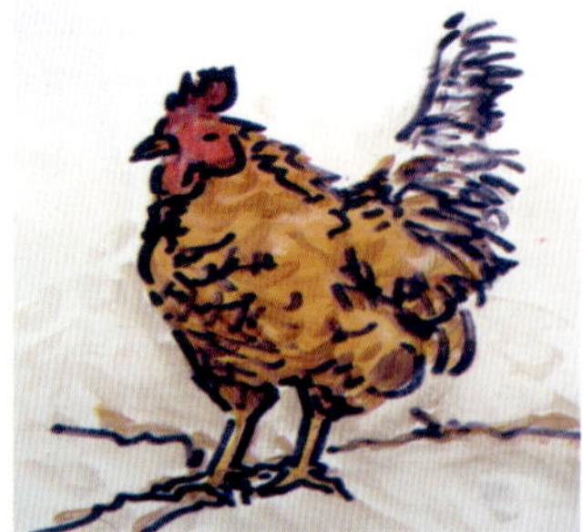

3 ⚬ Combine mediums

Alternatively, an ink pen could be used to add details and more information to a painting. Dipper pens and acrylic ink, or different types of markers could all be used. In this instance a chunky permanent ink marker was used.

Thinning

Discover how to use thin, diluted paint to create a transparent, watercolour appearance

1 ○ Moist surfaces

In this example, the paper was sponged first to make it stay wet longer and enable the paint to drift. On the damp paper, soft clouds and blue-green tree shapes were washed over the paper. When dry, these could be painted over with transparent glazes. They could also be subsequently covered or amended with opaque paint.

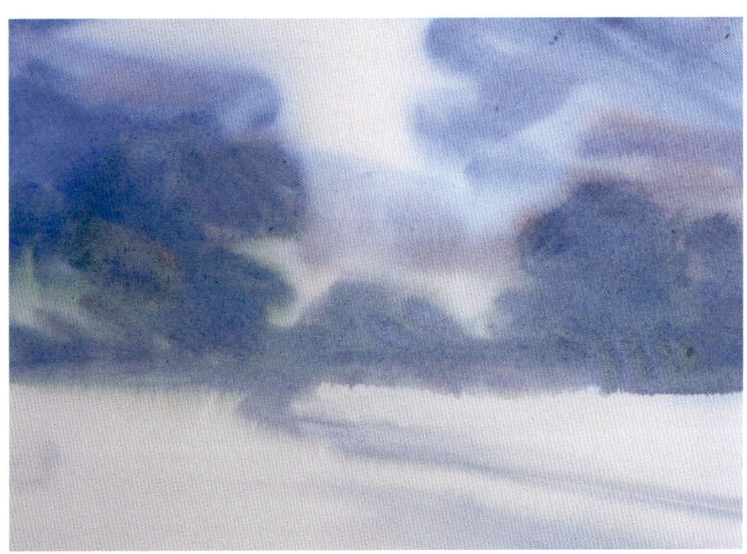

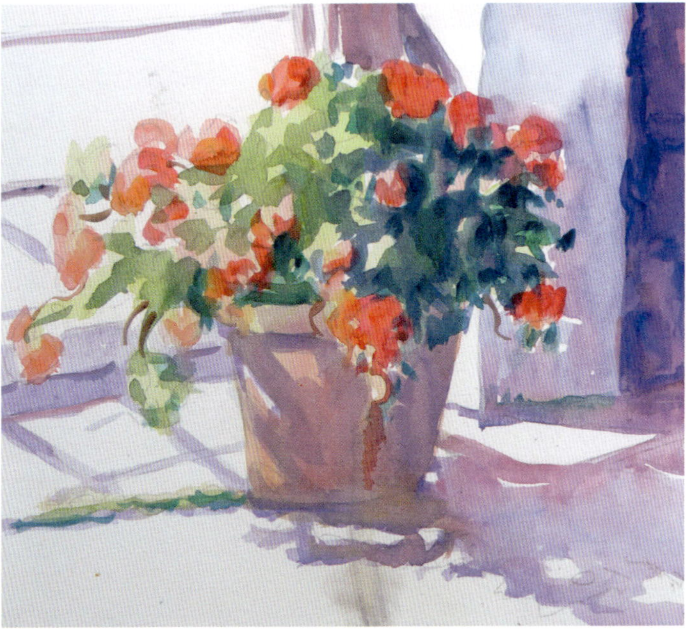

2 ○ Mimic mediums

Thinned transparent colours and glazes used in this particular painting give the scene a watercolour appearance.

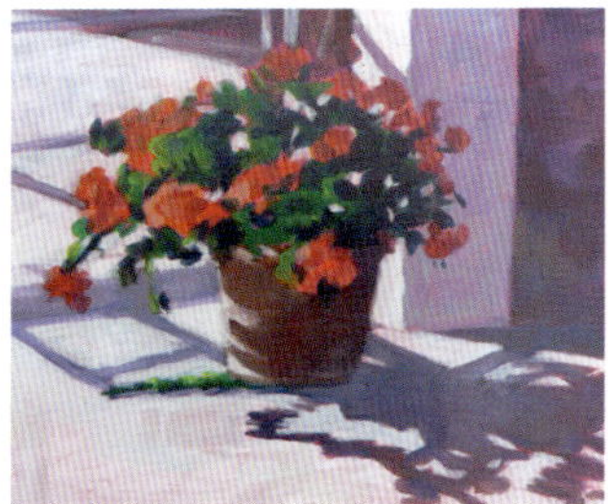

3 ○ Deepen the shadow

Here the painting was started with thin paint, and then subsequently amended using thick, opaque colour.

Glazing

Find out how glazing is an excellent technique to protect and even out the colours in your painting, or even to modify your original colours

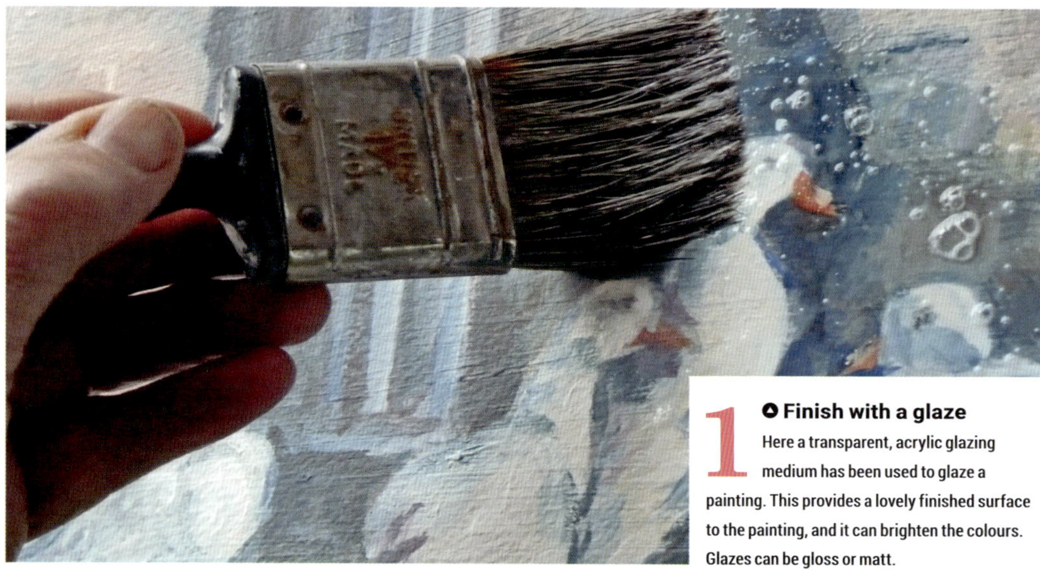

1 ◐ Finish with a glaze
Here a transparent, acrylic glazing medium has been used to glaze a painting. This provides a lovely finished surface to the painting, and it can brighten the colours. Glazes can be gloss or matt.

2 ◑ Colour effects
Used thinly and transparently, dried acrylic paint can be over layered with subsequent colours to change the underlying colour. Here we have yellow on red, creating orange, blue on red, orange and yellow, creating purple and green.

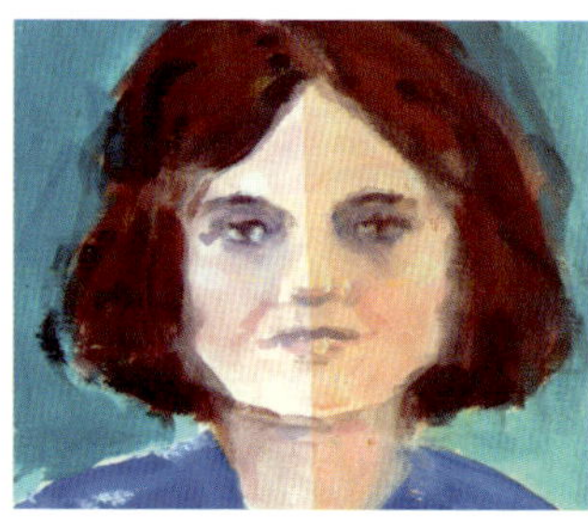

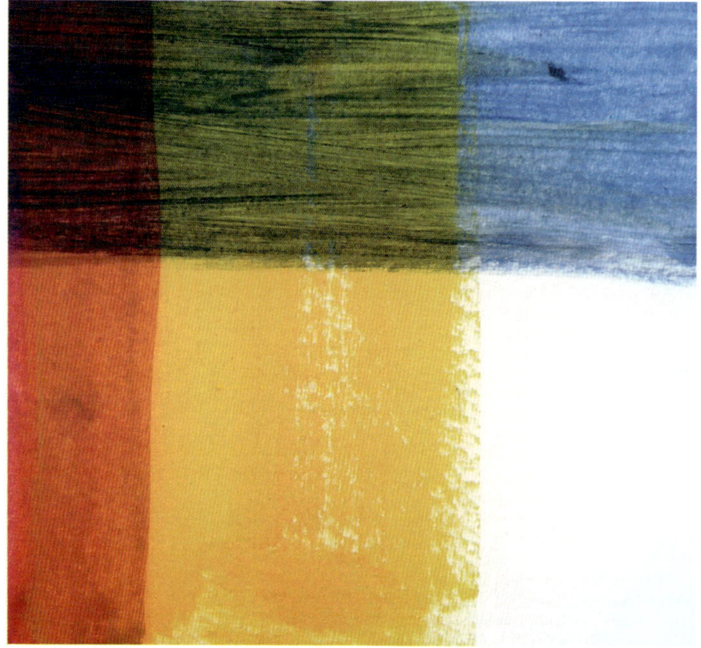

3 ◐ Warm the painting
Here a glaze of a warm skin colour has been thinly painted over a portrait, changing the skin tones.

Blending

It can be difficult with acrylics, but interactive paints can be used to allow more time for blending and experimenting

1 **◗ Blend it out**
Traditional acrylics dry very fast. This can be a problem if you prefer to work slowly, or if you like to have time to blend the colours, as with traditional oil painting. Interactive paints dry more slowly and can be reopened with water. Here a large brush is used to softly blend slower drying interactive colours together.

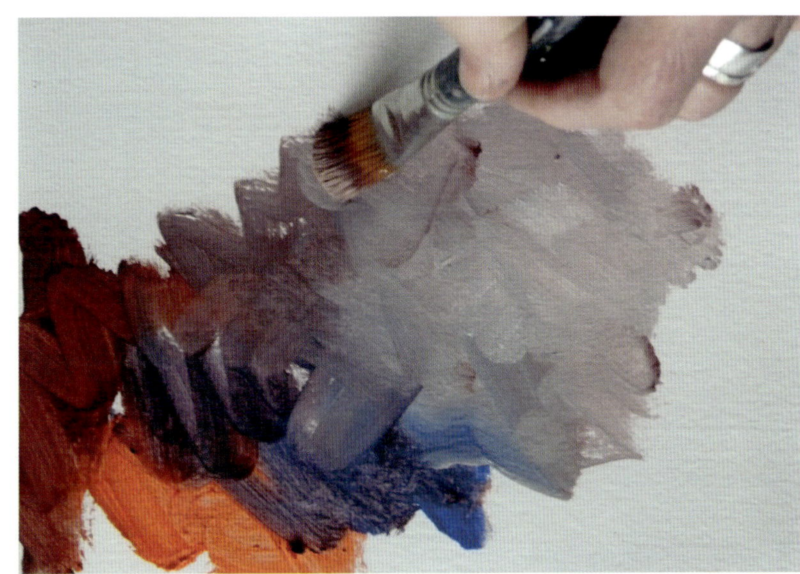

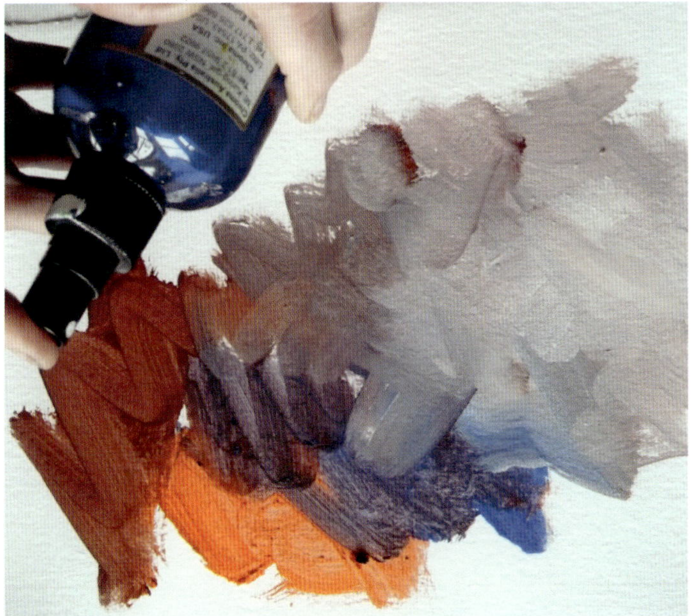

2 **◖ Lengthen drying time**
Water can be sprayed on to the paint to maintain blendability for longer. This is particularly useful for those who need to cover large areas, or require more time.

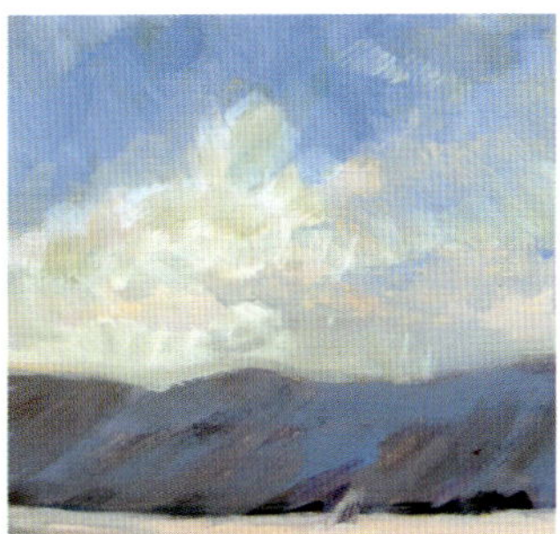

3 **◖ Subtle shades**
Here the colours are softly blended to create the subtle colour changes in the sky.

Lightening and darkening colours

Learn different ways to lighten and darken colours

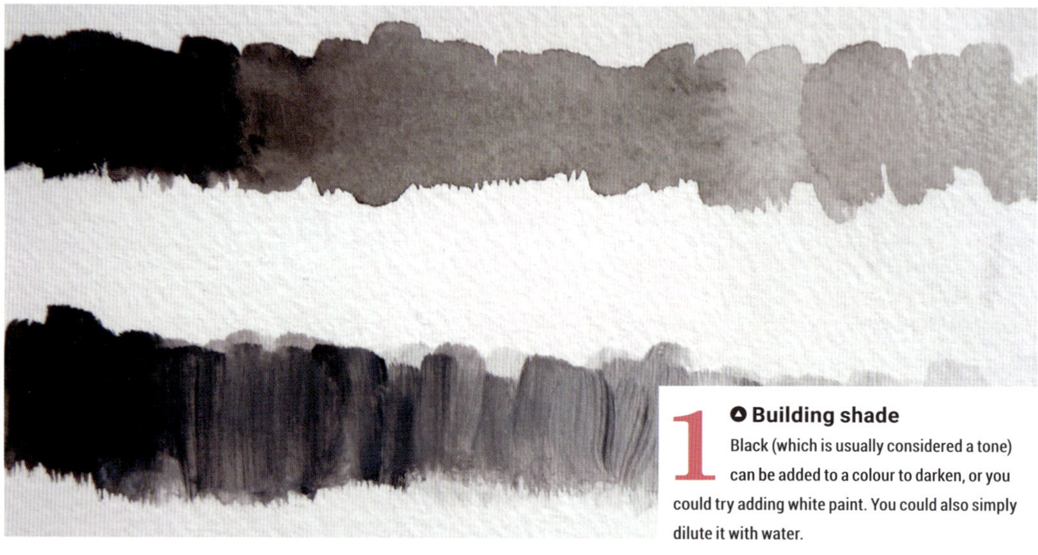

1   ⊙ **Building shade**
Black (which is usually considered a tone) can be added to a colour to darken, or you could try adding white paint. You could also simply dilute it with water.

2   ⊙ **Blend without black**
A bright, light yellow is darkened here with the addition of green, then the addition of blue. It can be useful for trees.

3   ⊙ **Natural tones**
Bright yellow is darkened here with the addition of red, and then darkened with the addition of purple. It can be useful for some flowers.

Experimenting

Acrylics are very versatile and combine well with other mediums

1 ▶ **Acrylic backgrounds**
Onto a dry, yellow, acrylic background, the flowers were drawn with chalk pastels and the background scribbled over loosely in blue chalk pastel. The original acrylic background could be used as a base colour for a quick pastel sketch, or used for a more completed pastel painting. Similarly, acrylics can form a dry base layer for other mediums like oils, or oil pastels.

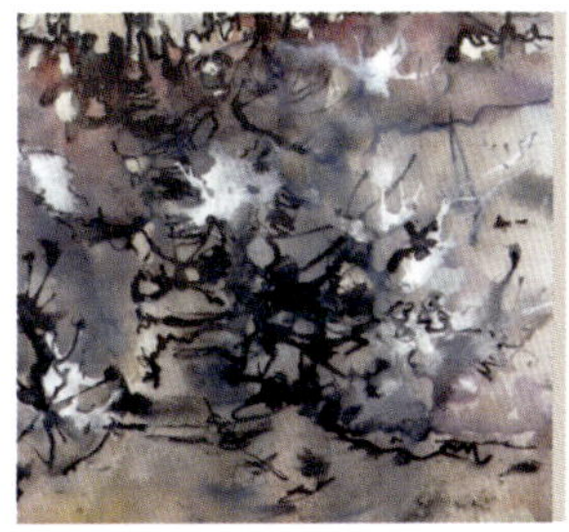

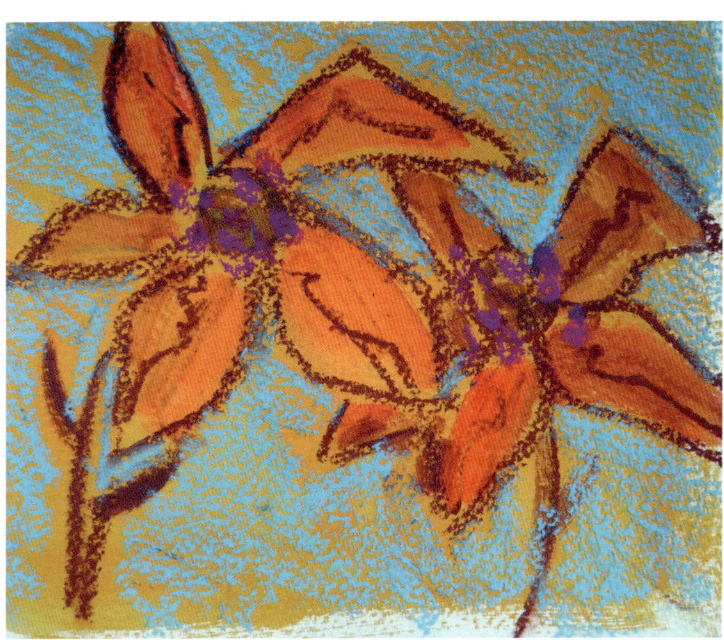

2 ▲ **Combine techniques**
Diluted, watery, acrylic paint was washed over dampened paper in a similar method to watercolour. Then black and white acrylic inks or diluted paint were dribbled or drawn onto the paper using pens and sharpened or blunt sticks. This creates interesting textures and colours.

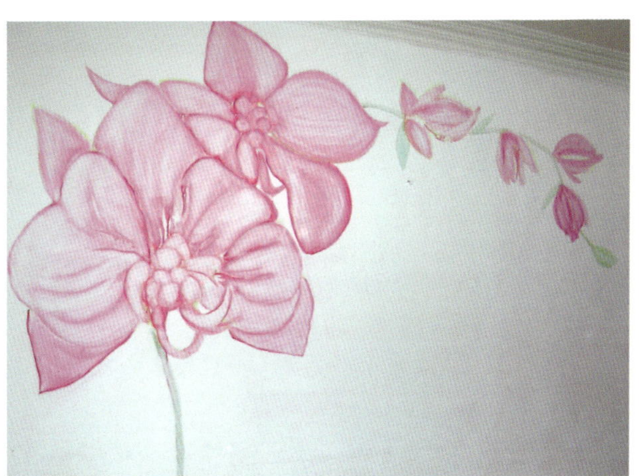

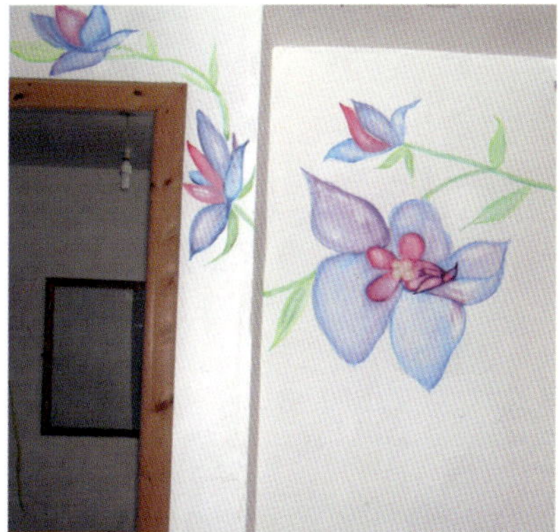

3 ◀ **The world is your canvas**
Murals can be fun. In the example a mixture of small and large ordinary household painting brushes and acrylic paints were used by my daughter to paint the large flower murals onto her walls. The walls had already been painted with ordinary, matt white, household emulsion paint.

Express your abstract scenes with texture

David Body describes how he paints colourful, expressive landscapes with layered acrylics and emulsion on canvas

When I create my paintings, they're all about colour, composition and memory of a place, rather than a faithful representation of somewhere. I like to have fun and use paint in a decorative way. When painting scenes like the one in this workshop, I tend to use houses for a compositional affect rather than reality, and I always paint places I know well – working this way gives me the freedom to be flexible. I find if I work from drawings or photos of places I get bogged down with the detail and realism.

I tend to reduce the landscape to a pattern of flat coloured blocks, so I can then play around with the composition, size and tone in an almost abstract way. Tone is also used to flatten out the painting by putting the darkest colours furthest away, and placing the lighter ones in the foreground. This flattens out the houses, removing perspective and making them all the same size. The opposite to what would be seen in real life!

I paint with heavy body acrylics and emulsion paints, which I get mixed for me as the colours are not readily available in the standard range. I start by laying out a basic colour palette of white, Yellow Ochre, Phthalo Blue (red hue), Cadmium Red, Alizarin Crimson, a mixed cyan, a mixed mauve emulsion paint (satin finish) and black. Sometimes I add Cadmium Yellow Deep and Chrome Green, too. I also use tester paint pots as they give ready-mixed clean colours, ideal for the underpainting.

The canvases I use are ready made and pre-primed and I give these a coat of flame-red matt emulsion for the background to give the painting a good colour key overall. This also means you can leave accidental areas showing through the painting to good effect.

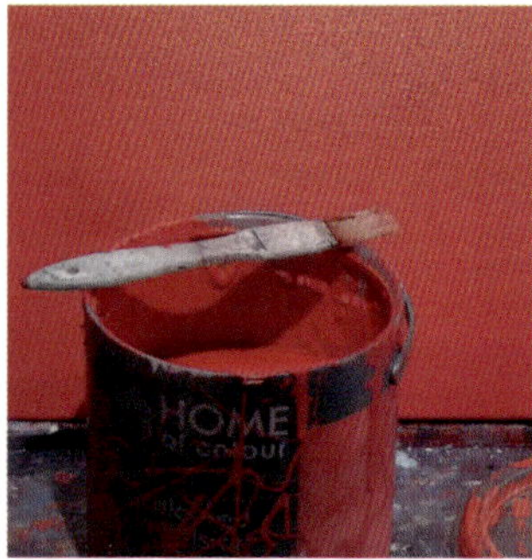

1 ❯ The first drawing

After the background has dried, it's time to paint the initial drawing. I do this using black paint, and use a fairly worn and pointed hog brush to lay out the outlines and composition. I also include some details, such as doors and windows on the houses.

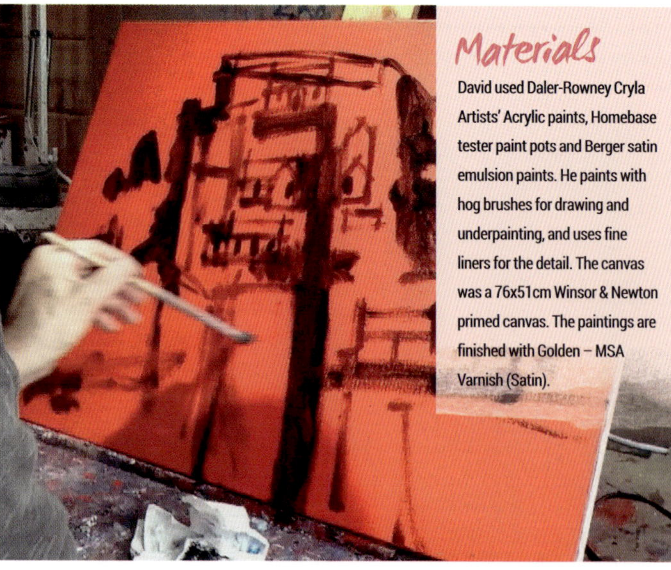

Materials

David used Daler-Rowney Cryla Artists' Acrylic paints, Homebase tester paint pots and Berger satin emulsion paints. He paints with hog brushes for drawing and underpainting, and uses fine liners for the detail. The canvas was a 76x51cm Winsor & Newton primed canvas. The paintings are finished with Golden – MSA Varnish (Satin).

2 ● The underpainting

I now add in the colour, as well as finalise the composition. I use a round hog brush and paint quickly. For the houses and finer details, I use smaller synthetic brushes. The same colours are used in different places over the canvas to give unity and balance.

Splat!

Use cardboard boxes to build a splash booth. It will help keep all the mess in one place (rather than all over you!).

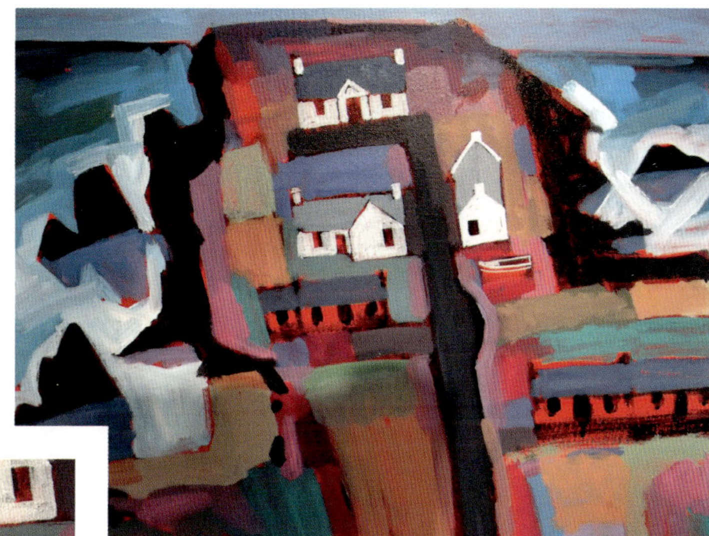

"Leave areas of canvas showing through the painting to good effect"

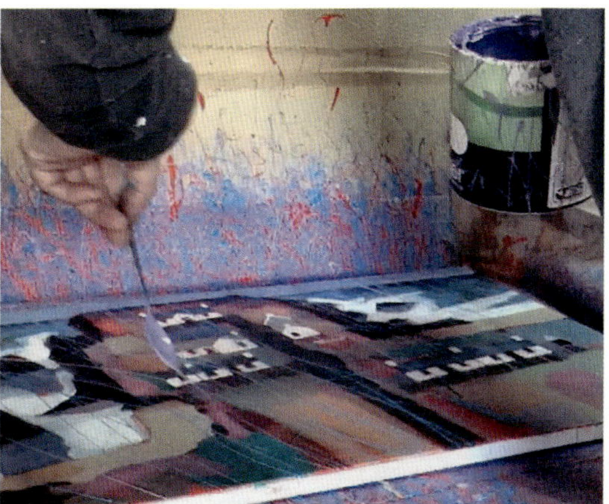

3 ● Texturing

Through pottery I've developed skills in working with texture and fluid glazes… techniques that I have also used in my painting. My trailing started off as pure texture using a grey paint on its own and was discovered by accident. I now use three main colours: cyan, mauve and red. I use a teaspoon to trail these paints.

4 ● Trail, flick and blot

The cyan and mauve colours are satin Berger paints I get mixed because they trail easily. However, the red is stiffer and more flicked about rather than trailed. It's a random process and any larger blobs are sponged off, as these would become too dominant. I work from top to bottom mostly, but I will use newspaper to mask off areas (such as the sky), and repeat the process over that area in a different direction.

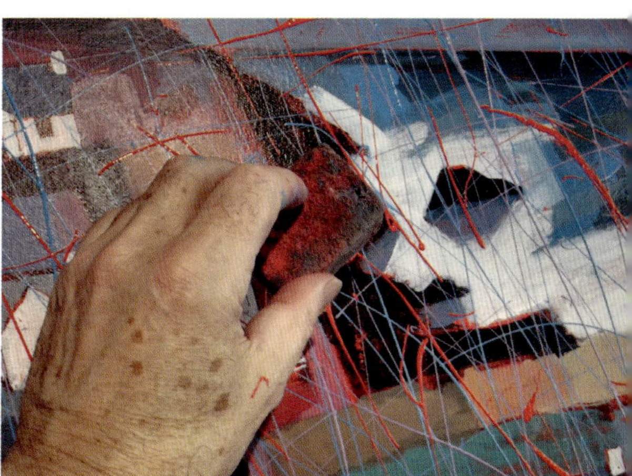

5 ▸ Work over the texture

I now do a second layer of painting – mostly with a palette knife where possible – using heavy body acrylics by themselves or with a mix of emulsion. The paint can be applied and then scraped back to reveal the textures underneath. Accidental areas of background colour are left showing through. The small unifying flashes of red give the painting warmth. I do not paint up to the edges.

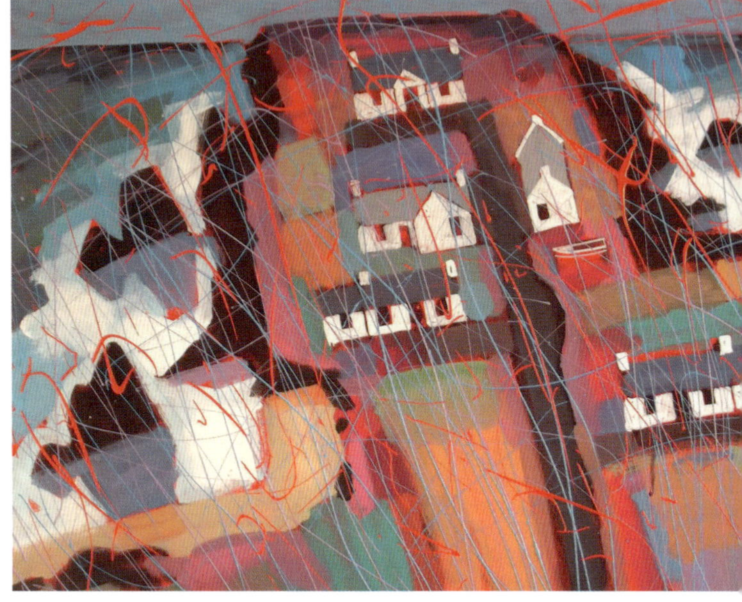

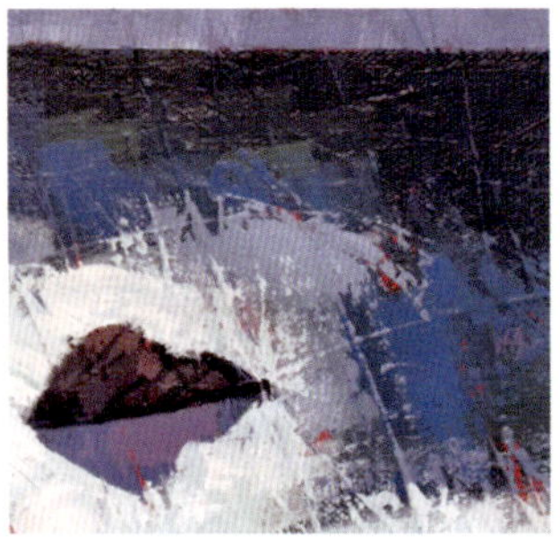

6 ◕ Layering colours

I now build up layers of paint, skimming them over one another to highlight the texture rather than making brush or palette knife marks. This offers a random texture that adds movement to the surface. To me, this suggests elements such as moving water, grass or wind and rain moving over the landscape. I am an impatient painter, so I use a hairdryer to speed up the drying process.

7 ◉ From dark to light

The red background darkens the initial underpainting, so even the same colour applied again will appear lighter. As the colours are built up, I work from dark to light. This brings out the texture to its best affect. The layers can be either a lighter version of the same colour or something completely different depending on what I'm trying to achieve or suggest.

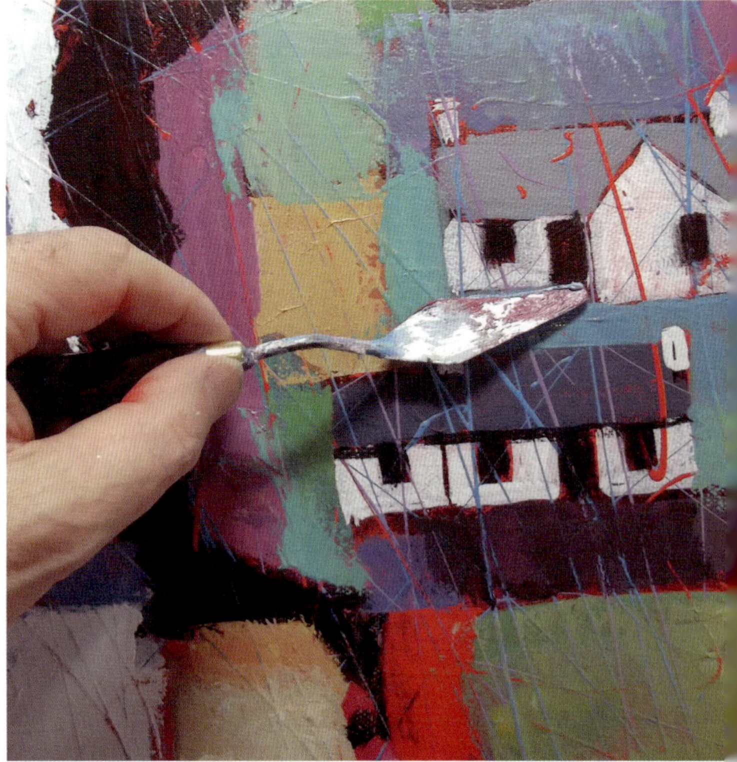

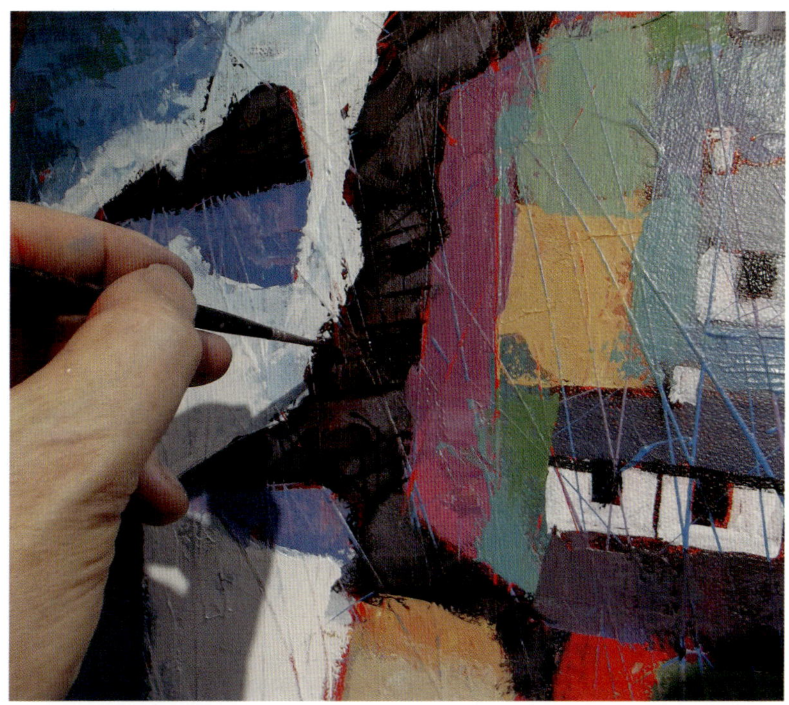

8 ▶ The detail

I paint as much as I can with a palette knife but for fine lines, such as the rock cracks, the seagulls and windows and doors in the houses, I use a very fine liner brush. These behave like a pen as they hold a lot of paint that is fed into a fine point.

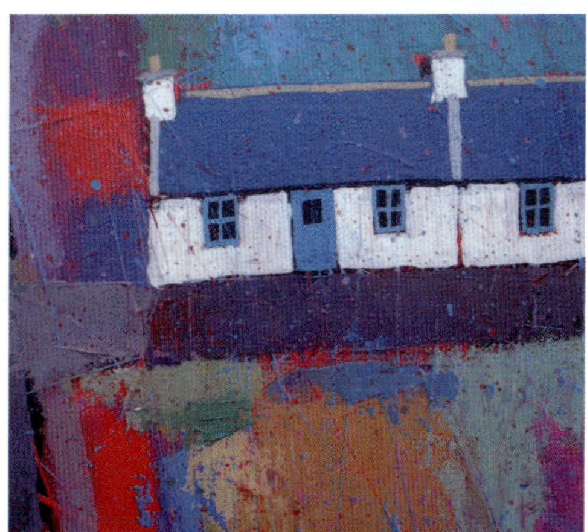

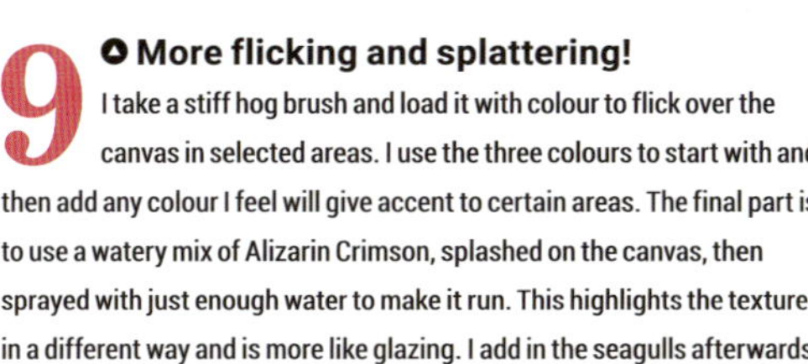

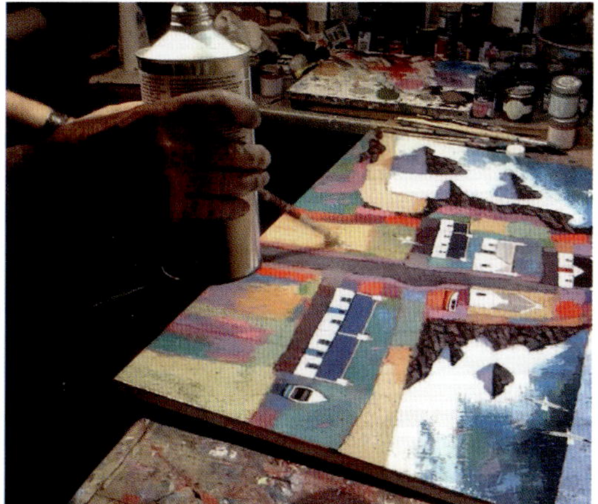

9 ▲ More flicking and splattering!

I take a stiff hog brush and load it with colour to flick over the canvas in selected areas. I use the three colours to start with and then add any colour I feel will give accent to certain areas. The final part is to use a watery mix of Alizarin Crimson, splashed on the canvas, then sprayed with just enough water to make it run. This highlights the texture in a different way and is more like glazing. I add in the seagulls afterwards.

10 ▲ Varnish

I find Golden MSA UV satin spirit varnish is the best for my work. It suggests on the tin that it should be thinned, but I get the best results using it as it comes. It needs to be used in a well-ventilated area. My studio used to be in the house, but because of the fumes, I now have a studio in the garden that was built last summer. This varnish also has UV-filtering properties to protect colours from fading.

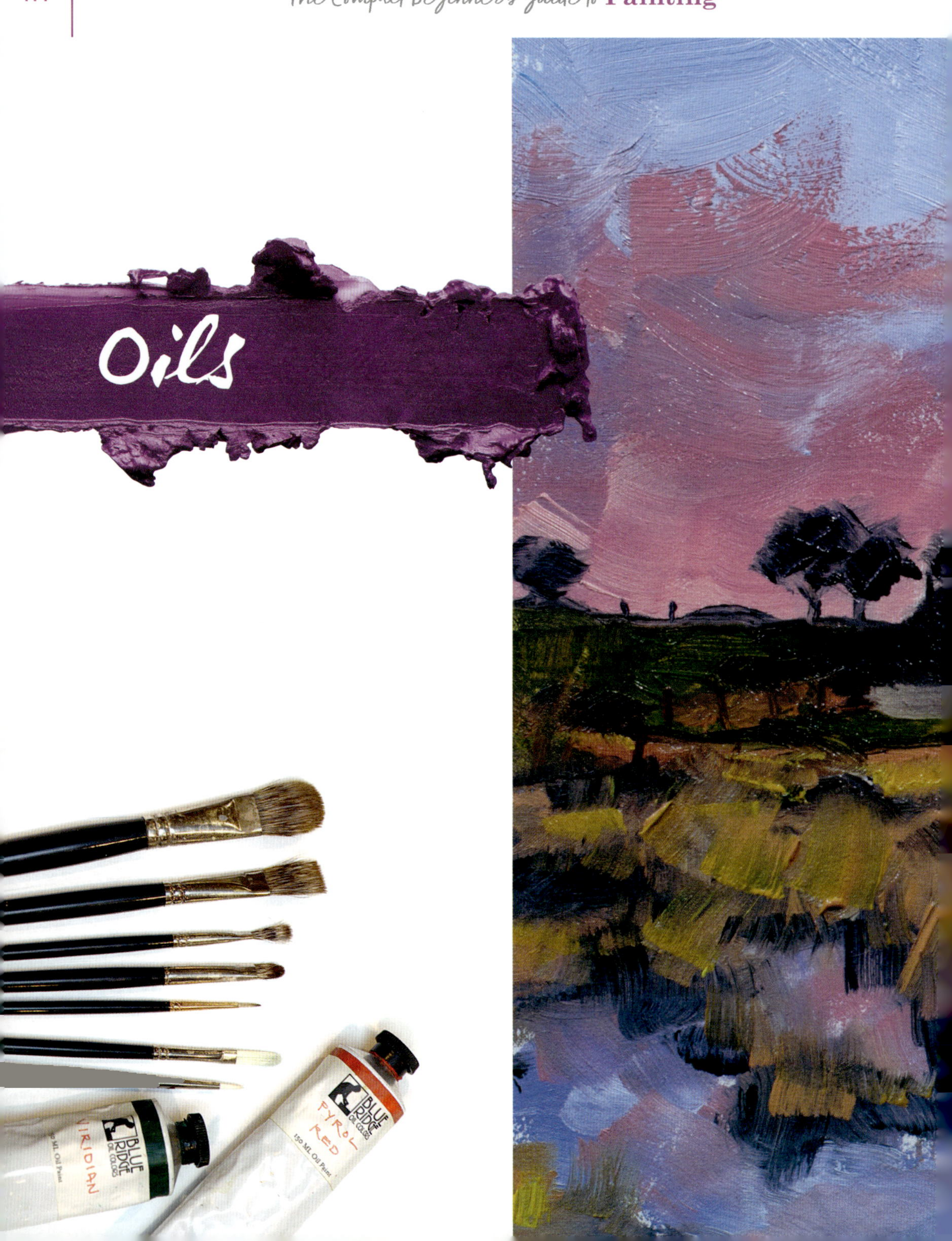

Oils

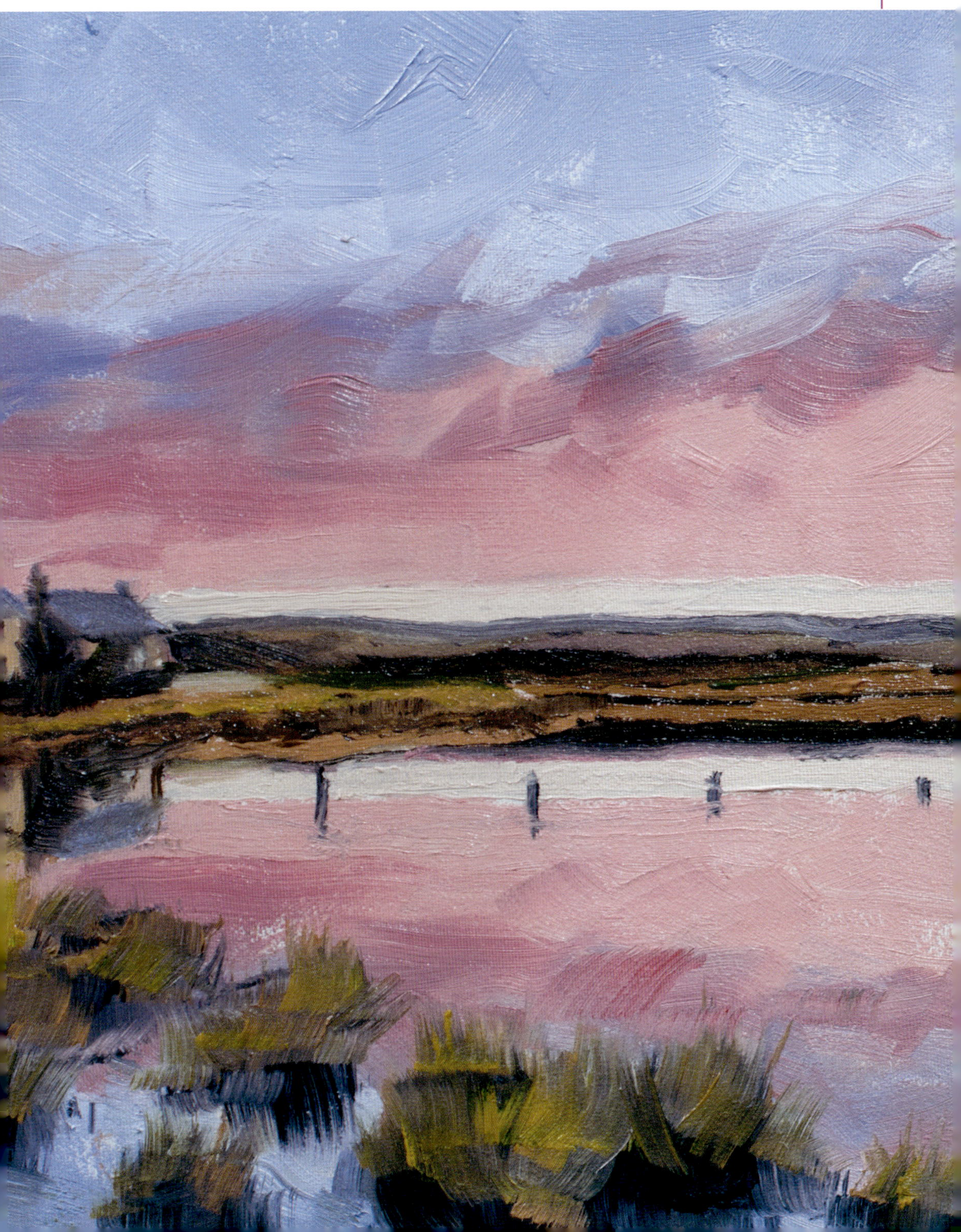

Get started with oils

In this tutorial, **Howard Lyon** explains how to get started in painting with oils, from choosing the right paint colours and brushes, to pulling together an essential kitbag

There's an undeserved mystique around oil painting that has put up some intimidating barriers for some artists wanting to use this wonderful medium. I hope to remove those concerns and provide a basic foundation of knowledge to help you get started.

Oil paint is pigment bound in a drying (siccative) oil. The most common is linseed oil extracted from flax seeds, but you'll also find paint bound in walnut, safflower or other oils. The pigments are generally the same as those found in watercolours, pastels and acrylics. Oil paints offer a richness of colour and its surface allows the creation of beautiful textures. You can paint thick or thin, directly or use glazes. Oils can be used on paper, wood, metal, plastic, canvas and many other surfaces.

If you're just getting started, don't get overwhelmed. Be patient with yourself and recognise that it'll take a little time to get the hang of this beautiful medium. Don't overcomplicate it, either.

To begin we'll go over the key materials needed for you to get started. Most art materials are sold in at least two grades: student and professional. Whenever possible, purchase pro-grade materials. I find the difference in price is offset because pro materials almost always last longer and the paint goes further.

1 ❂ Spectrum of colours

There are hundreds of colours to choose from, but start with a basic palette that covers the spectrum and will give you a good mix of warm and cool hues. Pro-grade oils will contain more pigment, which will result in more accurate colour mixing, and will be resistant to fading in sunlight.

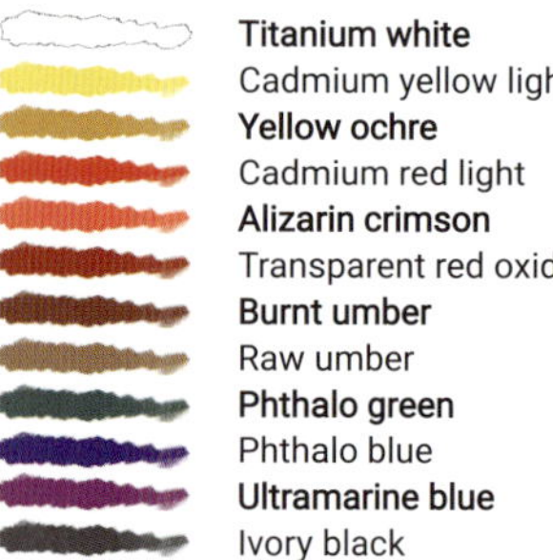

Titanium white
Cadmium yellow light
Yellow ochre
Cadmium red light
Alizarin crimson
Transparent red oxide
Burnt umber
Raw umber
Phthalo green
Phthalo blue
Ultramarine blue
Ivory black

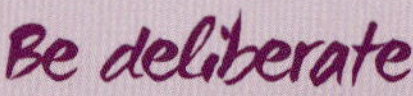

Be deliberate

Every stroke you make should have purpose. What shape, colour and value is the stroke you're trying to make? Stay focused and paint with intent.

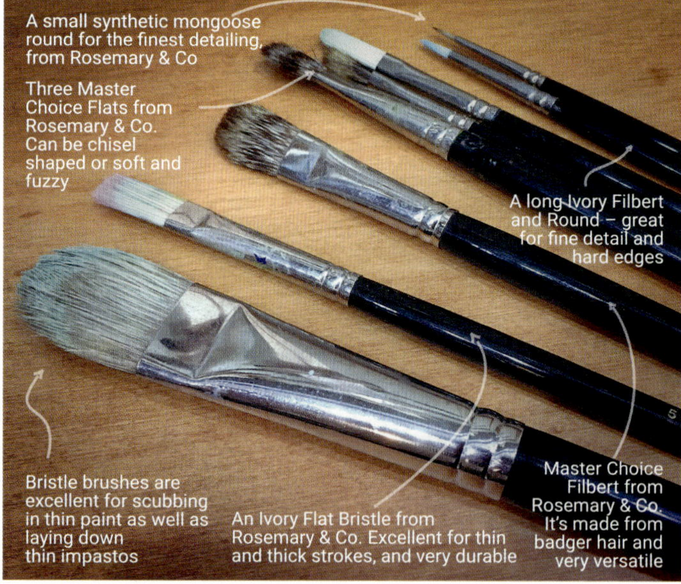

2 ❂ Oil painting requires a variety of brushes

I prefer Rosemary & Co. brushes, but I also recommend Silver Grand Prix and Trekell. Hog bristle brushes are versatile, not terribly expensive and allow for a variety of applications. Finer-haired brushes, both natural and synthetic, can give you an even smoother finish and make very fine detail possible.

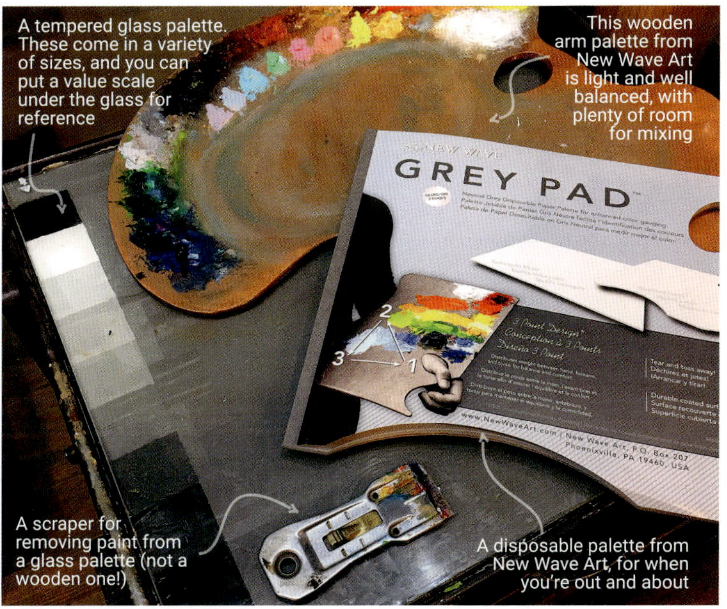

A tempered glass palette. These come in a variety of sizes, and you can put a value scale under the glass for reference

This wooden arm palette from New Wave Art is light and well balanced, with plenty of room for mixing

A scraper for removing paint from a glass palette (not a wooden one!)

A disposable palette from New Wave Art, for when you're out and about

3 ◖ Choose a palette for your paint

You'll need a palette for your paint. This can be a disposable one, a clean tabletop or a handheld wood palette, or a piece of glass that can be quickly scraped clean. Whatever you use, choose something that's large enough to allow for easy mixing and can be used ergonomically.

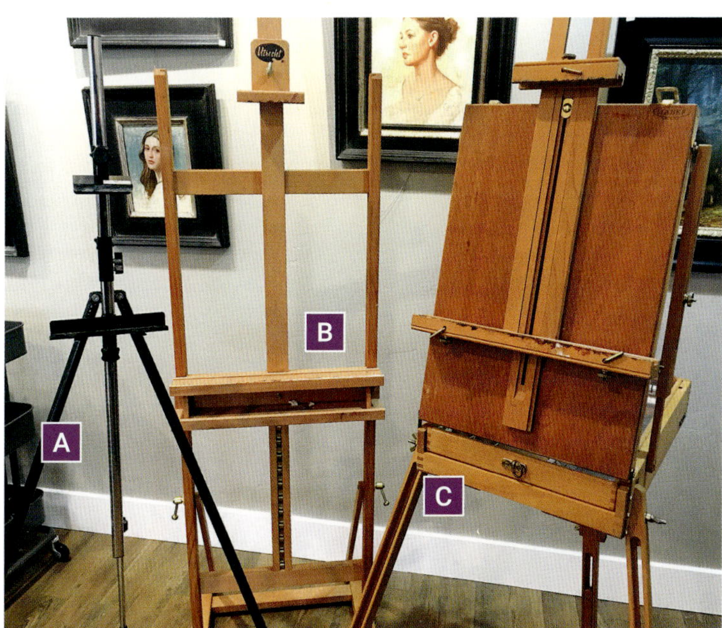

4 ◗ A surface to paint

The most common surfaces to paint on are canvas, linen and wood. You'll need to prime the surface with a gesso or ground to prevent the acids in the paint from contacting it directly. Acrylic gesso is easy to use and can be quickly applied with a brush or roller.

A wood hardboard panel is cheap and smooth, and easy to make

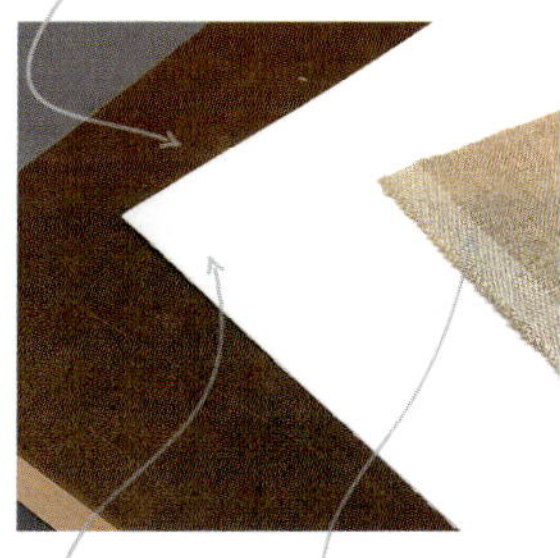

Paper from Arches that has been sized for oil painting

Raw linen before it's been sized or primed. Expensive, but has a beautiful texture, and is strong

5 ◖ A comfortable easel

A solid easel is important so that your work is stable, safe and remains at a good working height while you're painting. You can purchase small, metal tripod-style easels that can be used sitting or standing, or consider a folding wood easel, or larger studio models that are meant to remain in situ.

A Inexpensive, metal, tripod-style easel. Easy to carry and store, and can be used either when sitting or standing

B H-frame style easel for studio use. Broad price range and comes in various sizes

C French-style field easel. Limited canvas sizes, but is versatile and portable

Arrange and mix oils

Let's get started by covering how to get paint out on to your palette. I personally like to arrange my colours from the most intense shades to the less intense, grouped into warm and cool colours.

I've seen students squeeze out colour randomly and it becomes tricky to keep things organised as the painting progresses. Choose a layout, stick with it and you won't have to think about where your colours are.

I'll mix up a pile (or nut) of paint and make adjustments to the pile by mixing colour into a portion of it. If you remix the whole pile it can get away from you and then the whole nut is wasted. For example, if I have a base skin tone that I need to make cooler or warmer, I'll mix into the left and right sides of it, saving some of the original colour. You will find that your colours will stay cleaner if you can mix with two or three colours instead of six or seven. It also helps to reduce the intensity of your colours by mixing in a grey of the same value, instead of mixing in a complement or adding black.

In summary, mix until you have the right colour. Check it, adjust it and then start painting when you're happy.

1 ◑ Arrange your paint on the palette

It isn't critical how you arrange colours, as long as you're consistent so that you know where your colours are. Some artists pair warm and cool versions of each colour or arrange them in a ROYGBIV string with black and white at the ends. I recommend keeping things organised and consistent.

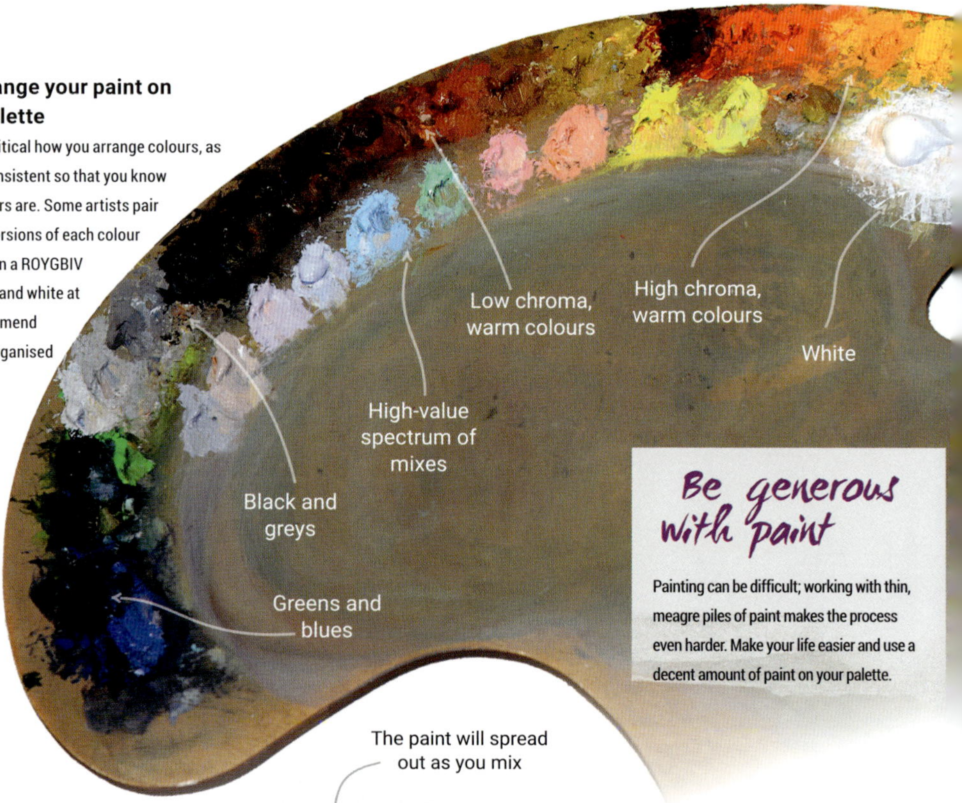

Be generous with paint

Painting can be difficult; working with thin, meagre piles of paint makes the process even harder. Make your life easier and use a decent amount of paint on your palette.

2 ◑ Mix on your palette

Use a palette knife rather than your brush to mix larger paint piles. This will help keep paint out of your brush ferrule (the metal collar that holds the bristles). Keep the mixed paint organised and if you need to, scrape your palette down so you have a clean space to mix colours.

The paint will spread out as you mix

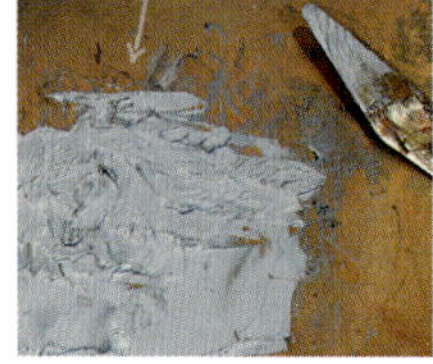

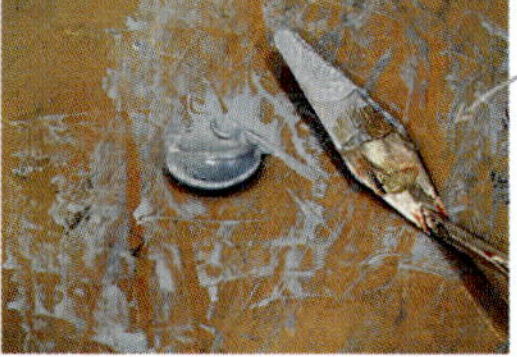

Use your palette knife to scrape the mixed paint back into a neat, compact pile

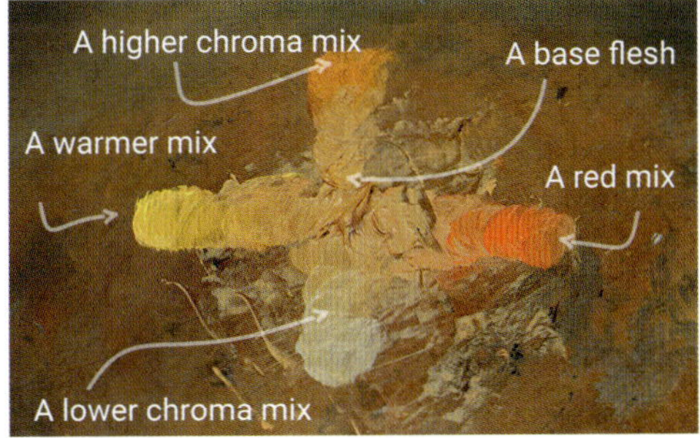

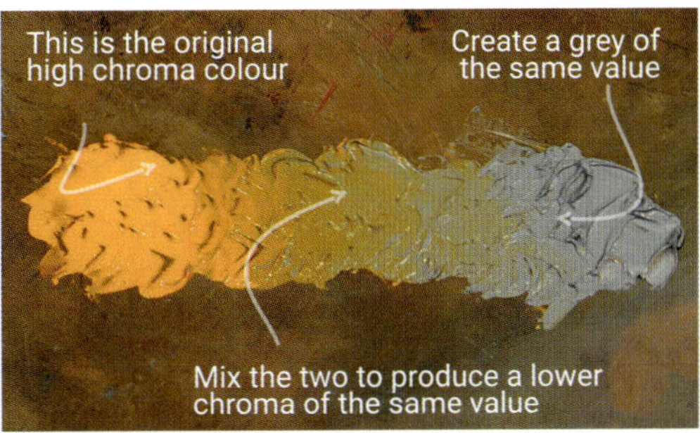

3 ◐ Keep your mixes versatile

When adjusting paint on your palette, mix into a portion of your pile, rather than the whole thing. The benefits are three-fold: it gives you more painting options, provides you with a visual history of your mixes, and if you mess the colour up you don't lose the whole pile.

4 ◐ Reduce the chroma

When painting from life, most colours out of the tube will be too intense. I find that it's best to reduce my colour by mixing in a grey of the same value, rather than mixing in a complement or black. Colours stay cleaner and you can control the values more easily.

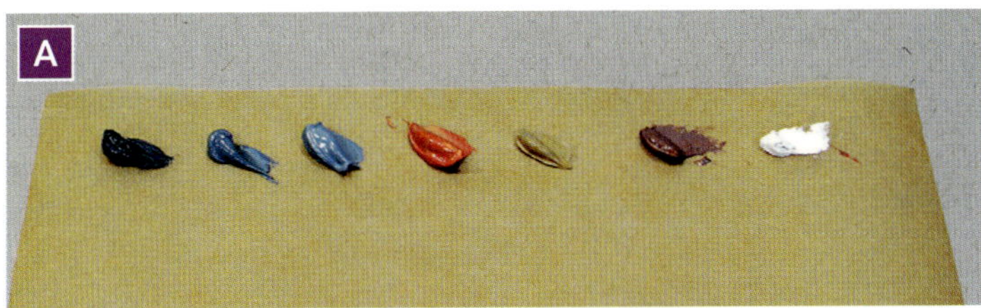

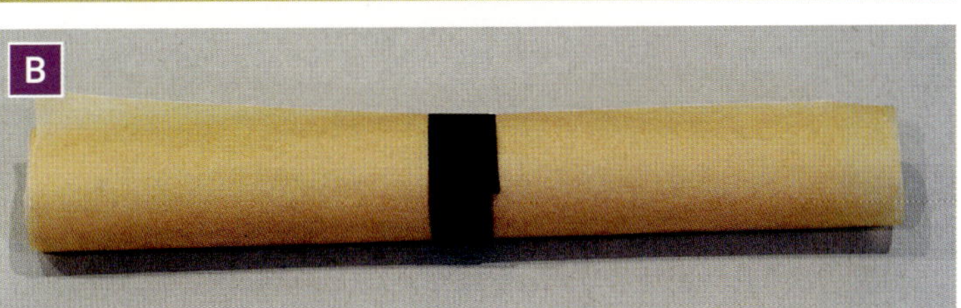

Take your time

Mixing the right colour and value at the beginning of your process makes it less daunting if you want to start over.

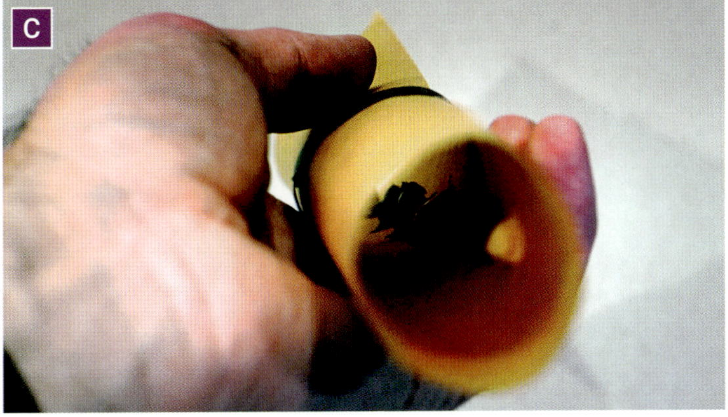

5 ◐ Store your paint

Extend your paint's life by keeping it in a freezer or fridge.

If your palette doesn't fit or space is limited, transfer your paint to wax paper and put all the paint in a row, then roll it up to reduce the amount of space it takes up.

From top to bottom…

A Transfer your paint to one end of the wax paper

B Carefully roll the paper and tape it

C Once rolled, your paint is compact and protected

How to apply oil paints

Oil paint is wonderfully versatile. It can be applied in thick, expressive impastos, or thinned down and used almost like watercolours. It can be brushed or scrubbed, knifed on or scratched out, applied in washes or painted in patches.

There are what seems like an endless variety of mediums and additives you can work with to create different effects. However, you can use oils without adding a medium. Most of my work is done with paint direct from the tube. Some mediums are added to shorten or lengthen drying times; others change the characteristics of the paint. Paint out of the tube is often called stiff or short, and will retain your brush stroke – especially with coarser brushes. If you add fluid medium, such as linseed oil or turpentine, it becomes what's known as long. It won't retain the peaks of the brush strokes, but will level out for a more smooth result.

Paintings are more interesting when you use a variety of techniques when it comes to applying paint. It's another form of contrast that provides variety and complexity in the medium, and it'll add dimension to your final work.

1 ❂ Different brush effects

Depending on what type of brush you use and how hard you press, oil paint can look very different from one stroke to the next. In addition, adding thinner or medium to the paint, as well as changing the angle of the brush, will alter the texture and impact of the mark.

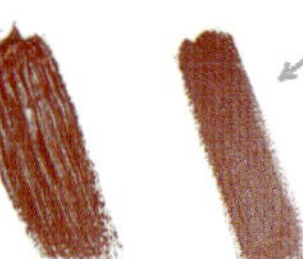

Paint applied thickly with a bristle brush – a 'short' paint stroke. Note its specularity

Paint applied thickly with a synthetic brush

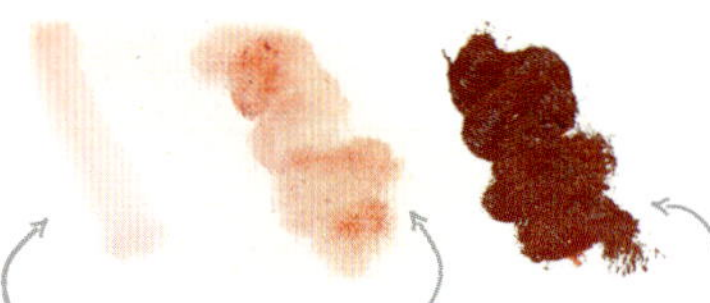

Paint that's thinned with Gamsol and then applied with a synthetic brush

Paint thinned with Gamsol, dabbed on with a bristle brush. Feel of watercolour

Paint applied thickly and then mopped on with a bristle brush

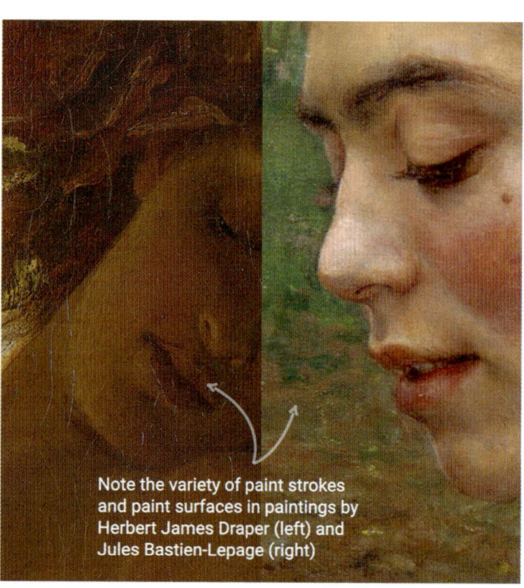

Note the variety of paint strokes and paint surfaces in paintings by Herbert James Draper (left) and Jules Bastien-Lepage (right)

2 ❂ Use palette knives

Palette knives aren't just for mixing paint. In fact, you'll see some knives marketed as 'painting knives'. Really, just use whatever gets the job done. I've used large, plastic putty trowels for creating rocky textures in some larger paintings.

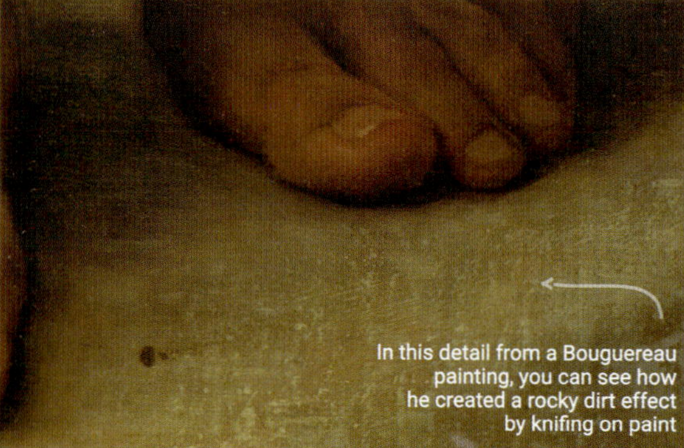

In this detail from a Bouguereau painting, you can see how he created a rocky dirt effect by knifing on paint

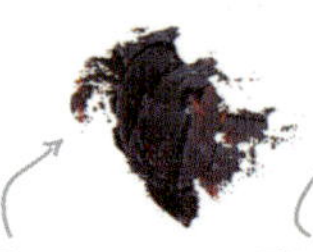

A generous amount of paint applied delicately with a knife

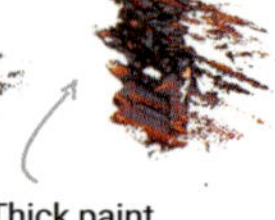

Thick paint applied with a knife by pressing straight down and lifting straight up

Paint scraped across the canvas. Notice how it describes the texture underneath

3 ⏺ Scrape the paint

Removing paint can sometimes be as effective as adding paint. I've used cotton swabs, old brushes with dry paint in them, rags, knives and toothpicks to remove paint for effect. There are also rubber-tipped scrapers sold in art stores that work well to this end.

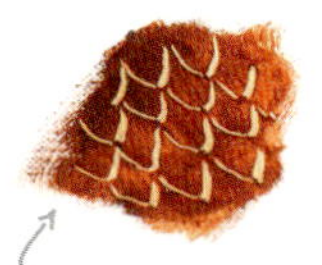

I've used a rubber-tipped colour shaper tool to add a scaly pattern to this paint swatch

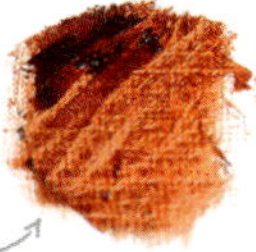

Apply paint and then subsequently scrape it off with a palette knife

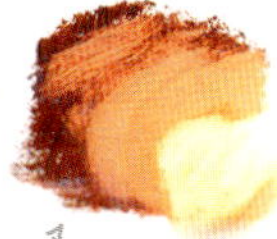

Wipe paint off using a paper towel and with varying pressure

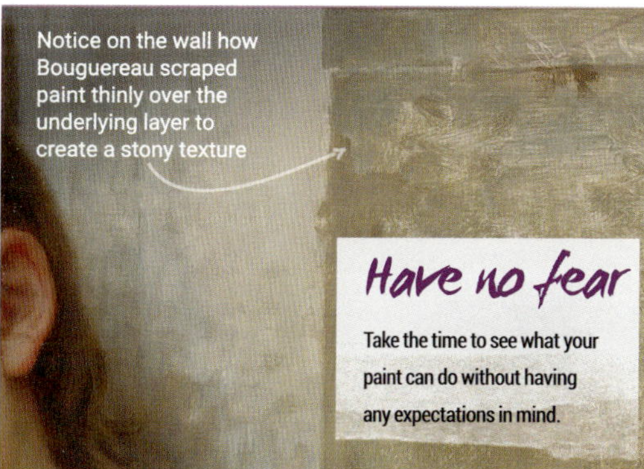

Have no fear

Take the time to see what your paint can do without having any expectations in mind.

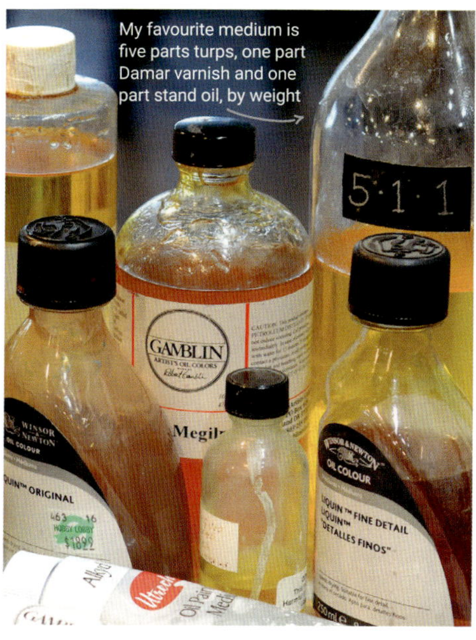

4 ⏶ Different mediums

Don't become overwhelmed by the variety of mediums out there. Here's a photo of some of the painting mediums that I've tried. Enjoy the different effects you can achieve, but don't be afraid to keep things simple or simply to experiment.

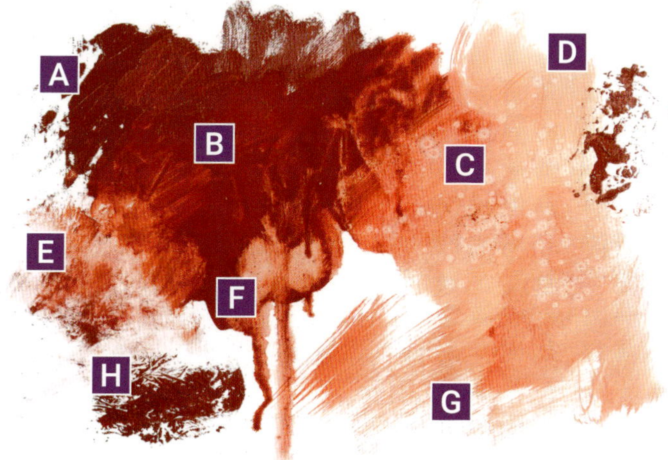

Let paint be paint

Oils are at their best when they're allowed to be paint. Don't work too hard to remove brush strokes and texture. Let the paint be a record of your actions on the canvas.

5 ⏺ Get creative

Don't feel limited to just the tools you find in the art store. In the past I've used tinfoil, plastic wrap, toothbrushes, my breath to blow paint around, fingers and other miscellaneous tools. Norman Rockwell used anything around at the time, including sand, fur and straw to add texture.

A. Paint applied with a palette knife
B. Paint applied with turpentine and a brush
C. Gamsol flicked into a thin film of paint, creating texture
D. Paint applied to tinfoil and then pressed on to the canvas
E. Paint applied with a soft paper towel
F. Paint allowed to drip with turpentine
G. Thin paint wiped on with a cloth
H. Paint applied to a piece of plastic wrap and then pressed to the canvas

Set up and stretch canvas

Cotton canvas, linen, wood panels, copper, paper, glass and stone are just some of the surfaces I've seen oil paintings on. Cotton is a cheap alternative to linen, but is less durable and not as strong.

If you stretch your own canvas then you can save a lot of money. Learning to do so isn't hard, but it takes a little practice to do it consistently. I recommend investing in a good pair of canvas pliers and an electric or pneumatic stapler to achieve consistent quality results.

Canvas, linen and panels are the most commonly available primed and unprimed surfaces. Priming your own can give you a lot of control, and it is another chance to save money and you can create textures that add to your painting.

Unless you're painting completely from imagination or from life, you'll need to gather reference. I'll often make little sculptures or wooden models to photograph. Your reference can never be too good, so go the extra mile.

I use a grid to transfer my drawing to the canvas or panel. Projectors and carbon paper are great tools, as long as they aren't replacements for time spent developing your drawing skills.

Once your drawing is accurate, ink or fix it, so that when you begin painting you won't scrub out all your hard work!

1 ○ Stretch your canvas

Cut your canvas with 2-2.5 inches overlap of the stretcher bars, then place a few staples in the middle of one side and stretch the opposite side. Move to the other sides and repeat. Work from the middles to the corners.

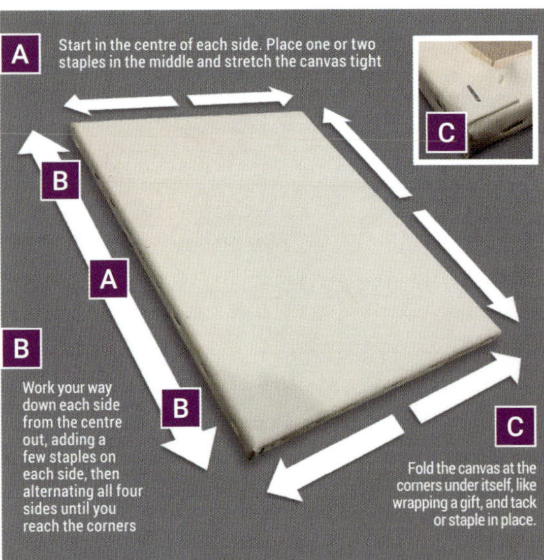

Thicker gessoes can be applied with a spatula. I bought this one on Amazon in the Kitchenware section

Putty and spackling knives are handy for producing a variety of textures when applying heavier acrylic gels and pastes

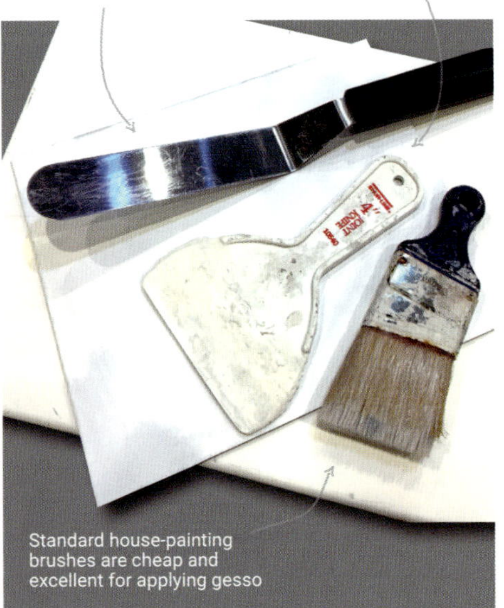

learn your craft

Taking the time to learn about the materials, processes and history of your craft can help you make the best decisions for your own work and give you a confidence boost.

2 ○ Gesso panels and canvas

Oil-based gessoes on canvas require sizing before applying. Rabbit skin glue is traditional, but you can use GAC 100 or PVA size, too. Acrylic gessoes and pastes don't require sizing and can be applied directly. Brushes, rollers and trowels are all useful for gessoing.

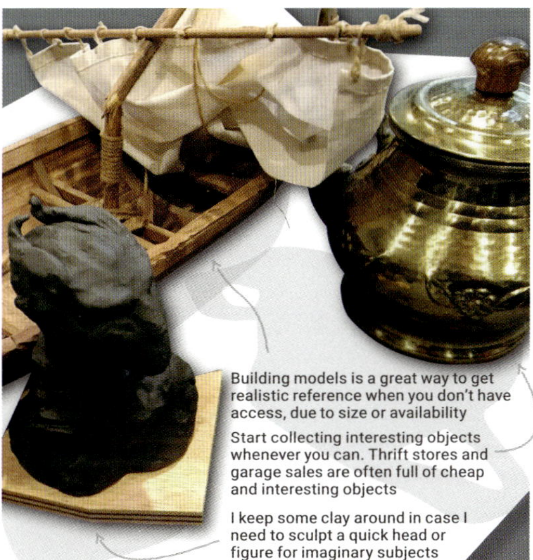

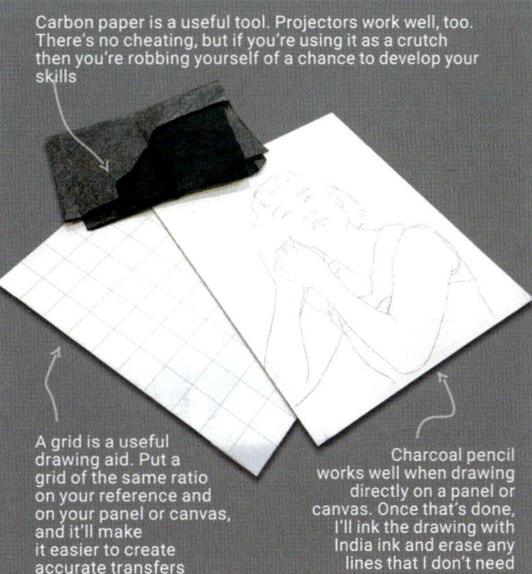

3 ◐ Gather the best reference

Take the time to learn how to use your camera. One of the biggest issues I see when reviewing student work is terrible reference that handicaps the work. Learn to make costumes and create models for reference. This is an invaluable and fun part of the process.

4 ◐ Transfer a drawing

Take your time when transferring your final drawing. A strong drawing is the basis of any good painting, so don't rush through this stage and have your work suffer. I think a grid is the best method because it'll reinforce your drawing skills.

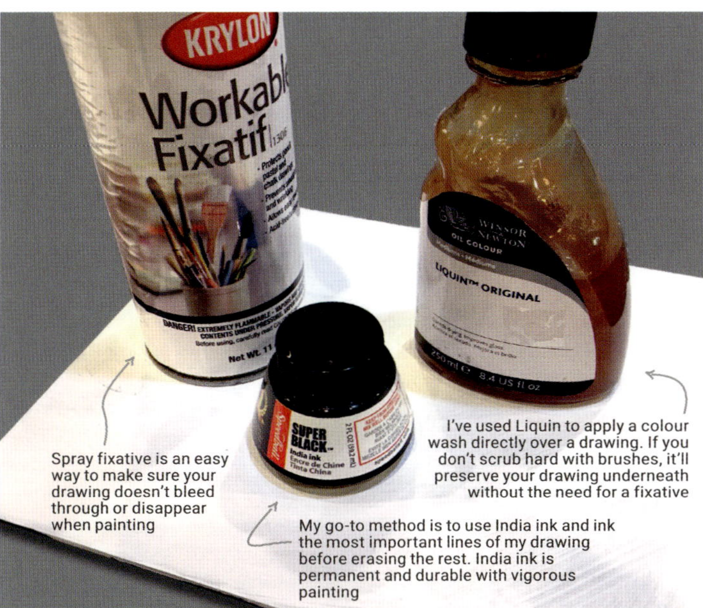

Spray fixative is an easy way to make sure your drawing doesn't bleed through or disappear when painting

My go-to method is to use India ink and ink the most important lines of my drawing before erasing the rest. India ink is permanent and durable with vigorous painting

I've used Liquin to apply a colour wash directly over a drawing. If you don't scrub hard with brushes, it'll preserve your drawing underneath without the need for a fixative

What will remain

Read up on art materials and ask other artists for advice. This could save you from buying unnecessary kit and media.

5 ◐ Secure your drawing

Once your drawing is done, it's a good idea to make sure that it's secured so that when you paint, it won't dissolve or smear. I like to go over my drawings with India ink. It enables me to scrub in paint or wipe off paint, and not remove the drawing.

How to clean oil paint from brushes

Learn how to get the most from your investment in artist brushes and keep them working at their best for longer

Tools do not make the artist, but quality tools really do help. If you're shelling out for the best-quality paints on the market, then why scrimp on poor-quality brushes? You always need to buy the best you can afford, so invest in the precious time you're spending on your art.

Good brushes are one of the best, and sometimes most costly, investments you'll make when kitting yourself out, so they deserve lots of TLC. Someone very wise once told me, 'If you look after your tools, your tools will look after you.' The golden rule is don't let the paint dry on your brush. Fear not, though – if the worst does happen, there is a chance you can still save it. One of the beauties of oil paint is its slow drying time, so this gives you a little more time, but it's still good practice to have a regular clean-up at the end of each studio day to keep your brushes in prime condition. In this article you'll learn how to look after your brushes and make sure you get the maximum return from your investment.

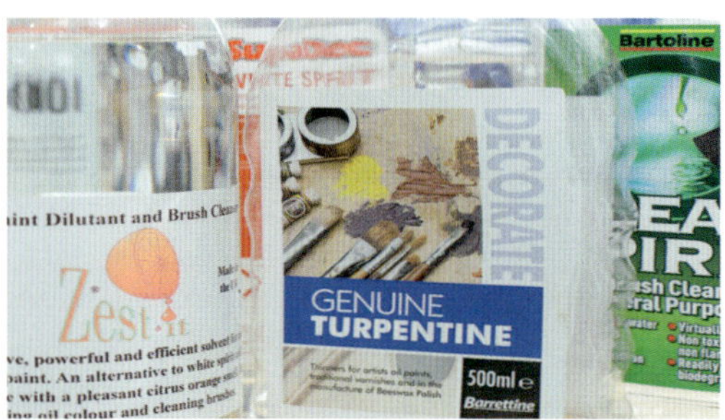

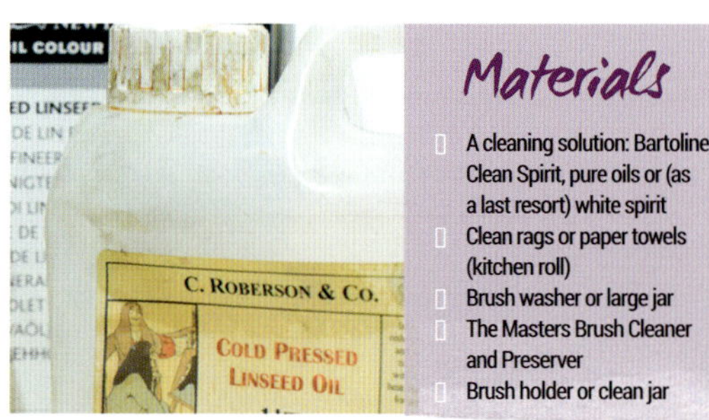

Materials

- A cleaning solution: Bartoline Clean Spirit, pure oils or (as a last resort) white spirit
- Clean rags or paper towels (kitchen roll)
- Brush washer or large jar
- The Masters Brush Cleaner and Preserver
- Brush holder or clean jar

1 ❂ Spirit of choice

Most people are familiar with cleaning paint using white spirit, but it's pretty horrible stuff. A safer and more eco alternative is Bartoline Clean Spirit, available at most good hardware stores. It can be used like white spirit but isn't flammable and doesn't have nasty fumes. Note: don't use clean spirit to dilute your oil paint, just use it for cleaning.

2 ❂ Keep it pure

The best solution for cleaning oil paint off brushes is pure oil itself, but it does take a bit more work. You can use linseed oil but this does dry quicker than other oils, so a better alternative is walnut oil or safflower oil. Linseed oil can be bought from most hardware stores and walnut and safflower oils from most supermarkets.

3 ❂ Give a sheet

Whether you choose spirit or oil, the cleaning process is the same. To begin with, you'll want to remove as much paint from the bristles as possible. Fold a clean cloth or paper towel around the ferrule of the brush and, holding between your thumb and forefinger, move the cloth to the end of the bristles, always moving away from the ferrule. Continue until very little paint shows on the cloth.

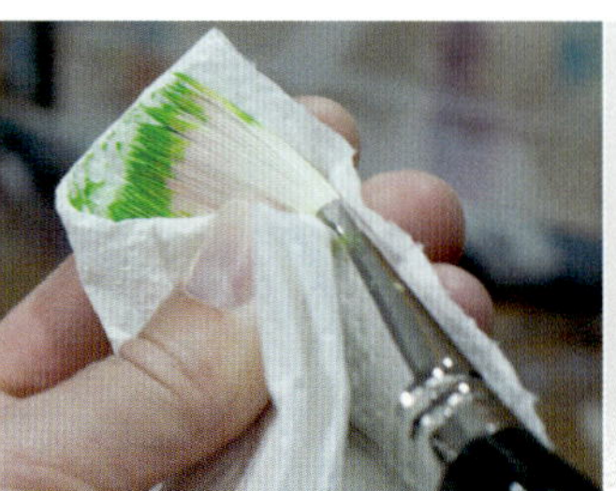

Ferrule them all!

Try not to get paint down inside the bristles where they protrude from the ferrule. If you do, clean it out ASAP. Once paint dries around the bristles inside the ferrule, the brush will splay and never regain its original shape. That's game over for the brush!

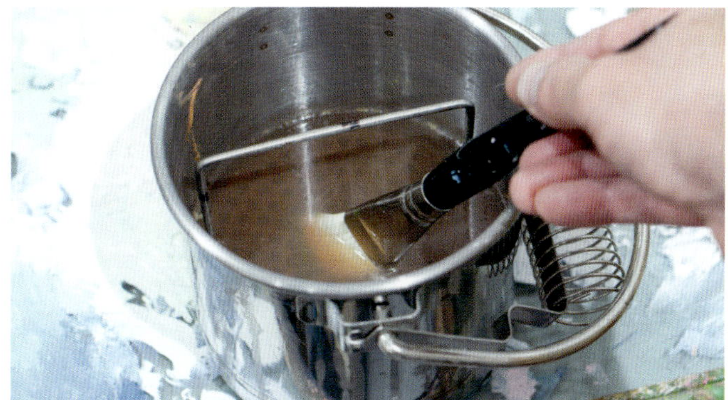

4 ❍ Going to pot

Here I've got my large metal brush-washer filled with Bartoline Clean Spirit. Gently run your brush back and forth across the submerged perforated-metal insert. This knocks off pigment from the bristles without swilling up the sediment at the bottom of the washer. The sediment can be periodically dredged. If you're using oil you'll need to repeat this step, wiping with a clean cloth each time, as described in step three. Alternatively, use an old jar.

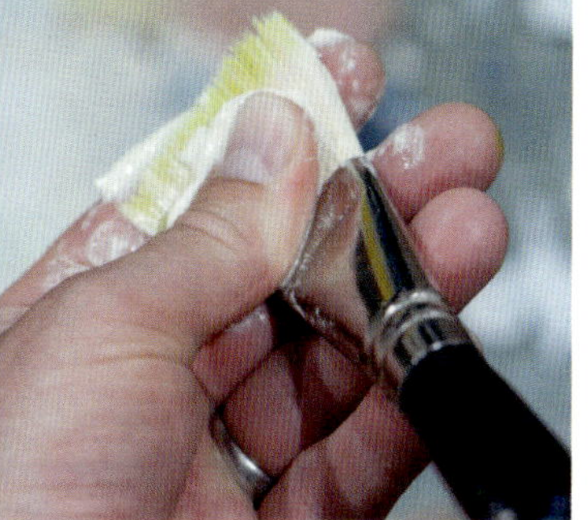

Reshape your brush

After cleaning your brushes, take the opportunity to reshape the bristles back into their original shape. Some artists like to use a little saliva for this, but don't put the brush in your mouth. Spit in your palm and reshape the bristles with a your fingers before washing your hands.

5 ❍ The secret is in the soap

My secret weapon in brush cleaning is The Masters Brush Cleaner and Preserver. This little gem isn't cheap but it's saved many a forgotten brush and more than paid for itself many times over. Work up a lather with your brush in the centre of the soap, then work the lather through the bristles with your thumb and forefingers, working from the ferrule out towards the ends of the bristles. Continue until no pigment can be seen in the lather.

6 ❍ Prepare to store

The last step is to rinse in clean water and reshape with your fingers before allowing to air-dry in a holder or pot. If storing for a longer period you can add some clean Masters soap lather and reshape with your fingers. The soap will dry holding the shape of the bristles hard until needed again. Always remember to leave brushes to dry in isolation. If the bristles dry misshaped it will be difficult to undo.

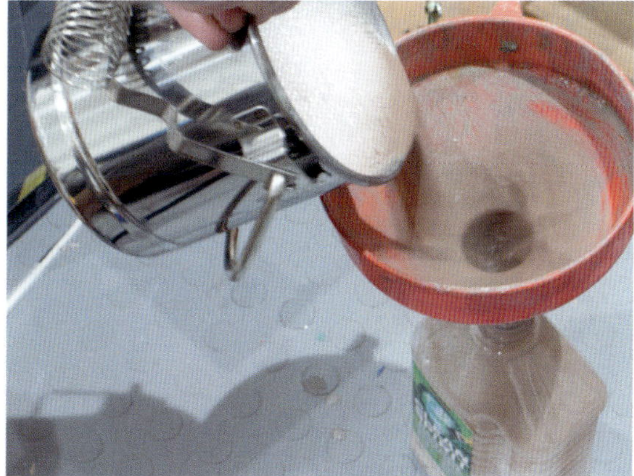

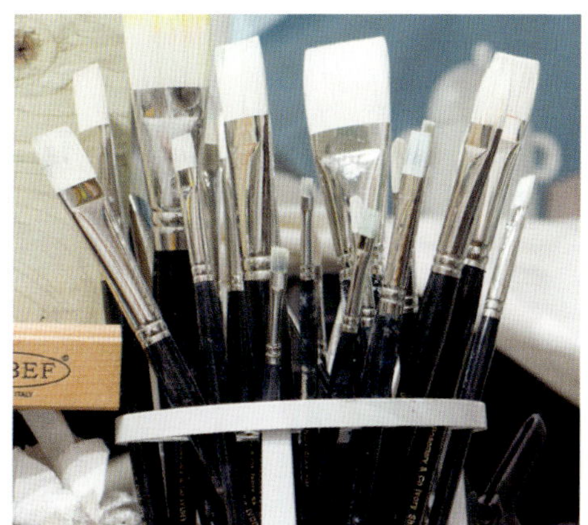

7 ❍ Save money, recycle

Although the clean spirit may be classed as biodegradable, the pigment remaining in the spirit could still be harmful to the environment. Take it to your local recycling centre, or even better, recycle it yourself. I keep empty clean spirit bottles that I pour the dirty 'wash' spirit into. Over time the pigment sinks to the bottom of the bottle, leaving reusable clean spirit above that can be carefully decanted, saving you money and the environment!

Work with a limited palette

Rob Lunn details how you can increase harmony in your colour mixes by stripping back your palette to just two reds, two blues and two yellows

Light seems colourless, but it is in fact made up of the full spectrum of colours. When we see the yellow of a pepper, it is because all the other colours in the spectrum are absorbed by the pepper, only the yellow light rays bounce off the pepper and are picked up by our eyes. So, what we are actually painting is not the pepper, but the light between the pepper and our eyes.

By re-creating the spectrum on our palette, the whole range of colours that occur within nature are opened up to us. The spectrum can be best represented by 12 colours, each representing a step around the full spectrum. The colour directly opposite a colour on the wheel is its complementary – that is to say, when put next to each other they make each other seem more colourful. When these colours are mixed, however, they cancel each other out and lower the saturation of each other and create a grey. To push this method, we're going to reduce the palette to six colours, plus white. Simply two blues, two reds and two yellows.

With these colours you will be able to mix your own blacks and browns, plus all the complementary colours we've omitted from the spectrum. The only downside of using a limited palette is not having the high levels of saturation you get from straight-out-of-the-tube colour, but nature isn't always that intense, depending on your subject, and the greater feeling of colour harmony outweighs this. All the paints recommended below are from Michael Harding and classed as non-toxic, plus I try not to use harmful spirits or additives.

A Ultramarine Blue

Michael Harding series 1

Ultramarine Blue is a lovely mid-blue with great warm tendencies. Before the discovery of this synthetic version in the 1820s, Lapis Lazuli Ultramarine Blue was one of the most expensive pigments in the world, hailing from the mountains of Afghanistan, and more expensive pound for pound than gold. The colour was reserved for only the most important people in paintings, and was traditionally the blue of Mary, mother of Jesus. It has an average drying time, leans more towards transparent and has excellent lightfastness. It produces lovely greens and beautiful violets, too. This is often my go-to blue for mixes.

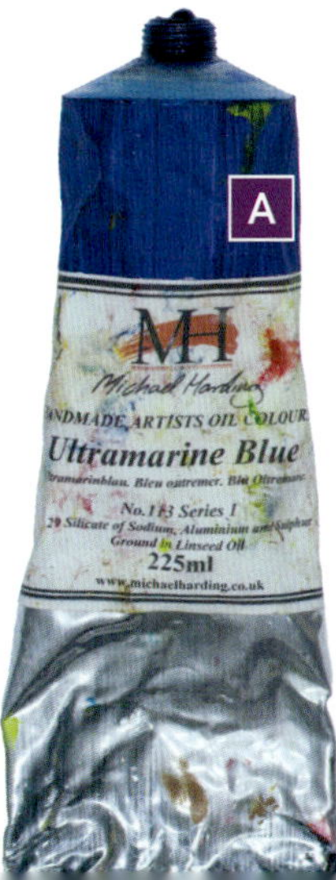
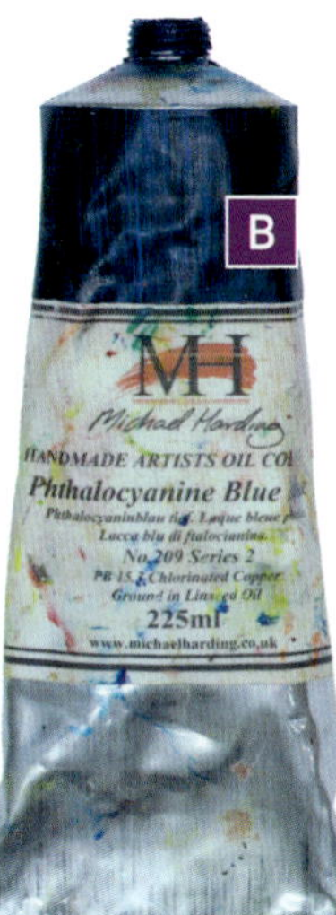
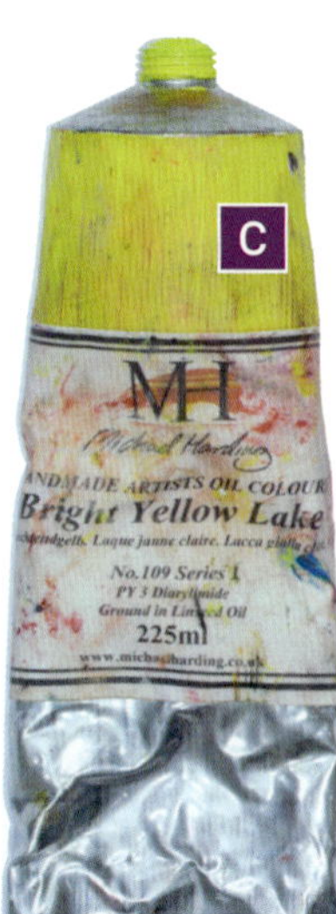

B 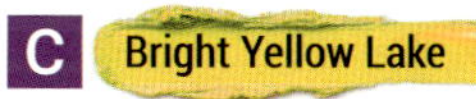 Phthalocyanine Blue Lake

Michael Harding series 2

Derived from Chlorinated Copper in 1935, Phthalocyanine (or 'Phthalo') Blue Lake is a power-house blue and is seen as a modern replacement for Prussian Blue. 'A little dab will do you' is recommended, as its extremely high tinting strength can easily overpower a mix. It is an intense blue that dries quickly and its transparency and excellent lightfastness make it great for glazes. This is a green-blue and great for those full-on greens that you really want to pop! Phthalo Blue Lake is a great wingman to Ultramarine Blue on your palette.

C 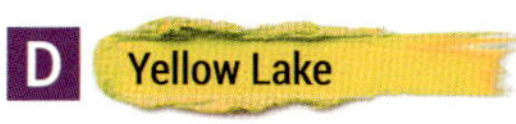 Bright Yellow Lake

Michael Harding series 1

Bright Yellow Lake is a powerful Arylide organic Lake pigment. It has a bottle green undertone when mixed and an incredibly high oil content and tinting strength. I use it as a non-toxic alternative to Cadmium Lemon Yellow, although it doesn't have the same covering strength when layered due to its high transparency. When you add Titanium White No.1 this yellow is almost luminous. With its high transparency and excellent lightfastness it's great for glazes, but it has a slow drying time. You may want to add Liquin to speed it up.

D 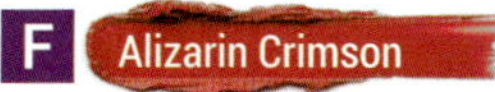 Yellow Lake

Michael Harding series 1

Yellow Lake is a warmer version of Bright Yellow Lake and what I use instead of Cadmium Yellow, although again, it doesn't have the same covering power as Cadmium when layering. Yellow Lake is transparent but with a strong tint power and excellent lightfastness. As with its Bright cousin, Yellow Lake has a slow drying time, which makes it great for mixing colours you want work back into. It makes amazing strong oranges and mixes well for punchy bright greens, too.

E 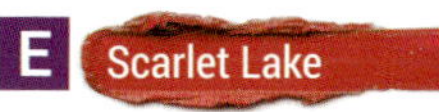 Scarlet Lake

Michael Harding series 2

Scarlet Lake is a strong and warm red belonging to the family of Napthol Red pigments, and is what I use in place of Cadmium Red. It is an organic red that has very high tinting power and can easily overpower a mix if added in too great a quantity, so go carefully. It has excellent lightfastness and is also more opaque than some of the other Lake colours, so take that into consideration when glazing or layering colours. It works great as a complementary to greens.

F 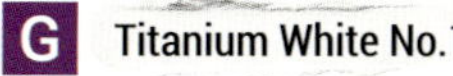 Alizarin Crimson

Michael Harding series 3

Alizarin Crimson is highly prized by portrait artists for the cool and smoky colour it adds to skin tones, although some have concerns about its lightfastness compared to more recent organic red pigments. I love the way Alizarin Crimson mixes with skin tones for depicting lips – it gives full and ruby tones without looking too 'painted on', making it ideal for male lips, where you might not want it to look like the subject is wearing lipstick. It's a good slow drier with good lightfastness and transparency.

G Titanium White No.1

Michael Harding series 3

Titanium White No.1 is buttery in consistency and the most brilliant white in the Michael Harding range. Ground with safflower oil, which extends its drying time, this Titanium White contains a small addition of Zinc White, which stops the tendency of Titanium White paints weeping oil to the surface whilst drying. That's the attention to detail you get from Michael Harding. Titanium No.1's qualities of drying very slowly, excellent lightfastness and super-high opacity make it my top choice of white for my palette.

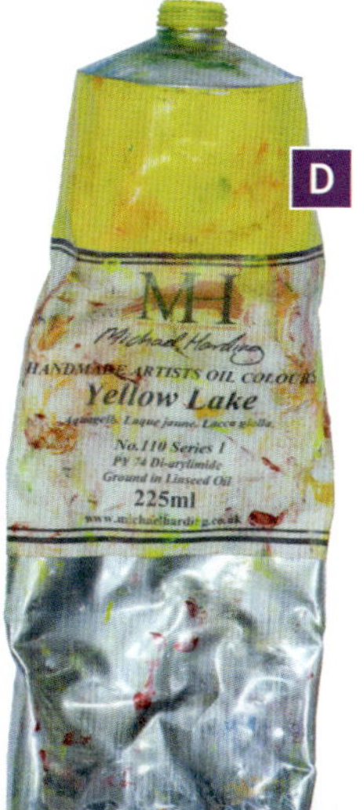

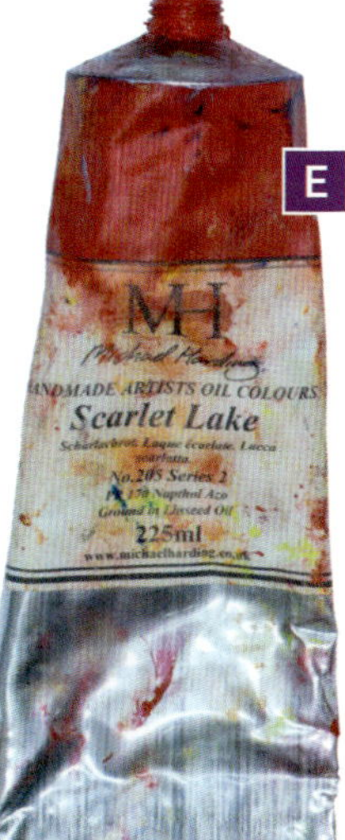

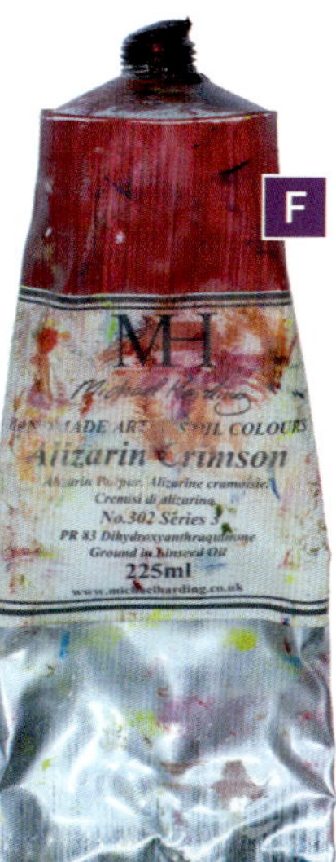

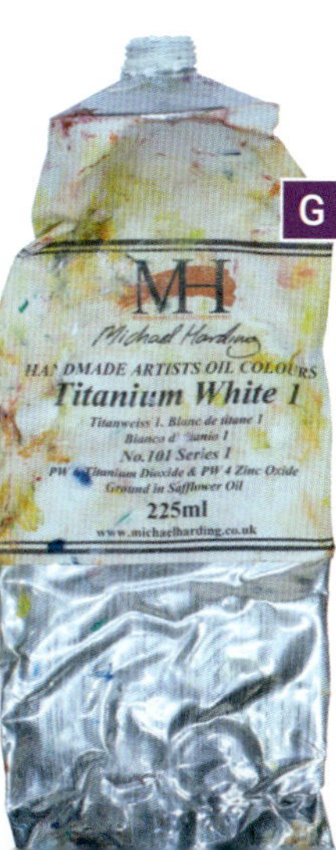

Perfect a sunset scene

Find out how to create warm and deep landscape scenes – particularly complex sunsets – with your limited colour palette

1 Blue skies ahead

The blue sky in this landscape sits above all the drama, so it was important to get just the right mix. The blue sky is reflected in the pool, so it had to sit well with surrounding colours to look authentic. I took Ultramarine Blue and tinted it down with Titanium White No.1. I wanted to add violet tones so I mixed in a little Alizarin Crimson. The blue of the sky also leaned towards the greens so I added a little Bright Yellow Lake to subtly shift it in that direction.

2 Peachy tones

As the sun gets lower in the sky, the rays of light have more atmosphere to travel through to reach your eyes. This tends to filter out more of the violets and blues, creating beautiful peachy-pink skies as in our subject. To re-create this, I mixed Scarlet Lake with Titanium White No.1. When mixing tints, add the dominant colour to the white, rather than adding white to the dominant colour – you'll save a lot of white paint. I then 'peached-up' my pink by adding small amounts of Bright Yellow Lake.

3 Deep shadows

In a painting with high notes of extreme colour, the composition needs to be balanced with dark tones. I increased harmony by combining a lot of these into one deep violet. These deep, dark tones need to be desaturated with a complementary colour – in this case, Bright Yellow Lake. I didn't want to go all the way to black, so I started with my warmer blue, Ultramarine. I then added Alizarin Crimson and Bright Yellow Lake to grey it down.

4 Golden grass

One of the strongest colours in the foreground, and counterpoint to the deep shadows, is the sunset on the foliage around the pool. I wanted this to be bright and sing out, but it's easy to go in too light and too high in saturation. I mix Scarlet Lake with Yellow Lake to create a strong and warm orange. As Scarlet Lake is the dominant colour, I greyed it down using Phthalo Blue Lake to create a strong desaturation while retaining a warm orange. Offer up your palette knife to your painting to see how your mix looks next its surrounding colours before you commit with a brush.

5 Green fields

A cool balancing colour to all those high notes and deep shadows is the green of the fields around the cottage. They lead the viewer's eye towards the cottage and out across the pool, so they're important elements. I wanted the green to be bright and full-bodied but it needed to be desaturated quite a bit so it didn't stand out like a sore thumb. I mixed Ultramarine Blue with Yellow Lake to make my strong green and then desaturated it with a little Alizarin Crimson. Go careful, though – it's all too easy to overdo it and mix a brown.

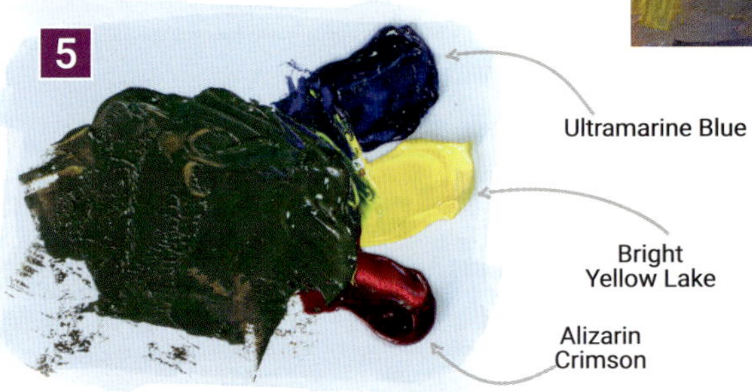

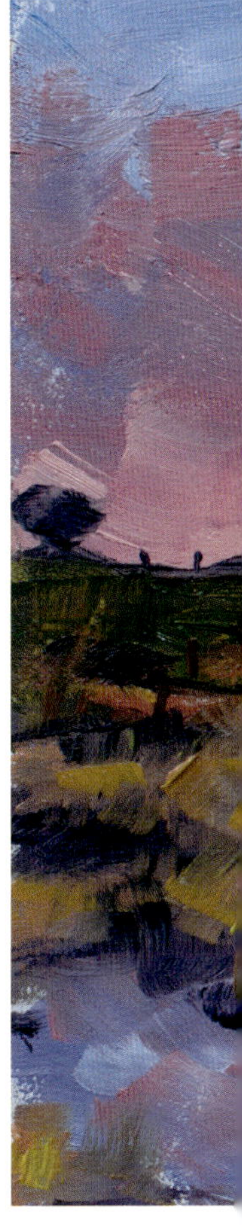

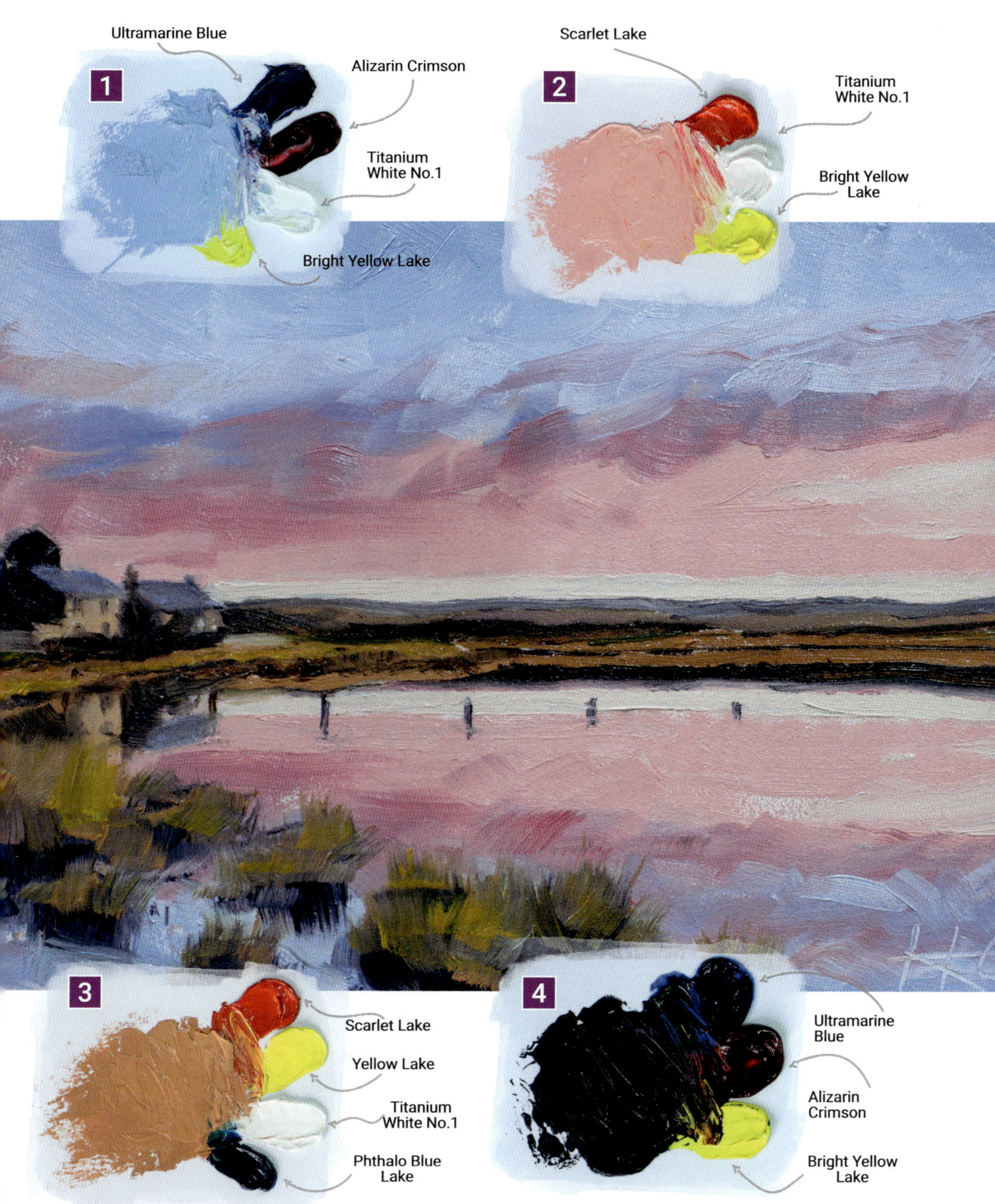
1
Ultramarine Blue
Alizarin Crimson
Titanium White No.1
Bright Yellow Lake

2
Scarlet Lake
Titanium White No.1
Bright Yellow Lake

3
Scarlet Lake
Yellow Lake
Titanium White No.1
Phthalo Blue Lake

4
Ultramarine Blue
Alizarin Crimson
Bright Yellow Lake

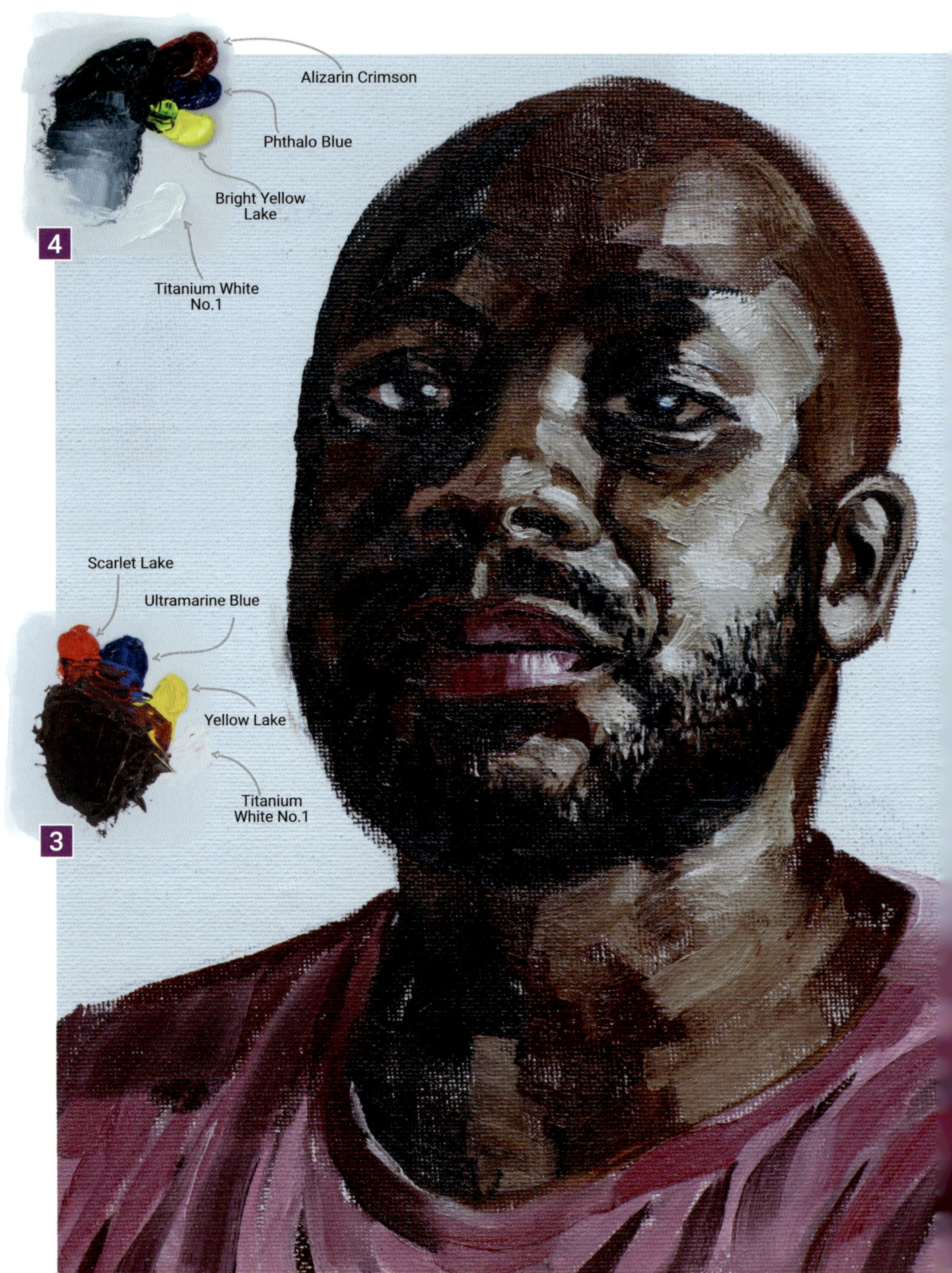
Alizarin Crimson
Phthalo Blue
Bright Yellow Lake
Titanium White No.1
4
Scarlet Lake
Ultramarine Blue
Yellow Lake
Titanium White No.1
3

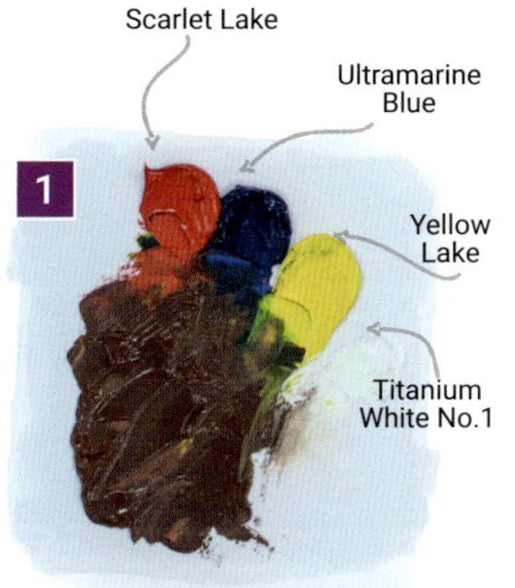

Darker skin tones

Learn how to approach mixing darker skin tones using a limited palette. Build from an initial local colour and push out extremes of light and dark, plus details

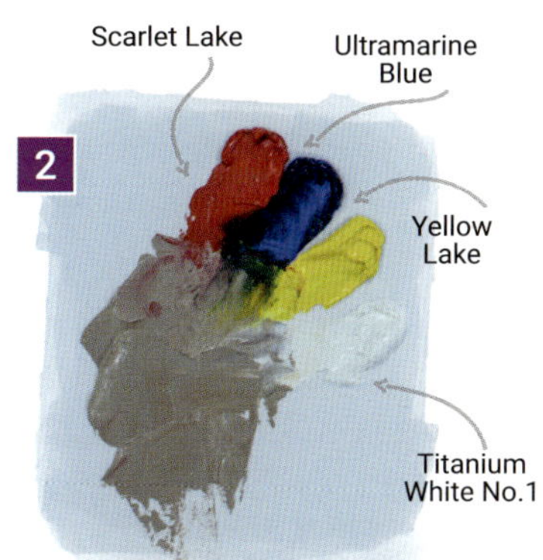

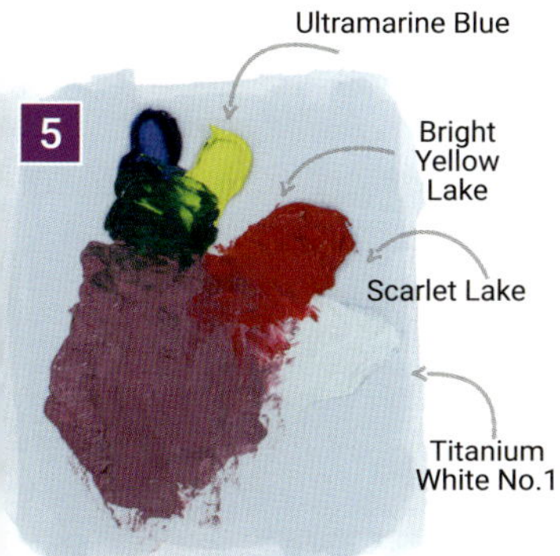

1 Mid-tone skin

All skin tones range from base colours of oranges through to browns. You first need to find the local colour of your subject – this is the midpoint of their skin tone. You can then push that midpoint to its lightest and its darkest points. Here I've mixed a brown with a fairly even balance of Scarlet Lake and Ultramarine Blue to create a violet, added heavy Yellow Lake to desaturate the violet, and a touch of Titanium White No.1 to cool it down a little.

3 Darkest skin tone

Adapt the midpoint again, but this time push it towards the darkest skin tones. Taking the same mix of Ultramarine Blue, Scarlet Lake, Yellow Lake and Titanium White No.1, we're now adding increasing amounts of Scarlet Lake and Ultramarine Blue. If you find the mix going too blue, too red or too violet, simply add more of the counter-balancing colour. Once you have these mixed, you can experiment adding additional colours.

2 Light skin tone

In this mix I want to push my midpoint mix towards the lightest skin tones. Take the same mix of Ultramarine Blue, Scarlet Lake, Yellow Lake and Titanium White No.1, but add increasing amounts of Yellow Lake and Titanium White No.1. If the mix starts to go too yellow, add small amounts of Scarlet Lake and Ultramarine Blue to bring it back in line. The Scarlet Lake and Ultramarine Blue combine to create a warm violet that you are then greying down with your warm Yellow Lake.

4 Hair

One of the most impressive examples of the 12-step and six-step colour wheel method is mixing your own blacks. As with the brown, we're going to mix a violet and then desaturate it with its complementary colour, but this time we'll be using all the cool versions of our colours. Mix the Alizarin Crimson and Phthalo Blue Lake into an even violet, then start to add Bright Yellow Lake to desaturate the violet into our black.

5 Lips

Lips are one of those tricky colour mixes to get right. If slightly overdone, they can have the tendency to look painted on. If underdone, a face can look washed-out and ill. Of course, if you're painting the portrait of a woman wearing make-up, this isn't a problem. I wanted a greyed-down pink that would work well for the t-shirt too, so I mixed some Scarlet Lake and Titanium White No.1, then mixed a green from Ultramarine Blue and Bright Yellow Lake as a complementary to desaturate the pink.

Paler skin tones

Expand upon the lesson learned in the first portrait by following the same approach on a different skin tone

1 Mid-tone skin

First I need to determine the mid skin tone of my subject. This can be tricky to determine. Try squinting at the subject. This reduces the range of tones you can see. I mixed Scarlet Lake and Ultramarine Blue to produce my warm violet and then reduced its saturation by adding increasing amounts of Yellow Lake to get my warm light brown. I then cooled and lightened the brown by adding Titanium White No.1.

2 Light skin tone

Use a tonal scale to judge whether you're reaching the desired tone. You can make these yourself by adding white to one end of a strip of card and black at the other end. Then mix a 50% grey and place halfway in between, and then 25% and 75% greys respectively. I used the same mix as in step one, but this time I added greater quantities of Yellow Lake and Titanium White No.1 until I reached the desired tone.

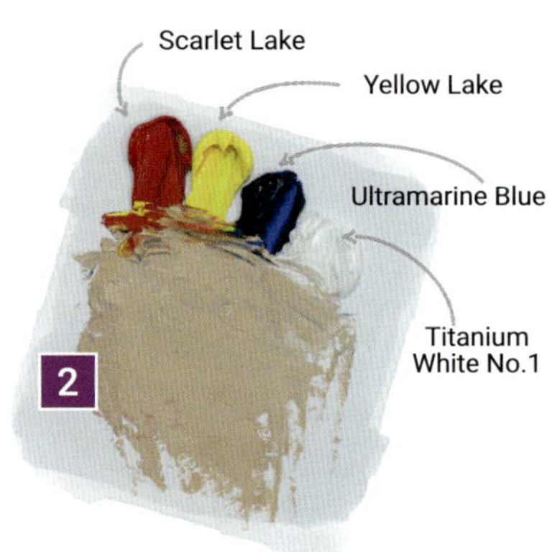

3 Darkest skin tone

The darker areas of our subject's skin tones have a more violet tendency, so we're going to have to shift our skin tone mix accordingly. I used Scarlet Lake and Ultramarine Blue to make a cool shade of violet that leant more towards the blues to keep it cooler, then added Yellow Lake to desaturate the violet and some Alizarin Crimson to add depth. I then lightened and cooled it down with a little Titanium White No.1.

4 Hair

The subject's hair is black in most places, but looks as if highlights are added too. I mixed Scarlet Lake and Ultramarine Blue to create a warm violet. I then added more Scarlet Lake to this mix to keep the violet warmer, then reduced its saturation and turned the violet into a warm brown by adding Yellow Lake. I then cooled and lightened the mix by adding small amounts of Titanium White No.1 until I reached the right colour.

5 Lips

In this portrait the subject has a very pronounced lip colour and I really wanted them to 'pop', but without overpowering the composition. In order to achieve this, the lip colour needed to be related to the skin tones, but also have its own sense of place in the painting. I mixed my violet but this time replaced Scarlet Lake with Alizarin Crimson to give the mix a deeper, more ruby red colour. I then added small amounts of Bright Yellow Lake and Titanium White No.1 to subtly reduce the saturation and lighten the colour.

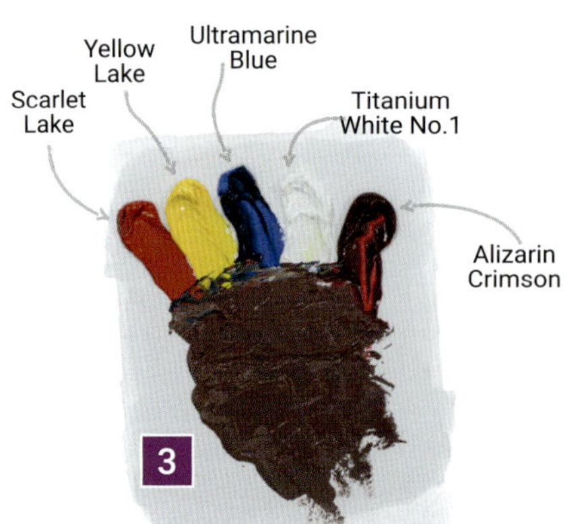

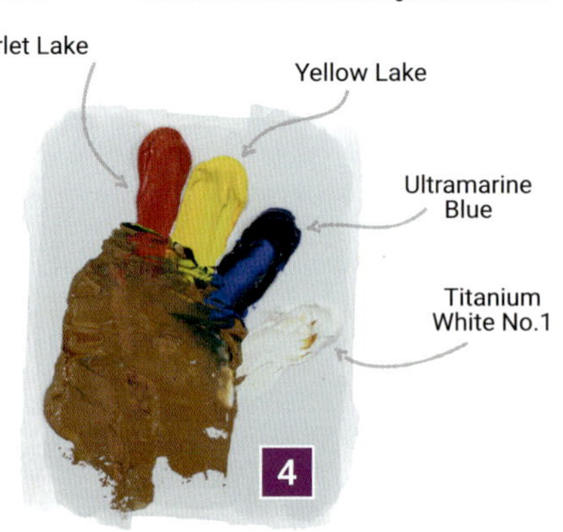

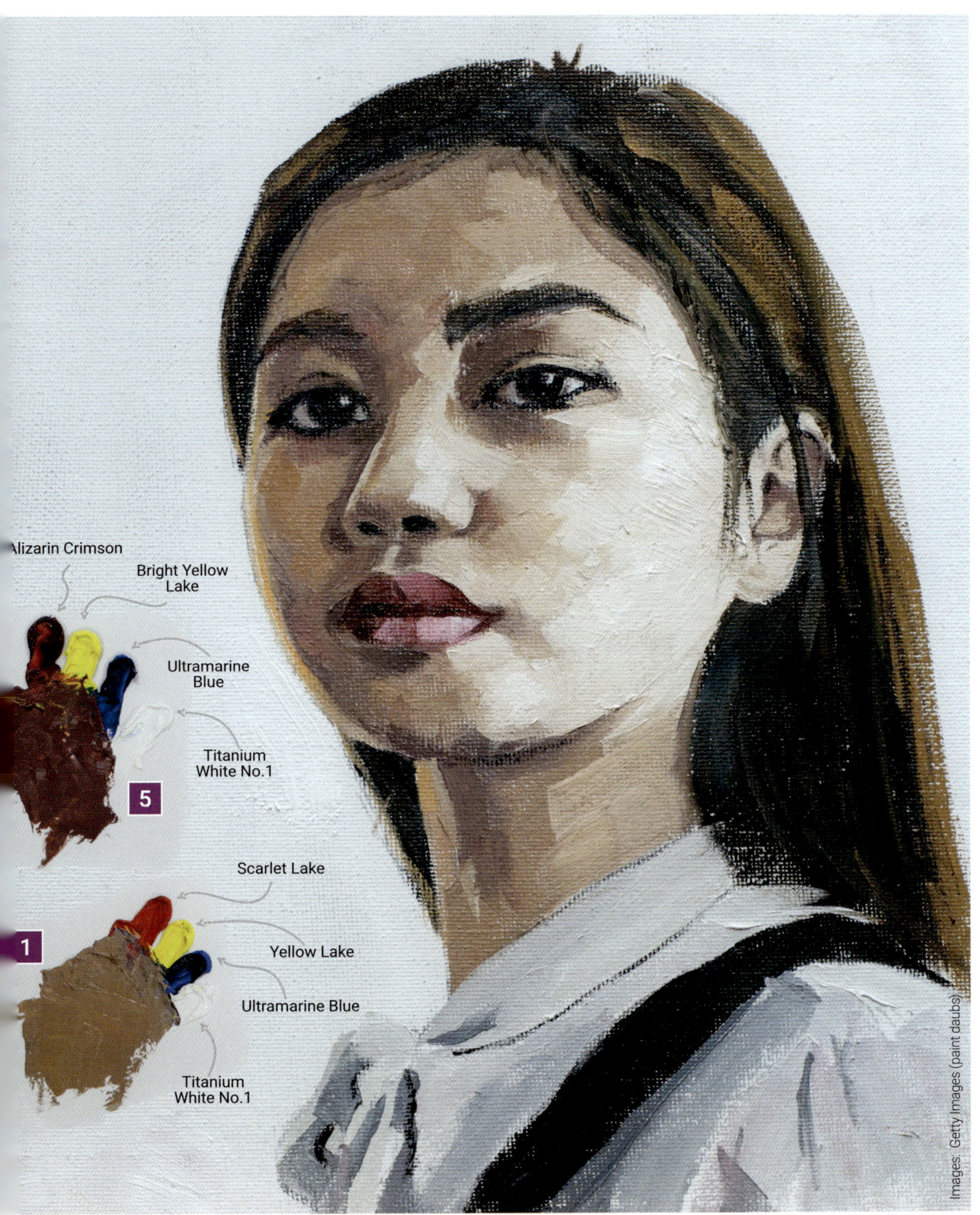
Alizarin Crimson
Bright Yellow Lake
Ultramarine Blue
Titanium White No.1
5
Scarlet Lake
Yellow Lake
Ultramarine Blue
Titanium White No.1
1

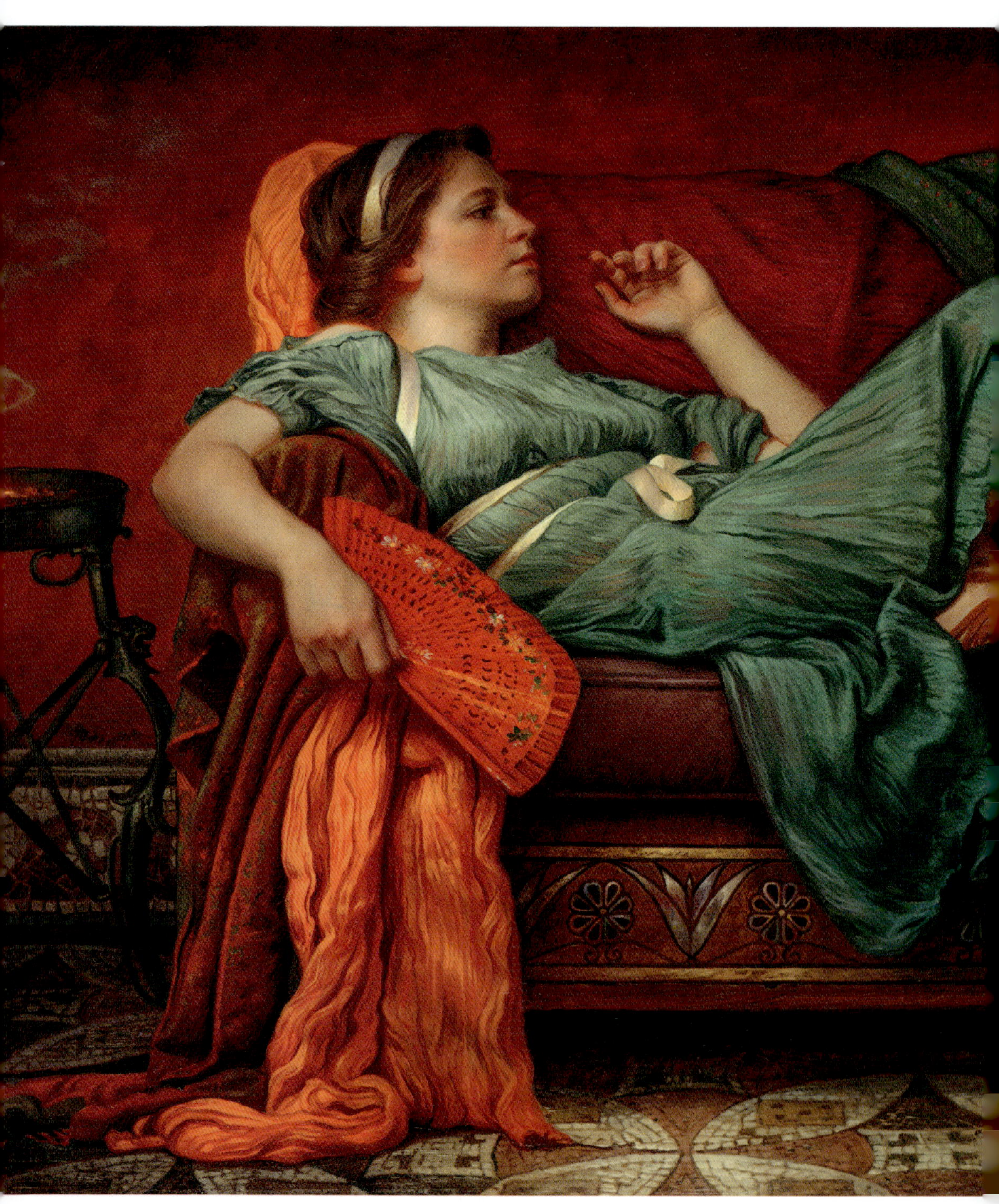

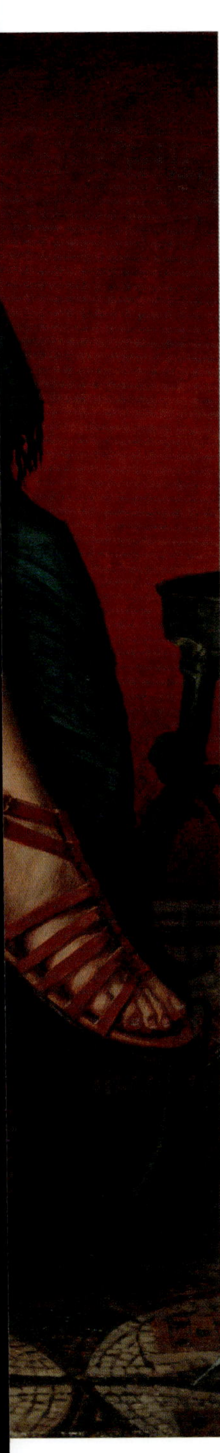

Paint like a 19th-century master

Howard Lyon draws inspiration from artists like Alma-Tadema and takes us through the process of creating a painting after their ideals

The 19th century was a wonderful time for art. Artists were held in high regard and the public was educated about art. There was a very high level of skilled technique on display thanks to the rigorous academic training available.

Artists like Lawrence Alma-Tadema, Frederic Leighton and William-Adolphe Bouguereau created works of great beauty and drew upon inspirations found in contemporary life, but especially antiquity. They all followed a similar process, creating thumbnails, detailed drawings, life studies, colour studies and then the final painting. A great amount of planning and effort was expended before brush ever met canvas.

We can learn a lot from these masters and not hurry through the process of creating a painting. Do not rush through the thumbnail stage. This is the best and easiest place to explore your composition. When I can, I like to let my sketches sit for a day or two and then come back with fresh eyes. Once the thumbnails are completed, I spend a little more time refining a sketch to flesh out the idea.

For this project I wanted to pay homage to the artists I love. I was lucky enough to have a friend, Birgitte Smoot, that was not only willing to model but also to help me with an authentic-looking costume. My friend, Erin Bjorn, made us a costume that was historically accurate. I can't overstate how much this helped elevate the whole effort from the beginning.

Paint what delights you and you will find an audience that feels the same way about your work. Follow me through these steps as I attempt to create a painting that echoes the masters I love and then go and create your own painting inspired by your favourite artists. You will learn more about them and yourself in the process.

Materials

Painted in Blue Ridge oil paints on a wood panel. Howard prefers Rosemary & Co brushes, and his New Wave Art Expressionist Confidant arm palette.

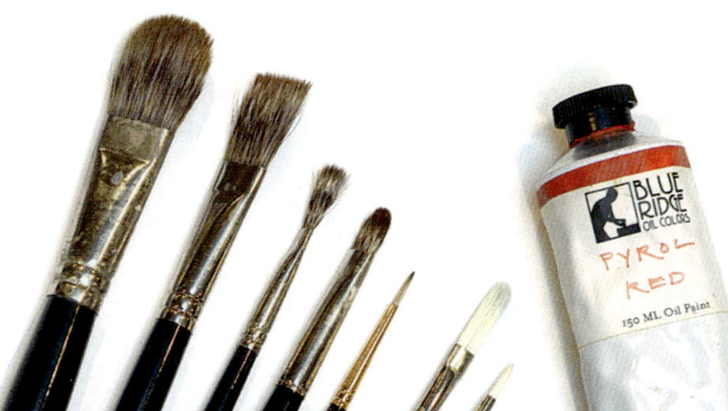

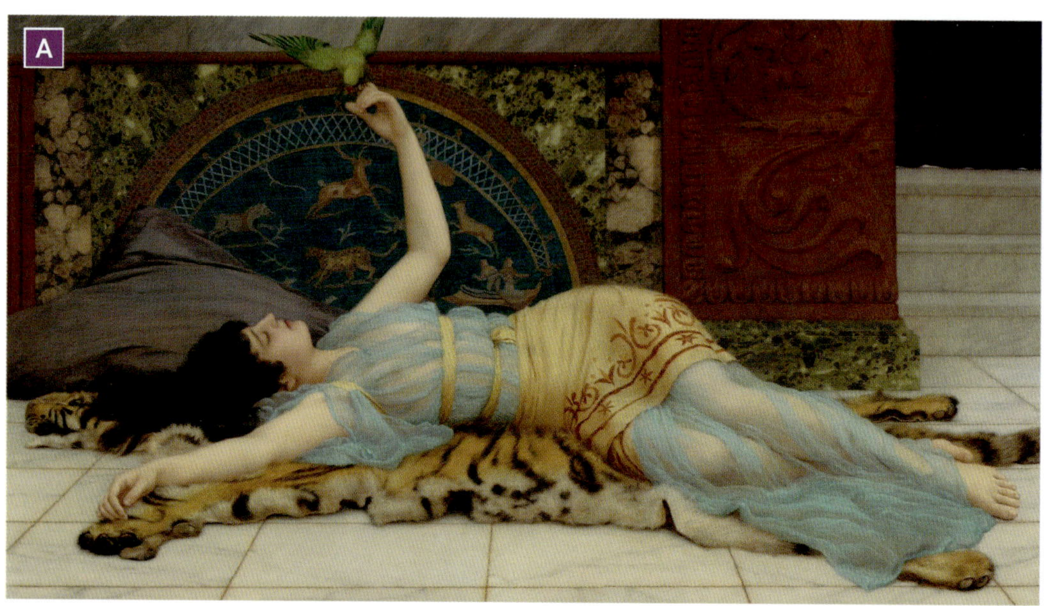

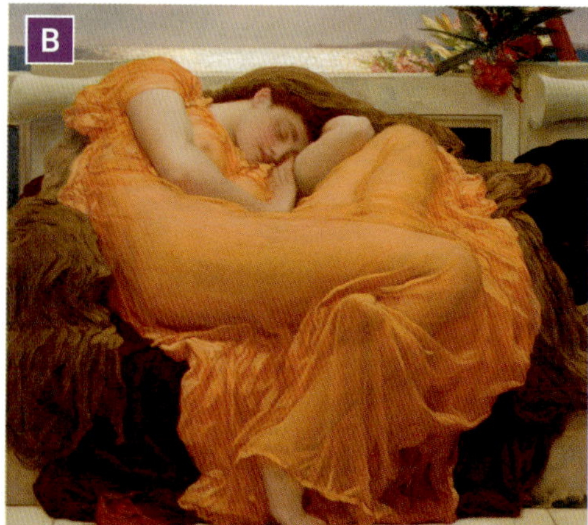

1 ◐ Find inspiration

Here are a few examples of the art I love from Leighton, Godward and Alma-Tadema. At this stage I am looking for inspiration for this painting. There is a richness in palette and a refinement of line that is very exciting. How can you not be inspired by such beauty?

A Dolce Far Niente (77.4 x 127 cm) by John William Godward, 1897

B Flaming June (120.6 x 120.6 cm) by Frederic Leighton, 1895Confidences

C (55.8 x 37.6 cm) by Alma-Tadema, 1869

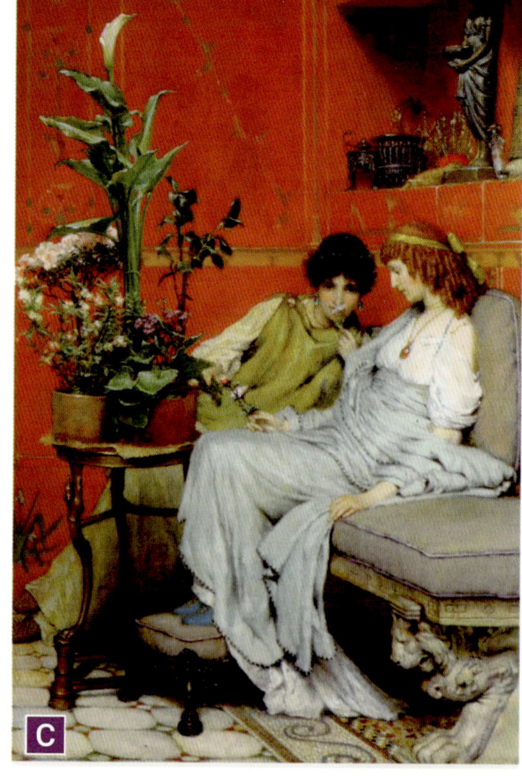

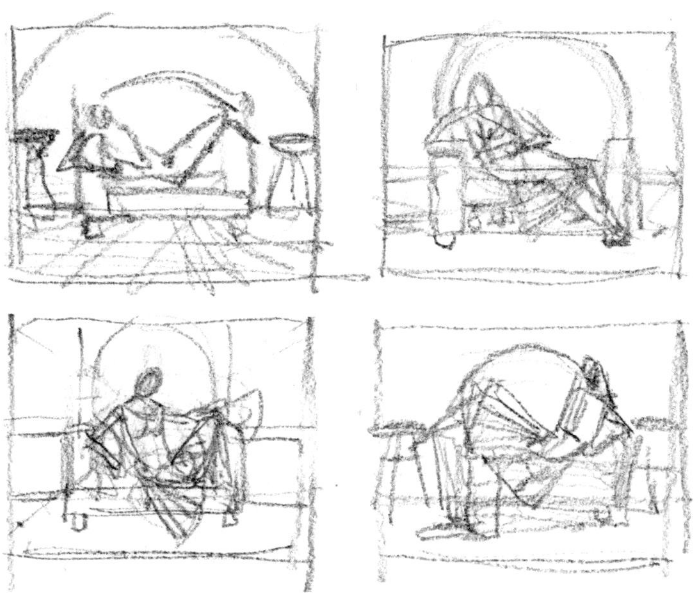

2 ⬤ Test composition and detail with thumbnails

I created many thumbnails for this painting. Here are four of them. You can see they aren't very pretty and only meaningful to me. A quick line or mark can represent a piece of furniture or figure. Imagination is important at this stage and adds a thrill as one imagines the possibilities!

3 ⬤ Create a sketch to solidify ideas

I like to take one of the thumbnails and take it further as a sketch. I did this one in Photoshop, but sometimes I will use charcoal or pencil. I like to mix up the materials and tools I use. The goal at this stage is to solidify the idea so that you can gather proper references and direct the model.

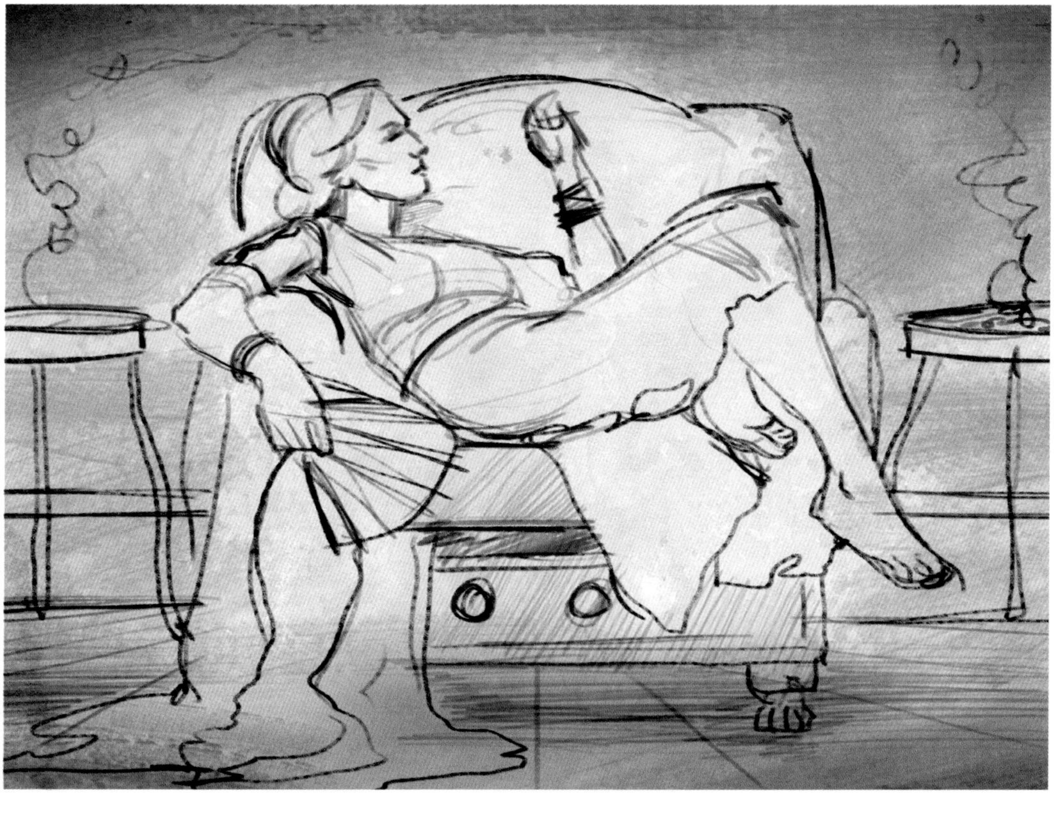

4 ⬤ Use photography as a tool

Unless you have the enviable means to have a model in your studio full-time, photography will most likely be an invaluable tool. Do what it takes to get the very best photo reference possible but don't be a slave to your photographs. You are the artist, not the camera. Trust your creativity and use all the tools at your fingertips.

Gathering references

I wanted to add some historically accurate details to my painting. The internet is another wonderful tool. I was able to find references for mosaics on the wall and floor as well as a bronze brazier. They gave me some authentic details to put in the painting and added significant visual richness.

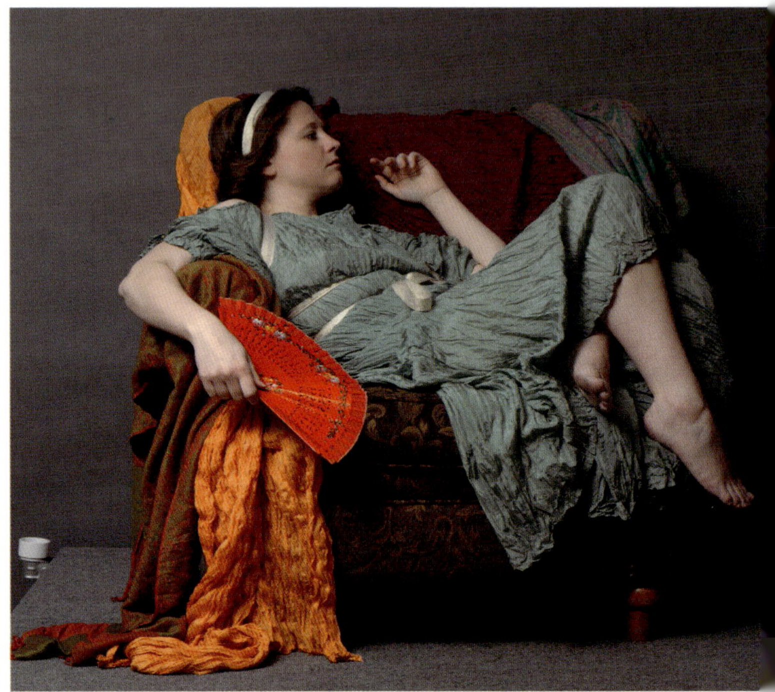

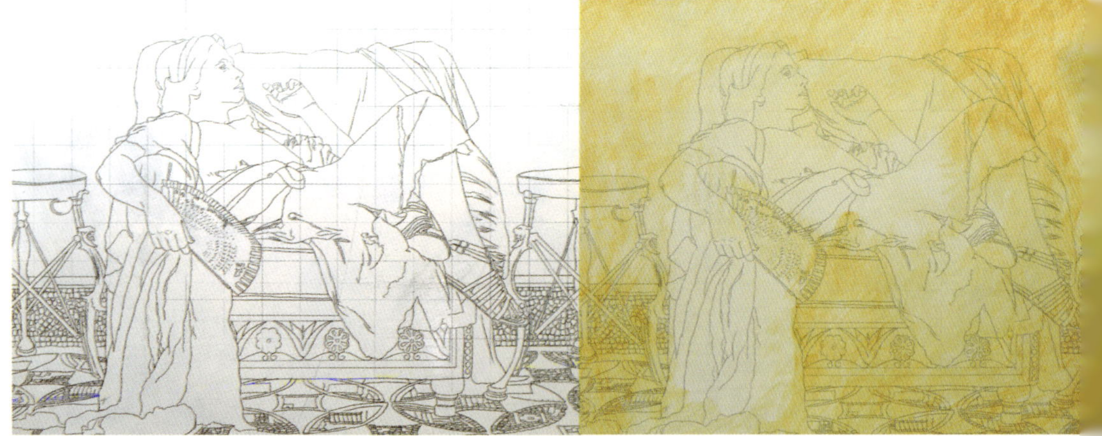

5 ⬤ Draw out the composition

The painting is 12x16 inches so I make a 1-inch grid on the panel and draw my composition. You don't need to draw every detail, though I draw in much of the mosaic hoping to take advantage of the dark lines in the final pass. Once it is drawn in, I ink the critical lines with a Pigma Micron pen.

6 ⬤ The imprimatura

I erase the pencil grid and start the imprimatura, or tinting the canvas with colour. This does a couple of things. It make it easier to judge the accuracy of subsequent layers of paint, and the warm colour will show through in places and help to add warmth and vibrancy in a subtle way.

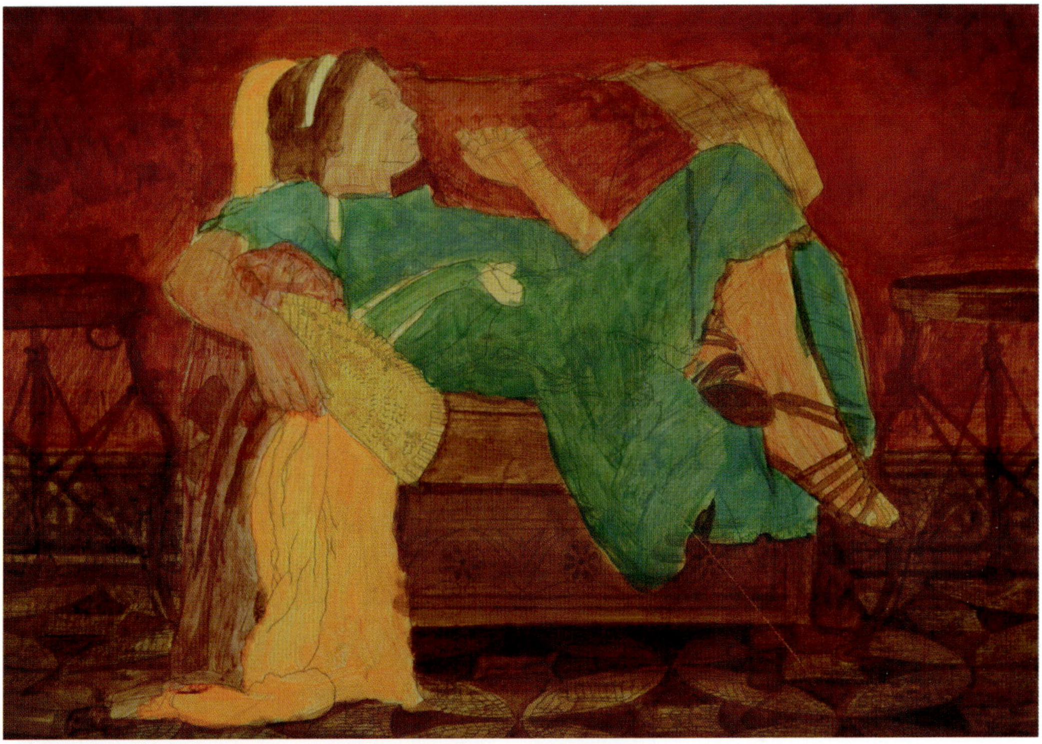

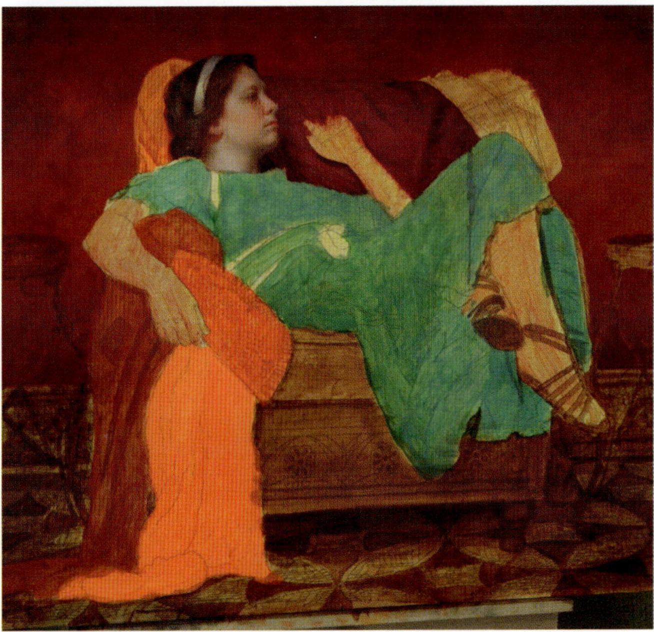

7 ◉ Apply a colour wash

I now apply a thin colour wash over the whole painting. I like to use a medium composed of five parts turpentine, one part damar varnish and one part stand oil. It makes the oil paint seem almost like watercolour and it dries quickly. It also keeps the paint semi-transparent, to allow the drawing to show through.

8 ◉ The first pass

The first pass of the painting is underway. I start with the head and hands. It lets me establish the quality and value range on what is usually the most important part of a painting containing figures. When painting flesh under cool daylight, I like to keep the shadows warm and lively.

9 ○ Pace your effort

When working through the first pass, it is important to remember that you will have the chance to go over everything again once it dries. Don't fall into the trap of trying to add all the polish and finish in the first stage. It takes some experience but you will soon learn when you are just pushing paint around and when you are actually making progress.

10 ○ First pass complete

The first pass is now complete. Notice that areas are still flat and washy, but the values and colours are well established. The fun part really begins where each stroke seems to make a big impact and you can choose what parts you want to focus on. I am about 80% of the way towards the finish at this point.

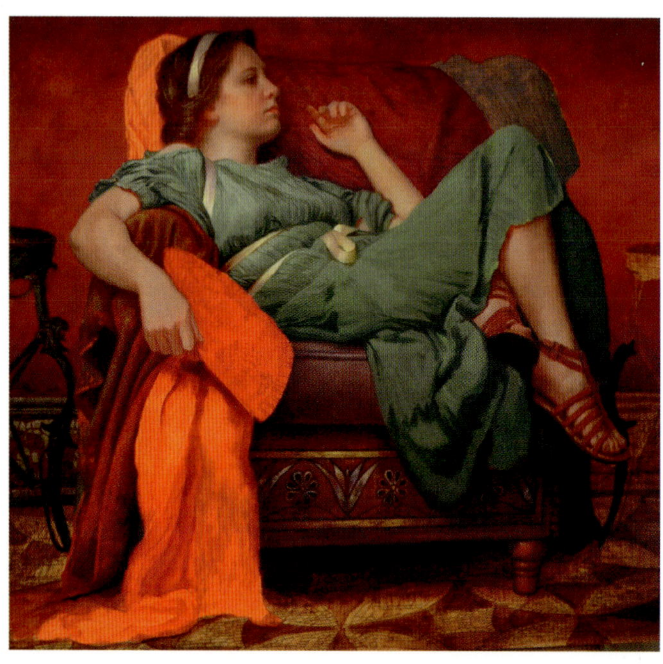

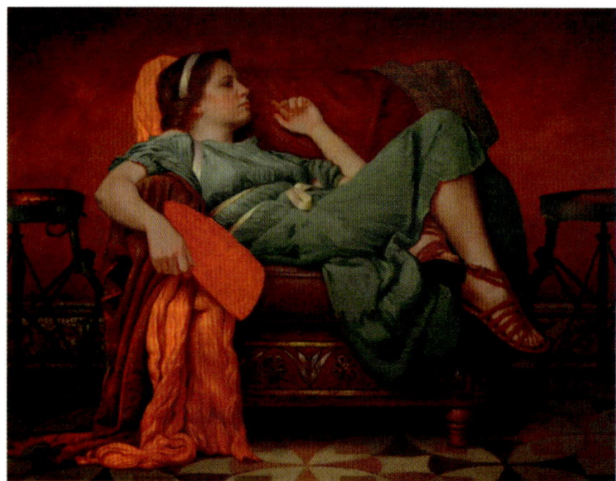

Paint with thought

Don't just make marks, be thoughtful about how you are applying paint. Think about the correct colour, value and shape with each stroke.

11 ○ Second pass

In my efforts to paint like my art heroes, I have to be meticulous with the details. For the smallest details, buy a medium sized round with a very fine tip. This will let you get all the detail you need and the brush will hold a good amount of paint.

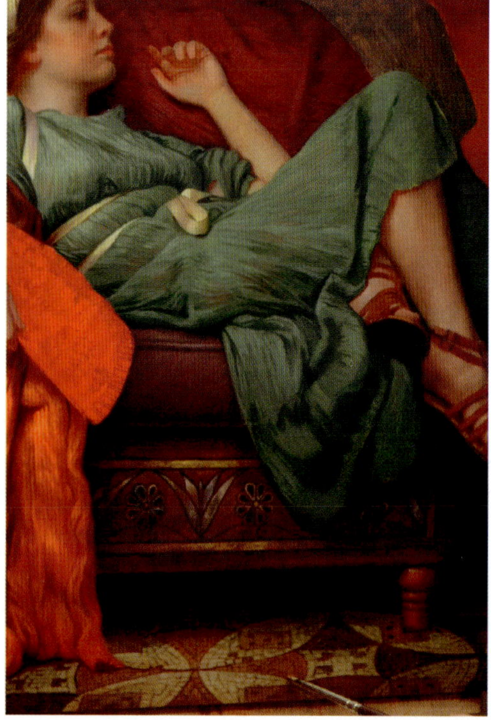

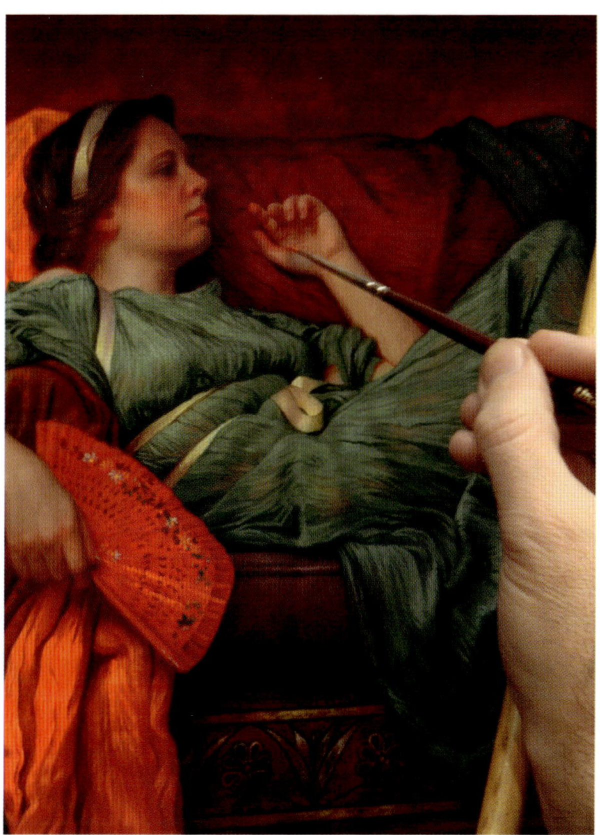

12 ◐ Apply the final touches

I am almost at the end of the painting. This is the stage to refine the delicate transitions and add in subtle details like the wrinkles in the hands and veins underneath the skin. I also glaze and intensify colours. I prefer to glaze with transparent colours and no medium.

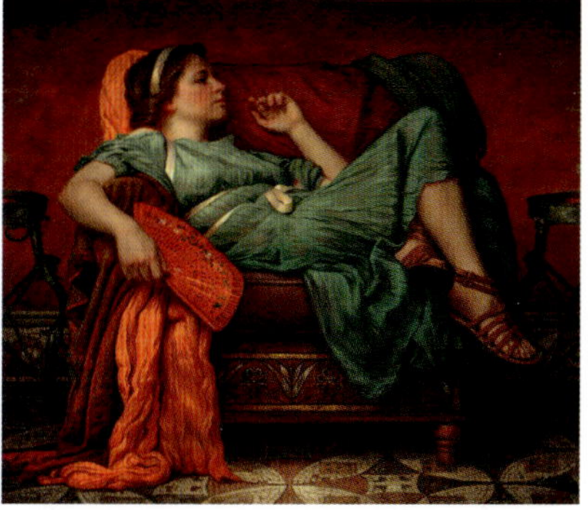

13 ◓ The end result

The painting is finished! I feel that I was able to create something that echoes the artists of the 19th century that I admire. I was aiming for a sense of classicism and elegance. The entire process from idea to finish took 48 hours, with 44 hours of painting time.

Do what you love

I worked for many years in the videogame industry and as a freelance illustrator, rarely painting what I wanted to paint. I needed to paint more from what inspires me. I have found that when I am inspired by the things I love, I love what I create.

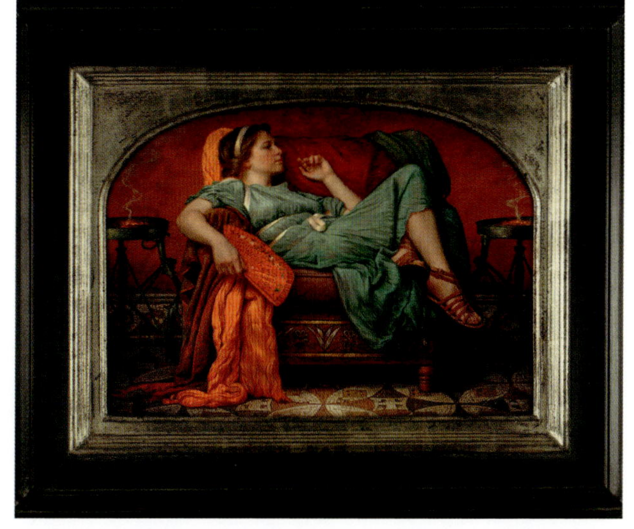

14 ◑ Frame your work

Don't forget to find a frame to enhance your artwork. I chose a frame from the talented people at Masterworks Frames. The frame is handmade and uses 16k gold leaf for a sense of history and grandeur. The arch of the frame was in the back of my mind as I composed the painting.

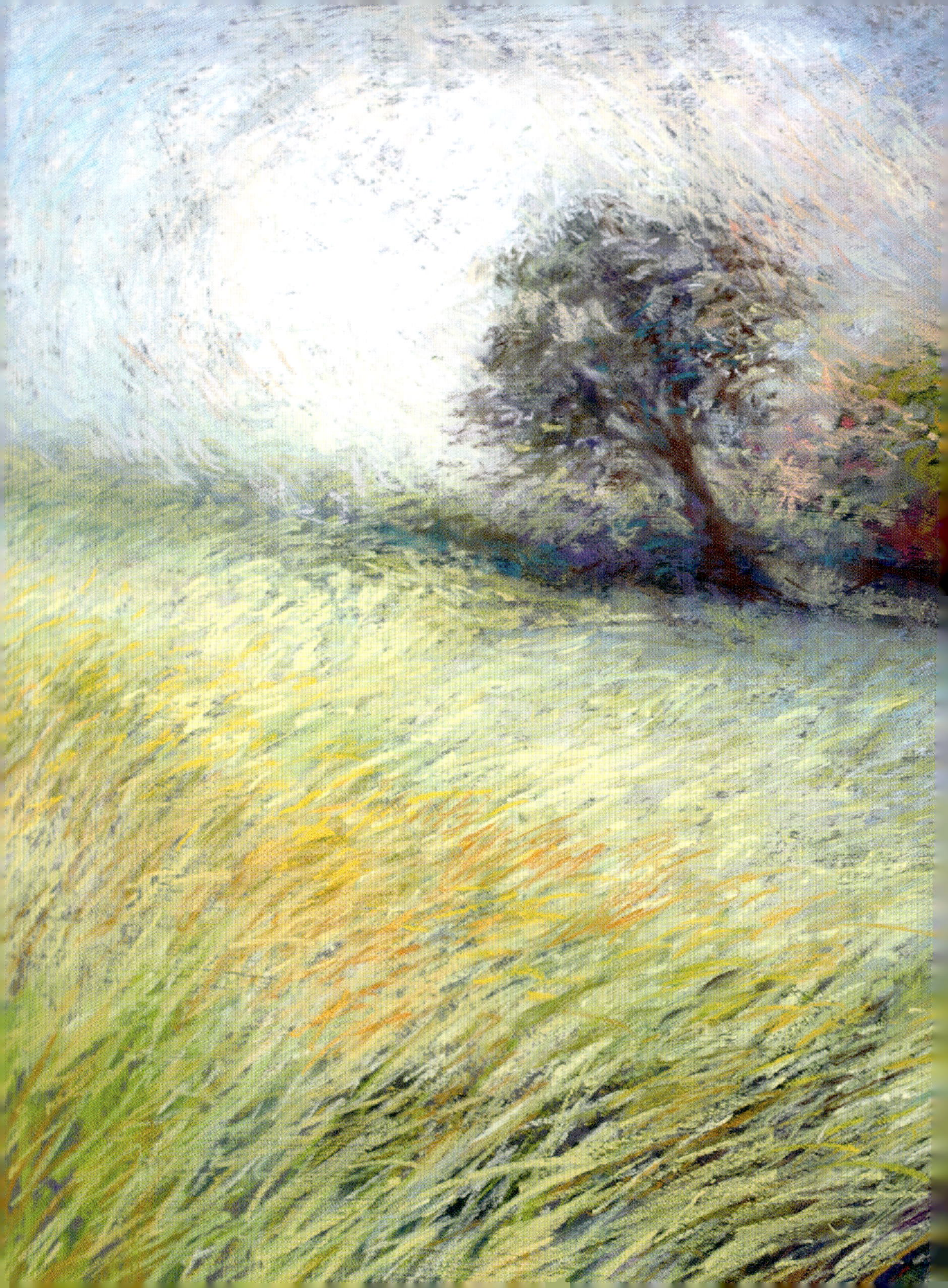

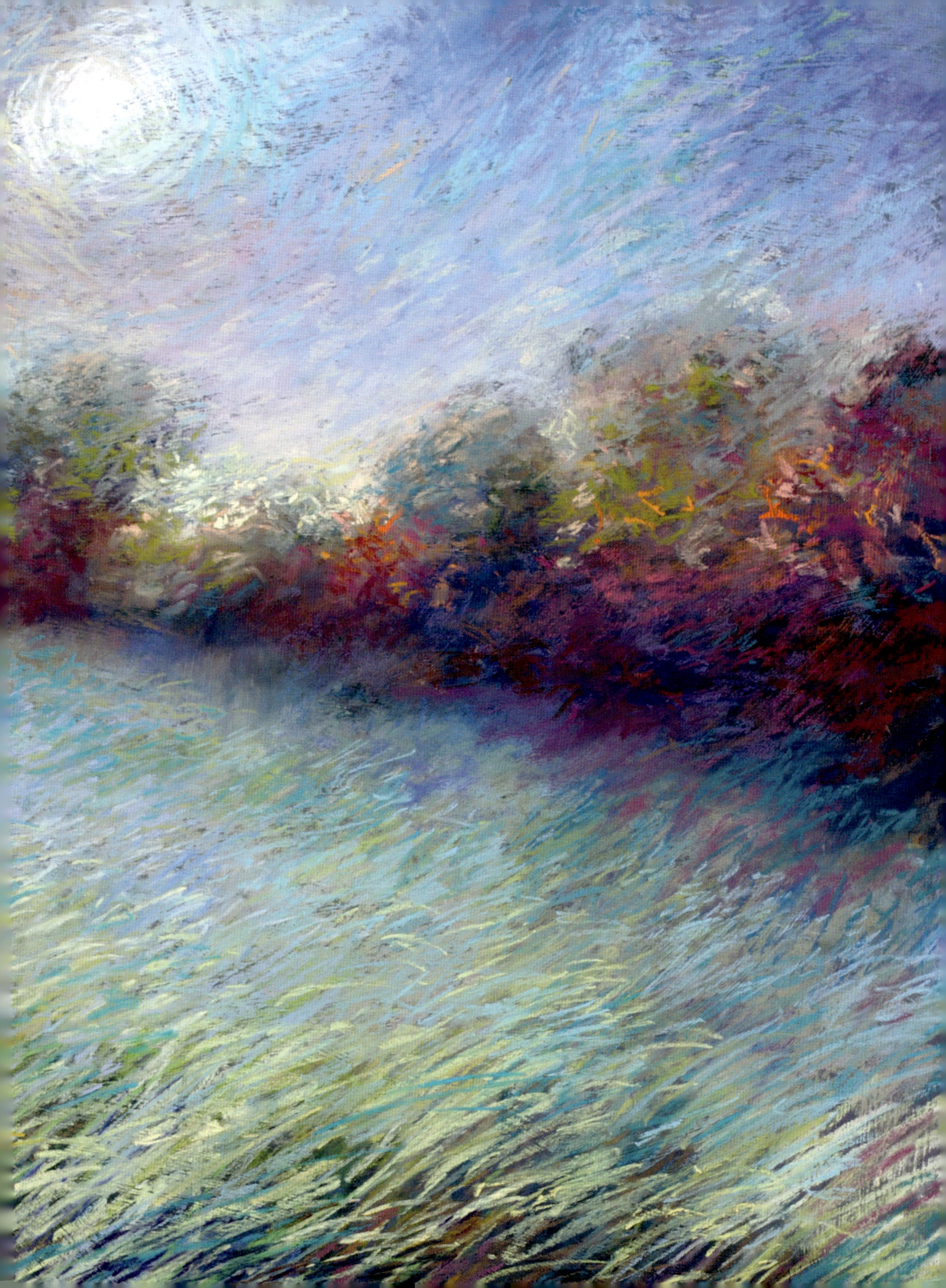